The Non-Smokers' Guide to Bed & Breakfasts

The Non-Smokers' Guide to Bed & Breakfasts

Robyn Martins, *Editor*

RUTLEDGE HILL PRESS

NASHVILLE, TENNESSEE

Published in Nashville, Tennessee, by Rutledge Hill Press, Inc.
513 Third Avenue South, Nashville, Tennessee 37210

Cover design and Book design by Harriette Bateman
Maps and selected illustrations by Tonya Pitkin Presley

Manufactured in the United States of America
1 2 3 4 5 6 — 94 93 92

Contents

Introduction ix
Alabama 3
Alaska 5
Arizona 9
Arkansas 19
California 21
Colorado 59
Connecticut 69
Delaware 73
District of Columbia 75
Florida 77
Georgia 83
Hawaii 87
Idaho 99
Illinois 101
Indiana 105
Iowa 109
Kansas 113
Kentucky 115
Louisiana 117
Maine 119
Maryland 131
Massachusetts 139
Michigan 159
Minnesota 165
Mississippi 169
Missouri 175

Montana 181
Nebraska 183
Nevada 185
New Hampshire 187
New Jersey 195
New Mexico 201
New York 207
North Carolina 221
North Dakota 227
Ohio 229
Oklahoma 233
Oregon 235
Pennsylvania 241
Rhode Island 263
South Carolina 267
South Dakota 273
Tennessee 275
Texas 279
Utah 283
Vermont 287
Virginia 299
Washington 307
West Virginia 317
Wisconsin 321
Wyoming 327
Canada 329
Puerto Rico 333

Introduction

Welcome to the first edition of *The Non-Smokers' Guide to Bed & Breakfasts*. This directory is a collection of bed and breakfasts and small inns across the country that are smoke-free. Specifically, they do not allow smoking indoors, although some allow smoking on porches or lawns.

While assembling this directory, the editor and publisher received a handful of letters proclaiming strong disagreement with non-smoking policies. However, many more bed and breakfast owners cheered for and encouraged the printing of this resource for non-smokers, making clear the need for such a directory.

This non-smoker's guide has been patterned after *The Annual Directory of American Bed & Breakfasts*, using the same format for quick reference and efficient travel planning. Each listing is presented alphabetically by state, city, and establishment name. The descriptions have been provided by the hosts. The publisher has not visited these B&Bs and is not responsible for inaccuracies.

Following the description is information that will be helpful when choosing a bed and breakfast. With this fact list, seen in the example below, you can quickly determine the number of rooms available, the number with private baths (PB), the number with shared baths (SB), and the cost range for two people sharing a room. Tax may or may not be included. Also, the "Credit Cards" and "Notes" correspond to the list at the bottom of each page. You may notice that the "Notes" are not in sequence. Number 7, which represents smoking, has been eliminated.

GREAT TOWN _____

Favorite Bed and Breakfast
123 Main Street, 10000
(800) 555-1234

This Colonial bed and breakfast is surrounded by five acres of colorful landscaping and gardens. Each guest room is individually decorated with antiques and family heirlooms. It is close to antique shops, restaurants, and outdoor activities. Breakfast includes homemade specialties and is served by the stone fireplace in the country kitchen.

Host: The Smith family
Rooms: 4 (2 PB; 2 SB) $65-80
Full Breakfast
Credit Cards: A, B
Notes: 2, 5, 8, 10, 11, 12, 13

Tips for B&B Travel

After choosing a bed and breakfast that appeals to you, it is important to call ahead for reservations and for information that may not be included in the description. For example, ask about local taxes as city and state taxes vary. Ask if dietary needs you may have can be accommodated. Confirm that your children or pets will be welcome. And ask for directions as many bed and breakfasts are off the beaten path.

Because many B&Bs are home to the hosts, remember to be respectful of their property and busy schedules. Most do not have the luxury of a large staff and have established certain policies to assure each guest a pleasant stay.

It is hoped that with *The Non-Smokers' Guide to Bed & Breakfasts* you will discover great places to visit and revisit; places where your desire for clean, breathable air will be respected; and places where your room will more often be filled with the aroma of baked-goods and fresh coffee than with the stale odor of tobacco smoke. It is hoped, too, that this guide will help you have a pleasant, memorable trip, whether it be a family vacation, a romantic getaway, or a business meeting.

The Non-Smokers' Guide to Bed & Breakfasts

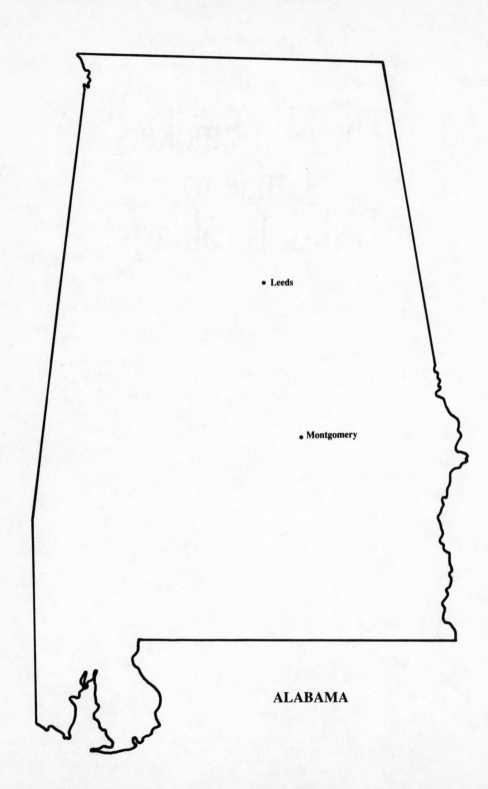

• Leeds

• Montgomery

ALABAMA

Alabama

LEEDS

Bed and Breakfast Birmingham

Route 2, Box 275, 35094
(205) 699-9841

This reservation service represents non-smoking bed and breakfasts across Alabama. Areas represented include Huntsville, Decatur, Arab, Anniston, Fort Payne, Birmingham, Franklin, Spanish Fort, Hayden, Corner, Columbiana, Leeds.

MONTGOMERY

Red Bluff Cottage

551 Clay Street, P. O. Box 1026, 36101
(205) 264-0056

This raised cottage, furnished with family antiques, is high above the Alabama River in Montgomery's historic Cottage Hill district, near the state capitol, Dexter Avenue King Memorial Baptist Church, the first white house of the Confederacy, the Civil Rights Memorial, and Old Alabama Town. It is convenient to the Alabama Shakespeare Festival Theater, the Museum of Fine Arts, and the expanded zoo.

Hosts: Mark and Anne Waldo
Rooms: 4 (PB) $55
Full Breakfast
Credit Cards: None
Notes: 2, 5, 8, 9, 14

Red Bluff Cottage

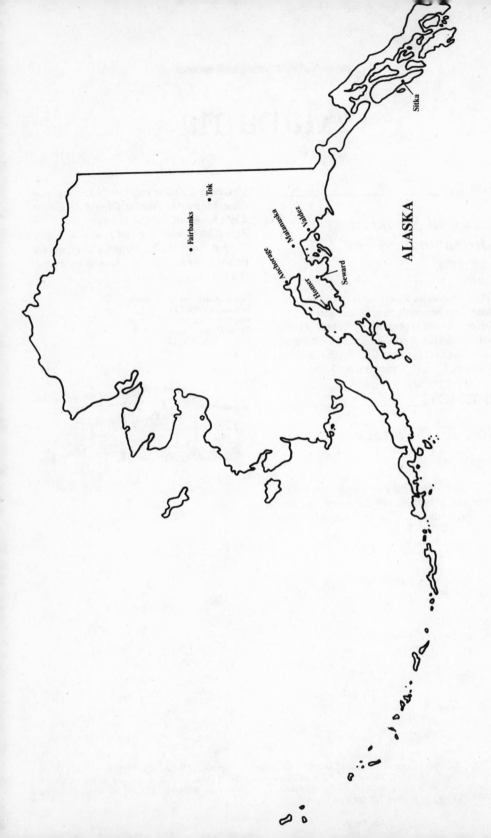

Alaska

ANCHORAGE

Accommodations Alaska Style
Stay With a Friend
3605 Arctic Boulevard, Suite 173, 99503
(907) 278-8800; FAX (907) 272-8800

This friendly reservation service has been providing accommodations since 1981 in Anchorage and other Alaska communities, particularly in Southcentral and the Kenai Peninsula. Whether you prefer to stay close to shops and restaurants, or a quieter hilltop location with views of Cook Inlet and Anchorage, you will receive personal attention by Jean Parsons, coordinator. Major credit cards accepted. $40 to $90.

FAIRBANKS

Alaska's 7 Gables Bed and Breakfast
P. O. Box 80488, 99708
(907) 479-0751

This spacious Tudor home offers 10,000 square feet of unique, custom, energy-efficient design. The entrance through the floral solarium into the foyer decorated with antique stained glass and an indoor waterfall is just part of the distinctive architecture. Other features, including cathedral ceilings, a wedding chapel, and wine cellar, give a quiet ambience. A gourmet breakfast is served daily. Laundry facilities, Jacuzzi, bikes, and luggage storage are available. Each room has a dormer, cable TV, and phone.

Hosts: Paul and Leicha Welton
Rooms: 9 (3 PB; 6 SB) $40-95
Full Breakfast
Credit Cards: A, B, D, E
Notes: 2, 5, 8, 9, 11, 13, 14

Beaver Bend Bed and Breakfast
231 Iditarod, 99701
(907) 452-3240

Beaver Bend Bed and Breakfast is by the scenic Chena River, with a beautiful country setting and convenient location. The hosts are 18-year Alaskan residents who are pleased to share their love for Alaska. Begin the day with a sourdough breakfast, and end it on the deck that overlooks the gardens, lawn, and river.

Hosts: Richard and Bonnie Reem
Rooms: 3 (1 PB; 2 SB) $55-60
Full Breakfast
Credit Cards: None
Notes: 2, 5, 8, 9, 13, 14

HOMER

Seaside Farm
58335 East End Road, 99603
(907) 235-7850

This original homesteader of a functioning ranch has opened her home and cabins to guests visiting Homer, the halibut fishing capital of the world where the road ends and the sea begins. The 40-acre ranch on a bluff has a spectacular panoramic view of Kachemak Bay. Access to beach, lovely landscaping, flowers, birds, huge berry

NOTES: Credit cards accepted: A Master Card; B Visa; C American Express; D Discover Card; E Diners Club; F Other; 2 Personal checks accepted; 3 Lunch available; 4 Dinner available; 5 Open all year; 6 Pets welcome; 8 Children welcome; 9 Social drinking allowed; 10 Tennis available; 11 Swimming available; 12 Golf available; 13 Skiing available; 14 May be booked through travel agents

patch, animals. Horseback trips available with advance arrangement. Camping (tent) $10. All private baths are outhouses.

Host: Mairiis Kilcher
Rooms: 7 (3 PB; 4 SB) $40-55 cabins; $55-75 rooms
Continental Breakfast
Credit Cards: A, B
Notes: 2, 6, 8, 9, 12, 14

MATANUSKA

Yukon Don's Bed and Breakfast Inn

HC31 5086, 99654
(904) 376-7472

This extraordinary Alaska inn has a 270-degree view of surrounding mountains and upper Knik arm. The five rooms each have a specific decor theme such as Hunting Room, Fishing Room, Iditarod Room. In addition, there is a 900-square-foot guest lounge complete with 25 years of collectible Alaskana. Selected as one of the top 50 inns in America in 1991 by *Inn Times*.

Host: Diane Mongeau
Rooms: 5 (1 PB; 4 SB) $80
Continental Breakfast
Credit Cards: None
Notes: 2, 5, 8, 9, 12, 13, 14

SEWARD

Swiss Chalet Bed and Breakfast

P. O. Box 1734, 99664
(907) 224-3939

Old-time Alaskans offer gracious hospitality and comfortable smoke-free atmosphere. Situated one block off Seward Highway by road to Exit Glacier, it is a five-minute walk to Le Barn Appetit Restaurant and a short ride to the boat harbor for tours in the magnificent Resurrection Bay and beyond. Apart-

ments are also available for day-by-day rentals. Seasonal service April 15 through October 15.

Hosts: Charlotte Freeman-Jones and Stan Jones
Rooms: 4 (2 PB; 2 SB) $50-75
Full or Continental Breakfast
Credit Cards: A, B
Note: 14

The White House Bed and Breakfast

P. O. Box 1157, 99664
(907) 224-3614

Guest rooms are finely wallpapered to country taste and have views of surrounding forest and mountains from windows covered by unique insulated shades resembling small quilts when extended, ensuring a good night's rest in the land of the midnight sun. Common area of cable TV room and fully equipped kitchen is exclusively for guest use. All guest rooms are on the second level of what was once a boat repair shop.

Hosts: Tom and Annette Reese
Rooms: 5 (3 PB; 2 SB) $41-72
Continental Breakfast
Credit Cards: A, B
Notes: 2, 5, 8, 9, 13, 14

SITKA

Biorka Bed and Breakfast

611 Biorka Street, 99835
(907) 747-3111

This Alaskan home offers a private bath and entrance. Guests walk easily to local attractions, restaurants, and shops. A hearty breakfast is served with a view of the mountains. Phones and cable TV are available.

Hosts: Steve and Stephanie Vieira
Rooms: 2 (PB) $55-65
Continental Breakfast
Credit Cards: A, B, E
Notes: 2, 5, 10, 11

NOTES: Credit cards accepted: A Master Card; B Visa; C American Express; D Discover Card; E Diners Club; F Other;
2 Personal checks accepted; 3 Lunch available; 4 Dinner available; 5 Open all year; 6 Pets welcome; 8 Children

TOK

VALDEZ

The Stage Stop
P.O. Box 69, 99780
(907) 883-5338

A bed and breakfast for people and horses.
A private cabin and two large rooms with
king and queen beds are available. Enjoy a
full country breakfast and a quiet location.
A new barn and corrals are available for
horses.

Host: Mary Dale Underwood
Rooms: 3 (SB) $45-65
Full Breakfast
Credit Cards: None
Notes: 2, 5, 6, 8, 9, 14

Gussie's Lowe Street Inn
P. O. Box 64, 99686
(907) 835-4448

This deluxe room has a private bath, cable
TV, VCR, fireplace, and excellent queen
Hide-a-bed. A queen room and single room
share a bath. All rooms have phones. No
stairs.

Hosts: Bob and Joanne LaRae
Rooms: 3 (1 PB; 2 SB) $60-65
Full Breakfast
Credit Cards: A, B, D
Notes: 10, 11

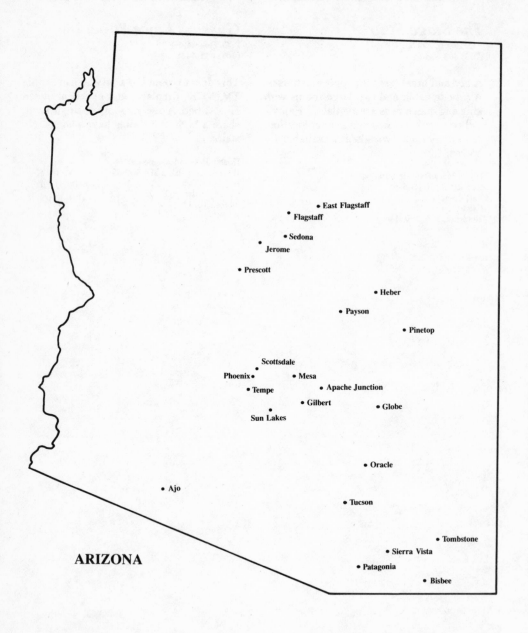

East Flagstaff
Flagstaff
Sedona
Jerome
Prescott
Heber
Payson
Pinetop
Scottsdale
Phoenix • Mesa
Tempe
Apache Junction
Gilbert
Sun Lakes
Globe
Oracle
Ajo
Tucson
Tombstone
Sierra Vista
Patagonia
Bisbee

ARIZONA

Arizona

AJO

Mi Casa Su Casa #291

P. O. Box 950, Tempe, 85280-0950
(602) 990-0682; (800) 456-0682

A white farmhouse with landscaped grounds and spacious interior. The pride of the inn is its stately dining room. It is four blocks from the Spanish-style plaza and shops. Furnishings reflect rich Arizona traditions. Full breakfast. $49-59.

APACHE JUNCTION

Mi Casa Su Casa #306

P.O. Box 950, Tempe, 85280-0950
(602) 990-0682; (800) 456-0682

Situated on the western face of Superstition Mountain, the ten-acre ranch blends seclusion with diverse recreational activities. The exterior is board-and-bat design of the buildings of the Old West. Riding stables are nearby. Breakfast is full on weekends, continental weekdays. Two-night minimum stay. $71.

BISBEE

Mi Casa Su Casa #2552

P. O. Box 950, Tempe, 85280-0950
(602) 990-0682; (800) 456-0682

Step back in time and enjoy collections of art, antiques, and collectibles in a turn-of-the-century home with hardwood floors on a quiet street. No children. Full breakfast. $55-65.

Old Style Homestays #255

P. O. Box 13603, Tucson, 85732
(602) 790-2399

Visit the historical mining town 25 miles from Tombstone and stay in this 1920 vintage Mediterranean-style home with balconies and terraces near the quaint, Switzerlandlike business district. $40-60.

The Petra
Bed and Breakfast

818 Tombstone Canyon, 85603
(602) 432-2996; (800) 537-4333

The Petra offers a peaceful, relaxing setting to travelers in historic Old Bisbee. The rooms are large and comfortably furnished. Each has a private bath. A delicious southwestern breakfast is served family-style. There is ample parking in front, and a handicapped ramp in the rear.

Hosts: Frank and Rosalind Peters
Rooms: 10 (PB) $40-45
Full Breakfast
Credit Cards: A, B, C
Notes: 2, 5, 6, 8, 9, 12

EAST FLAGSTAFF

Mi Casa Su Casa #257

P. O. Box 950, Tempe, 85280-0950
(602) 990-0682; (800) 456-0682

This large, passive solar home in the pines is at the foot of Mount Elden. Mountain hiking directly behind the house. Contemporary decor. Self-catering continental breakfast. Two night minimum. $85.

NOTES: Credit cards accepted: A Master Card; B Visa; C American Express; D Discover Card; E Diners Club; F Other; 2 Personal checks accepted; 3 Lunch available; 4 Dinner available; 5 Open all year; 6 Pets welcome; 8 Children welcome; 9 Social drinking allowed; 10 Tennis available; 11 Swimming available; 12 Golf available; 13 Skiing available; 14 May be booked through travel agents

FLAGSTAFF

Dierker House
423 West Cherry, 86001
(602) 774-3249

A lovely old house listed on the National Register of Historic Places, this bed and breakfast has three rooms that share a private entrance, sitting room, and sunny guest kitchen. Guests enjoy large beds, antiques, and many extras.

Host: Dorothea Dierker
Rooms: 3 (SB) $40 plus
Full Breakfast
Credit Cards: None
Notes: 2, 5, 9, 10, 11, 12, 14

Mi Casa Su Casa #100
P. O. Box 950, Tempe, 85280-0950
(602) 990-0682; (800) 456-0682

Split-level ranch house built in 1967 near the scenic route to the Grand Canyon, San Francisco Peaks, the Northern Arizona Museum, Lowell Observatory. Traditional decor. Full breakfast. $50.

GILBERT

Mi Casa Su Casa #283
P. O. Box 950, Tempe, 85280-0950
(602) 990-0682; (800) 456-0682

Large mature trees give a park setting to this quiet rural ranch home on several acres with quilts and some antiques. Arabian horses and peacocks add to the enchantment. Near old mines and lakes. Full breakfast. $55-60.

GLOBE

Mi Casa Su Casa #302
P. O. Box 950, Tempe, 85280-0950
(602) 990-0682; (800) 456-0682

In a rural area outside the city limits on a seven-acre horse farm, both the main house and the guest house have pleasing southwestern-style furnishings. The area has something for everyone. Two-night minimum stay. Continental breakfast. $65.

HEBER

Mi Casa Su Casa #258
P. O. Box 950, Tempe, 85280-0950
(602) 990-0682; (800) 456-0682

Ponderosa pines surround this rustic home adjoining the Sitgreaves National Forest. Collectibles, antiques, quilts, hanging baskets, wild flowers, and elevated deck with panoramic view. Full breakfast. $55.

JEROME

Mi Casa Su Casa #285
P. O. Box 950, Tempe, 85280-0950
(602) 990-0682; (800) 456-0682

A two-story home perched on the side of Mingus Mountain has a view that won't quit. Within walking distance of Jerome's arts and crafts shops and mining museum. Furnished with Early American and English antiques. Full breakfast. $55-75.

MESA

Mi Casa Su Casa #1
P. O. Box 950, Tempe, 85280-0950
(602) 990-0682; (800) 456-0682

Nestled in a large citrus grove is a self-contained cottage built in 1975 to match the handsome ranch-style main house. Easy driving to shopping malls, golf courses, Tempe, Scottsdale, Phoenix, Superstition Mountains. Three-night minimum stay. Self-catered breakfast. $65.

Mi Casa Su Casa #220

P. O. Box 950, Tempe, 85280-0950
(602) 990-0682; (800) 456-0682

The decor of this Spanish-style stucco house is traditional with a Scandinavian touch. One mile to golf, three miles to Chicago Cubs spring training. Easy drive to Superstition Mountains. Full breakfast. $40.

Mi Casa Su Casa #229

P. O. Box 950, Tempe, 85280-0950
(602) 990-0682; (800) 456-0682

The Chicago Cubs practice baseball only one and one-half blocks from this spacious new home. Host specializes in sticky buns, homemade breads, and jams. Two-night minimum stay. Full breakfast. $40-50.

ORACLE

Old Pueblo Homestays

P. O. Box 13603, Tucson, 85732
(602) 790-2399

A Spanish hideaway with red tile roofs and courtyard with a trickling fountain is just 35 minutes from Tucson. Catalina Mountain country has spectacular views and clear starry nights. $50.

Triangle L Ranch
Bed and Breakfast Retreat

P. O. Box 900, 85623
(602) 896-2804; (800) 266-2804

This lovely 1880s homestead ranch is situated in the high desert/oak woodland 30 miles north of Tucson. Guest accommodations consist of four private cottages tucked away among the oaks. A country breakfast is served in the main ranch house. Birds and wildlife abound. The Triangle L is near Aravaipa Canyon wilderness area, Bio-

sphere 2, San Pedro Riparian birding areas, Indian ruins, hiking, and horseback riding.

Hosts: Tom and Margot Beeston
Rooms: 4 (PB) $55-75
Full Breakfast
Credit Cards: None
Notes: 2, 5, 8, 9, 14

PATAGONIA

Mi Casa Su Casa #1624

P. O. Box 950, Tempe, 85280-0950
(602) 990-0682; (800) 456- 0682

Guests write that this guest house is "absolutely charming." Originally built in 1930-40, it was remodeled in 1986. One hour from Tucson, 20 minutes from Nogales, Mexico. Full breakfast. $60.

PAYSON

Mi Casa Su Casa #47

P. O. Box 950, Tempe, 85280-0950
(602) 990-0682; (800) 456-0682

Three miles south of Payson is this very large A-frame home with three levels adjacent to a national forest. The home features comfortable contemporary decor. Barbecue, picnic areas, and horseshoe pits available. Two-night minimum stay. Continental breakfast. $50.

PHOENIX

Mi Casa Su Casa #127

P. O. Box 950, Tempe, 85280-0950
(602) 990-0682; (800) 456-0682

Built in 1984, this upscale patio home is situated in a small complex in a pleasant area shaded by tall trees with a scenic canal and jogging path one block away. Contemporary decor. Full breakfast. Two-night minimum stay. $50.

welcome; 9 Social drinking allowed; 10 Tennis available; 11 Swimming available; 12 Golf available; 13 Skiing available; 14 May be booked through travel agents

Mi Casa Su Casa #165

P. O. Box 950, Tempe, 85280-0950
(602) 990-0682; (800) 456-0682

This Spanish-style house is at the foot of a mountain on a quiet cul-de-sac ten minutes from downtown Phoenix, 20 minutes from Scottsdale. Three-night minimum stay. Self-catering continental breakfast. $55.

Mi Casa Su Casa #268

P. O. Box 950, Tempe, 85280-0950
(602) 990-0682; (800) 456-0682

This exceptional bed and breakfast retreat offers gracious accommodations with delightful quiet ambience. Enjoy nearby golf, parks with lighted tennis courts, riding stables, and Turf Paradise with thoroughbred racing. Full breakfast. $55.

Mi Casa Su Casa #269

P. O. Box 950, Tempe, 85280-0950
(602) 990-0682; (800) 456-0682

This large immaculate house with four bedrooms and two baths is two miles from Paradise Valley Mall and near many activities: golf, tennis, shopping, art galleries, horse shows, and racing. Continental breakfast. Two-night minimum stay. $45.

Westways Private Resort Bed and Breakfast

P. O. Box 41624, 85080
(602) 582-3868

Westways, winner of numerous domestic and international awards, has casual western comfort with a touch of class, where guests preserve their privacy. The contemporary, southwestern, Mediterranean-style establishment is situated on one acre of designer-landscaped land surrounded by the desert mountain preserve. Guest rooms are individually decorated with area furnishings of oak, rattan, and leather.

Host: Darrell Trapp
Rooms: 6 (PB) $49-122
Full Breakfast
Credit Cards: A, B, C
Notes: 2, 3, 4, 5, 9, 10, 11, 12, 14

PINETOP

Mi Casa Su Casa #113

P. O. Box 950, Tempe, 85280-0950
(602) 990-0682; (800) 456-0682

This log-sided ranch-style home was built in 1988 on a long mountain lot with pines in a quiet area with no street lights. The interior is done in American Primitive antiques. Will loan bicycles. Two-night minimum stay. Full breakfast. $35-75.

PRESCOTT

The Marks House Victorian Bed and Breakfast Inn

203 East Union Street, 86303
(602) 778-4632

An elegant Queen Anne Victorian home decorated in the 1890s style takes guests back to a bygone era when entertaining in style meant high tea in the parlor. With a wonderful view of historic Prescott, the inn is close to shopping, restaurants, antiquing, museums, and outdoor sports. Listed on the National Register of Historic Places, the house was built in 1894 by Jake Marks, a colorful figure in territorial Arizona.

Hosts: Dottie and Harold Viehweg
Rooms: 4 (PB) $75-110
Full Breakfast
Credit Cards: A, B
Notes: 2, 5, 10, 11, 12, 13

Westways Private Resort Bed and Breakfast

NOTES: Credit cards accepted: A Master Card; B Visa; C American Express; D Discover Card; E Diners Club; F Other; 2 Personal checks accepted; 3 Lunch available; 4 Dinner available; 5 Open all year; 6 Pets welcome; 8 Children

Mi Casa Su Casa #106

P. O. Box 950, Tempe, 85280-0950
(602) 990-0682; (800) 456-0682

A California architect designed this spacious two-story home on top of a hill in a serene setting. The house has many windows and glass doors to take advantage of the 360-degree views. Ten minutes from downtown Prescott. Full breakfast. $95.

Prescott Country Inn Bed and Breakfast

503 South Montezuma, U.S. Highway 89, 86303
(602) 445-7991; (800) 362-4759 reservations

You will snuggle under quilted comforters on king or queen beds in individual two-, three-, or four-room cottage suites, some with fireplace and all with private baths and entrances. A charming blend of old and new offering the extraordinary relaxing privacy of breakfast brought to your cottage, porch, or patio. Each cottage is equipped with refrigerator, stove, or microwave, coffee maker, color cable TV, phones, and much more. Free separate health club, spa, pool, and tennis.

Hosts: Morris and Sue Faulkner
Rooms: 12 (PB) $59-109
Expanded Continental Breakfast
Credit Cards: A, B
Notes: 2, 5, 8, 9, 10, 11, 12

SCOTTSDALE

Mi Casa Su Casa #46

P. O. Box 950, Tempe, 85280-0950
(602) 990-0682; (800) 456-0682

This ranch style home is furnished in traditional decor with antiques. Near desert botanical gardens, Phoenix Zoo, hiking, jogging. Quick access to Phoenix, Tempe, Old Scottsdale. Continental breakfast. $40.

Mi Casa Su Casa #217

P. O. Box 950, Tempe, 85280-0950
(602) 990-0682; (800) 456-0682

This handsome home offers a private balcony with a view of the McDowell Mountains. Near golf, tennis, jogging. Minutes to Taliesen West, the Mayo Clinic, fifteen minutes to downtown. Continental breakfast weekdays, full on weekends. Two-night minimum stay. $58.

Mi Casa Su Casa #227

P. O. Box 950, Tempe, 85280-0950
(602) 990-0682; (800) 456-0682

Walk under the adobe arch into an authentic southwestern adobe home built in 1986 on two acres of land with a variety of desert flora and fauna. Near Taliesen West, the Mayo Clinic, fine dining, and golf. Two-night minimum stay. Full breakfast. $65.

SEDONA

Mi Casa Su Casa #186

P. O. Box 950, Tempe, 85280-0950
(602) 990-0682; (800) 456-0682

This large, ranch-style home in a quiet setting features a honeymoon suite with a wood-burning stove and whirlpool tub. Other rooms are decorated thematically. Common room has a fireplace, TV, games, books. Full breakfast. Two-night minimum stay. $50-75.

Mi Casa Su Casa #317

P. O. Box 950, Tempe, 85280-0950
(602) 990-0682; (800) 456-0682

This ranch-style house has a view of the Sugar Loaf red rock formation. A separate apartment is connected to the main house and has a private entrance. Full breakfast. $55.

welcome; 9 Social drinking allowed; 10 Tennis available; 11 Swimming available; 12 Golf available; 13 Skiing available; 14 May be booked through travel agents

Sipapu Lodge
P. O. Box 552, 86336
(602) 282-2833

Anasazi Indian culture is evident throughout this ranch-style house constructed of local red rock and surrounded by natural vegetation. Hosts are knowledgeable about area history and geography. Unique, original recipes are a specialty. The host is a craftsman and potter whose original pieces are on display, along with local Indian artifacts. Guests enjoy true southwestern hospitality.

Host: Lea Pace
Rooms: 5 (3 PB; 2 SB) $57-87
Full Breakfast
Credit Cards: None
Notes: 2, 5, 6, 8, 9

SIERRA VISTA

Mi Casa Su Casa #30
P. O. Box 950, Tempe, 85280-0950
(602) 990-0682; (800) 456-0682

Enjoy casual living at 5,000 feet on a small ranch situated in the foothills of the Huachuca Mountains with magnificent views of the valley and surrounding mountains. Easy driving to Tombstone, Bisbee, Chiricahua Mountains, Cochise Stronghold. Two-night minimum stay. Full breakfast. $55.

SUN LAKES

Old Pueblo Homestays #115
P. O. Box 13603, Tucson, 85732
(602) 790-2399

This planned recreational area has several golf courses, tennis, swimming, fishing, shopping, and is close to spring training fields. $65-85.

TEMPE

Mi Casa Su Casa #290
P. O. Box 950, 85280-0950
(602) 990-0682; (800) 456-0682

This residence features landscaped desert front yard, wooded back yard with fruit and shade trees, and traditional decor with some antiques. Near golf, tennis, handball, fitness centers. Two blocks from public transportation. Full breakfast. $55.

TOMBSTONE

Old Pueblo Homestays #112
P. O. Box 13603, Tucson, 85732
(602) 790-2399

This one-hundred-year-old house is one block from the famous OK Corral and has a front porch with swing, high ceilings, antique furnishings, Tiffany lamp, and wrought iron bed. $45.

TUCSON

The Brimstone Butterfly
940 North Olsen Avenue, 85719
(602) 322-9157; (800) 323-9157

This elegant adobe home built in the 1930s is situated in a tree-lined neighborhood just two blocks from the university and cancer research center. Cozy accommodations with privacy easily access the lushly landscaped pool. Numerous amenities give a resort quality in an exclusive private home.

Host: Marie Johnstone
Rooms: 3 (PB) $95
Full Breakfast
Credit Cards: None
Notes: 2, 5, 8, 10, 11, 12, 13, 14

NOTES: Credit cards accepted: A Master Card; B Visa; C American Express; D Discover Card; E Diners Club; F Other;
2 Personal checks accepted; 3 Lunch available; 4 Dinner available; 5 Open all year; 6 Pets welcome; 8 Children

El Presidio
Bed and Breakfast Inn
297 North Main Avenue, 85701
(602) 623-6151

Experience southwestern charm in a garden
oasis with the romance of a country inn. A
Victorian adobe, the loyally restored 1879
inn is a splendid example of American Territorial and is on the National Register of
Historic Places. Garden courtyards with Old
World ambience surround four suites and
guest houses. All have fine antique furnishings, phones, and TV. Close to museums,
restaurants, downtown Tucson.

Host: Patti Toci
Rooms: 4 (PB) $65-95
Full Breakfast
Credit Cards: None
Notes: 2, 5, 9, 10, 11, 12, 13, 14

El Presidio Bed and Breakfast Inn

Mi Casa Su Casa #223
P. O. Box 950, Tempe, 85280-0950
(602) 990-0682; (800) 456-0682

Ski on Mt. Lemmon in the morning and sun
by the pool in the afternoon, enjoying panoramic mountain and city views, surrounded
by 20 acres. The guest cottage is a smaller
version of the main house with southwestern decor. Two-night minimum stay. Full
breakfast. $85-105.

Old Pueblo Homestays #3
P. O. Box 13603, 85732
(602) 790-2399

This quiet desert retreat is near the base of
Mt. Lemmon yet has easy access to the city.
The ranch-style home is decorated with a
blend of traditional and antiques and has a
pool. $45.

Old Pueblo Homestays #4
P. O. Box 13603, 85732
(602) 790-2399

Enjoy a spectacular view of the mountains
and a striking view of the city. Rooms are
tastefully decorated with cherry and walnut
antiques and Oriental rugs. $45-90.

Old Pueblo Homestays #7
P. O. Box 13603, 85732
(602) 790-2399

This spacious ranch-style home is on four
desert acres in the northeast foothills with a
view of the Catalina Mountains. Close to
fine dining and shopping. $65-75.

Old Pueblo Homestays #9
P. O. Box 13603, 85732
(602) 790-2399

This guest house featuring Swedish and
southwestern touches has a pool, stone fireplace, and cable TV. Two-night minimum
stay. $85.

Old Pueblo Homestays #10
P. O. Box 13603, 85732
(602) 790-2399

Nestled against the Catalina Mountains and
high above the city, guests enjoy the city
view. Pools and Jacuzzi. Near La Paloma
and Ventana Canyon Resorts. $50.

welcome; 9 Social drinking allowed; 10 Tennis available; 11 Swimming available; 12 Golf available; 13 Skiing
available; 14 May be booked through travel agents

Old Pueblo Homestays #14

P. O. Box 13603, 85732
(602) 790-2399

This home is situated on a residential cul-de-sac on the northeast side. Guests enjoy a bird's eye view of the mountains from a private patio. $50.

Old Pueblo Homestays #16

P. O. Box 13603, 85732
(602) 790-2399

A family residence built around a lovely courtyard, the home is situated in a quiet neighborhood within walking distance of the University of Arizona. $75-85.

Old Pueblo Homestays #20

P. O. Box 13603, 85732
(602) 790-2399

This adobe home features over 50 arches and an interior courtyard. Rooms have private entrances and patios overlooking the desert landscape. Refrigerator, microwave, spa. $55-65.

Old Pueblo Homestays #22

P. O. Box 13603, 85732
(602) 790-2399

With a relaxed, friendly atmosphere, this home is near desert and mountain hiking trails and has easy access to community center and downtown Tucson. $40-50.

Old Pueblo Homestays #23

P. O. Box 13603, 85732
(602) 790-2399

A neighborhood park surrounded by pleasant homes is the setting for this inviting offering close to shopping, restaurants, churches, theaters, and doctors. $40.

Old Pueblo Homestays #24

P. O. Box 13603, 85732
(602) 790-2399

Enjoy a panoramic view of the ever-changing Catalina Mountains in a quiet country setting where quail, rabbits, hummingbirds, and roadrunners abound at this passive solar, rammed earth and adobe home. $60.

Old Pueblo Homestays #25

P. O. Box 13603, 85732
(602) 790-2399

Bird watchers' paradise. Relax among stately saguaros in this Sonoran Desert foothill home and experience splendid bird watching from guest rooms and the adjacent desert oasis. $55.

Old Pueblo Homestays #26

P. O. Box 13603, 85732
(602) 790-2399

One guest room is furnished with western accessories, one is furnished traditionally at this home close to bus lines and restaurants. $40.

Old Pueblo Homestays #30

P. O. Box 13603, 85732
(602) 790-2399

Situated in the foothills between the Santa Catalina Mountains and midtown Tucson, this home offers a covered porch with swing, patio, and spa. $60.

Old Pueblo Homestays #33

P. O. Box 13603, 85732
(602) 790-2399

A restful, cozy retreat is situated in a quiet residential area near Sabino and Pima Canyons, Colossal Cave, and the Santa Catalina

---

NOTES: Credit cards accepted: A Master Card; B Visa; C American Express; D Discover Card; E Diners Club; F Other;
2 Personal checks accepted; 3 Lunch available; 4 Dinner available; 5 Open all year; 6 Pets welcome; 8 Children

Mountains. Short walk to an Olympic-size pool open to the public. $45.

Old Pueblo Homestays #39
P. O. Box 13603, 85732
(602) 790-2399

Enjoy the warmth and friendliness of family, but with privacy, security, and relaxation. The upscale, peaceful neighborhood is only minutes from top-class resorts and near Sabino Canyon. $60.

Old Pueblo Homestays #46
P. O. Box 13603, 85732
(602) 790-2399

Situated on 20 acres in the foothills of the Santa Catalina Mountains, this hacienda is only two miles from the city limits. There are two rooms in the main house and a separate guest house. $40-105.

Old Pueblo Homestays #50
P. O. Box 13603, 85732
(602) 790-2399

Desert living at its best, this beautiful home is set in a lovely rural area with mountain vistas. Hosts stock refrigerator with breakfast foods. $60-80.

Old Pueblo Homestays #60
P. O. Box 13603, 85732
(602) 790-2399

The owners have meticulously restored this house and gardens in a historical district close to restaurants, museums, art galleries, shopping, University of Arizona, and freeway access. $85-105.

Old Pueblo Homestays #61
P. O. Box 13603, 85732
(602) 790-2399

An unobstructed view of the Santa Catalina Mountains beckons from this charming home in the foothills, where wildlife and rare birds feed. Enjoy a morning swim at this home on a strategic north-south street. $65.

Quail's Nest
Bed and Breakfast
1416 North Richey, 85716
(602) 325-8938

This comfortable, attractively furnished home near east midtown Tucson is ten minutes from downtown, University of Arizona, University Medical Center, has easy access to airport, is two blocks to city bus and 30 minutes to Old Tucson and Arizona-Sonora Desert Museum. A warm welcome awaits guests.

Host: Wanda Marts
Rooms: 2 (1 PB; 1 SB) $45
Full Breakfast
Credit Cards: None
Notes: 6, 8

welcome; 9 Social drinking allowed; 10 Tennis available; 11 Swimming available; 12 Golf available; 13 Skiing available; 14 May be booked through travel agents

Eureka Springs

Jasper

ARKANSAS

Arkansas

Heart of the Hills
5 Summit, 72632
(501) 253-7468

Enter this 1883 home in the historic district and step back in time to antique-filled rooms, porch swing, lemonade, or hot cider. Guests may slow to the pace of a bygone era with a beautiful walk downtown or step on the trolley in front of the house. Begin the day with a gourmet breakfast, and end the evening with a scrumptuous homemade dessert.

Host: Jan Jacobs Weber
Rooms: 4 (PB) $60-80
Full Breakfast
Credit Cards: A, B
Notes: 2, 5, 8, 9, 10, 11, 12

The Heartstone Inn and Cottages
35 Kingshighway, 72632
(501) 253-8916

Nationally acclaimed, award-winning bed and breakfast inn. Antiques, quilts, all private baths, private entrances, cable TV, full gourmet breakfasts. Licensed massage therapist on duty. "Best breakfast in the Ozarks," *The New York Times.* "Perfect inn," *Country Home* magazine. In historic district and on trolley route. Off-street parking.

Hosts: Iris and Bill Simantel
Rooms: 10 (PB) $58-105
Cottages: 2
Full Breakfast
Credit Cards: A, B, C
Notes: 2, 8, 9

Singleton House Bed and Breakfast
11 Singleton, 72632
(501) 253-9111

This 1890s Victorian inn with a touch of magic is whimsically decorated with folk art, antiques, and eclectic treasures. Four light and airy guest rooms with private baths are available. Enjoy a full breakfast on the balcony overlooking woods, fantasy wildflower garden, and goldfish pond. Historic district location; walk one block down wooded footpath, or ride the trolley to shops and cafes. Passion play, dinner train, and bath house reservations. Also, a romantic guest cottage is available at a separate location.

Host: Barbara Gavron
Rooms: 4 (PB) $55-75
Cottage: 1
Full Breakfast
Credit Cards: A, B, C, D
Notes: 2, 5, 8, 9, 11, 12, 14

The Heartstone Inn and Cottages

NOTES: Credit cards accepted: A Master Card; B Visa; C American Express; D Discover Card; E Diners Club; F Other; 2 Personal checks accepted; 3 Lunch available; 4 Dinner available; 5 Open all year; 6 Pets welcome; 8 Children welcome; 9 Social drinking allowed; 10 Tennis available; 11 Swimming available; 12 Golf available; 13 Skiing available; 14 May be booked through travel agents

Sunnyside Inn
5 Ridgeway, 72632
(501) 253-6638

The Sunnyside Inn is an 1883 Victorian mansion situated on the national historic loop in Eureka Springs. It depicts the majesty of Queen Anne architecture. Characteristically, it features three-story bay windows. Up to 14 guests may be lavished in antique luxury, served breakfast on Haviland china and the finest silver. Guests enjoy warmth, laughter, and gracious living.

Hosts: Mary Capps and Jamie Eccleston
Rooms: 5 (PB) $80-150
Full Breakfast
Credit Cards: A, B
Notes: 2, 5, 9, 12, 14

JASPER

Brambly Hedge Cottage
HCR 31, Box 39, 72641
(501) 446-5849

Country French Victorian elegance in the rugged Ozarks. Guests delight in breakfast on the deck while watching clouds far below this mountaintop home right on scenic Highway 7. The house resembles an English Cotswold cottage. The thick-walled living room is a homestead log cabin. Minutes from Buffalo National River float trips, hiking trails, Dogpatch, craft shops. A short distance to Eureka Springs, Branson (Missouri), major lakes.

Hosts: Jacquelyn and Billy Smyers
Rooms: 1 (PB) $50-65
Full Breakfast
Credit Cards: None
Notes: 2, 5, 9, 11

California

Garratt Mansion

900 Union Street, 94501
(510) 521-4779

Only 15 miles to San Francisco or Berkely
on the tranquil island of Alameda, Garratt
Mansion offers the convenience of home
and the service of a five-star hotel, but with
the peace of a retreat. Guests enjoy a blend
of privacy and hospitality. Rooms are large
and comfortable, and breakfasts are nutri-
tious and filling.

Hosts: Royce and Betty Gladden
Rooms: 6 (3 PB; 3 SB) $70-120
Full Breakfast
Credit Cards: A, B, C, E
Notes: 2, 5, 8, 10, 11, 12, 14

Webster House

1238 Versailles Avenue, 94501
(415) 523-9697

Webster House is the 22nd historical monument in the city. Quaint, enchanting 1854
Gothic revival cottage is the oldest house on
the island of Alameda. Nestled in coastal
redwoods and scrub oaks, with a large deck,
waterfall, fountain. Irish cream liqueur or
champagne available; afternoon tea and
evening snack. Near beach, golf, tennis,
fishing, shopping, and bicycling. Twenty
minutes from San Francisco.

Hosts: Andrew and Susan McCormack
Rooms: 6 (2 PB: 4 SB) $75-105
Full Breakfast
Credit Cards: None
Notes: 2, 3, 5, 8, 9, 10, 11, 12, 14

Garratt Mansion

Eye Openers Bed and Breakfast Reservations

P. O. Box 694, 91003
(213) 684-4428; (818) 797-2055

This reservation service matches guest requests with bed and breakfast home stays
and inns throughout California. 150 accommodations to choose from with private and
shared baths. Many near tennis, swimming,
golf, and skiing. Breakfast varies. $35-150.

Anaheim Bed and Breakfast

1327 South Hickory, 92805
(714) 533-1884

Anaheim Bed and Breakfast is less than one
mile from Disneyland and the Anaheim
Convention Center. It is situated in a residential area close to the I-5 Santa Ana free-

welcome; 9 Social drinking allowed; 10 Tennis available; 11 Swimming available; 12 Golf available; 13 Skiing
available; 14 May be booked through travel agents

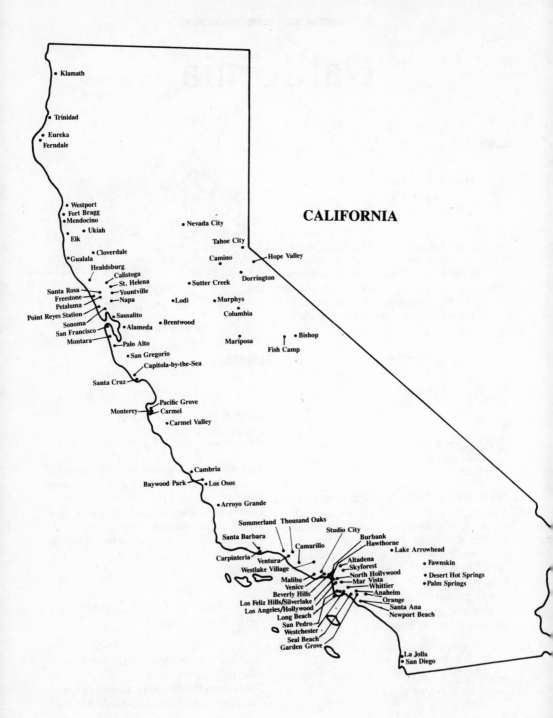

CALIFORNIA

Klamath

Trinidad

Eureka
Ferndale

Westport
Fort Bragg
Mendocino
Ukiah
Elk
Cloverdale
Gualala
Healdsburg
Calistoga
St. Helena
Santa Rosa
Yountville
Freestone
Napa
Petaluma
Point Reyes Station
Sausalito
Sonoma
Alameda
Brentwood
San Francisco
Montara
Palo Alto
San Gregorio
Capitola-by-the-Sea
Santa Cruz

Nevada City
Tahoe City
Camino
Hope Valley
Sutter Creek
Dorrington
Lodi
Murphys
Columbia
Mariposa
Bishop
Fish Camp

Pacific Grove
Monterey
Carmel
Carmel Valley

Cambria
Baywood Park
Los Osos

Arroyo Grande

Summerland
Thousand Oaks
Santa Barbara
Studio City
Burbank
Camarillo
Hawthorne
Lake Arrowhead
Carpinteria
Altadena
Fawnskin
Ventura
Skyforest
Westlake Village
North Hollywood
Desert Hot Springs
Malibu
Mar Vista
Palm Springs
Venice
Whittier
Beverly Hills
Anaheim
Los Feliz Hills/Silverlake
Orange
Los Angeles/Hollywood
Santa Ana
Long Beach
Newport Beach
San Pedro
Westchester
Seal Beach
Garden Grove
La Jolla
San Diego

way. The neighborhood is one of the oldest in Anaheim. The owner of the home lives on the premises and speaks English and German fluently.

Host: Margot E. Palmgren
Rooms: 3 (SB) $40
Full Breakfast
Credit Cards: None
Notes: 2, 5, 8

Anaheim Country Inn
856 South Walnut Street, 92802
(800) 755-7801

Step back in time and enjoy the Anaheim Country Inn, graced by beveled, leaded-glass windows and charming turn-of-the-century furnishings. It is situated on spacious grounds in a quiet residential neighborhood near the Disneyland and Anaheim Convention Center area. Off-street parking and hot tub are available.

Hosts: Lois Ramont and Marilyn Watson
Rooms: 9 (6 PB; 3 SB) $55-80
Full Breakfast
Credit Cards: A, B, C, D
Notes: 2, 5, 9, 10, 12, 14

Bed and Breakfast International #501
P. O. Box 282910, San Francisco, 94128
(415) 696-1690; FAX (415) 696-1699

This is a perfect location for visiting Disneyland, Knott's Berry Farm, and other tourist attractions in southern California. This is a large, two-story home that is ideal for a famiy. The guest room has an adjacent sitting room with a fireplace. $55.

Bed and Breakfast International #504
P. O. Box 282910, San Francisco, 94128
(415) 696-1690; FAX (415) 696-1699

This traditional southern California home is centrally situated for tourists, close to Disneyland, Universal Studios, Knott's Berry Farm. There is a lovely pool and gazebo in the back, and one room has a private entrance. Host can offer a 35% discount on tickets for Disneyland with advance notice. $60-80.

Bed and Breakfast of Los Angeles 01
32074 Waterside Lane, Westlake Village, 91361
(818) 889-8870

This spacious home has two guest rooms, all nicely decorated in country style. There is a spa on the patio; bus line is two blocks away. $50.

Anaheim Country Inn

Bed and Breakfast of Los Angeles 02
32074 Waterside Lane, Westlake Village, 91361
(818) 889-8870

This home is less than one mile from Disneyland. Three guest rooms share two baths in the hall. Bus line is two blocks away. $55.

APTOS

Apple Lane Inn
6265 Soquel Drive, 95003
(408) 475-6868

A secluded 1870s Victorian farmhouse on three acres of rolling meadows and towering trees is just minutes from downtown and beaches. Enjoy an authentic farm with barn, horses, and orchards, vegetable and formal gardens, sunny patio, Victorian gazebo, and lush lawns. Guest rooms offer period antiques, William Morris wallpapers, and fresh flowers. Player piano, darts, horseshoes, croquet, and game room are available.

Hosts: Doug and Diana Groom
Rooms: 5 (3 PB; 2 SB) $70-125
Full Breakfast
Credit Cards: A, B, D
Notes: 2, 5, 8, 9, 10, 11, 12

ARROYO GRANDE

Bed and Breakfast of Los Angeles
32074 Waterside Lane, Westlake Village, 91361
(818) 889-8870

This three-story inn is just off the freeway and offers today's convenience with yesterday's charm. Seven guest rooms with queen beds and private baths. Full breakfast. $95-165.

BAYWOOD PARK

Baywood Bed and Breakfast Inn
1370 Second Street, 93402
(805) 528-8888

This contemporary inn situated on Morro Bay has 15 suites with beautiful bay views, fireplaces, kitchenettes, phones, and private baths. Each suite is decorated in a different theme: Victorian, country, frontier,

Williamsburg. It is close to Hearst Castle and Montano de Oro State Park.

Hosts: Pam and John Cutmore
Rooms: 15 (PB) $80-120
Continental Breakfast
Credit Cards: None
Notes: 2, 3, 5, 8, 9, 12

BEVERLY HILLS

Bed and Breakfast of Los Angeles 01
32074 Waterside Lane, Westlake Village, 91361
(818) 889-8870

This spacious ground-floor condominium is in the heart of Beverly Hills. The guest room has twin beds, TV, private bath, and garden view. Near bus line. Underground parking is available. $50.

Bed and Breakfast of Los Angeles 02
32074 Waterside Lane, Westlake Village, 91361
(818) 889-8870

One mile from Sunset, this English country style cottage has a massive fireplace, small yard with spa, and guest room with sitting area. Two-night minimum stay.

BISHOP

The Chalfant House Bed and Breakfast
213 Academy, 93514
(619) 872-1790

This historic turn-of-the-century inn stands among towering mountains just one block off Highway 395. Each of the six guest rooms has a private bath, antiques, homemade quilts, ceiling fans, and central air conditioning. Guests are served hot and cold drinks during afternoon tea, and ice cream sundaes in the evening in the parlor.

Restaurants, theater, and park are within walking distance. Historic tours are given on request.

Hosts: Fred and Sally Manecke
Rooms: 6 (PB) $60-75
Full Breakfast
Credit Cards: C
Notes: 2, 5, 8, 9, 10, 11, 12, 13

The Chalfant House Bed and Breakfast

BURBANK

Bed and Breakfast of Los Angeles 01

32074 Waterside Lane, Westlake Village, 91361
(818) 889-8870

There are two guest rooms with a shared bath in this ranch-style home with covered patio and pool. Children over 16 welcome. Near bus line. $40.

Bed and Breakfast of Los Angeles 02

32074 Waterside Lane, Westlake Village, 91361
(818) 889-8870

This pool-side cottage has facilities for limited food preparation, TV, patio, and barbecue. The busline is two blocks away. Married couples only. $50.

BRENTWOOD

Bed and Breakfast of Los Angeles

32074 Waterside Lane, Westlake Village, 91361
(818) 889-8870

Near Santa Monica, this two-story redwood townhome with patio looks out onto woods, yet it is only ten minutes to Beverly Hills. $50.

CALISTOGA

Calistoga Wishing Well Inn

2653 Foothill Boulevard (Highway 128), 94515
(707) 942-5534

A country estate among the vineyards with elegant period interiors is situated on four acres in a historical setting. Enjoy gourmet breakfast featuring homegrown fruits and preserves, complimentary wine, and hors d'oeuvres served individually by the pool with a magnificent view of Mount Saint Helens, on your private sundeck, or fireside in the parlor. TV and spa.

Hosts: Marina and Keith Dinsmoor
Rooms: 3 (PB) $100-125
Full Breakfast
Credit Cards: ·A, B
Notes: 2, 5, 8, 9, 10, 11, 12, 14

Quail Mountain Bed and Breakfast

4455 North Saint Helena Highway, 94515
(707) 942-0316

This secluded luxury retreat is situated on 26 heavily wooded acres with a vineyard 300 feet above the Napa Valley. Guest rooms are decorated with art work and antiques

welcome; 9 Social drinking allowed; 10 Tennis available; 11 Swimming available; 12 Golf available; 13 Skiing available; 14 May be booked through travel agents

and have king beds and private decks. Breakfast and complimentary wine are served in the solarium, the common guest sitting room. There are a pool and hot tub on the premises.

Hosts: Don and Alma Swiers
Rooms: 3 (PB) $90-110
Full Breakfast
Credit Cards: A, B
Notes: 2, 5, 9, 10, 11, 12, 14

CAMARILLO

Bed and Breakfast of Los Angeles

32074 Waterside Lane, Westlake Village, 91361
(818) 889-8870

Enjoy acres of orchards, pleasant yard with a spa, and stables for elegant horses. Guest rooms share a bath in the hall. Children over seven or infants welcome. $45.

CAMBRIA

Bed and Breakfast of Los Angeles

32074 Waterside Lane, Westlake Village, 91361
(818) 889-8870

This 1873 Greek Revival-style home has been restored and offers six guest rooms with private baths. It is seven miles to Hearst Castle. Children over 13 welcome. $75.

Pickford House Bed and Breakfast

2555 MacLeod Way, 93428
(805) 927-8619

Pickford House offers eight large rooms, some with fireplaces and views of mountains and valleys. All have large beds and TVs. Wine and tea served at 5:00 PM. Rooms are named after movie stars who visited Hearst Castle when Hearst lived there. Hearst Castle is just seven miles north.

Beaches are nearby for fishing and jade or shell collecting. Also, 23 vineyards are nearby.

Host: Anna Larsen
Rooms: 8 (PB) $75-115
Full Breakfast
Credit Cards: A, B
Notes: 5, 8, 9, 11

CAMINO

Camino Hotel-Seven Mile House

P.O. Box 1197, 4103 Carson Road, 95709
(916) 644-7740

Situated in the heart of the Apple Hill area of the Mother Lode, the historic Camino Hotel is perched at an elevation of 3,000 feet along the old Carson Wagon Trail. Historically restored in the fall of 1990, the hotel offers ten intimate sleeping rooms, sun porch, and a cheery parlor with warm stove for cold winter days. Evening dessert and breakfast are served in the parlor or on the sun porch overlooking town.

Hosts: Paula Nobert and John Eddy
Rooms: 10 (3 PB; 7 S2B) $55-85
Expanded Continental Breakfast
Credit Cards: A, B, C, E
Notes: 2, 5, 8, 11, 12, 13, 14

CAPITOLA-BY-THE-SEA

The Inn at Depot Hill

250 Monterey Avenue, 95010
(408) 462-3376

Sophistication and elegance describe this inn in the quaint Mediterranean-style beachside resort of Capitola-by-the-Sea. Buy a ticket to romance, illusion, and escapism. Stay in Portofino, Stratford-on-Avon, Delft, Sissinghurst, or Paris. Each of eight suites has a fireplace. Most have private patios and Jacuzzis. All rooms are unique.

NOTES: Credit cards accepted: A Master Card; B Visa; C American Express; D Discover Card; E Diners Club; F Other; 2 Personal checks accepted; 3 Lunch available; 4 Dinner available; 5 Open all year; 6 Pets welcome; 8 Children

Host: Suzie Lankes
Rooms: 8 (PB) $155-250
Full Breakfast
Credit Cards: A, B, C
Notes: 2, 5, 9, 10, 11, 12, 14

CARMEL

Bed and Breakfast International #203

P. O. Box 282910, San Francisco, 94128
(415) 696-1690; FAX (415) 696-1699

This large contemporary home with several decks is surrounded by hills. The studio guest house has a wood-burning fireplace and private entrance. There is a hot tub for guest use. Breakfast is served in the guest house. $88.

Bed and Breakfast International #205

P. O. Box 282910, San Francisco, 94128
(415) 696-1690; FAX (415) 696-1699

This spacious modern home has four fireplaces and contemporary design. The guest room has a private entrance, fireplace, and view of Point Lobos. Breakfast is prepared in the main house. $95.

Bed and Breakfast International #207

P. O. Box 282910, San Francisco, 94128
(415) 696-1690; FAX (415) 696-1699

Situated on the east side of Highway 1, five minutes from Carmel Beach, this contemporary town house features fine art and tasteful furnishings. The guest room has a queen bed and private bath. A pool is available for guest use. $78.

Monte Verde Inn

Ocean and Monte Verde, P.O. Box 394, 93921
(408) 624-6046; (800) 328-7707

This is a charming country inn with a warm ambience and gracious hospitality. Lovely gardens and terraces are tucked away for guests to enjoy. Close to shops and beach. A continental breakfast is served, and on-premises parking is available.

Host: Ernest Aylaian
Rooms: 10 (PB) $85-145
Continental Breakfast
Credit Cards: A, B, C
Notes: 2, 5, 8, 9, 10, 11, 12, 14

The Stonehouse Inn

Eighth below Monte Verde, 93921
(408) 624-4569

A touch of old Carmel. Experience this luxurious country house in a quiet neighborhood setting. The Stonehouse Inn offers a tastefully restored turn-of-the-century vacation retreat. The original owner often invited well-known artists and writers to stay in her home. Each room bears a distinct character reminiscent of the artist or writer for whom it was named.

Host: Barbara Cooke
Rooms: 6 (S3B) $90-125
Expanded Continental Breakfast
Credit Cards: A, B
Notes: 2, 5, 9, 10, 11, 12, 14

CARMEL VALLEY

Hilltop House

11685 McCarthy Road, 93924
(408) 659-3060

This peaceful, private mountain retreat overlooks sunny Carmel Valley, just 20 minutes away from Monterey Peninsula's natural attractions, cultural activities, and fine restaurants. The comfortable two-room guest suite has a wood-burning fireplace, and guests enjoy a 40-foot pool and hot tub, extensive flower and sculpture gardens. Ideal for a couple, traveling friends, or a family group.

welcome; 9 Social drinking allowed; 10 Tennis available; 11 Swimming available; 12 Golf available; 13 Skiing available; 14 May be booked through travel agents

Hosts: Margaret and Richard Mayer
Rooms: 2 (SB) $65-75
Full Breakfast
Credit Cards: None
Notes: 2, 5, 9, 10, 11, 12

CARPINTERIA

Carpinteria Beach Condo
1825 Cravens Lane, 93013
(805) 684-1579

A self-catering bed and breakfast in a two-room condo across the street from the "world's safest beach." The unit can sleep four in a queen bed and two single beds. Color TV, pool, outside barbecue, complete minikitchen. The host family invites guests to visit their semi-tropical fruit ranch two miles away. Visit the orchard farms, see a polo game, or play a game of tennis at the Polo and Racquet Club.

Hosts: Bev and Don Schroeder
Rooms: 2 (SB) $60-65
Continental Breakfast
Credit Cards: None
Notes: 2, 5, 8, 9, 10, 11, 12

Columbia City Hotel

CLOVERDALE

Ye Olde Shelford House Bed and Breakfast
29955 River Road, 95425
(800) 833-6479

This circa 1885 country Victorian home is situated in the wine country with a wrap-around porch, hot tub, pool, bicycles, and recreation room. Guest rooms are filled with antiques, flowers, homemade quilts, and dolls. Horse-drawn surrey rides ($60) or antique car wine tour ($55) with picnic lunch are available.

Hosts: Ina and Al Sauder
Rooms: 6 (4 PB; 2 SB) $85-110
Full Breakfast
Credit Cards: A, B, D
Notes: 2, 8, 9, 10, 11, 12, 14

COLUMBIA

Columbia City Hotel
Main Street, Columbia State Historic Park, 95310
(209) 532-1479

Small and intimate, the hotel conveys a genuine feeling of the Gold Rush era. The City Hotel has provided hospitality to wayfarers for over 130 years and is dedicated to maintaining the quality and excellence of food and service for which it has been known throughout its history. A living museum, Columbia is the best-preserved Gold Rush town in California.

Host: Tom Bender
Rooms: 9 (PB) $65-85
Continental Breakfast
Credit Cards: A, B, C
Notes: 2, 3, 4, 5, 8, 9, 10, 11, 12, 13, 14

DESERT HOT SPRINGS

Bed and Breakfast of Los Angeles
32074 Waterside Lane, Westlake Village, 91361
(818) 889-8870

NOTES: Credit cards accepted: A Master Card; B Visa; C American Express; D Discover Card; E Diners Club; F Other; 2 Personal checks accepted; 3 Lunch available; 4 Dinner available; 5 Open all year; 6 Pets welcome; 8 Children

Two guest rooms share a bath and another has a private bath. All rooms have views of the mountains and are decorated with country charm. Pool and Jacuzzi. Closed summers. $50.

DORRINGTON

Dorrington Hotel and Restaurant

3431 Highway 4, P. O. Box 4307, 95223
(209) 795-5800

Built in 1860 by John and Rebecca Gardner, the hotel was a stage coach stop on the Big Trees Carson Valley Road. Noted for its ice cold spring, it was called Cold Spring Ranch until 1902, when Rebecca's maiden name was submitted to the postal department and the town became known as Dorrington. The old legend persists that Rebecca's ghost still haunts the hotel.

Hosts: Bonnie and Ardan Saville
Rooms: 5 (SB) $75
Continental Breakfast
Credit Cards: A, B
Notes: 2, 3, 4, 5, 10, 11, 12, 13

ELK

Elk Cove Inn

6300 South Highway 1, P.O. Box 367, 95432
(707) 877-3321

1883 Mansard Victorian atop a bluff overlooking the Mendocino coastline. Four ocean-view cabins, two with Victorian fireplaces, have large bay windows and skylights. Three new additions to the main house have large dormer windows and window seats for ocean viewing. French and German specialties for a complete breakfast are served in the ocean-view dining rooms of the main house. Private staircase to beach below the inn.

Host: Hildrun-Uta Triebess
Rooms: 7 (PB) $108-138
Full Breakfast

Credit Cards: None
Notes: 2, 5, 9, 10, 12

An Elegant Victorian Mansion

EUREKA

An Elegant Victorian Mansion

1406 C Street, 95501
(707) 444-3144; (707) 442-5594

With opulence, grace, and grandeur, this national historic landmark is the most elegant home in Eureka. Noted for its outstanding quality, elegance, and highly personalized service, the Elegant Victorian is a cherished world of warmth, good cheer, and spirited camaraderie. Gracious and helpful in every way, the innkeepers are the consumate perfection of what one would expect in world-class innkeepers.

Hosts: Doug and Lily Vieyra
Rooms: 3 (1 PB; 2 SB) $55-85
Full Breakfast
Credit Cards: A, B
Notes: 2, 3, 5, 9, 10, 11, 12, 14

A Weaver's Inn

1440 B Street, 95501
(707) 443-8119

This Queen Anne Colonial Revival house was built in 1883 and remodeled in 1907. Placed in a spacious fenced garden, it is airy

welcome; 9 Social drinking allowed; 10 Tennis available; 11 Swimming available; 12 Golf available; 13 Skiing available; 14 May be booked through travel agents

and light, but cozy and warm when veiled by wisps of fog. Many fine restaurants are within walking distance, and the Victorian parlor offers a piano and elegant relaxation. Guests enjoy croquet, Japanese gardens, and colorful flowers.

Hosts: Bob and Dorothy Swendeman
Rooms: 4 (2 PB; 2 SB) $65-85
Full Breakfast
Credit Cards: A, B, C
Notes: 2, 5, 6, 8, 9, 12, 14

The Gingerbread Mansion

FAWNSKIN

The Inn at Fawnskin Bed and Breakfast

880 Canyon Road, P.O. Box 378, 92333
(714) 866-3200

This is a beautiful custom contemporary log home situated on the peaceful north shore of Big Bear Lake featuring a livingroom with a big rock fireplace and baby grand piano; library; game room with large TV, movie library, and wet bar; dining room; and gazebo with spa. The grand suite includes a huge rock fireplace, private deck, and bath.

Hosts: G. B. and Susie Sneed
Rooms: 4 (2 PB; 2 SB) $75-155

Full Breakfast
Credit Cards: A, B
Notes: 2, 3, 4, 5, 9, 10, 11, 12, 13

FERNDALE

The Gingerbread Mansion

400 Berding, 95536
(707) 786-4006

The Gingerbread Mansion is well-named for its striking Victorian architecture trimmed with gingerbread. A dramatic English garden is wonderful for strolling and relaxing on a quiet afternoon. The Mansion has nine guest rooms, four parlors, and a large dining room—all beautifully decorated in antiques. It is situated a short block from Main Street in the Victorian village of Ferndale, with its art galleries, mercantile, unique gift shops, and live theater.

Host: Ken Torbert
Rooms: 9 (PB) $70-175
Continental Breakfast
Credit Cards: A, B
Notes: 2, 5, 9, 14

FISH CAMP

Karen's Bed and Breakfast Yosemite Inn

1144 Railroad Avenue, P. O. Box 8, 93623
(800) 346-1443

The inn is only two miles from the south entrance to Yosemite National Park. Nestled amid the towering pines and whispering cedars at 5,000 feet, guests find a unique blend of contemporary and country living. Experience the splendor of each season in Yosemite. Spectacular views, hiking, fishing, golfing, skiing, swimming, ice skating, horseback riding, museums, art galleries, and fine dining await.

Hosts: Karen Bergh and Lee Morse
Rooms: 3 (PB) $85
Full Breakfast
Credit Cards: None
Notes: 2, 5, 8, 12, 13, 14

Karen's Bed and Breakfast Yosemite Inn

FORT BRAGG

The Grey Whale Inn

615 North Main Street, 95437
(707) 964-0640; (800) 382-7244

The inn, a Mendocino Coast landmark since 1915, is furnished with yesterday's treasures and today's comforts. Each room offers a special amenity: ocean, garden, or town view; fireplace; private deck; double-size whirlpool tub; or wheelchair access. In-room phones, several TVs. The staff is helpful in a relaxed manner, and the inn is situated close to beaches, downtown, Skunk Train depot, Noyo harbor, restaurants, and theaters.

Host: Colette Bailey
Rooms: 14 (PB) $80-176
Full Breakfast
Credit Cards: A, B, D
Notes: 2, 5, 9, 10, 11, 12, 14

Pudding Creek Inn

700 North Main Street, 95437
(707) 964-9529

Situated at the north end of historic Fort Bragg, the inn consists of two Victorian homes connected by an enclosed garden court. The homes were built by a Russian count in 1884. Each room is appointed in a Victorian manner, some with fireplaces. A parlor with a fireplace and a breakfast room complete the inn.

Hosts: Garry and Carole Anloff
Rooms: 10 (PB) $65-115
Full Breakfast
Credit Cards: A, B, C
Notes: 2, 10, 12, 14

FREESTONE

Green Apple Inn

520 Bohemian Highway, 95472
(707) 874-2526

An 1860s New England-style farmhouse set in a meadow backed by redwoods, this inn is situated on five acres in the designated historic district of Freestone between Bodega Bay and the Russian River. There are several excellent restaurants and small family wineries in the area. In the village itself are several unique shops.

Hosts: Rogers and Rosemary Hoffman
Rooms: 4 (PB) $82-92
Full Breakfast
Credit Cards: A, B
Notes: 2, 5, 6, 8 (over 6), 10, 11, 12, 14

The Grey Whale Inn

GARDEN GROVE

Bed and Breakfast of Los Angeles

32074 Waterside Lane, Westlake Village, 91361
(818) 889-8870

This lovely older home offers three guest rooms with private baths, one with a fireplace and balcony. $45-54.

welcome; 9 Social drinking allowed; 10 Tennis available; 11 Swimming available; 12 Golf available; 13 Skiing available; 14 May be booked through travel agents

GUALALA

North Coast Country Inn

34591 South Highway 1, 95445
(707) 884-4537

The inn features rustic redwood buildings on a forested hillside overlooking the Pacific Ocean, fireplaces, minikitchens, decks, authentic antiques, romantic hot tub under the pines, and hilltop gazebo garden. It is near beaches, hiking, golf, tennis, state parks, and restaurants.

Hosts: Loren and Nancy Flanagan
Rooms: 4 (PB) $115
Full Breakfast
Credit Cards: A, B, C
Notes: 2, 5, 9, 10, 12, 14

HAWTHORNE

Bed and Breakfast of Los Angeles

32074 Waterside Lane, Westlake Village, 91361
(818) 889-8870

This home is just minutes from the airport and beaches, and the bus line is nearby. Private or shared bath available. $40-45.

HEALDSBURG

Bed and Breakfast of Los Angeles

32074 Waterside Lane, Westlake Village, 91361
(818) 889-8870

This Italianate 1869 Victorian town house is convenient to wineries and golf and has rooms with private or shared bath. $50-90.

HOLLYWOOD

Bed and Breakfast of Los Angeles

32074 Waterside Lane, Westlake Village, 91361
(818) 889-8870

Two blocks north of Sunset in a quiet neighborhood, this home offers two upstairs bedrooms with private bath. The larger room has a sun deck overlooking the yard. $45.

HOPE VALLEY

Sorensen's Resort

14255 Highway 88, 96120
(916) 694-2203

Sorensen's is an all-season resort situated in Hope Valley 20 minutes south of Lake Tahoe and offering 17 cozy cabins, three of which are bed and breakfast. The restaurant serves breakfast, lunch, and dinner daily. A wood-burning sauna is available for guests.

Hosts: John and Patty Brissenden
Rooms: 27 (26 PB; 1 SB) $50-225
Continental Breakfast
Credit Cards: A, B
Notes: 2, 3, 4, 5, 8, 9, 10, 11, 12, 13, 14

KLAMATH

Requa Inn

451 Requa Road, 95548
(707) 482-8205

Situated in the heart of the Redwood National Park on the Klamath River, Requa Inn is just one mile from the ocean. Beaches and hiking trails are nearby. Some rooms have a view of the river. The lobby features a fireplace, and the dining room overlooks the river. Reservations guaranteed with credit card, three-day cancellation notice. Closed January.

Hosts: Paul and Donna Hamby
Rooms: 10 (PB) $50-75
Full Breakfast
Credit Cards: A, B, C
Notes: 4, 9, 11, 12

NOTES: Credit cards accepted: A Master Card; B Visa; C American Express; D Discover Card; E Diners Club; F Other; 2 Personal checks accepted; 3 Lunch available; 4 Dinner available; 5 Open all year; 6 Pets welcome; 8 Children

LA JOLLA—SEE ALSO SAN DIEGO

Bed and Breakfast of Los Angeles

32074 Waterside Lane, Westlake Village, 91361
(818) 889-8870

One block from Windansea surfing beach, this charming beach house offers four guest rooms decorated in a variety of styles. Children over 13 welcome. Two-night minimum stay. $70-105.

LAKE ARROWHEAD

Bed and Breakfast of Los Angeles 01

32074 Waterside Lane, Westlake Village, 91361
(818) 889-8870

On the West Shore, this home is a short distance from the village of Blue Jay and has four guest rooms with private baths and individual decor. $70-120.

Bed and Breakfast of Los Angeles 02

32074 Waterside Lane, Westlake Village, 91361
(818) 889-8870

This three-story estate built in the 1940s has six guest rooms, three suites, and a separate cabin. Weekday discounts. $95-175.

LODI

Wine and Roses Country Inn

2505 West Turner Road, 95242
(209) 334-6988

Converted to a charming, romantic country inn with nine elegant suites filled with handmade comforters, antiques, and fresh flowers, this 1902 estate is secluded on five acres

of towering trees and old-fashioned flower gardens. Walk to lake with swimming, boating, and fishing. Five minutes to wine tasting, golf, tennis, health club. Delta Waterways, Gold Country, and Sacramento are close by.

Hosts: Kris Cromwell; Del and Sherri Smith
Rooms: 9 (PB) $85-115
Continental and Full Breakfast
Credit Cards: A, B, C
Notes: 2, 4, 5, 9, 10, 11, 12, 14

LONG BEACH

Bed and Breakfast of Los Angeles 01

32074 Waterside Lane, Westlake Village, 91361
(818) 889-8870

This restored home of Captain James Appleton and his wife, Rose, has five guest rooms with private baths and telephones. It is ten blocks to the ocean, one block to bus lines. Chidren over 12 welcome. $60-80.

Bed and Breakfast of Los Angeles 02

32074 Waterside Lane, Westlake Village, 91361
(818) 889-8870

This classic box-style Victorian has guest rooms on the second floor that share two baths. The bus line is one block away. Children over 16 welcome. $60.

Wine and Roses Country Inn

LOS ANGELES _____

Bed and Breakfast of Los Angeles 01

32074 Waterside Lane, Westlake Village, 91361
(818) 889-8870

On the National Register of Historic Places, this 1910 Craftsman home is beautifully restored. Two upstairs rooms share a bath; one has a small sun porch. Easy access to downtown. $45-50.

Bed and Breakfast of Los Angeles 02

32074 Waterside Lane, Westlake Village, 91361
(818) 889-8870

This high-rise apartment has a balcony overlooking Wilshire Boulevard. Two guest rooms each with a private bath. Children over six welcome. $65.

Bed and Breakfast of Los Angeles 03

32074 Waterside Lane, Westlake Village, 91361
(818) 889-8870

Just south of Melrose, this comfortable duplex has two guest rooms with shared bath. Enjoy the downstairs fireplace, and make use of the full kitchen. $40; whole house $70.

Bed and Breakfast of Los Angeles 04

32074 Waterside Lane, Westlake Village, 91361
(818) 889-8870

This fascinating historic home has beautiful woodwork, leaded windows, and exquisite detail. Five guest rooms are available with a variety of beds. $55-100.

Bed and Breakfast of Los Angeles 05

32074 Waterside Lane, Westlake Village, 91361
(818) 889-8870

Beautifully restored and furnished, this Craftsman-style home offers five rooms. A car is essential. $60-85.

Bed and Breakfast of Los Angeles 06

32074 Waterside Lane, Westlake Village, 91361
(818) 889-8870

Time stands still in this 1902 home facing a park. Leaded windows, paneling, period furnishings, and an atmosphere of genteel living. Five rooms all have private baths. $70-100.

West Hollywood Spanish Villa

449 North Detroit Street, 90036
(213) 938-4794

Enjoy comfortable accommodations in a quiet villa and converse with the host in a friendly atmosphere. The villa is on an attractive street in a convenient location, not far from downtown, Beverly Center, Hollywood Hills, CBS studios, and the beach. Bus stops are within walking distance.

Host: Suzanne Moultout
Room: 1 (PB) $55
Continental Breakfast
Credit Cards: None
Notes: 5, 14

LOS FELIZ HILLS _____

Bed and Breakfast of Los Angeles

32074 Waterside Lane, Westlake Village, 91361
(818) 889-8870

NOTES: Credit cards accepted: A Master Card; B Visa; C American Express; D Discover Card; E Diners Club; F Other; 2 Personal checks accepted; 3 Lunch available; 4 Dinner available; 5 Open all year; 6 Pets welcome; 8 Children

Just minutes from downtown, this two-story Art Deco home with lush gardens has two guest rooms, each with a balcony, one with a private bath. Bus lines and restaurants are nearby. $60.

LOS OSOS

Gerarda's
1056 Bay Oaks Drive, 93402
(805) 528-3973

Guests are welcomed by a Dutch-born hostess who speaks Dutch, Indonesian, Japanese, and several other languages. Situated near state parks, Morro Bay, Hearst Castle, San Luis Obispo, universities, and shopping centers. The immediate area offers tennis, hiking, scuba diving, and golf.

Host: Gerarda Ondang
Rooms: 3 (1 PB; 2 SB) $42
Full Breakfast
Credit Cards: None
Notes: 2, 5, 8, 9, 10, 11, 12

MALIBU

Bed and Breakfast of Los Angeles 01
32074 Waterside Lane, Westlake Village, 91361
(818) 889-8870

Walk the path beside the driveway to this cottage built behind the garage with a view through the canyon to the ocean. Livingroom with Hide-a-bed, bedrooms, kitchen, and balcony. Two-night minimum stay. $65.

Bed and Breakfast of Los Angeles 02
32074 Waterside Lane, Westlake Village, 91361
(818) 889-8870

This contemporary home has views up and down the coastline. A private upstairs suite has views of the mountains. Two downstairs rooms share a bath. One mile to the beach. $40-60.

MARINA DEL REY

Bed and Breakfast of Los Angeles
32074 Waterside Lane, Westlake Village, 91361
(818) 889-8870

Light and airy, this upstairs studio has a private entrance, full kitchen, and roof deck. It is an easy walk to shops and restaurants and one mile to the ocean. $75.

MARIPOSA

Oak Meadows, too
5263 Highway 140, P. O. Box 619, 95338
(209) 742-6161

Oak Meadows, too is just a short drive to Yosemite National Park. This bed and breakfast has turn-of-the-century charm. A stone fireplace greets arriving guests in the parlor. Comfortable rooms are decorated with handmade quilts, brass bedboards, and charming wallpapers. The California State Mining & Mineral Museum is nearby.

Hosts: Frank Ross and Kaaren Black
Rooms: 6 (PB) $59-69
Continental Breakfast
Credit Cards: A, B
Notes: 2, 5, 13, 14

MAR VISTA

Bed and Breakfast of Los Angeles
32074 Waterside Lane, Westlake Village, 91361
(818) 889-8870

Two guest rooms, each with a single bed, share two baths with host. Patio and bikes available. Children over five welcome. $50.

welcome; 9 Social drinking allowed; 10 Tennis available; 11 Swimming available; 12 Golf available; 13 Skiing available; 14 May be booked through travel agents

MENDOCINO

The Headlands Inn
Corner of Howard and Albion Streets
P.O. Box 132, 95460
(707) 937-4431

An 1868 Victorian home, the Headlands Inn is centrally situated within the historic preservation district. All rooms have fireplaces and large beds, some with spectacular ocean views overlooking English-style garden. Afternoon tea is served, with nuts, cookies, mineral waters. Two parlors feature numerous unusual antiques. Handicapped access cottage available. Open weekends, reserve 6 to 8 weeks in advance.

Hosts: Pat and Rod Stofle
Rooms: 5 (PB) $98-150
Full Breakfast
Credit Cards: None
Notes: 2, 5, 8, 9, 10, 11, 12

John Dougherty House
571 Ukiah Street, P. O. Box 817, 95460
(707) 937-5266

This 1867 saltbox is in a historic district. Furnished with antiques, stenciled walls, and wood-burning stoves, the house offers some of the best ocean views in Mendocino and is within walking distance of beaches, shops, and restaurants. It offers a quiet, peaceful night's sleep seldom experienced in today's urban lifestyle. Park the car and visit the California of 120 years ago.

Hosts: David and Marion Wells
Rooms: 6 (PB) $95-140
Full Breakfast
Credit Cards: None
Notes: 2, 5, 9, 10, 11, 14

Mendocino Village Inn
Box 626, 95460
(707) 937-0246

Hummingbirds, Picassos, 1882 Victorian, French roast coffee, fuchsias, fireplaces, Vivaldi, country breakfasts, Pacific surf, bokharas, fresh blackberries, four-poster beds, migrating whales, Chardonnay. "A bed and breakfast inn well done."

Hosts: Sue and Tom Allen
Rooms: 12 (10 PB; 2 SB) $59-130
Full Breakfast
Credit Cards: A, B
Notes: 2, 5, 9, 10, 12

MONTARA

Goose and Turrets Bed and Breakfast
835 George Street, P. O. Box 937, 94037-0937
(415) 728-5451

Geese on the pond, hummingbirds in the fuchsias, Bach on the tape deck, bread baking in the oven, a wood fire in the livingroom, down comforters to cuddle under, and sounds of surf and foghorns in the distance. This 1908 Italian villa in a large garden is only 20 minutes from San Francisco airport, 25 miles from downtown San Francisco, and one-half mile from the beach. Nous parlons français.

Hosts: Raymond and Emily Hoche-Mong
Rooms: 5 (PB) $88-104
Full Breakfast
Credit Cards: A, B, C, D
Notes: 2, 5, 8, 9, 10, 11, 12, 14

Goose and Turrets Bed and Breakfast

NOTES: Credit cards accepted: A Master Card; B Visa; C American Express; D Discover Card; E Diners Club; F Other; 2 Personal checks accepted; 3 Lunch available; 4 Dinner available; 5 Open all year; 6 Pets welcome; 8 Children

Montara Bed and Breakfast

P. O. Box 493, 94037
(415) 728-3946

This lovely bed and breakfast home is in a semi-rural area just 20 miles south of San Francisco on the scenic California coast. Facilities consist of a two-room suite with private entrance, fireplace, TV, stereo, ocean view, and phone. The beautifully decorated contemporary rustic redwood home is one-half mile from Montara State Beach, with walking trails nearby.

Hosts: Bill and Peggy Bechtell
Suite: 1 (PB) $80
Full Breakfast
Credit Cards: A, B
Notes: 2, 5, 9, 11, 12, 14

MONTEREY

Bed and Breakfast International #204

P. O. Box 282910, San Francisco, 94128
(415) 696-1690 ; FAX (415) 696-1699

Three homes situated on the southern end of Monterey are modestly priced. Two have views of the Bay; all have shared baths. $50-60.

Bed and Breakfast International #206

P. O. Box 282910, San Francisco, 94128
(415) 696-1690; FAX (415) 696-1699

This contemporary redwood home in an exclusive area features a breakfast room encircled in glass and extending into the garden. There is a fireplace and view of the ocean from the livingroom. $88-98.

Del Monte Beach Inn

1110 Del Monte Avenue, 93940
(408) 649-4410

The inn offers all the charm and comfort of a quaint European bed and breakfast at affordable rates in an ideal location. Situated near the heart of Monterey and just across the boulevard from the beach. Guests are never more than a few minutes away from the best the peninsula has to offer. Take a scenic drive down Highway 1 to the Big Sur coast or golf at some of the world's finest courses.

Hosts: Lisa and Ken Hardy
Rooms: 18 (2 PB; 16 SB) $40-75
Expanded Continental Breakfast
Credit Cards: A, B
Notes: 2, 5, 8, 9, 10, 11, 12, 14

Dunbar House, 1880

MURPHYS

Dunbar House, 1880

271 Jones Street, P. O. Box 1375, 95247
(209) 728-2897

Dunbar House, 1880 is a large Italianate-style home with comfortable country furnishings situated in the Gold Rush town of Murphys. Guests are greeted with afternoon snacks, lemonade, or coffee. A chilled bottle of local wine is waiting in the guest's room. All rooms have queen beds and fireplaces. Breakfast is served in the rooms, in the dining room by the fire, or in the century-old gardens.

Hosts: Barbara and Bob Costa
Rooms: 4 (PB) $95

Full Breakfast
Credit Cards: A, B
Notes: 2, 5, 9, 10, 11, 12, 13, 14

NAPA

Arbor Guest House
1436 G Street, 94559
(707) 252-8144

This 1906 Colonial transition home and carriage house have been completely restored. Rooms are beautifully appointed with antiques and queen beds. One room has a spa. For guests seeking privacy, the carriage house bed and sitting rooms, both with fireplaces, are most fitting. Breakfast is served on the garden patios, in the dining room, or in the carriage house. The inn is conveniently close to valley attractions.

Hosts: Rosemary and Bruce Logan
Rooms: 5 (PB) $85-135
Full Breakfast
Credit Cards: A, B
Notes: 2, 5, 9, 10, 11, 12, 14

Beazley House
1910 First Street, 94559
(707) 257-1649

Stroll past verdant lawns and bright flowers, and sense the hospitality of Beazley House. The landmark 1902 mansion is a chocolate brown masterpiece. The view from each room reveals beautiful gardens. Some rooms have private spa and fireplace. Napa's first bed and breakfast is still its best. Call for the color brochure.

Hosts: Jim and Carol Beazley
Rooms: 10 (PB) $105-175
Full Breakfast
Credit Cards: A, B, D
Notes: 2, 5, 9, 10, 11, 12, 14

Bed and Breakfast International #303
P. O. Box 282910, San Francisco, 94128
(415) 696-1690; FAX (415) 696-1699

Situated in Old Town Napa, this English country home built in 1892 is close to many wineries. The house has been renovated and furnished with heirloom-quality antiques. $85.

Churchill Manor
485 Brown Street, 94559
(707) 253-7733

Churchill Manor is an 1889 three-story Victorian mansion designated as a national historic landmark. It rests on an acre of beautifully landscaped grounds and is surrounded by a large veranda supported by Greek Revival columns. Other features include original redwood carved ceilings, Corinthian columns, fireplaces, marble-floored sunroom, and grand piano. The entire home is furnished with antiques, Oriental rugs, and brass and crystal chandeliers.

Host: Joanna Guidotti
Rooms: 10 (PB) $75-145
Full Breakfast
Credit Cards: A, B
Notes: 2, 5, 9, 10, 11, 12, 14

Napa Valley Reservations Unlimited
1819 Tanen Street, Suite B, 94559
(707) 252-1985

This reservation service specializes in accommodations in an around the Napa valley. Using the travel dates and other information provided by guests, such as price range, bed size, city or county, agents will arrange for suitable accommodations. More than 1,000 accommodations are represented, ranging from $65 to $600. This is a no-fee service.

Old World Inn
1301 Jefferson Street, 94559
(707) 257-0112

NOTES: Credit cards accepted: A Master Card; B Visa; C American Express; D Discover Card; E Diners Club; F Other; 2 Personal checks accepted; 3 Lunch available; 4 Dinner available; 5 Open all year; 6 Pets welcome; 8 Children

This romantic 1906 Victorian home was built as the private residence of E. W. Doughty, a prominent contractor who virtually built Old Town Napa. The charming interior is graced by enchanting wooden pillars, brightly appointed rooms, stenciled walls, and claw foot tubs. Guests are pampered with afternoon tea, relaxing wine and cheese, and a chocolate lover's dessert buffet. To end a most enjoyable visit, an outdoor Jacuzzi is available.

Host: Diane M. Dumaine
Rooms: 8 (PB) $82-137
Full Breakfast
Credit Cards: A, B, C, D
Note: 2

Downey House Bed and Breakfast

Tall Timbers Chalet
1012 Darms Lane, 94558
(707) 252-7810

The chalet is made up of 1944 rustic, white-washed country cottages off Highway 29. Walking trails, golf, bicycle rentals, wineries, and restaurants are nearby. The cottages are reminiscent of places in Austria and Switzerland: squeaky clean with lace curtains, papered walls, and carpets in light, fresh colors. The grounds are studded with evergreens and fruit trees.

Hosts: Mary and Serge Montes
Rooms: 8 (PB) $105-125
Continental Breakfast
Credit Cards: A, B, C, F
Notes: 2, 5, 8, 9, 11, 12, 14

Wine Country Reservations
P. O. Box 5059, 94581-0059
(707) 257-7757

This reservation service offers the finest bed and breakfast accommodations in the wine country. Over 90 inns utilize this service with prices ranging from $65 to $300.

NEVADA CITY

Downey House Bed and Breakfast
517 West Broad Street, 95959
(916) 265-2815; (800) 258-2815

A restored 1870 Eastlake Victorian, one block from the historic downtown with its quaint shops, wonderful restaurants, galleries, live theater, and horse-drawn carriages. Downey House serves a breakfast buffet, and wine, coffee, tea and homemade cookies in the afternoon. Parlor, sun room with view, garden entrance room, garden with waterfall and lily pond, and the veranda provide places to relax.

Host: Miriam Wright
Rooms: 6 (PB) $70-90
Full Breakfast
Credit Cards: A, B
Notes: 2, 5, 8, 10, 11, 12, 13, 14

The Parsonage Bed and Breakfast
427 Broad Street, 95959
(916) 265-9478

The Parsonage opened in 1986 after extensive renovations. The house dates back more than 100 years and served for 80 years as the home for the local Methodist minister and his family. Cozy guest rooms, parlor, dining and family rooms are lovingly furnished with antiques from the innkeeper's pioneer family. Breakfast is served on the veranda or in the formal dining room.

welcome; 9 Social drinking allowed; 10 Tennis available; 11 Swimming available; 12 Golf available; 13 Skiing available; 14 May be booked through travel agents

Hosts: Deborah Dane and Rebecca Worthington
Rooms: 3 (PB) $65-90
Expanded Continental Breakfast
Credit Cards: A, B
Notes: 2, 5, 8, 9, 11, 12, 13, 14

NEWPORT BEACH

Doryman's Inn

2102 West Oceanfront, 92663
(714) 675-7300

This is a Victorian French country-style oceanfront bed and breakfast. All rooms have Italian marble sunken Jacuzzi tubs along with touch-button fireplaces in front of four-poster canopy king-size beds. A beautiful oceanfront sun deck offers a view of the sunset. Breakfast is served in bed. More than 200 restaurants and shops are within five blocks of the hotel. Full concierge service available; transportation arranged.

Host: Michael D. Palitz
Rooms: 10 (PB) $135-275
Full Breakfast
Credit Cards: A, B, C, D, E
Notes: 2, 4, 5, 9, 10, 11, 12, 13, 14

The Little Inn on the Bay

617 Lido Park Drive, 92663
(714) 673-8800

This is the only property on the waterfront in Newport Beach. Each room in this charming country inn is oriented to beautiful Newport Bay. The decor has authentically reproduced furniture and fixtures of early 1800s New England. Stroll to restaurants, antiques, boutiques, and ocean beach. Complimentary bicycles, wine, cheese, hors d'oeuvres, and milk and cookies are offered.

Host: Herrick Hanson
Rooms: 29 (PB) $98-180
Continental Breakfast
Credit Cards: A, B, C, D, E
Notes: 5, 9, 11, 12

NORTH HOLLYWOOD

Bed and Breakfast of Los Angeles

32074 Waterside Lane, Westlake Village, 91361
(818) 889-8870

This small home with a nice patio has a convenient location near the bus line. No children. $35.

La Maida House and Bungalows

11159 La Maida Street, 91601
(818) 769-3857

Set in a quiet, residential neighborhood, this historic landmark house is centrally situated in the Los Angeles area and convenient to the freeway system. The home boasts extensive use of marble, oak, mahogany, tile, and stained glass. Luxurious public rooms and airy bedrooms include antiques, Oriental rugs, and primitive art gathered from around the world. Fresh flowers, evening apéritifs, and turndown service are complimentary.

Host: Megan Timothy
Rooms: 11 (PB) $80-210
Expanded Continental Breakfast
Credit Cards: A, B
Notes: 2, 4, 5, 9, 10, 11, 12, 13

The Little Inn on the Bay

NOTES: Credit cards accepted: A Master Card; B Visa; C American Express; D Discover Card; E Diners Club; F Other;
2 Personal checks accepted; 3 Lunch available; 4 Dinner available; 5 Open all year; 6 Pets welcome; 8 Children

NORTHRIDGE

Bed and Breakfast of Los Angeles 01
32074 Waterside Lane, Westlake Village, 91361
(818) 889-8870

Miniature horses are raised on this secluded ranch in the middle of the San Fernando Valley. A separate guest wing offers two antique twin four-poster beds and private bath and entrance. $50.

Bed and Breakfast of Los Angeles 02
32074 Waterside Lane, Westlake Village, 91361
(818) 889-8870

On one-half acre of trees, this country style home has a pool and paddle tennis court, stained glass, and art work. The bus line is two blocks away. $45.

Bed and Breakfast of Los Angeles 03
32074 Waterside Lane, Westlake Village, 91361
(818) 889-8870

This contemporary home is filled with treasures from bygone times. The master bedroom has an antique double bed. Married couples only. $50.

ORANGE

Bed and Breakfast of Los Angeles
32074 Waterside Lane, Westlake Village, 91361
(818) 889-8870

Just five miles from Disneyland, this beautiful contemporary home has a view of the hills from the pool/spa area. Three rooms share two baths. $50.

PACIFIC GROVE

Bed and Breakfast of Los Angeles 01
32074 Waterside Lane, Westlake Village, 91361
(818) 889-8870

This Victorian mansion is furnished with antiques and is only a stroll to the beach. There are 22 rooms, most with private baths. $100-200.

Bed and Breakfast of Los Angeles 02
32074 Waterside Lane, Westlake Village, 91361
(818) 889-8870

This romantic Queen Anne mansion was built in 1888. The main house and carriage house offer a variety of accommodations, some with fireplaces or ocean views. $85-140.

The Martine Inn
255 Ocean View Boulevard, 93950
(408) 373-3388

Built in the 1890s, this grand old house overlooks the magnificent rocky coastline of Pacific Grove on Monterey Bay. Each of the 19 rooms has a private bath and is elegantly furnished with authentic museum-quality furnishings. Breakfast is served on old Sheffield silver, Victorian-style china, crystal, and lace. Read in the library, watch otters from the sitting rooms, or play pool in the game room.

Hosts: Don and Marion Martine
Rooms: 19 (PB)
Full Breakfast
Credit Cards: A, B
Notes: 2, 5, 9, 14

The Old Saint Angela Inn
321 Central Avenue, 93950
(408) 372-3246

welcome; 9 Social drinking allowed; 10 Tennis available; 11 Swimming available; 12 Golf available; 13 Skiing available; 14 May be booked through travel agents

The Old Saint Angela Inn was born as a fine country home in 1910, converted to a rectory, then a convent in 1928, and is now a cozy inn overlooking the natural beauty of Monterey Bay. Within this historic Cape Cod home are rooms of distinctive individuality and warmth to provide comfort and serenity, with country pine furniture and soft quilts, fresh flowers, and fine linens. Near restaurants and shopping areas, Cannery Row, aquarium, beaches, and parks.

Hosts: Don and Barbara Foster
Rooms: 9 (6 PB; 3 SB) $90-150
Full Breakfast
Credit Cards: A, B
Notes: 2, 5, 9, 10, 11, 12, 14

Roserox Country Inn by-the-Sea
557 Ocean View Boulevard, 93950
(408) 373-7673

A historic country Victorian mansion set on the edge of the Pacific shoreline, the home was built in 1904 for Doctor Julia Platt, mayor of Pacific Grove. Today, Roserox is a charming, intimate four-story inn with eight guest rooms with spectacular ocean-front views. Breakfast is served in bed, the country French morning room, or on the ocean patio. A delightful wine and cheese hour is observed in the parlor.

Host: Dawn Vyette Browncroft
Rooms: 8 (SB) $125-205
Full Breakfast
Credit Cards: None
Notes: 2, 3, 4, 5, 9, 10, 11, 12, 14

PALM SPRINGS

Bed and Breakfast of Los Angeles
32074 Waterside Lane, Westlake Village, 91361
(818) 889-8870

Next to the tennis club, this small inn offers a one-bedroom suite, a two-bedroom suite, and a studio, all with kitchens and baths. $95.

Casa Cody Bed and Breakfast Country Inn
175 South Cahuilla Road, 92262
(619) 320-9346

This romantic, historic hideaway is nestled against the spectacular San Jacinto mountains in the heart of Palm Springs village. Beautifully redecorated in Sante Fe decor, 17 hacienda-style units include motel rooms, studios, one- and two-bedroom suites with private patios. Features include fireplaces, fully equipped tiled kitchens, cable TV, phones, pools, and spa.

Roserox Country Inn by-the-Sea

Host: Therese Hayes
Rooms: 17 (PB) $35-160
Continental Breakfast
Credit Cards: A, B, C
Notes: 2, 5, 6, 8, 9, 10, 11, 12, 14

PALO ALTO

Adella Villa

P. O. Box 4528, 94309
(415) 321-5195; FAX (415) 325-5121

A secluded one-acre estate built in the 1920s
features luxury accommodations: private
baths, robes, heated pool, bicycle, gorgeous
neighborhood. It is only 30 minutes to San
Francisco. Tours are given by arrangement.
Formal gardens combined with serenity
blend to make a guest's stay very enjoyable.

Hosts: Scott and Tricia Young
Rooms: 3 (PB) $95
Full Breakfast
Credit Cards: A, B, C, E
Notes: 2, 5, 9, 10, 11, 12, 14

PETALUMA

The 7th Street Inn

525 Seventh Street, 94952
(707) 769-0480

The 7th Street Inn is a charming Victorian
lady conveniently situated on Petaluma's
historic west side, 13 blocks from shops and
restaurants. The inn offers four lovely guest
rooms, including a romantic water tower.
Breakfast is served in the dining room, and
evening snacks are available. Special rates
for midweek and business travelers are available.

Hosts: Mark and Terry Antell
Rooms: 4 (PB) $75-125
Full Breakfast
Credit Cards: A, B
Notes: 2, 5, 8, 9, 10, 12, 14

POINT REYES STATION

The Country House

P. O. Box 98, 94956
(415) 663-1627

Country House is a California ranch house
on the mesa overlooking Point Reyes Station. Two suites share a large country kitchen
and livingroom. A third suite is separate
and totally private, with fireplace, loft, and
deck. Homegrown and whole-grain foods
are served. English garden, ridge views,
orchard, cable TV. Reservations required.
Seven-day cancellation notice.

Host: Ewell McIsaac
Rooms: 3 (PB) $75-90
Full Breakfast
Credit Cards: None
Notes: 2, 5, 8, 9, 11, 14

The Country House

Knob Hill

40 Knob Hill Road; P. O. Box 1108, 94956
(415) 663-1784

This custom-designed cottage has a queen
bed, wood-burning stove, and private deck,
as well as a cozy double room with separate
entrance, bath, and secluded garden area.
Spectacular views of the Inverness Ridge.
Easy walk the back way through fields to
restaurant and shops. Direct access to Point
Reyes National Seashore, which offers hiking, swimming, horseback riding, bird
watching, fishing, and bicycling.

Host: Janet Schlitt
Rooms: 2 (PB) $60-105
Continental Breakfast
Credit Cards: None
Notes: 2, 5, 8, 9, 11

The Neon Rose

P. O. Box 632, 94956
(415) 663-9143

A unique guest cottage overlooking Tomales Bay is available for dreams, private moments, and quiet times. One bedroom, livingroom, fully equipped kitchen, Jacuzzi, wood-burning stove, cable TV, stereo, private garden with direct access to Point Reyes National Seashore. Breakfast foods available for guest preparation.

Host: Sandy Fields
Room: 1 (PB) $125-135
Continental Breakfast
Credit Cards: A, B
Notes: 2, 5

Terri's Homestay

83 Sunnyside Drive, 94956
(415) 663-1289

High atop Inverness Ridge this sunny, secluded trailside bed and breakfast offers magnificent views, colorful Central American decor, and natural fiber bedding, as well as a private entrance. Near Old Town, museums, and restaurants. It is on the Sacramento Old House Tour and is furnished in antiques.

Hosts: Terri Elaine and Richard Lailer
Room: 1 (PB) $50-60
Expanded Continental Breakfast
Credit Cards: None
Notes: 2, 5, 8, 9, 11, 14

PORTOLA

Upper Feather Bed and Breakfast

256 Commercial Street, 96122
(916)832-0107

Casual country atmosphere in an old-fashioned small town. No TV, radio, or phones in your room, but there are popcorn, jigsaw puzzles, games, and relaxation. Walk to restaurants, a wild and scenic river, and railroad museum. You can even drive a locomotive. Only one hour from Reno, Nevada.

Hosts: Jon and Lynne Haman
Rooms: 6 (SB) $40
Full Breakfast
Credit Cards: None
Notes: 2, 5, 6, 8, 9, 10, 11, 12, 13

REDDING

Palisades Paradise Bed and Breakfast

1200 Palisades Avenue, 96003
(916) 223-5305

Enjoy a breathtaking view of the Sacramento River, city, and surrounding mountains from this beautiful, newly decorated, contemporary home with a garden spa, fireplace, wide-screen TV, VCR, and homelike atmosphere. Palisades Paradise is a serene setting for a quiet, romantic hideaway, yet convenient to shopping and Interstate 5. Water skiing and river rafting are also nearby.

Host: Gail Goetz
Rooms: 2 (SB) $55-65
Full Breakfast
Credit CArds: A, B, C
Notes: 2, 5, 9, 10, 12, 13, 14

ST. HELENA

Asplund Country Inn Bed and Breakfast

726 Rossi Road, 94574
(707) 963-4614

The inn offers European-style bed and breakfast with personal hospitality and privacy in a comfortable environment nestled in lush gardens with views from multilevel terraces

NOTES: Credit cards accepted: A Master Card; B Visa; C American Express; D Discover Card; E Diners Club; F Other; 2 Personal checks accepted; 3 Lunch available; 4 Dinner available; 5 Open all year; 6 Pets welcome; 8 Children

of vineyards and rolling hills. Volleyball, badminton, croquet, barbecue facilities. Peaceful, quiet, and serene.

Host: Elsie Asplund Hudale
Rooms: 3 (1 PB; 2 SB) $75-95
Full Breakfast
Credit Cards: A, B, C
Notes: 2, 5, 8, 9, 10, 11, 12, 14

Bartels Ranch and Country Inn

1200 Conn Valley Road, 94574
(707) 963-4001; FAX (707) 963-5100

Situated in the heart of the world-famous Napa Valley wine country. Secluded, romantic, elegant country estate overlooking a "100-acre valley with a 10,000-acre view." Honeymoon "Heart of the Valley" suite with sunken Jacuzzi, sauna, shower, stone fireplace, and silver service. Award-winning accommodations, expansive entertainment room, pool table, fireplace, library, and terraces overlooking the vineyard. Poolside lounging, bicycles, refrigerator, TV, and phone available. Tailored itinerary provided; champagne and afternoon refreshments are served. Nearby wineries, lake, golf, tennis, fishing, boating, and mineral spas.

Host: Jamie Bartels
Rooms: 3 (PB) $99-275
Expanded Continental Breakfast
Credit Cards: A, B, C
Notes: 2, 3, 4, 5, 9, 10, 11, 12, 14

Hilltop House Bed and Breakfast

P. O. Box 726, 94574
(707) 944-0880

Poised at the very top of the ridge that separates the famous wine regions of Napa and Sonoma, Hilltop House is a country retreat with all the comforts of home and a view that must be seen to be believed. The contemporary home was built with this mountain panorama in mind, and the vast deck allows guests to enjoy it at their leisure. From this vantage point, sunrises and sunsets are simply amazing.

Hosts: Bill and Annette Gevarter
Rooms: 3 (PB) $95-165
Full Breakfast
Credit Cards: A, B, C
Notes: 2, 5, 9, 14

SAN DIEGO

Windansea Beach Bed and Breakfast

P. O. Box 91223, 92169
(619) 456-9634

This bed and breakfast is situated one block from the ocean at La Jolla's famous Windansea Beach, and is within walking distance of restaurants and shops. The private residence features elegant furnishings with inn-quality decor and service. It is a short drive to Sea World, zoo, Coronoda, and Del Mar. Public transportation is available. Come and be pampered.

Host: Sherry Cash
Rooms: 3 (2 PB; 1 SB) $75-105
Full Breakfast
Credit Cards: None
Notes: 5, 9, 10, 11, 12, 14

SAN FRANCISCO

Art Center Bed and Breakfast

1902 Filbert Street, 94123
(415) 567-1526; (800) 821-3877

Enjoy a stay on the rim of the bay in the quiet ambience of the Marina and just a 20-minute stroll to Fisherman's Wharf. All rooms have queen beds, private entrances, kitchens, or coffee bars, and some have fireplaces, writing/dressing rooms, whirlpool bath, and enclosed deck off the garden. Near restaurants and transportation to all attractions.

Hosts: George and Helvi Wamsley
Rooms: 5 (PB) $65-115
Full Breakfast
Credit Cards: A, B, C, D, E
Notes: 2, 5, 9, 10, 12, 14

Art Center Bed and Breakfast

Bed and Breakfast International #101

P. O. Box 282910, 94128
(415) 696-1690; FAX (415) 696-1699

Situated on Russian Hill, this charming garden apartment has been professionally decorated and has glass doors that open onto the patio. It is one block from the cable cars. $85.

Bed and Breakfast International #102

P. O. Box 282910, 94128
(415) 696-1690; FAX (415) 696-1699

These accommodations are ideally situated in a modernized Victorian building near the North Beach area on Telegraph Hill and within walking distance of Fisherman's Wharf. Two rooms share a bath. $58-68.

Bed and Breakfast International #103

P. O. Box 282910, 94128
(415) 696-1690; FAX (415) 696-1699

This three-story turn-of-the-century home has been featured in *Sunset* magazine. It is situated only 15 minutes from Union Square and Ocean Beach and is within walking distance of Golden Gate Park. $60-70.

Bed and Breakfast International #104

P. O. Box 282910, 94128
(415) 696-1690; FAX (415) 696-1699

Exceptionaly well-decorated, this 1880 Victorian offers a guest room, studio, or carriage house in the back garden. All rooms open onto a beautifully landscaped garden in the Pacific Heights neighborhood. $95-175.

Bed and Breakfast International #105

P. O. Box 282910, 94128
(415) 696-1690; FAX (415) 696-1699

This 1876 Victorian is eclectically decorated and close to shops and restaurants in Pacific Heights. Room with private bath and minikitchen and sitting room $70; guest cottage with fully equipped kitchen. $85.

Bed and Breakfast of Los Angeles 01

32074 Waterside Lane, Westlake Village, 91361
(818) 889-8870

In the financial district, six rooms with elegant decor all have private baths; some have fireplaces. Meeting facilities are available. $145-160.

Bed and Breakfast of Los Angeles 02

32074 Waterside Lane, Westlake Village, 91361
(818) 889-8870

NOTES: Credit cards accepted: A Master Card; B Visa; C American Express; D Discover Card; E Diners Club; F Other; 2 Personal checks accepted; 3 Lunch available; 4 Dinner available; 5 Open all year; 6 Pets welcome; 8 Children

In the financial district is this inn with six rooms with private baths, some with fireplaces, beautifully furnished in French country antiques. $105-155.

Bed and Breakfast of Los Angeles 03
32074 Waterside Lane, Westlake Village, 91361
(818) 889-8870

This beautifully restored Victorian mansion is in Alamo Square between the civic center and the park. An impressive English tudor home next door offers a variety of rooms. Meetings and parties can be accommodated. $75-250.

Bed and Breakfast of Los Angeles 04
32074 Waterside Lane, Westlake Village, 91361
(818) 889-8870

This large, typical San Francisco flat with two guest rooms is near the bay. Guests enjoy full use of facilities. $55.

Bed and Breakfast of Los Angeles 05
32074 Waterside Lane, Westlake Village, 91361
(818) 889-8870

Enjoy views of Twin Peaks and Diamond Heights in this typical San Francisco flat. Shared bath. $55.

Casa Arguello
225 Arguello Boulevard, 94118
(415) 752-9482

Casa Arguello is a family-run bed and breakfast which prides itself on friendliness and cleanliness. It is situated in a nice neighborhood within walking distance of restaurants and shops, five blocks north of Golden Gate Park, convenient to the Golden Gate Bridge. There is public transportation right on the corner of Arguello to take guests to Union Square in 15 minutes.

Host: Emma Baires
Rooms: 5 (3 PB; 2 SB) $50-75
Continental Breakfast
Credit Cards: None
Notes: 2, 5, 8, 9, 10, 11, 12

The Chateau Tivoli Bed and Breakfast

The Chateau Tivoli Bed and Breakfast
1057 Steiner Street, 97230
(415) 776-5462; (800) 228-1647

Guests travel back to San Francisco's romantic golden age of opulence. They are surrounded by antiques and art from the estates of the Vanderbilts, Getty, and de Gaulle. The restoration of the mansion required five years to complete. It is now referred to as the greatest "painted lady" in the world, having 22 colors and gold leaf on the exterior. The rooms and suites feature canopy beds, marble baths, views, fireplaces, stained glass, and towers; each facet contributing to the atmosphere that makes staying here an unforgettable experience.

Hosts: Rodney, Bill, and Siobhan
Rooms: 8 (4 PB: 4 SB) $80-200
Expanded Continental Breakfast Monday-Friday;
   Full Breakfast Saturday-Sunday
Credit Cards: A, B, C
Notes: 2, 4, 5, 9, 10, 11, 12, 14

welcome; 9 Social drinking allowed; 10 Tennis available; 11 Swimming available; 12 Golf available; 13 Skiing available; 14 May be booked through travel agents

Cornell Hotel

715 Bush Street, 94108
(415) 421-3154; (800) 232-9698 reservations

Centrally situated between Union Square
and Nob Hill, renowned for its cuisine and
reasonable prices. The Cornell Hotel offers
a delightful taste of France in the heart of
San Francisco. Special deal available: one
week's stay with seven breakfasts and five
dinners served in Restaurant Jeanne d'Arc
on premises.

Host: Claude Lambert
Rooms: 58 (42 PB; 16 SB) $55-85
Full Breakfast
Credit Cards: A, B, C, E
Notes: 4, 5, 10, 11, 12, 14

The Inn at Union Square

440 Post Street, 94102
(415) 397-3510; (800) AT-THE-INN
FAX (415) 989-0529

The Inn at Union Square is an elegant small
hotel in the heart of downtown San Francisco. The financial and theater districts are
a short walk from the hotel's front door. The
city's fabled cable car is one-half block
away, and can make traveling to view historical sites convenient and fun. The inn
provides breakfast of flaky croissants, muffins, fresh juice and fruit, and coffee served
in bed or in the lobbies located on each floor.
Enjoy the afternoon tea served with fresh
cakes and crisp cucumber sandwiches or
hors d'oeuvres and wine served every day.

Host: Brooks Bayly
Rooms: 30 (PB) $110-180; $145-375 suites
Continental Breakfast
Credit Cards: A, B, C
Note: 2, 5, 8, 9, 11, 14

Pine Mews

P.O. Box 282910, 94128-2910
(415) 696-1690

Exceptional accommodations in the back of
an 1880 Victorian. All three guest quarters
have private entrances and open onto the
garden. There is a spacious, elegantly appointed carriage house with grand piano,
fireplace, and formal dining area; a large
studio with fireplace facing the sleeping
area; and a smaller guest room with private
bath. Situated in one of San Francisco's
nicest neighborhoods, Pacific Heights. Close
to wonderful shops and restaurants on Union
and Fillmore streets.

Rooms: 3 (PB) $65-175
Continental Breakfast
Credit Cards: A, B, C
Notes: 5, 9, 14

Red Victorian Inn Bed and Breakfast

1665 Haight Street, 94117
(415) 864-1978; FAX (415) 863-3293

San Francisco's colorful Red Victorian Bed
and Breakfast is upstairs above the Global
Village Center, where breakfast is shared
by wonderful guests from all over the world,
often creative folks who are involved in
peace, ecology, and world friendship. It is
situated near the Golden Gate Park in the
bohemian Haight/Ashbury district. Guest
rooms celebrate the diverse neighborhood
and culture.

Hosts: Sami Sunchild, Sally McReynolds, and John
  Drake
Rooms: 14 (4 PB; 10 SB) $65-125
Continental Breakfast
Credit Cards: A, B, C
Notes: 5, 14

Washington Square Inn

1660 Stockton Street, 94133
(415) 981-4220; (800) 388-0220

Situated in the heart of the city's Italian
district on historic Washington Square, the

inn offers imaginatively and tastefully furnished rooms with French and English antiques and an intimate parlor with fireplace where complimentary tea and hors d'oeuvres are served. Walking distance to Telegraph Hill, Fisherman's Wharf, Chinatown, financial district, restaurants, shops and markets, cable car line. Concierge service available.

Host: Brooks Bayly
Rooms: 15 (10 PB; 5 SB) $85-175
Continental Breakfast
Credit Cards: A, B, C
Notes: 2, 5, 8, 9, 14

SAN GREGORIO

Rancho San Gregorio
Route 1, Box 54, 94074
(415) 747-0810

Rancho San Gregorio is an early California-style country retreat on 15 acres with a creek and is near ocean beaches, wildlife reserves, and redwood parks. It features American oak antiques, wood-burning stoves, barn, gazebo, gardens, down quilts, robes, complimentary snacks and beverages, country breakfast with homegrown and local products. Close to San Francisco and Bay area locations off Ocean Highway 1.

Hosts: Bud and Lee Raynor
Rooms: 4 (PB) $65-125
Full Breakfast
Credit Cards: A, B, C
Notes: 2, 5, 8, 9, 11, 12, 14

SAN PEDRO

Bed and Breakfast of Los Angeles 01
32074 Waterside Lane, Westlake Village, 91361
(818) 889-8870

These cottages were the site of the movie *Swing Shift*. Breakfast is served at the elegant Grand House next door or brought to guests. Children over 14 welcome. $105.

Bed and Breakfast of Los Angeles 02
32074 Waterside Lane, Westlake Village, 91361
(818) 889-8870

This sprawling contemporary home on a hillside has views of the ocean and Catalina. Guest rooms are in a separate wing. Beach and tidepools are three blocks away. $45.

SANTA ANA

Bed and Breakfast of Los Angeles 01
32074 Waterside Lane, Westlake Village, 91361
(818) 889-8870

Enjoy this newly redecorated home. The guest room has an antique double bed and large bath in the private hall. Disneyland is 10 minutes away; bus line is four blocks away. $55.

Bed and Breakfast of Los Angeles 02
32074 Waterside Lane, Westlake Village, 91361
(818) 889-8870

This marvelous Craftsman home has spacious rooms and the elegance of an earlier time. Two upstairs rooms share a hall bath. Guests enjoy the pool and patio. Children over seven welcome. $65.

SANTA BARBARA

Bed and Breakfast at Valli's View
340 North Sierra Vista Road, 93108
(805) 969-1272

This beautiful home is nestled in the foothills of Montecito. The charming guest room overlooks the mountains and has a color TV. Spacious back patios offer lounges for

welcome; 9 Social drinking allowed; 10 Tennis available; 11 Swimming available; 12 Golf available; 13 Skiing available; 14 May be booked through travel agents

sunning and a porch swing for relaxing. Shady fern gardens surround the hillside deck with a magnificent view of the valley and mountains. The livingroom offers a fireplace and grand piano. Awaken to song-birds and the aroma of Dutch babies in the oven.

Hosts: Valli and Larry Stevens
Room: 1 (PB) $65
Full Breakfast
Credit Cards: None
Notes: 2, 5, 6 (outside), 8, 9, 10, 11, 12

Bed and Breakfast at Valli's View

Bed and Breakfast of Los Angeles 01

32074 Waterside Lane, Westlake Village, 91361
(818) 889-8870

Lots of light and charm are found in the French country-style inn with nine guest rooms and private baths. Two blocks to the beach and harbor. $85-155.

Bed and Breakfast of Los Angeles 02

32074 Waterside Lane, Westlake Village, 91361
(818) 889-8870

This beautiful Eastlake-style Victorian home is secluded in an acre of English gardens, yet just a five-minute walk to restaurants, theaters, and shops. Children over 12 welcome. $90-140.

Bed and Breakfast of Los Angeles 03

32074 Waterside Lane, Westlake Village, 91361
(818) 889-8870

This hilltop home with ocean views, pool, and spa offers two guest rooms with shared bath and private entrances. Breakfast is served poolside in nice weather. $85.

Bed and Breakfast of Los Angeles 04

32074 Waterside Lane, Westlake Village, 91361
(818) 889-8870

Only one-half block from the beach, this 1912 home has been lovingly restored. One room has a private bath; four more share two baths. Next door are four more guest rooms. Children over 13 welcome. $70-115.

Blue Quail Inn and Cottages

1908 Bath Street, 93101
(805) 687-2300; (800) 676-1622 U.S.A.
(800) 549-1622 CA

Choose from cottages and suites in a delightfully relaxing country setting close to town and beaches, and just three blocks to Sansum Clinic/Cottage Hospital. Breakfast is served in the main house dining room or in the gardens. Afternoon light hors d'oeuvres with wine and late-evening sweets and hot spiced apple cider are served. Bicycles are also offered. Picnic lunches and gift certificates available.

Host: Jeanise Suding Eaton
Rooms: 9 (7 PB; 2 SB) $74-125
Full Breakfast
Credit Cards: A, B, C
Notes: 2, 3, 5, 8, 9, 10, 11, 12, 14

Cheshire Cat Inn

36 West Valerio Street, 93101
(805) 569-1610

Two Victorians separated by a flower-filled red brick patio overlooking a gazebo and garden make a delightful setting for the delicious full breakfast that is served year-round, weather permitting. Guest rooms are decorated with Laura Ashley wallpapers and fabrics, some having fireplaces, Jacuzzis, and private patios. Rates include use of mountain bikes and wine and cheese on Saturday evenings.

Host: Midge Goeden
Rooms: 14 (PB) $119
Full Breakfast
Credit Cards: A, B
Notes: 2, 5, 9, 10, 11, 12, 14

The Old Yacht Club Inn

431 Corona Del Mar Drive, 93103
(805) 962-1277; (800) 676-1676 U.S.A.
(800) 549-1676 CA

Situated within one block of the city's nicest beaches, the inn is housed in two buildings: a 1912 California Craftsman and a mid-1920s early California-style dwelling. The inn is known for its hospitality and fine food. Rates include complimentary wine in the evening, bicycles, beach chairs, and towels.

Hosts: Nancy Donaldson, Lu Caruso, and Sandy Hunt
Rooms: 9 (PB) $75-135
Full Breakfast
Credit Cards: A, B, C, D
Notes: 2, 4 (Saturday only), 5, 8, 9, 10, 11, 12, 14

Simpson House Inn

121 East Arrellaga, 93101
(805) 963-7067

This 1874 Victorian estate is secluded on an acre of gardens, yet a five-minute walk to historic Santa Barbara and the shops, res-taurants, and theaters. Six elegant guest rooms are decorated with antiques, English lace, and flowers. Some rooms have large private decks. Spacious common areas open onto large porches overlooking the gardens. Wine and hors d'oeuvres and afternoon tea are served on the veranda. Bicycles and croquet are available.

Host: Gillean Wilson
Rooms: 6 (PB) $76-145
Full Breakfast
Credit Cards: A, B, C
Notes: 2, 5, 10, 11, 12, 14

SANTA CRUZ

Babbling Brook Inn

1025 Laurel Street, 95060
(408) 427-2437; (800) 866-1131
FAX (408) 427-2457

This secluded inn built in 1909 is on the original foundation of the first grist mill built in 1796 and an 1870s tannery. Before the Portolla expedition, there was an Ohlone Indian fishing village on the site, and three burial caves remain. Oldest and largest in the county, the inn has 12 rooms with fireplaces or jet tubs, phones, TVs, private entrances, and decks with views.

Host: Helen King
Rooms: 12 (PB) $85-135
Full Breakfast
Credit Cards: A, B, C, D, E
Notes: 2, 5, 8 (over 11), 9, 10, 11, 12, 14

Simpson House Inn

Bed and Breakfast International #201

P. O. Box 282910, San Francisco, 94128
(415) 696-1690; FAX (415) 696-1699

This home is in a spectacular setting over-looking the Santa Cruz Mountains. Guests have full use of the two-bedroom house with fireplace, deck, and hot tub. $125.

Bed and Breakfast International #202

P. O. Box 282910, San Francisco, 94128
(415) 696-1690; FAX (415) 696-1699

Guest quarters are in a former carriage house behind an 1875 Victorian home just a few minutes from the ocean and Santa Cruz by car. The house features patios, hot tub, and fireplaces. $80-95.

Bed and Breakfast of Los Angeles

32074 Waterside Lane, Westlake Village, 91361
(818) 889-8870

Twelve unique rooms in country French decor are set on one acre of gardens and streams. All rooms have private baths and entries, some with balconies and fireplaces. Children over 12 welcome. $75-115.

The Darling House—A Bed and Breakfast Inn by the Sea

314 West Cliff Drive, 95060
(408) 458-1958

Darling House is a 1910 oceanside architec-tural masterpiece designed by William Weeks, lighted by the rising sun through beveled glass, Tiffany lamps, and open hearths. The spacious lawns, rose gardens, citrus orchard, towering palms, and expan-sive ocean view verandas create colorful California splendor in an atmosphere of peaceful elegance. Stroll to secluded beaches, lighthouse, wharf, and boardwalk. Soak in the hot tub and sleep secure.

Host: Darrell Darling
Rooms: 7 (1 PB; 6 SB) $85-195
Continental Breakfast
Credit Cards: A, B, C, D
Notes: 2, 5, 8, 9, 10, 11, 12, 14

SANTA ROSA

Melitta Station Inn

5850 Melita Road, 95409
(707) 538-7712

A turn-of-the-century railroad station, now a rustic American country bed and breakfast in the Valley of the Moon. Furnished in antiques and country collectibles, with a superb breakfast served in the warm, cozy sitting room. Situated on a country road five miles from central Santa Rosa, it is conve-nient to many of the area's finest wineries and restaurants. Within minutes of three parks offering hiking, jogging, biking, ten-nis, and other activities.

Hosts: Diane and Vic
Rooms: 6 (4 PB; 2 SB) $70-90
Full Breakfast
Credit Cards: A, B
Notes: 2, 5, 8 (prior arrangement), 10, 12

Pygmalion House Bed and Breakfast

331 Orange Street, 95407
(707) 526-3407

Pygmalion House is ideally situated in a secluded residential street in Santa Rosa's historic old town. This fine example of Queen Anne Victorian architecture was built in the 1880s and withstood the great earth-quake of 1906. The interior is bright with flowers amid a charming combination of furnishings. Pygmalion House is within walking distance of Railroad Square, popular for its specialty shops and fine restaurants.

Host: Lola Wright
Rooms: 5 (PB) $50-70
Full Breakfast
Credit Cards: A, B, C
Notes: 2, 5, 9, 10, 12, 14

Pygmalion House Bed and Breakfast

SAUSALITO

Bed and Breakfast International #108
P. O. Box 282910, San Francisco, 94128
(415) 696-1690; (415) 696-1699

Three houseboats are docked five minutes north of the Golden Gate Bridge and minutes from interesting shops and restaurants in downtown Sausalito. Two are unhosted; one offers breakfast. $98.

The Butterfly Tree
P. O. Box 790, 94966
(415) 383-8447

Situated at Muir Beach, the Butterfly Tree is within walking distance of the beach and is surrounded by the Golden Gate National Recreation Area. There are hiking trails, wildflowers, birds, Muir Woods, and an abundance of natural beauty. The monarch butterfly returns here each year. Secluded, fragile environment appropriate for restful hideaway or spiritual retreat.

Host: Karla Andersdatter
Rooms: 2 (PB) $95-115
Full Breakfast
Credit Cards: None
Notes: 2, 5, 6 (some restrictions), 8 (some restrictions), 9

SEAL BEACH

Bed and Breakfast of Los Angeles
32074 Waterside Lane, Westlake Village, 91361
(818) 889-8870

An impressive three-story beachfront home has three guest rooms with private baths. On the lower level is a spa and fireplace. The rear garden leads to the beach. No children. $75.

Seal Beach Inn and Gardens
212 Fifth Street, 90740
(213) 493-2416

One block from the beach are 23 elegant and comfortable guest rooms featured in a restored vintage inn with lush and peaceful gardens. Gourmet breakfast is served in the French tea room. Complimentary wine, cheese, and crackers are served in the library in the evening. Swimming pool and board games are available. Eighteen restaurants are within walking distance.

Host: Marjorie Bettenhausen Schmaehl
Rooms: 23 (PB) $98-145
Full Breakfast
Credit Cards: A, B, C, E
Notes: 2, 11, 14

SILVERLAKE

Bed and Breakfast of Los Angeles
32074 Waterside Lane, Westlake Village, 91361
(818) 889-8870

welcome; 9 Social drinking allowed; 10 Tennis available; 11 Swimming available; 12 Golf available; 13 Skiing available; 14 May be booked through travel agents

This second-floor apartment has an outside entrance, bath, bedroom, livingroom with two couches, and a minikitchen. Bus line is four blocks away. Children over 12 welcome. $65.

SKYFOREST

Storybook Inn
28717 Highway 18, P.O. Box 362, 92385
(714) 336-1483

Storybook Inn has nine elegantly decorated rooms with private baths and a separate rustic three-bedroom cabin with wood-burning fireplace. All but two rooms have a spectacular 100-mile view. The price of the room includes a full home-cooked breakfast and complimentary wine and hors d'oeuvres served from 5:30 to 7:00 P.M., including friendly attentive service. A conference room accommodates 15 to 20 people, and a wedding gazebo is available overlooking the magnificent terrain. Hiking trails and private picnics are also available.

Hosts: John and Kathleen Wooley
Rooms: 9 (PB) $105-200
Cabin: 1
Credit Cards: A, B, D
Notes: 2, 5, 8, 9, 10, 11, 12, 13, 14

SONOMA

Bed and Breakfast International #301
P. O. Box 282910, San Francisco, 94128
(415) 696-1690; FAX (415) 696-1699

In the heart of Sonoma within walking distance of the plaza is this old stonecutter's cottage with a Franklin stove and a garden setting studded with giant oaks. Breakfast is served in the main house. $115.

STUDIO CITY

Bed and Breakfast of Los Angeles 01
32074 Waterside Lane, Westlake Village, 91361
(818) 889-8870

Stained glass, skylights, and country charm are in every room. Guests also enjoy the enclosed garden and patio with pool. No children. $55.

Bed and Breakfast of Los Angeles 02
32074 Waterside Lane, Westlake Village, 91361
(818) 889-8870

An upstairs suite offers privacy at this home within walking distance of Universal Studios, restaurants, and bus line. Two-night minimum stay. Children over five welcome. $50.

SUMMERLAND

Summerland Inn
2161 Ortega Hill Road, P. O. Box 1209, 93067
(805) 969-5225

Summerland Inn has ten rooms with private baths, phones, and TVs. Summerland Beach is a five-minute stroll from the inn. Antique stores, local shops, and restaurants are within walking distance. Santa Barbara attractions and tours are a ten-minute drive from the inn.

Host: James R. Farned
Rooms: 10 (PB) $55-120
Continental Breakfast
Credit Cards: A, B, C, D, E
Notes: 2, 5, 8, 10, 11, 12, 14

NOTES: Credit cards accepted: A Master Card; B Visa; C American Express; D Discover Card; E Diners Club; F Other; 2 Personal checks accepted; 3 Lunch available; 4 Dinner available; 5 Open all year; 6 Pets welcome; 8 Children

SUTTER CREEK

Sutter Creek Inn

75 Main Steet, P.O. Box 385, 95685
(209) 267-5606

The inn has 19 rooms with private baths,
electric blankets, and air conditioning. Ten
rooms have fireplaces. Four have swinging
beds that can be stabilized. The large old
livingroom is filled with books, games, and
a piano. A hot breakfast is served by the
fireplace. A one-half acre lawn surrounds
the inn with garden furniture and hammocks.
Handwriting analysis, massage, and
reflexology upon request.

Host: Jane Way
Rooms: 19 (PB) $45-97
Full Breakfast
Credit Cards: None
Notes: 2, 5, 9, 10, 11, 12, 13, 14

TAHOE CITY

Bed and Breakfast International #404

P. O. Box 282910, San Francisco, 94128
(415) 696-1690; FAX (415) 696-1699

This large alpine-style house has beautiful
views of Lake Tahoe. Guest rooms are on
the second floor. Close to casinos, ski areas,
and lakefront. $65.

Bed and Breakfast of Los Angeles

32074 Waterside Lane, Westlake Village, 91361
(818) 889-8870

Built in the 1920s, this stone lakefront home
has a massive fireplace and stone arches,
three patios, pine trees, private pier. Many
ski areas and casinos are nearby. Children
over 12 welcome. $75.

Cottage Inn at Lake Tahoe

1690 West Lake Boulevard, P. O. Box 66, 96145
(916) 581-4073

The Cottage Inn has two acres of woods and
access to three acres of beach. The cottages
are single-level with private bath and entrance. The main house is open to guests,
offering a fireplace, coffee, tea, wine, and
home-baked goodies. Two miles south of
Tahoe City at Lake Tahoe off Highway 89.

Hosts: Jim and Suni Kreft
Rooms: 15 (PB) $90-120
Full Breakfast
Credit Cards: A, B, E
Notes: 2, 5, 8, 9, 10, 11, 12, 13

THOUSAND OAKS

Bed and Breakfast of Los Angeles

32074 Waterside Lane, Westlake Village, 91361
(818) 889-8870

Overlooking a regional park, this decorator-
perfect home has a great patio with pool,
spa, and fire pit. Upstairs guest rooms share
a bath. School-age children welcome. $40.

TRINIDAD

The Lost Whale Bed and Breakfast Inn

3452 Patrick's Point Drive, 95570
(707) 677-3425

Enjoy the only bed and breakfast in California with a private beach on four breathtaking acres overlooking a spectacular coastline. A scenic wooded trail leads down to a
primitive cove of tidepools and barking sea
lions. Afternoon tea; hot tub overlooking
the ocean. Thirty minutes north of Eureka.
"A whale of an inn," Jerry Hulse, *Los Angeles Times*.

welcome; 9 Social drinking allowed; 10 Tennis available; 11 Swimming available; 12 Golf available; 13 Skiing
available; 14 May be booked through travel agents

Hosts: Susanne Lakin and Lee Miller
Rooms: 6 (4 PB; 2 SB) $85-120
Full Breakfast
Credit Cards: A, B
Notes: 2, 5, 8, 9, 11, 12, 14

Trinidad Bed and Breakfast

560 Edwards Street, P. O. Box 849, 95570
(707) 677-0840

This Cape Cod-style home overlooks beautiful Trinidad Bay. The inn offers spectacular views of the rugged coastline and fishing harbor below from two suites, one with a fireplace, and two upstairs bedrooms. Surrounded by dozens of beaches, trails, and redwood parks, the inn is within walking distance of restaurants and shops. Suite guests enjoy the luxury of breakfast delivered. Other guests share a family-style table.

Hosts: Paul and Carol Kirk
Rooms: 4 (PB) $105-145
Full Breakfast
Credit Cards: A, B, D
Notes: 2, 5, 9, 10, 12

UKIAH

Vichy Springs Resort

2605 Vichy Springs Road, 95482
(707) 462-9515

Vichy Springs features naturally sparking 90-degree mineral baths; a communal 104-degree pool; Olypmic-size pool; and 700 private acres with trails and roads for hiking, jogging, picnicking, and mountain bicycling. A quiet healing environment describes Vichy's idyllic setting. Swedish massage, reflexology, herbal facials, and accupressure are offered.

Host: Gilbert Ashoff
Rooms: 14 (PB) $95-150
Expanded Continental Breakfast
Credit Cards: A, B, C, D, E, F
Notes: 2, 5, 8, 9, 10, 11, 12, 14

VENICE

Bed and Breakfast International #502

P. O. Box 282910, San Francisco, 94128
(415) 696-1690; FAX (415) 696-1699

Guest quarters are an addition with a deck on the second floor of a renovatd 1920s California bungalo. Contemporary furnishings in blue and white with natural wood. Close to Venice boardwalk and Santa Monica pier. $75.

Bed and Breakfast of Los Angeles 01

32074 Waterside Lane, Westlake Village, 91361
(818) 889-8870

This pleasant family home offers two guest rooms with twin beds and shared bath. The bus line is two blocks away. Babies or children over five welcome. $45.

Bed and Breakfast of Los Angeles 02

32074 Waterside Lane, Westlake Village, 91361
(818) 889-8870

One block from the beach, this turn-of-the-century home has rooms decorated in several motifs. Private baths or four rooms share two large baths. Children over ten welcome. Two-night minimum stay. $75-150.

VENTURA

Bed and Breakfast of Los Angeles 01

32074 Waterside Lane, Westlake Village, 91361
(818) 889-8870

NOTES: Credit cards accepted: A Master Card; B Visa; C American Express; D Discover Card; E Diners Club; F Other;
2 Personal checks accepted; 3 Lunch available; 4 Dinner available; 5 Open all year; 6 Pets welcome; 8 Children

Just steps from the sand, this home offers a guest room with a double bed and a den with a queen futon. Bath in the hall. No children except babies. $65.

Bed and Breakfast of Los Angeles 02
32074 Waterside Lane, Westlake Village, 91361
(818) 889-8870

This Cape Cod-style Victorian home is within walking distance of restaurants and just a few blocks from the beach. Five guest rooms are decorated in styles that represent different countries. $75.

"La Mer" European Romantic Get-a-Way
411 Poli Street, 93001
(805) 643-3600

La Mer, three blocks from the beach on a hillside overlooking the Pacific coastline, is a Victorian Cape Cod historical landmark built in 1890. Each accommodation represents a European country. The inn is decorated with European antiques and features private entrances. There is complimentary wine or champagne on arrival. Midweek packages are available with therapeutic massages, European dinners, and carriage rides.

Hosts: Mike and Gisela Baida
Rooms: 5 (PB) $105-155
Full Breakfast
Credit Cards: A, B
Notes: 2, 3, 5, 9, 10, 11, 12, 14

WESTCHESTER

Bed and Breakfast of Los Angeles 01
32074 Waterside Lane, Westlake Village, 91361
(818) 889-8870

Extensively remodeled, this bungalow offers two guest rooms sharing a hall bath with host family. Easy access to the beach. $45.

Bed and Breakfast of Los Angeles 02
32074 Waterside Lane, Westlake Village, 91361
(818) 889-8870

This country-style bungalow is near the airport, bus lines, restaurant, tennis, and golf. The guest room has twin beds and shares a bath with host. $45.

WEST HOLLYWOOD

Bed and Breakfast of Los Angeles
32074 Waterside Lane, Westlake Village, 91361
(818) 889-8870

This bungalow has been completely redone to accommodate guests. The host lives to the rear. One bedroom has a private entrance and bath; the others share a bath. No children. $45-65.

WESTLAKE VILLAGE

Bed and Breakfast of Los Angeles
32074 Waterside Lane, 91361
(818) 889-8870

This Spanish-style home on a quiet cul-de-sac has a guest room and private bath in a separate hallway. Community pool and tennis are nearby. $45.

WESTPORT

Howard Creek Ranch
40501 North Highway One, P. O. Box 121, 95488
(707) 964-6725

welcome; 9 Social drinking allowed; 10 Tennis available; 11 Swimming available; 12 Golf available; 13 Skiing available; 14 May be booked through travel agents

Howard Creek Ranch is a historic 1867 oceanfront ranch bordered by miles of beach and mountains in a spectacular wilderness area on the Mendocino Coast. There is excellent hiking and bicycling in the area. Guests enjoy flower gardens, antiques, fireplaces, swinging bridge, hot tub, sauna, horseback riding. German, Dutch, Italian, and Spanish are spoken.

Hosts: Charles (Sunny) and Sally Grigg
Rooms: 8 (5 PB; 3 SB) $50-115
Full Breakfast
Credit Cards: A, B
Notes: 2, 5, 6 (by prior arrangement), 9

Howard Creek Ranch

WHITTIER

Coleen's California Casa

P. O. Box 9302, 90608
(213) 699-8427

This home is convenient to the freeway system yet feels like a rural area. The peacefulness is enhanced by the luxurious patio where guests enjoy sunshine and breakfast. Some rooms have private entrances. Excellent hiking is available in the nearby canyon. The deck offers an enchanting view of the city in the evenings. Los Angeles is only 30 minutes away.

Host: Coleen Davis
Rooms: 4 (3 PB; 1 SB) $55-65
Full Breakfast
Credit Cards: None
Notes: 2, 3, 4 (by arrangement), 5, 8, 9, 10, 11, 12, 14

YOUNTVILLE

Oleander House

7433 Saint Helena Highway
P. O. Box 2937, 94599-2937
(707) 944-8315

This country French two-story home recently featured in the the *New York Times* combines the best of Old World design with modern amenities. It is conveniently situated in the heart of the Napa Valley and just a short walk from the well-known restaurant, Mustard's Grill. Guests enjoy Laura Ashley wallpaper and fabrics, balcony, fireplace, rose garden, patio with spa, well-appointed common area, and elegant dining room.

Hosts: John and Louise Packard
Rooms: 4 (PB) $115-145
Full Breakfast
Credit Cards: A, B
Notes: 2, 5, 9, 10, 11, 12, 14

Colorado

ARVADA

On Golden Pond

7831 Eldridge, 80005
(303) 424-2296

On Golden Pond is nestled in the foothills only 15 miles west of Denver. The custom-built, two-story brick home is situated on ten acres with dramatic views of mountains, prairies, and downtown Denver. Enjoy European hospitality with breakfast served on the deck or indoors. Each room opens onto a deck or patio. Other features include a honeymoon suite, in-room hot tubs, fireplaces, airport transit, TVs, room service, whirlpool, playground, game room, fishing, and gazebo.

Host: Kathy Kula
Rooms: 6 (PB) $40-80
Full Breakfast
Credit Cards: A, B
Notes: 2, 5, 8, 9, 10, 11, 12, 14

BOULDER

Briar Rose
Bed and Breakfast

2151 Arapahoe Avenue, 80302
(303) 442-3007

This 1892 Victorian country cottage and carriage house are decorated with period antiques, fresh flowers, "fedderbet" down comforters, fine linens, and original art. Breakfast is served in the dining room or guest rooms. Afternoon tea trays and shortbread cookies are served. Beautiful gardens surround the inn.

Hosts: Bob and Margaret Weisenbach
Rooms: 9 (PB) $78-105
Continental Breakfast
Credit Cards: A, B, C, E
Notes: 2, 5, 8, 9, 10, 11, 12, 13, 14

CARBONDALE

Ambiance Inn

66 North Second Street, 81623
(303) 963-3597

The Ambiance Inn is a contemporary chalet style home offering one suite and three rooms. Year-round activities are numerous in the area. Aspen and Snowmass are just 35 minutes away. Glenwood Springs and the world's largest hot springs are just ten minutes away. Gold-medal fishing, white-water rafting, golf, horseback riding, cross country and alpine skiing are nearby.

Hosts: Norma and Robert Morris
Rooms: 5 (PB) $60-100
Full Breakfast
Credit Cards: A, B
Notes: 2, 4, 5, 8, 9, 11, 12, 13, 14

The Biggerstaff House

0318 Lions Ridge Road, 81623
(303) 963-3605

This country home, filled with antiques and family heirlooms, is in the Aspen Roaring Fork Valley and within minutes of Aspen, Snowmass, and Sunlight ski areas. The historic towns of Redstone, Marble, and Glenwood Springs are also nearby. Each room has a beautiful view of Mount Sopris. Two rooms have private balconies. The guest lounge, furnished in wicker, has

welcome; 9 Social drinking allowed; 10 Tennis available; 11 Swimming available; 12 Golf available; 13 Skiing available; 14 May be booked through travel agents

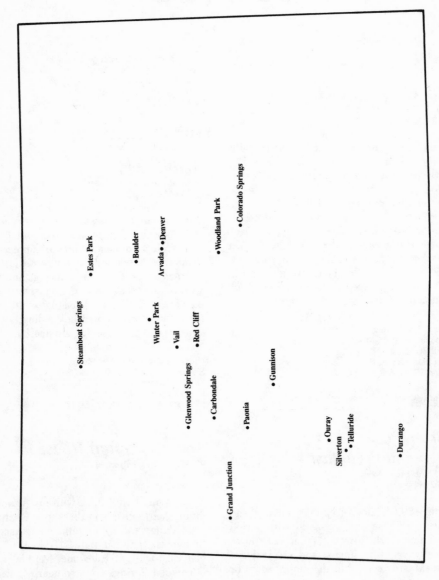

COLORADO

snacks, books, games, phone, and its own balcony.

Hosts: Jack and Jane E. Van Horn
Rooms: 4 (S2.5B) $50
Full Breakfast
Credit Cards: A, B
Notes: 2, 8 (over 12), 10, 11, 12, 13, 14

COLORADO SPRINGS

Hearthstone Inn
506 North Cascade, 80903
(719) 473-4413; (800) 521-1885

The Hearthstone Inn is an elegantly restored 1885 mansion near the heart of Colorado Springs. Twenty-three rooms with private baths, all furnished with Victorian antiques. Three rooms have private porches, and three have wood-burning fireplaces. A conference room is available for seminars and executive retreats of about 35 people. Full gourmet breakfast, changing daily, is part of the warmth and friendliness of this in-town country inn.

Hosts: Dot Williams and Ruth Williams
Rooms: 25 (23 PB; 2 SB) $60-120
Full Breakfast
Credit Cards: A, B, C
Notes: 2, 5, 10, 11, 12, 13, 14

Holden House
1102 West Pikes Peak Avenue, 80904
(719) 471-3980

This historic 1902 storybook Victorian and 1906 carriage house are filled with antiques and family treasures. Five lovely guest rooms (three suites) boast feather pillows, period furnishings, and individual decor. There is a romantic atmosphere with tubs for two and fireplaces. The common rooms have fireplace, TV, and phone. Holden House is just one mile west of downtown near the historic district, shopping, restaurants, and attractions. Immaculate accommodations and warm hospitality. Not suitable for children.

Hosts: Sallie and Welling Clark
Rooms: 5 (PB) $57-85
Full Breakfast
Credit Cards: A, B, C, D
Notes: 2, 5, 9, 10, 11, 12, 13, 14

Tudor Manor
1332 North Cascade Avenue, 80903
(719) 633-1409

This stately 1929 Tudor-style house is elegantly decorated in period antiques with an emphasis on comfort and hospitality. Four spacious rooms with adjoining full baths. Two rooms have sun porches. A cozy library is available with rare books and Colorado railroad memorabilia. The house is close to Colorado College, jogging trails, museums, tennis, and golf. The evening appetizer tray is complimentary.

Hearthstone Inn

NOTES: Credit cards accepted: A Master Card; B Visa; C American Express; D Discover Card; E Diners Club; F Other; 2 Personal checks accepted; 3 Lunch available; 4 Dinner available; 5 Open all year; 6 Pets welcome; 8 Children welcome; 9 Social drinking allowed; 10 Tennis available; 11 Swimming available; 12 Golf available; 13 Skiing available; 14 May be booked through travel agents

Hosts: Vernon "Biff" and Marlene Hallenbeck
Rooms: 4 (2 PB; 2 SB) $59-79
Full Breakfast
Credit Cards: None
Notes: 2, 5, 9, 10, 11, 12, 14

DENVER

Bed and Breakfast Rocky Mountain, Inc.

906 South Pearl Street, 80209
(800) 733-8415

Representing more than 230 inns and homestays in the Rocky Mountain region, a majority of them nonsmoking. From rustic to elegant, in town, or with spectacular mountain views, each inn is approved and inspected. Services include door-to-door transportation from Denver airport to many of the inns, special dinners, lift tickets for many ski areas, and dietary considerations. Coordinators: Cheryl, Beth, Marie, and June.

Castle Marne Bed and Breakfast

1572 Race Street, 80206
(303) 331-0621; (800) 92-MARNE

This historic Victorian mansion built in 1889 is now a luxury urban inn situated near the intersection of Routes 40 and 287, 20 blocks east of downtown. Nine distinctive guest rooms or suites are available, each with period antiques and family heirlooms. Guest suites feature fireplaces and Jacuzzi tubs. The original character of the mansion is evident with hand-rubbed woods, circular stained glass, and ornate fireplaces. Afternoon tea is served.

Host: The Peiker family
Rooms: 9 (PB) $75-145
Full Breakfast
Credit Cards: A, B, C, D, E
Notes: 2, 5, 10, 11, 12, 13, 14

Queen Anne Inn Luxury Bed and Breakfast

2147 Tremont Place, 80205
(303) 296-6666 information
(800) 432-INNS reservations

This is an award-winning 1879 Victorian in the downtown historic district offering luxurious, elegant surroundings. Horse-drawn carriage rides, museums, art galleries, shopping, restaurants, cultural events, historic districts, lakes, streams, bike paths, and parks are available.

Hosts: Chuck and Ann Hillestad
Rooms: 10 (PB) $64-124
Expanded Continental Breakfast
Credit Cards: A, B, C, D, F
Notes: 2, 5, 9, 10, 11, 12, 13, 14

DURANGO

Gable House

805 Fifth Avenue, 81301
(303) 247-4982

Gable House is a very large three-story Queen Ann Victorian home on a tree-lined street. Spacious rooms display antique furnishings and double beds, sharing two baths down the hall. The house is just five blocks from the Durango-Silverton narrow gauge train and is within walking distance of downtown restaurants and shops. Open June, July, and August. By reservation only.

Hosts: Heather and Jeffrey Bryson
Rooms: 2 (SB) $55
Full or Continental Breakfast
Credit Cards: F
Notes: 2, 9, 10, 11, 12

Penny's Place

1041 County Road 307, 81301
(303) 247-8928

Penny's Place is 11 miles from Durango on 26 acres of rolling countryside overlooking the spectacular La Plata Mountains. There are deer and meadowlarks visiting most days. A king room has a private entrance and deck. A spiral staircase joins this room to the common room, which has a hot tub, satellite TV, and wood-burning stove. A stay of several days is recommended to see the wonderful sites of the area.

Host: Penny O'Keefe
Rooms: 3 (1 PB; 2 SB) $49-70
Full Breakfast
Credit Cards: A, B
Notes: 2, 5, 10, 12, 13, 14

River House Bed and Breakfast

495 Animas View Drive, 81301
(303) 247-4775

River House is a southwestern private home with large atrium, six bedrooms, antique snooker table, three fireplaces, and spacious Colorado environment. Healthy gourmet breakfasts are served. Across from Animas River and near hot spring, hiking, and narrow gauge train, it specializes in weddings, reunions, health retreats, and family gatherings.

Host: Crystal Carroll
Rooms: 6 (PB) $45-65
Full Breakfast
Credit Cards: A, B
Notes: 2, 5, 8, 9, 10, 11, 12, 13

ESTES PARK

RiverSong Bed and Breakfast

P. O. Box 1910, 80517
(303) 586-4666

RiverSong is a romantic inn secluded at the end of a country road. It has 27 wooded acres with a rushing river, skating pond, and hiking trails. The inn offers spectacular views of the snowcapped peaks of Rocky Moun-

tain National Park, fireplaces, tubs for two, romantic candlelight dinners, and gentle deer grazing on wildflower-adorned slopes.

Hosts: Gary and Sue Mansfield
Rooms: 9 (PB) $ 85-150
Full Breakfast
Credit Cards: A, B
Notes: 2, 4, 5, 9, 10, 11, 12, 13, 14

GLENWOOD SPRINGS

The Kaiser House

932 Cooper Avenue, 81601
(303) 945-8827

In the center of the "spa of the Rockies," The Kaiser House features turn-of-the-century charm with 20th-century conveniences. Situated on the corner of 10th and Cooper Avenue, the inn is close to parks, shops, and restaurants and to Hot Springs Pool and Vapor Caves. Enjoy a gourmet breakfast in the spacious dining room or sunny breakfast area before hitting the slopes in the winter. In the summer, enjoy brunch on the private patio.

Hosts: Glen and Ingrid Eash
Rooms: 7 (PB) $52-120
Full Breakfast
Credit Cards: A, B
Notes: 2, 5, 9, 10, 11, 12, 13, 14

RiverSong Bed and Breakfast

GRAND JUNCTION

Junction Country Inn Bed and Breakfast

861 Grand Avenue, 81501
(303) 241-2817

A wonderful getaway for couples and families, Junction Country Inn is minutes away from biking, hiking, rafting, and skiing. Kids of all ages will enjoy Grand Junction's dinosaur and children's museums. Shop for antiques, sample fine wines, or spend an evening enjoying the theater or symphony. A restful night's sleep awaits you at the beautifully decorated inn.

Host: The Bloom Family
Rooms: 4 (2 PB; 2 SB) $30-59
Full Breakfast
Credit Cards: A, B, C
Notes: 2, 5, 8, 10, 11, 12, 13, 14

GUNNISON

Mary Lawrence Inn

601 North Taylor, 81230
(303) 641-3343

Make this Victorian home the center of your excurions through Gunnison country. The mountains, rivers, and lakes are extraordinary. Golf, swimming, rafting, fishing, and biking possibilities are tremendous. The inn is decorated with imagination and furnished with antiques and collectibles. Fly fishing and mystery weekends are offered. Great ski package available for Crested Butte skiing.

Hosts: Les and Tom Bushman
Rooms: 5 (3 PB; 2 SB) $46-68
Full Breakfast
Credit Cards: A, B
Notes: 2, 5, 8, 10, 11, 12, 13, 14

OURAY

The Damn Yankee Bed and Breakfast

100 Sixth Avenue, 81427
(800) 845-7512

The inn is situated just two blocks from the center of town, yet bordered by a relaxing mountain stream. Each room has a private entrance and cable TV. All rooms adjoin a central foyer and third-floor observatory. Enjoy the common parlor with a baby grand piano and the outdoor hot tub under a gazebo. Upon check-in, you will find fresh fruit in your room, and complimentary beverages and snacks are served in the afternoon.

Hosts: Mike and Joyce Manley
Rooms: 8 (PB) $58-145
Full Breakfast
Credit Cards: A, B, C
Notes: 2, 5, 10, 11, 13, 14

PAONIA

Agape Inn

206 Rio Grande, P.O. Box 640, 81428
(303) 527-4004

This turn-of-the-century Victorian home was built in 1896 and completely remodeled during the last two years. A full country breakfast is served, from sourdough pancakes to German pancakes, with hot apples or Mexican omelets and fresh coffee cakes or muffins.

Hosts: Jim and Norma Shutts
Rooms: 3 (1 PB; 2SB) $40
Full Breakfast
Credit Cards: None
Notes: 2, 5, 8

NOTES: Credit cards accepted: A Master Card; B Visa; C American Express; D Discover Card; E Diners Club; F Other; 2 Personal checks accepted; 3 Lunch available; 4 Dinner available; 5 Open all year; 6 Pets welcome; 8 Children

The Pilgrim's Inn
101 Eagle Street, P. O. Box 151, 81649
(303) 827-5333

The Pilgrim's Inn is a quiet turn-of-the-century Victorian home, newly restored and filled with books, antiques, Asian art, and the work of local painters and photographers. Just 15 miles from Vail and across the street from the Tenth Mountain Trail hut system, the inn makes a great base camp for alpine and Nordic skiing, mountain biking, bicycle touring, hiking, or camping. Guests enjoy the hot tub and time to write, meditate, or photograph.

Host: Michael Wasmer
Rooms: 4 (2 PB; 2 SB) $60-90
Full Breakfast
Credit Cards: A, B
Notes: 2, 8, 12, 13, 14

SILVERTON

Christopher House Bed and Breakfast
821 Empire Street P. O. Box 241, 81433
(303) 387-5857 June-September
(904) 567-7549 October-May

This charming 1894 Victorian home has original golden oak woodwork, parlor fireplace, and antiques throughout. All rooms offer comfortable mattresses, wall-to-wall carpeting, and a mountain view. Guests are warmly welcomed with mints and fresh wildflowers. Breakfast is served to Irish music. The house is conveniently situated four blocks from the town's narrow gauge train depot, Old West shops, restaurants, and riding stable.

Hosts: Howard and Eileen Swonger
Rooms: 4 (1 PB; 3 SB) $42-52
Full Breakfast
Credit Cards: None
Notes: 2, 8, 9, 10, 12, 13, 14

STEAMBOAT SPRINGS

Oak Street Bed and Breakfast
702 Oak Street, Box 772434, 80477

Experience mountain charm and southern hospitality in the heart of Steamboat Springs. Each room is uniquely decorated with antiques and all have TVs, VCRs, and private baths. Breakfast includes homemade bread, souffles, quiches, fruit salads, juices, and coffee.

Hosts: Jill Coit and Julie English
Rooms: 12 (11 PB; 1 SB) $55 summer; $90 winter
Full Breakfast
Credit Cards: A, B
Notes: 2, 5, 8, 9, 10, 11, 12, 13, 14

Scandinavian Lodge
2883 Burgess Creek Road
P. O. Box 774484, 80477
(303) 879-0517; (800) 233-8102

Secluded in a pine forest on the side of Mount Werner, the Scandinavian Lodge offers breathtaking views of 60 miles. The unique location offers romantic seclusion while maintaining accessibility to the numerous recreational activities that Steamboat Springs has to offer. Ski in the winter or ride mountain bikes along the ski trails in the summer. The atmosphere is European, and the food is very Swedish.

Host: The Olsson Family
Rooms: 28 (PB) $49-109
Full Breakfast
Credit Cards: None
Notes: 2, 3, 4, 5, 6, 8, 9, 10, 11, 13, 14

TELLURIDE

Johnstone Inn
403 West Colorado, Box 546, 81435
(303) 728-6395; (800) 752-1901

A true, historic Victorian bed and breakfast, the inn is situated in one of the most beautiful and historic towns in Colorado. Comfortable, romantic rooms offer queen beds and plump comforters. All have marble and brass private baths. Winter evenings include après ski served in the parlor around the fireplace. The hot tub is under the clear Colorado sky. It is a short walk to restaurants and ski lifts.

Host: Bill Schiffbauer
Rooms: 8 (PB) $70-115
Full Breakfast
Credit Cards: A, B, C
Notes: 2, 9, 13, 14

San Sophia

330 West Pacific Avenue, P. O. Box 1825, 81435
(800) 537-4781

Situated in a ski resort town, this 16-room nouveau Victorian inn is one-half block from the ski lift and San Miguel River. Hiking and biking trails lead into the surrounding 13,000-foot mountains. Rooms have brass beds, tubs for two, TV, and views. The library has an evening deck; the dining room has a deck and views toward Telluride Peak and the Ingram Waterfall. Jacuzzi in gazebo and roof-top observatory are also available.

Hosts: Dianne and Gary Eschman
Rooms: 16 (PB) $85-175
Full Breakfast
Credit Cards: A, B, C
Notes: 2, 5, 9, 13, 14

VAIL

Bed and Breakfast Vail/ Ski Areas

P.O. Box 491, 81658
(303) 949-1212; (800) 748-2666

Come and enjoy the warmth and charm of Colorado mountain ski areas. This reservation service offers unique lodging in mountain homes and log and adobe inns. Centrally located or nestled on a hillside, choose from private rooms and suites, full breakfast, hot tubs, après ski refreshments, and free bus shuttle. Summer or winter, Vail offers many recreational activities, restaurants, and internationally known shops. More than 45 accommodations represented ranging from $45 to $145. Kathy Fagan-Westerberg, coordinator.

Johnstone Inn

WINTER PARK

Englemann Pines

P. O. Box 1305, 80482
(303) 726-4632; (800) 992-9512

Enjoy old-fashioned elegance in this contemporary mountain home with spectacular views of pine trees and mountains from many windows. There is a separate TV room, reading/game room, and kitchen for guest use, and the refrigerator is always stocked with complimentary beer, wine, and soft drinks. Gourmet breakfasts feature fresh fruit, Swiss specialties, and a variety of entrees.

Hosts: Margaret and Heinz Engel
Rooms: 6 (2 PB; 4 SB) $75-95
Full Breakfast
Credit Cards: A, B, C
Notes: 2, 5, 8, 9, 10, 11, 12, 13, 14

WOODLAND PARK

Pikes Peak Paradise

236 Pinecrest Road, P. O. Box 5760, 80866
(719) 687-6656; (800) 728-8282

Situated next to a national forest in the mountains 20 minutes west of Colorado Springs, Pikes Peak Paradise offers luxury accommodations in a romantic, peaceful, and private setting. Full gourmet breakfast is served in bed, on the patio, or in the dining room. Enjoy an incredible view of Pikes Peak, private entrances, hot tub, and complimentary snacks.

Hosts: Tim Stoddard, Martin Meier, and Priscilla Arthur
Rooms: 4 (2 PB; 2 SB) $75-110
Full Breakfast
Credit Cards: A, B, C, D
Notes: 2, 5, 9, 10, 11, 12, 13, 14

welcome; 9 Social drinking allowed; 10 Tennis available; 11 Swimming available; 12 Golf available; 13 Skiing available; 14 May be booked through travel agents

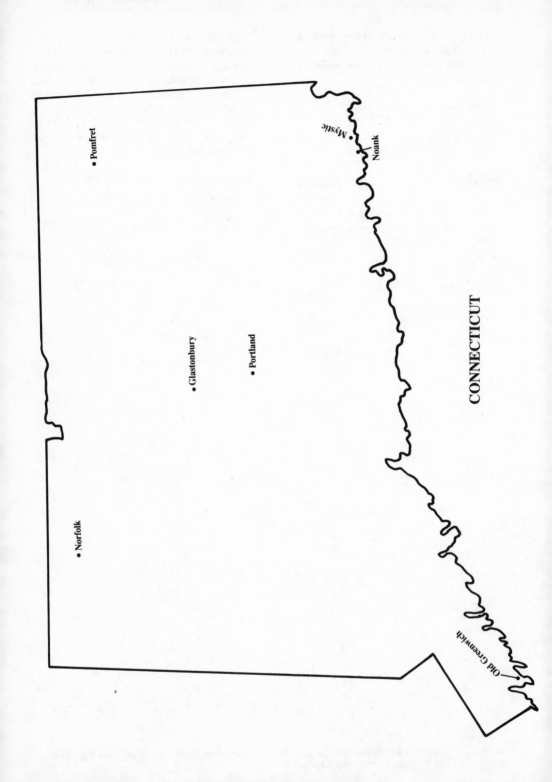

CONNECTICUT

Connecticut

Butternut Farm

1654 Main Street, 06033
(203) 633-7197

An 18th-century architectural jewel, Butternut Farm is furnished with period antiques and features prize-winning dairy goats, pigeons, and chickens; trees; and herb garden. Quality Americana meets the eye throughout. Each bedroom is decorated with attention to detail. Two suites have fireplaces. The interior of the classic Colonial house was painstakingly restored to its original condition.

Host: Don Reid
Rooms: 5 (3 PB; 2 SB) $65-83
Full Breakfast
Credit Cards: A, B, C
Notes: 2, 5, 8, 9, 10, 11, 12, 13

MYSTIC

Adams House

382 Cow Hill Road, 06355
(203) 572-9551

Adams House is a 1790-era house with three old-fashioned fireplaces in two bedrooms and the dining room. It is situated in a quaint country setting minutes away from downtown Mystic and the famous Mystic drawbridge. Adams House is surrounded by lush greenery and flower gardens. The carriage house is a self-contained separate unit.

Host: Mary Adams
Rooms: 7 (PB) $65-135
Continental Breakfast

Credit Cards: A, B, D
Notes: 2, 5, 9, 10, 11, 12, 14

Comolli's House

36 Bruggeman Place, 06355
(203) 536-8723

This immaculate home situated on a quiet hill overlooking the Mystic seaport complex is convenient to Olde Mistick Village and aquarium. Sightseeing, sporting activities, shopping, and restaurant information are provided. Guest rooms are cozy in winter and cool in summer. Color TV is furnished. Comolli's House has accommodations for discriminating adults and children over 12.

Host: Dorothy Comolli
Rooms: 2 (PB) $60-90
Continental Breakfast
Credit Cards: None

Red Brook Inn

P.O. Box 237, 06372
(203) 572-0349

The Red Brook Inn welcomes guests to the charm and beauty of early New England. Two Colonial buildings are situated on seven acres of woodlands and surrounded by ancient stone walls. Eleven guest rooms are furnished with period American antiques, some with canopy beds, seven with working fireplaces.

Host: Ruth Keyes
Rooms: 11 (PB) $95-179
Full Breakfast
Credit Cards: A, B
Notes: 2, 4, 5, 8, 9, 10, 11, 12

NOTES: Credit cards accepted: A Master Card; B Visa; C American Express; D Discover Card; E Diners Club; F Other; 2 Personal checks accepted; 3 Lunch available; 4 Dinner available; 5 Open all year; 6 Pets welcome; 8 Children welcome; 9 Social drinking allowed; 10 Tennis available; 11 Swimming available; 12 Golf available; 13 Skiing available; 14 May be booked through travel agents

Steamboat Inn

73 Steamboat Wharf, 06355
(203) 536-8300

Luxurious lodging directly on the Mystic River in historic downtown Mystic village. Many shops, restaurants, and historic homes are just steps away. All rooms have a river view, fireplace, and personal whirlpool. Romantic weekend packages are available.

Host: Kitty Saletnik
Rooms: 6 (PB) $95-185
Expanded Continental Breakfast
Credit Cards: A, B, C
Notes: 2, 5, 8, 9, 11, 12, 14

Weaver's House

NOANK

The Palmer Inn

25 Church Street, 06340
(203) 572-9000

Take a step back in time and enjoy gracious seaside lodging. Craftsmen skillfully built this elegant mansion at the turn of the century. Guests enjoy afternoon tea in the Victorian parlor. Antique furnishings, fireplaces, mahogany staircase, original wall coverings, stained-glass windows, and individually decorated guest rooms will enhance your stay. It is only two miles to Mystic shops and attractions.

Host: Patricia White
Rooms: 6 (PB) $105-175
Continental Breakfast
Credit Cards: A, B
Notes: 2, 5, 10, 11, 12

NORFOLK

Weaver's House

Route 44, 06058
(203) 542-5108

Enjoy simple hospitality in an 1898 house in a village with hills and forests. There is swimming in the village pond, hiking in four areas, biking, cross country skiing, summer music festival, excellent free student recitals, the Appalachian Trail, canoeing, horseback riding, horse and buggy rides, downhill skiing, and antiquing. Adjacent to the Berkshires.

Hosts: Judy and Arnold Tsukroff
Rooms: 4 (SB) $48-58
Full Breakfast
Credit Cards: A, B
Notes: 2, 5, 9, 10, 11, 13

OLD GREENWICH

Harbor House Inn

165 Shore Road, 06870
(203) 637-0145

This lovely inn is situated in a quiet residential area. Each room has a refrigerator, coffee maker, and color TV. Guests may use a fully equipped kitchen. Harbor House is one mile from a charming New England town, and the beach is within walking distance. Antique shops, restaurants, and the train are also close by.

Hosts: Dolly Stuttig and Dawn Browne
Rooms: 23 (17 PB; 6 SB) $50-75
Continental Breakfast
Credit Cards: None
Notes: 2, 5, 8, 9, 10, 11, 12

NOTES: Credit cards accepted: A Master Card; B Visa; C American Express; D Discover Card; E Diners Club; F Other; 2 Personal checks accepted; 3 Lunch available; 4 Dinner available; 5 Open all year; 6 Pets welcome; 8 Children

POMFRET

Inn at Gwyn Gareg
Route 44, 06230

Once a garden estate of European aristo-
crats, this is now a luxury inn on 30 acres
with gardens, ponds, orchards, greenhouse,
and stables. The residence radiates wealth
and opulence. The Inn at Gwyn Gareg serves
as an extraordinary haven for guests.

Host: George
Rooms: 13 (12 PB; 1 SB) $85-145
Continental Breakfast
Credit Cards: A, B, E
Notes: 2, 4, 5, 9, 10, 11, 12, 14

The Croft

PORTLAND

The Croft
7 Penny Corner Road, 06480
(203) 342-1856

An 1822 Colonial in a picturesque New
England setting. Two suites; one with a

kitchen, living/dining area, and one or two
bedrooms. The other with one bedroom and
a dining nook. Both have private baths,
phones, TVs, and private entrances. The
house is typical of those built during the
early 19th century, with low ceilings and
pleasant surroundings, including open fields,
barns, and an herb garden. Convenient to
Wesleyan University. A 30-minute drive to
Connecticut shoreline and Long Island
Sound.

Host: Elaine R. Hinze
Suites: 2 (PB) $55-75
Full Breakfast
Credit Cards: None
Notes: 2, 5, 8, 9, 10, 12, 13, 14

TOLLAND

The Tolland Inn
63 Tolland Green, 06084-0717
(203) 872-0800

Built in 1800 and accommodating guests
during a bustling post road era, The Tolland
Inn still stands on the historic town green.
Purchased in 1985 by the Beechings and
restored throughout, the inn now offers seven
guest rooms, including a kitchen suite and
three common rooms. Susan is a teacher
and third generation innkeeper from Nantucket. Steve is a fine furniture maker
working at the inn. His work is seen throughout the inn along with antiques.

Hosts: Susan and Stephen Beeching
Rooms: 7 (5 PB; 2 SB) $50-70
Expanded Continental Breakfast
Credit Cards: A, B, C
Notes: 2, 5, 9, 10, 11, 12, 14

welcome; 9 Social drinking allowed; 10 Tennis available; 11 Swimming available; 12 Golf available; 13 Skiing
available; 14 May be booked through travel agents

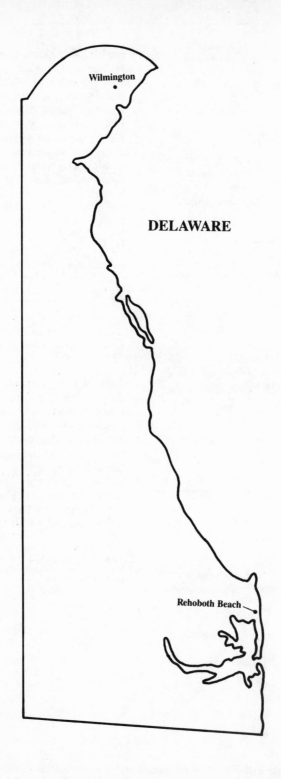

Wilmington

DELAWARE

Rehoboth Beach

Delaware

_____

Tembo Bed and Breakfast
100 Laurel Street, 19971
(302) 227-3360

Tempo is a cozy beach cottage framed by
old shade trees, brick walls, and gardens.
Situated one block from a wide, sandy beach,
guests find shops, restaurants, and attractions within easy walking distance. Enjoy
Early American furnishings, hand-braided
rugs, antiques, art, and an elephant collection. Rooms are bright and airy.

Hosts: Don and Gerry Cooper
Rooms: 6 (1 PB; 5 SB) $50-100
Continental Breakfast
Credit Cards: None
Notes: 2, 5, 9, 10, 11, 12

WILMINGTON _____

A Small Wonder
Bed and Breakfast
213 West Crest Road, 19803
(302) 764-0789

Enjoy the award-winning hospitality and
landscaping of this gracious suburban home
convenient to DuPont Chateau country, busi-
nesses, and historic attractions. Double and
king beds, air conditioning, outdoor spa and
pool, TV/VCR, phone, use of entire home,
and garden. Near Interstate 95, Winterthur
Museum and Gardens, Nemours Estate,
Hagley Museum, and Eleutherian Mills,
Longwood Gardens, and Rockwood Estate.

Hosts: Dot and Art Brill
Rooms: 2 (PB) $ 60-65
Full Breakfast
Credit Cards: A, B, C
Notes: 2, 5, 8 (over 9), 9, 10, 11, 12, 14

Bed and Breakfast
of Delaware
3650 Silverside Road, Box 177, 19810
(302) 479-9500; (800) 233-4689

This reservation service provides an elegant
alternative to commercial lodging. Guests
stay in manor homes, farms, carriage houses,
inns, and homestays throughout the
Brandywine Valley, Delaware, Maryland,
Virginia, and Pennsylvania. One hundred
accommodations represented. Mill Alford,
coordinator. $60-95.

NOTES: Credit cards accepted: A MasterCard; B Visa; C American Express; D Discover Card; E Diners Club; F Other;
2 Personal checks accepted; 3 Lunch available; 4 Dinner available; 5 Open all year; 6 Pets welcome; 8 Children
welcome; 9 Social drinking allowed; 10 Tennis available; 11 Swimming available; 12 Golf available; 13 Skiing
available; 14 May be booked through travel agents

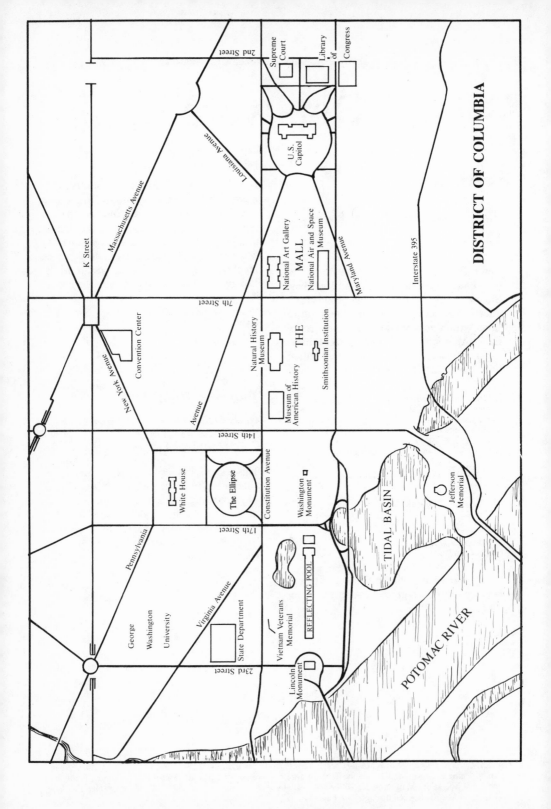

DISTRICT OF COLUMBIA

District of Columbia

The Bed and Breakfast League, Ltd. #1

P.O. Box 9490, 20016
(202) 363-7767

The Park House is a charming late-Victorian house within a ten-minute walk of the U.S. Capitol and the Library of Congress. It is three blocks from the Capitol South Metro stop and within walking distance of the east end of the mall and several Smithsonian museums. There are three guest rooms; one with private bath and two that share a bath. An expanded continental breakfast is served in the dining room. $65-95.

The Bed and Breakfast League, Ltd. #2

P.O. Box 9490, 20016
(202) 363-7767

This unhosted one-bedroom apartment is just eight blocks east of the U.S. Capitol and two blocks from the oldest remaining farmers' market in the city. Accommodations include one bedroom, with private bath, large closet, living/dining room with a queen pullout bed, and a Pullman kitchen with washer and dryer. The kitchen is stocked for continental breakfast. $60-105.

The Bed and Breakfast League, Ltd. #3

P.O. Box 9490, 20016
(202) 363-7767

This late-Victorian home built in 1900 and completely restored by the hosts is in the DuPont Circle section of the city. The six guest rooms have high ceilings, most of the original woodwork, antique furnishings, lovely linens, and sitting areas. Breakfast is served in the dining room or in guest rooms with advance notice. Three shared baths. Resident cat. $65-70.

The Bed and Breakfast League, Ltd. #4

P.O. Box 9490, 20016
(202) 363-7767

Situated in the heart of Georgetown, this two-room suite offers both space and privacy within a short walk of every restaurant and shop you would want to visit. There is one bedroom, a private bath, sitting room with color TV and wet bar, and supplies for continental breakfast. $65-70.

The Bed and Breakfast League, Ltd. #5

P.O. Box 9490, 20016
(202) 363-7767

Just ten minutes from Georgetown and five minutes from American University and the Potomac River is this handsome house built on the side of a hill. Two guest rooms with private baths (one bath in hall), and use of den with wet bar. Close to bus service to downtown and the mall. $60-70.

NOTES: Credit cards accepted: A Master Card; B Visa; C American Express; D Discover Card; E Diners Club; F Other; 2 Personal checks accepted; 3 Lunch available; 4 Dinner available; 5 Open all year; 6 Pets welcome; 8 Children welcome; 9 Social drinking allowed; 10 Tennis available; 11 Swimming available; 12 Golf available; 13 Skiing available; 14 May be booked through travel agents

The Reeds

Bed and Breakfast Limited
P. O. Box 12011, 20005
(202) 328-3510

This is a restored Victorian home, circa
1887, decorated with period and Art Nouveau
antiques and featuring original woodwork,
fireplaces, stained-glass windows, Victorian-style lattice porch, and garden with
fountains. It is situated ten blocks from the
White House and close to restaurants and
public transportation.

Hosts: Charles and Jackie Reed
Rooms: 6 (1 PB; 5 SB) $55-85
Expanded Continental Breakfast
Credit Cards: A, B, C, E
Notes: 5, 8, 10, 11, 12, 14

The Reeds

Florida

Florida House Inn

20 and 22 South Third Street, P. O. Box 688, 32034
(904) 261-3300; (800) 258-3301

Situated on Amelia Island in the heart of the 50-block historic district of Fernandina Beach, Florida House Inn is steps away from a Victorian seaport village. Built in 1857 as a tourist hotel, the inn offers today's guests the same large porches and 11 rooms, some with fireplaces, country pine and oak antiques, handmade rugs, and quilts throughout. Local airport and marina pickup available. Handicapped accessible.

Hosts: Bob and Karen Warner
Rooms: 11 (PB) $55-125
Full Breakfast
Credit Cards: A, B, C, E
Notes: 2, 3, 4, 5, 8, 9, 10, 11, 12, 14

Deer Run
Bed and Breakfast

P. O. Box 431, 33043
(305) 872-2015

Deer Run is a Florida cracker-style home nestled in lush, native trees on the oceanfront, furnished with antiques, wicker, and rattan. Upstairs rooms have high ceilings, Bahama fans, and French doors, plus air conditioning. Breakfast is served on the veranda overlooking the ocean.

Host: Sue Abbott
Rooms: 2 (PB) $85-95
Full Breakfast
Credit Cards: None
Notes: 2, 5, 9, 10, 11, 12

Historic Island Hotel

Main Street (Second and B Streets), 32625
(904) 543-5111

Set in a small fishing and arts community, the hotel features a wraparound veranda, Jamaican architecture, and romantic character. The Gourmet-Natural Foods Restaurant specializes in fresh seafood and strong vegetarian menu. There is an art collection and classical music in the dining room. Suitable for weddings, reunions, and anniversaries. Therapeutic massage available in hotel.

Hosts: Marcia Rogers and Daniela Taylor
Rooms: 10 (6 PB; 4 SB) $75-105
Full Breakfast
Credit Cards: A, B
Notes: 2, 4, 8, 9, 10, 11

The Son's Shady Brook
Bed and Breakfast

P.O. Box 551, 33521
(904) 748-7867

Enjoy a refreshing change in a rural setting offering solitude, tranquility, and therapeutic picturesque surroundings. This easy-to-find modern house is on 21 secluded wooded acres overlooking a spring-fed creek. Guests enjoy piano, library, and fireplace within an hour from Orlando and Tampa. A relaxing retreat for elderly, handicapped, newlyweds, and others.

welcome; 9 Social drinking allowed; 10 Tennis available; 11 Swimming available; 12 Golf available; 13 Skiing available; 14 May be booked through travel agents

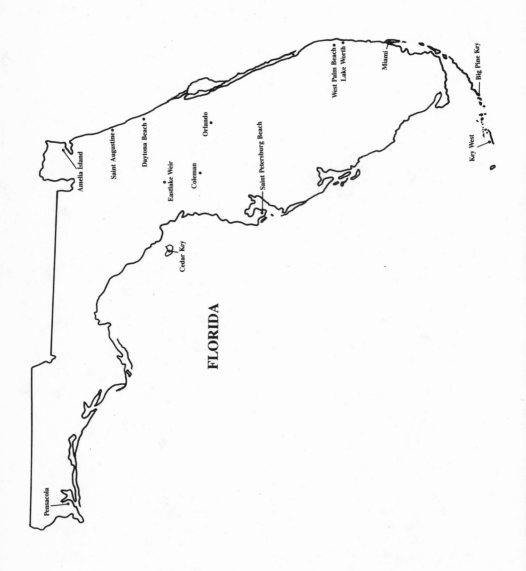

FLORIDA

Pensacola

Amelia Island
Saint Augustine
Daytona Beach
Eastlake Weir
Coleman
Orlando
Cedar Key
Saint Petersburg Beach
West Palm Beach
Lake Worth
Miami
Big Pine Key
Key West

Host: Jean Lake Martin
Rooms: 4 (PB) $40-60
Full Breakfast
Credit Cards: A, B, C
Notes: 2, 3 (prior arrangement), 4 (prior arrangement), 5, 10, 12

DAYTONA BEACH

Live Oak Inn

444-448 South Beach Street, 32114-5004
(904) 252-4667; (800) 253-INNS
FAX (904) 252-1871

Listed on the National Register of Historic Places, the inn offers 16 rooms, most with Jacuzzis, and porches with views of historic garden or marina. Flowers and fruit are presented in each room, and a beverage is served upon your arrival. Fine dining and afternoon tea and coffee are provided. Special services for business travelers include meeting rooms. Golf package available. AAA rated excellent.

Hosts: Vinton and Sandra Fisher
Rooms: 16 (PB) $60-170
Full and Continental Breakfast
Credit Cards: A, B, C
Notes: 2, 3, 4, 5, 8 (over 12), 9, 10, 11, 12, 14

Whispers Bed and Breakfast

EASTLAKE WEIR

Lakeside Country Inn Bed and Breakfast

P. O. Box 71, 32133
(904) 288-1396

This quaint 100-year-old residence overlooks beautiful Lake Weir, a 5,600-acre recreational lake. A canoe is available for guest use. The home was built as a hotel and has irreplaceable woods on the inside, with an upstairs veranda with magnificent views. This is a unique Florida experience with excellent hiking and biking nearby.

Hosts: Bill and Sandy Bodner
Rooms: 5 (2 PB; 3 SB) $50-60
Full Breakfast
Credit Cards: None
Notes: 2, 5, 9, 11, 12, 14

KEY WEST

Whispers Bed and Breakfast

409 William Street, 33040
(305) 294-5969

This beautifully restored and maintained 1866 inn offers guests romantic, antique-filled rooms and gourmet breakfast creations served in the tropical garden. The inn is situated perfectly—an easy walk or bicycle to anything in Old Town. As seen in *Colonial Homes* magazine.

Hosts: Les and Marilyn Tipton
Rooms: 6 (S3B) $69-120
Full Breakfast
Credit Cards: A, B, C
Notes: 5, 9, 10, 11, 12

LAKE WORTH

The Matthews Bed and Breakfast

3150 Gulfstream Road, 33461
(407) 965-0068

NOTES: Credit cards accepted: A Master Card; B Visa; C American Express; D Discover Card; E Diners Club; F Other; 2 Personal checks accepted; 3 Lunch available; 4 Dinner available; 5 Open all year; 6 Pets welcome; 8 Children welcome; 9 Social drinking allowed; 10 Tennis available; 11 Swimming available; 12 Golf available; 13 Skiing available; 14 May be booked through travel agents

This contemporary home offering a choice of double or king beds is surrounded by flowers and fruit trees and is within eight miles of West Palm airport. (Transportation available.) A rented car will help you enjoy many tourist attractions within a short driving distance, such as the ocean, beautiful Japanese gardens, Flagler Museum and Zoo, shopping malls. Barbecue, lawn darts, and bicycles available. November 1 through April 30.

Hosts: Vern and Beryl Matthews
Rooms: 1 (PB) $55
Full Breakfast
Credit Cards: None

MIAMI

Bed and Breakfast Company—Tropical Florida
P.O. Box 262, 33243
(305) 661-3270; FAX (305) 661-3270

The Bed and Breakfast Company is a reservation service for over 100 bed and breakfast homes all over Florida. Host homes include mansions on historic properties, homes along the ocean or Gulf of Mexico, in woodland retreats, and on private residential islands. Guests are welcomed by all the warmth and comforts of southern hospitality. $40-115; $5 surcharge for stays under three nights.

ORLANDO

PerriHouse Bed and Breakfast
10417 State Road 535, 32819
(407) 780-4830; (800) 780-4830

PerriHouse is a private and secluded country estate on 20 acres conveniently nestled right in Disneyland's backyard. All that Disneyland and Orlando have to offer is only minutes away. The hosts will gladly point the way. Indulge in a few quiet moments while being treated with personal

hospitality. Cool off in the pool or relax in the Jacuzzi. Each room is lavishly furnished and has an outside entrance.

Hosts: Nick and Angi Perretti
Rooms: 4 (PB) $65-85
Continental Breakfast
Credit Cards: None
Notes: 2, 5, 8, 9, 11, 12, 14

The Kenwood Inn

PENSACOLA

Homestead Village Inn
7830 Pine Forest Road, 32526
(904) 944-4816

This beautiful inn is centrally situated in historic Pensacola, home of the Naval Aviation Museum and America's most beautiful white sand beaches. The inn features homemade desserts in the evening, an eight-course breakfast, Williamsburg-style rooms, cable TV, phones, and a new Mennonite full-service restaurant.

Hosts: Neil and Jeanne Liechty
Rooms: 6 (PB) $59-79
Full Breakfast
Credit Cards: A, B, C
Notes: 2, 3, 4, 5, 8, 9, 10, 11, 12, 14

SAINT AUGUSTINE

Castle Garden
15 Shenandoah Street, 32084
(904) 829-3839

NOTES: Credit cards accepted: A Master Card; B Visa; C American Express; D Discover Card; E Diners Club; F Other; 2 Personal checks accepted; 3 Lunch available; 4 Dinner available; 5 Open all year; 6 Pets welcome; 8 Children

Unique 100-year-old coquina house restored to perfection. This former Warden Castle carriage house boasts four guest rooms, each tastefully decorated with its own special charm and antiques. There are also two honeymoon suites complete with sunken bedrooms, Jacuzzi tub, and all of life's little pleasures. Stroll down romantic Water Street along the coastal waterway or relax on the portico. Weddings are performed in the outdoor garden or indoor chapel. Bicycles, chocolates, wine, and private parking are provided.

Host: Bruce Kloeckner
Rooms: 6 (PB) $55-150
Full Breakfast
Credit Cards: A, B, C, D
Notes: 2, 3, 4, 5, 8, 9, 10, 11, 12, 14

The Kenwood Inn

38 Marine Street 32084
(904) 824-2116

For more than a century this lovely old Victorian building has received visitors to Saint Augustine. The inn was built between 1865 and 1885 as a private boarding house and has maintained the charm and character of the one-hundred-year tradition while providing the comforts of home. The inn is within walking distance of many fine restaurants and all historic sights.

Hosts: Mark, Kerrianne, and Caitlin Constant
Rooms: 14 (PB) $55-85
Continental Breakfast
Credit Cards: A, B, D
Notes: 2, 5, 9, 10, 11, 12

Old City House Inn and Restaurant

115 Cordova Street, 32084
(904) 826-0113

The inn is just one year old and situated in the heart of the historic district within walking distance of interesting and beautiful parts of the nation's oldest city. A veranda and courtyard serve as common rooms. Bi-

cycles and wine are complimentary. Reduced midweek rates. Full service restaurant on premises.

Hosts: Alice and Bob Compton
Rooms: 5 (PB) $60-95
Full Breakfast
Credit Cards: A, B, C
Notes: 2, 3, 4, 5, 8, 9, 10, 11, 12, 14

Old Powder House Inn

38 Cordova Street, 32084
(904) 824-4149; (800) 447-4149

This two-story Victorian structure is situated in the heart of the historic area. Horse and buggies tour by the inn with echoes of the past. Enjoy period antiques with today's convenience, high tea, wine, hors d'oeuvres, Jacuzzi, bicycles, private parking, cable TV. Hosts offer family hospitality and knowledge of local sites and restaurants. Special packages available for weddings, anniversaries, and birthdays.

Hosts: Mike and Connie Emerson
Rooms: 9 (PB) $59-98
Full Breakfast
Credit Cards: A, B
Notes: 2 (Florida), 3, 4, 5, 9, 10, 11, 12

St. Francis Inn

St. Francis Inn

279 Saint George Street, 32084
(904) 824-6068

Built in 1791, the St. Francis Inn is one of the oldest inns in the United States. The beautiful Spanish Colonial building and courtyard provide a peaceful setting for traditional hospitality and modern conveniences. Accommodations range from double rooms to suites to a five-room cottage. Central air conditioning, pool, cable TV, and complimentary use of inn bicycles are available.

Host: Marie Register
Rooms: 14 (PB) $49-118
Expanded Continental Breakfast
Credit Cards: A, B
Notes: 2, 5, 8, 9, 10, 11, 12, 14

SAINT PETERSBURG BEACH _____

Bernard's Swanhome
8690 Gulf Boulevard, 33706
(813) 360-5245

Situated on the waterfront with dock and good fishing and heated spa, one-third mile to the white sand of the Gulf of Mexico. Laundry and kitchen privileges available. TV and phones in room. Discount for families, and the seventh night is free.

Hosts: Ron and Danie Bernard
Rooms: 3 (1 PB; 2 SB) $45
Continental Breakfast
Credit Cards: C
Notes: 5, 8, 9, 10, 11, 12, 13, 14

WEST PALM BEACH _____

Hibiscus House
501 30th Street, 33407
(407) 863-5633

Hibiscus House is situated in a charming historic neighborhood near the Intracoastal Waterway with convenient access to the ocean, Palm Beach International Airport, and Palm Beach with its fabulous homes and shopping. The home, built in 1921, offers elegant surroundings with period furnishings and antiques. One suite is available.

Host: Raleigh Hill
Rooms: 6 (PB) $55-90
Full Breakfast
Credit Cards: None
Notes: 2, 5, 8, 9, 10, 11, 12, 14

West Palm Beach Bed and Breakfast
419 32nd Street, P. O. Box 8581, 33407
(800) 736-4064

This is a cozy Key West-style cottage built in the 1930s with all the modern conveniences of today: air conditioning, paddle fans, cable TV. Hosts have retained the charm of Old World Florida with white wicker furniture in a colorful Caribbean decor. Sun by the lush tropical pool, ride complimentary bicycles, or just relax and kick off your sandals. Centrally situated.

Hosts: Dennis Keimel and Ron Seitz
Rooms: 3 (PB) $55-75
Expanded Continental Breakfast
Credit Cards: None
Notes: 2, 5, 6, 8, 9, 10, 11, 12, 14

Georgia

Hilltop House

Bed and Breakfast Atlanta
1801 Piedmont Avenue #208, 30324
(404) 875-0525; (800) 967-3224

This architecturally interesting home built
about 1910 is in a neighborhood of winding
streets and parks. Situated in the heart of
midtown Atlanta, it is within walking distance of Woodruff Arts Center, High Museum, Botanical Gardens, Colony Square,
and many desirable shops and restaurants.
One room has king bed, the other has twin
beds.

Rooms: 2 (1 PB; 1 SB) $72-80
Expanded Continental Breakfast
Credit Cards: A, B, C, D, E
Notes: 9, 10

Hilltop House

The Woodruff
Bed and Breakfast

223 Ponce de Leon Avenue, 30308
(800) 473-9449

A 1915 Victorian home built by prominent
neurologist Dr. William Orr, the inn has 12
lovely bedrooms decorated with antiques
and 11 baths. It is situated in historic midtown Atlanta and convenient to theatrical,
historical, cultural, and sporting activities.
A southern breakfast is featured with grits.
The home is restored, managed, lived in,
and owned by the hosts.

Hosts: Joan and Douglas Jones
Rooms: 12 (8 PB; 4 SB) $68.50-125
Full Breakfast
Credit Cards: A, B, C
Notes: 2, 5, 8, 9, 12, 14

CHICKAMAUGA

Gordon-Lee Mansion

217 Cove Road, 30707
(404) 375-4728

Step back in time and enter this antebellum
plantation house of museum quality, circa
1847. Used during the battle of Chickamauga
as a Union headquarters and hospital, the
mansion is furnished with period antiques
in the atmosphere of early southern aristoc-
racy. It is listed on the National Register of
Historic Places. The seven-acre setting is
just three miles from the Chickamauga-
Chattanooga National Military Park and 20

welcome; 9 Social drinking allowed; 10 Tennis available; 11 Swimming available; 12 Golf available; 13 Skiing
available; 14 May be booked through travel agents

- Fort Oglethorpe
- Chickamauga

Flowery Branch •   • Commerce

• Atlanta

• Hamilton

Saint Marys

GEORGIA

minutes from downtown Chattanooga, Tennessee. Wine and cheese are complimentary.

Host: Richard Barclift
Rooms: 5 (4 PB; 1 SB) $60-72
Expanded Continental Breakfast
Credit Cards: A, B
Notes: 2, 5, 9, 10, 12, 14

COMMERCE

The Pittman House

103 Homer Street, 30529
(404) 335-3823

The Pittman House is vintage Colonial with a wraparound porch that invites rocking. The circa 1890s house has a split parlor interior with four bedrooms upstairs and is completely furnished in period antiques. It is a gracious old house from a gracious period of history and is lovingly restored to today's comforts.

Hosts: Tom and Dot Tomberlin
Rooms: 4 (2 PB; 2 SB) $50
Full Breakfast
Credit Cards: A, B
Notes: 2, 5, 8, 10, 11, 12, 14

FLOWERY BRANCH

Whitworth Inn

6593 McEver Road, 30542
(404) 967-2386

This newly constructed country inn on five wooded acres is near Lake Lanier Islands and just 30 minutes northeast of Atlanta at the foothills of the northeast Georgia mountains. It is close to championship golf courses, marinas, beaches and waterparks, Chateau Elan Winery, and Road Atlanta Raceway. Country breakfast is served in a sunny, spacious dining room. Ideal for catered parties and meetings.

Hosts: Kenneth and Christine Jonick
Rooms: 8 (PB) $55-65

Full Breakfast
Credit Cards: A, B
Notes: 2, 5, 8, 10, 12, 14

FORT OGLETHORPE

Captain's Quarters Bed and Breakfast

13 Barnhardt Circle, 30742
(404) 858-0624

Built in 1902 as a home for two army captains, this totally renovated home stands ready for guest enjoyment. It is situated adjacent to Chickamauga-Chattanooga National Military Park and 15-30 minutes away from all Chattanooga, Tennessee, attractions, just off Highway 27, six miles from Exit 141 on Interstate 75.

Hosts: Pam Humphrey and Ann Gilbert
Rooms: 4 (PB) $50-75
Full Breakfast
Credit Cards: A, B, C
Notes: 2, 5

HAMILTON

Wedgwood Bed and Breakfast

Highway 27 and Mobley Drive
P. O. Box 115, 31811
(404) 628-5659

Situated six miles south of Callaway Gardens, this 1850 home is decorated in Wedgwood blue with white stenciling. Enjoy the piano in the livingroom, view a classic movie on the VCR in the den, read in the library, swing on the screened porch, or doze in a hammock in the gazebo under pecan trees. Roosevelt's Little White House is nearby.

Host: Janice Neuffer
Rooms 3 (1 PB; 2 SB) $55-70
Full Breakfast
Credit Cards: None
Notes: 2, 5, 8, 9, 10, 11, 12, 14

NOTES: Credit cards accepted: A Master Card; B Visa; C American Express; D Discover Card; E Diners Club; F Other; 2 Personal checks accepted; 3 Lunch available; 4 Dinner available; 5 Open all year; 6 Pets welcome; 8 Children welcome; 9 Social drinking allowed; 10 Tennis available; 11 Swimming available; 12 Golf available; 13 Skiing available; 14 May be booked through travel agents

SAINT MARYS _____

The Historic Spencer House Inn

101 East Bryant Street, 31558
(912) 882-1872

The Historic Spencer House Inn is decorated with fine antiques and beautiful reproductions. Selected fabrics and furnishings
breathe new life into the big, sunny inn.
Original mouldings and wide-planked
wooden floors add warmth and beauty. Saint
Marys is located along Georgia's Colonial
coast and is billed as the nation's second
oldest city. Cumberland Island National
Seashore is just east of Saint Marys.

Host: Rena Schumaker Provo
Rooms: 14 (PB) $60-87
Continental Breakfast
Credit Cards: A, B
Notes: 5, 8, 9, 10, 11, 12

The Historic Spencer House Inn

Hawaii

Bed and Breakfast Honolulu (Statewide) COOPJ

3242 Kaohinani Drive, Honolulu, 96817
(808) 795-7533; (800) 288-4666
FAX (808) 595-2030

Enjoy the view of the entire coastline from this sugar plantation camp-style house. Close to Rainbow Falls, pools, boiling pots, and caves. $45.

Bed and Breakfast Honolulu (Statewide) KEGLS

3242 Kaohinani Drive, Honolulu, 96817
(808) 585-7533; (800) 288-4666
FAX (808) 595-2030

Only a five-minute walk from the center of Hilo, these accommodations offer two guest rooms and a private livingroom with a view of the ocean, Hilo Bay, and the mountains. $45.

Bed and Breakfast Honolulu (Statewide) SMALM

3242 Kaohinani Drive, Honolulu, 96817
(808) 795-7533; (800) 288-4666
FAX (808) 595-2030

This house, with a stone fireplace and screened Japanese tea room, was once the home of a Japanese ambassador. Across the street from the ocean. $60.

Bed and Breakfast Honolulu (Statewide) VINYM

3242 Kaohinani Drive, Honolulu, 96817
(808) 795-7533; (800) 288-4666
FAX (808) 595-2030

This air-conditioned condominium overlooks the famous white sands beaches. Enjoy sauna, billiards, and tennis. Some of the island's best restaurants and shopping are nearby. $70.

Bed and Breakfast Honolulu (Statewide) FREIS

3242 Kaohinani Drive, Honolulu, 96817
(808) 795-7533; (800) 288-4666
FAX (808) 595-2030

At this beautiful brand-new two-story home, guests enjoy a special "aloha" breakfast served in the family room that is furnished with piano, pool table, big screen TV, and refrigerator. $50.

Bed and Breakfast Honolulu (Statewide) HORNJ

3242 Kaohinani Drive, Honolulu, 96817
(808) 795-7533; (800) 288-4666
FAX (808) 595-2030

welcome; 9 Social drinking allowed; 10 Tennis available; 11 Swimming available; 12 Golf available; 13 Skiing available; 14 May be booked through travel agents

HAWAII

Princeville
Kilauea
Anahola
Kapaa
Poipu
Lihue
Koloa
KAUAI

North Shore
Kaneohe
Kailua
Lanikai
Hawaii Kai
OAHU

Kalului
Haiku
Upcountry
Hana
MAUI
Lahaina
Kihei

Kohala
Kamuela
HAWAII
Hilo
Pahoa-Kehena Beach
Volcano
Kailua/Kona

This renovated 50-year-old home has four guest rooms and sits on more than an acre of tropical gardens. Enjoy sunning at the pool or the ocean view from the gazebo. $50.

HAWAII—KOHALA

Bed and Breakfast Honolulu (Statewide) AROSP

3242 Kaohinani Drive, Honolulu, 96817
(808) 795-7533; (800) 288-4666
FAX (808) 595-2030

On the north shore of the big island, this large landscaped old plantation manager's home has two guest rooms, one with a private entrance and a shared bath. $50.

HAWAII—KONA

Bed and Breakfast Honolulu (Statewide) CANNT

3242 Kaohinani Drive, Honolulu, 96817
(808) 795-7533; (800) 288-4666
FAX (808) 595-2030

This is a complete studio on the Kona coast. Enjoy a private view of the blue Pacific from the lanai. $60.

Bed and Breakfast Honolulu (Statewide) CRONN

3242 Kaohinani Drive, Honolulu, 96817
(808) 795-7533; (800) 288-4666
FAX (808) 595-2030

Accommodations include a main house and apartment with a separate entrance. All rooms have private baths. $45.

Bed and Breakfast Honolulu (Statewide) DITTE

3242 Kaohinani Drive, Honolulu, 96817
(808) 795-7533; (800) 288-4666
FAX (808) 595-2030

Guests stay in a bedroom with a king bed and private bath only five minutes from Kailua-Kona. Breakfast is served on the lanai overlooking the ocean. $55.

Bed and Breakfast Honolulu (Statewide) GOODS

3242 Kaohinani Drive, Honolulu, 96817
(808) 795-7533; (800) 288-4666
FAX (808) 595-2030

Ten miles from the Kona airport, this guest room is in a quiet residential area with an ocean view and a view of Kailua town from the lanai. Three-night minimum stay. $55.

Bed and Breakfast Honolulu (Statewide) OBERJ

3242 Kaohinani Drive, Honolulu, 96817
(808) 795-7533; (800) 288-4666
FAX (808) 595-2030

Right at the Captain Cook monument is a brand-new accommodation with one bedroom and adjacent sitting room. Two-night minimum stay. $65.

Bed and Breakfast Honolulu (Statewide) ROSEJ

3242 Kaohinani Drive, Honolulu, 96817
(808) 795-7533; (800) 288-4666
FAX (808) 595-2030

In the Captain Cook area is this bed and breakfast with a kitchen stocked with a hearty continental breakfast for guests to enjoy at their leisure. Near shopping and restaurants. $50.

Bed and Breakfast Honolulu (Statewide) TOYJ

3242 Kaohinani Drive, Honolulu, 96817
(808) 795-7533; (800) 288-4666
FAX (808) 595-2030

NOTES: Credit cards accepted: A MasterCard; B Visa; C American Express; D Discover Card; E Diners Club; F Other; 2 Personal checks accepted; 3 Lunch available; 4 Dinner available; 5 Open all year; 6 Pets welcome; 8 Children welcome; 9 Social drinking allowed; 10 Tennis available; 11 Swimming available; 12 Golf available; 13 Skiing available; 14 May be booked through travel agents

This completely private apartment has a sweeping view of Kona's sunsets. The breakfast alcove has a toaster oven, refrigerator, and microwave. Kona coffee, tropical fruit, and local specialties are furnished. $60.

HAWAII—PAHOA-KEHENA BEACH

Kalani Honua by the Sea
Rural Route 2, Box 4500, 96778
(808) 965-7828; (800) 800-6886

Kolani Honua provides an environment where the spirit of aloha flourishes. Situated on 20 secluded acres bordered by lush jungle and rugged coastline forged by ancient lava flows, Kalani Honua offers an authentic experience of rural Hawaii. Far from city life, close to the ocean playground of dolphins and whales, the lodge offers simple, comfortable accommodations.

Hosts: Richard Koob and Madilyn Sandra
Rooms: 40 (13 PB; 27 SB) $58-80
Continental Breakfast
Credit Cards: A, B, C, E, F
Notes: 2, 3, 4, 5, 8, 9, 10, 11, 12, 13, 14

HAWAII—VOLCANO

Bed and Breakfast Honolulu (Statewide) JACKB
3242 Kaohinani Drive, Honolulu, 96817
(808) 795-7533; (800) 288-4666
FAX (808) 595-2030

At Volcano Village is this complete three-bedroom cottage with well-equipped kitchen, large livingroom, covered deck, and hibachi. Hiking, picnicking, and golf nearby. $55.

Bed and Breakfast Honolulu (Statewide) PEDES 1
3242 Kaohinani Drive, Honolulu, 96817
(808) 795-7533; (800) 288-4666
FAX (808) 595-2030

Situated just one mile from Volcano National Park, this bed and breakfast is surrounded by fruit trees and many native trees. Rooms have a lovely view of the natural setting. $56.

Kalani Honua by the Sea

Bed and Breakfast Honolulu (Statewide) WOLDR
3242 Kaohinani Drive, Honolulu, 96817
(808) 795-7533; (800) 288-4666
FAX (808) 595-2030

This home is situated in the village of Volcano and has rooms with large bright windows looking out on the lush green tropical foliage. $50.

Volcano Bed and Breakfast
19-3950 Keonelehua Street, P. O. Box 22, 96785
(808) 967-7779; (800) 733-7713

The 1920s three-story home that is Volcano Bed and Breakfast offers a peaceful setting and a safe haven that draws visitors from all over the world. Guest rooms look out onto tree ferns, fragrant ginger, and surrounding native ohia forest. Various nearby activities include Hawaii Volcanoes National Park's hiking trails and spectacular lava flows. Christian hosts provide an abundance of information.

Hosts: Jim and Sandy Pedersen
Rooms: 3 (SB) $50-55
Full Breakfast
Credit Cards: A, B
Notes: 2, 5, 8, 10, 11, 12, 14

NOTES: Credit cards accepted: A Master Card; B Visa; C American Express; D Discover Card; E Diners Club; F Other; 2 Personal checks accepted; 3 Lunch available; 4 Dinner available; 5 Open all year; 6 Pets welcome; 8 Children

KAUAI—ANAHOLA

Bed and Breakfast Honolulu (Statewide) SKAGJH

3242 Kaohinani Drive, Honolulu, 96817
(808) 795-7533; (800) 288-4666
FAX (808) 595-2030

This completely private studio is across the street from the beach and has easy access to all sightseeing and touring. A continental breakfast is stocked for guests to enjoy at their leisure. $70.

KAUAI—KAPAA

Bed and Breakfast Honolulu (Statewide) BAUMT

3242 Kaohinani Drive, Honolulu, 96817
(808) 795-7533; (800) 288-4666
FAX (808) 595-2030

Just past Opaekaa Falls is this new 600-square-foot guest cottage with deck. Falls can be seen from the deck. Breads and fruit provided for breakfast. Light cooking facilities. $65.

Bed and Breakfast Honolulu (Statewide) NEUMM

3242 Kaohinani Drive, Honolulu, 96817
(808) 795-7533; (800) 288-4666
FAX (808) 595-2030

This four-level home offers a guest suite with a livingroom, kitchen, bedroom, bath, and private entrance, and a spectacular view of the ocean. The beach is a ten-minute drive away. $75.

Kauai Calls Bed and Breakfast

Bed and Breakfast Honolulu (Statewide) SCHEJ

3242 Kaohinani Drive, Honolulu, 96817
(808) 795-7533; (800) 288-4666
FAX (808) 595-2030

This studio is under the eyebrow of the sleeping giant and very private. Guests enjoy the best of both mountains and sea. Only five minutes from Lydgate Park. $55.

Bed and Breakfast Honolulu (Statewide) SMITR

3242 Kaohinani Drive, Honolulu, 96817
(808) 795-7533; (800) 288-4666
FAX (808) 595-2030

Two units are available in a 90-year-old plantation home, and there are two one-bedroom condominiums on the beach. The home is a landscaping showpiece. $50.

Bed and Breakfast Honolulu (Statewide) TAYLG

3242 Kaohinani Drive, Honolulu, 96817
(808) 795-7533; (800) 288-4666
FAX (808) 595-2030

Three acres of rolling hills overlook the ocean and mountains. The large solar Jacuzzi offers green mountain vistas. The grounds have ample space for solitude. $45.

Kauai Calls Bed and Breakfast

5972 Heamoi Place, 96746
(808) 822-9699

Situated in Wailua Valley, behind the Coco Palms Hotel, near Fern Grotto and Lydgate Park on the ocean. Two guest rooms have private entrances and Jacuzzi for guests only. Waterfalls, craters, canyons, hiking nearby. Breakfast features fresh ground Kona coffee, fruits, and pastries prepared to

welcome; 9 Social drinking allowed; 10 Tennis available; 11 Swimming available; 12 Golf available; 13 Skiing available; 14 May be booked through travel agents

arouse your tastebuds. Three-night minimum stay.

Hosts: Joy and Earle Schertell
Rooms: 2 (PB) $60-80
Full Breakfast
Credit Cards: None
Notes: 2 (for reservation only), 5, 8 (over 12), 9, 10, 11, 12, 14

KAUAI—KILAUEA

Bed and Breakfast Honolulu (Statewide)WINKJ

3242 Kaohinani Drive, Honolulu, 96817
(808) 795-7533; (800) 288-4666
FAX (808) 595-2030

Overlooking the Kilauea Valley on the north shore of Kauai, the guest room has a spectacular view of the island and is only five minutes from several secluded beaches. Horseback riding, tennis, golf nearby. $65.

KAUAI—KOLOA

Bed and Breakfast Honolulu (Statewide) GOOCK

3242 Kaohinani Drive, Honolulu, 96817
(808) 795-7533; (800) 288-4666
FAX (808) 595-2030

Centrally situated, only five minutes from beaches of Poipu, 15 minutes from downtown Lihue. Loan of beach and sports equipment. Light cooking facilities. $65.

Poipu Bed and Breakfast Inn ·

2720 Hoonani Road, 96756
(808) 742-1146; (800) 552-0095

This award-winning, renovated 1933 plantation inn is in a garden setting one block from the water. Just a few doors away, the new oceanfront inn offers spectacular ocean views, rooms or suites with private baths, TVs, VCRs, and ceiling fans. Some rooms have whirlpool tubs, kitchenettes, air condi-

tioning, and one is handicapped accessible. Tropical breakfast buffet, afternoon tea, free video movies and popcorn, games, barbecue, laundry facilities, and maid service are provided.

Hosts: Dotti Cichon and B. Young
Rooms: 8 (PB) $50-195
Expanded Continental Breakfast
Credit Cards: A, B, C, D, E, F
Notes: 2, 5, 8, 9, 10, 11, 12, 14

Poipu Bed and Breakfast Inn

KAUAI—LIHUE

Bed and Breakfast Honolulu (Statewide) ZAIML

3242 Kaohinani Drive, Honolulu, 96817
(808) 795-7533; (800) 288-4666
FAX (808) 595-2030

This lovely cottage is only two minutes from the airport and is 20 minutes to sunny beaches of Poipu. Guests enjoy use of barbecue pit. Breakfast fixings provided. Three-night minimum stay. $45.

Z's Bed and Breakfast

3296 Uluhui Street, P.O. Box 1365, 96766-5365
(808) 245-2665; (808) 245-4039

Two minutes from the airport is this single-bedroom apartment with livingroom, queen bed, queen Hide-a-bed, microwave, refrigerator, coffee maker, private entrance. Situated in the heart of town, central to all points of interest on the island. TV, stereo, phone available upon request.

NOTES: Credit cards accepted: A Master Card; B Visa; C American Express; D Discover Card; E Diners Club; F Other; 2 Personal checks accepted; 3 Lunch available; 4 Dinner available; 5 Open all year; 6 Pets welcome; 8 Children

Host: Lani Zaimi Camacho
Room: 1 (PB) $60
Continental Breakfast
Credit Cards: None
Notes: 2, 5, 8, 9, 10, 11, 12

KAUAI—POIPU

Bed and Breakfast Honolulu (Statewide) JOHNJ

3242 Kaohinani Drive, Honolulu, 96817
(808) 795-7533; (800) 288-4666
FAX (808) 595-2030

This deluxe master bedroom has a cathedral ceiling, king bed, and color TV. Enjoy the view of the ocean from a private lanai in a lush green setting with beautiful landscaping. $65.

Bed and Breakfast Honolulu (Statewide) KNUDV 1

3242 Kaohinani Drive, Honolulu, 96817
(808) 795-7533; (800) 288-4666
FAX (808) 595-2030

This guest ranch sits atop a secluded hill. A century-old home, it was brought down from the mountains and restored. The view of the ocean is panoramic. $75.

Bed and Breakfast Honolulu (Statewide) LEVII

3242 Kaohinani Drive, Honolulu, 96817
(808) 795-7533; (800) 288-4666
FAX (808) 595-2030

This apartment has two bedrooms with private entrances and a shared bath. The home sits in a very tropical setting with an array of Hawaiian foliage and sweeping mountain and ocean views. $50.

Pua Hale and the Garden Suite

2381 Kipuka Street, Koloa, 96756
(808) 742-1700; (800) 745-7414

Pua Hale is a beautifully decorated Japanese-style 750-square-foot house at Poipu Beach. Complete kitchen, laundry room, livingroom, dining room, and king-sized bedroom with a deluxe Japanese-style sunken bath. There is a yard fenced with a profusion of tropical flowers in a quiet residential neighborhood. There is also a 500-square-foot garden suite with complete kitchen, living and dining area, bedroom, and bath with sunken tub. Opens to lanai facing a garden with fruit trees and flowers.

Hosts: Walter Briant and Carol Ann Davis
Suites: 2 (PB) $70-100; $450-650 weekly
Four-night minimum stay
Continental Breakfast
Credit Cards: None
Notes: 2, 10, 11, 12, 14

KAUAI—PRINCEVILLE

Bed and Breakfast Honolulu (Statewide) BARNC 1

3242 Kaohinani Drive, Honolulu, 96817
(808) 795-7533; (800) 288-4666
FAX (808) 595-2030

A lovely home in the Hanalei area offers three units, including an apartment with light cooking. Sunset and waterfall views are dramatic from the cathedral windows. Only 100 yards to the beach. $70.

Bed and Breakfast Honolulu (Statewide) FISHJ

3242 Kaohinani Drive, Honolulu, 96817
(808) 795-7533; (800) 288-4666
FAX (808) 595-2030

Three guest rooms all have private baths, one has a private entrance. This condominium is situated on the third hole of the golf course. Walk to town or to the ocean. $55.

welcome; 9 Social drinking allowed; 10 Tennis available; 11 Swimming available; 12 Golf available; 13 Skiing available; 14 May be booked through travel agents

Hale 'Aha Bed and Breakfast in Paradise
P. O. Box 3370, 96722
(800) 826-6733

Bed and Breakfast in Paradise is situated on Princeville's championship golf course overlooking the blue Pacific. Private decks, entrances, refrigerators, TVs are included with all guest rooms. Enjoy the panoramic view in new, peaceful, affordable luxury. Great for honeymoons and vacations.

Hosts: Herb and Ruth Bockelman
Rooms: 4 (PB) $80-180
Expanded Continental Breakfast
Credit Cards: None
Notes: 2, 10, 11, 12, 14

MAUI—HAIKU

Haikuleana Bed and Breakfast, Plantation Style
69 Haiku Road, 96708
(808) 575-2890

Experience mid-19th century charm at this totally renovated Hawaiian plantation home. An all-glass livingroom enhances the lush botanical surroundings in a country setting only 15 minutes from quaint shops and the airport and one and one-half miles from the famous Hoo Kipa Beach. Wainscoting, 12-foot ceilings, wood floors, antiques, and old wicker abound.

Hosts: Frederick J. Fox, Jr., and family
Rooms: 3 (PB) $80
Full Breakfast
Credit Cards: None
Notes: 2, 5, 8 (over 6), 9, 10, 11, 12, 14

MAUI—HANA

Bed and Breakfast Honolulu (Statewide) KAIAJ 1
3242 Kaohinani Drive, Honolulu, 96817
(808) 795-7533; (800) 288-4666
FAX (808) 595-2030

Guests may roam the gardens of this working fruit and flower farm or even pull a few weeds. Kerosene lamps, no electricity, TV, or phone. $60.

Kaia Ranch and Company
P. O. Box 404, 96713
(808) 248-7725

Experience a Hawaiian country farm on 27 private, quite acres. Exotic tropical flowers and fruits are grown in a parklike setting. Guests are welcome to walk and picnic. An adjacent trail leads to scenic ocean cliffs. Guest room consists of spacious enclosed patio with kerosene lamps. Two-night minimum stay.

Hosts: John and Joloyce Kaia
Room: 1 (SB) $90
Full Breakfast
Credit Cards: None
Notes: 5, 10, 11

Haikuleana Bed and Breakfast, Plantation Style

MAUI—KALULUI

Bed and Breakfast Honolulu (Statewide) ROBEE
3242 Kaohinani Drive, Honolulu, 96817
(808) 795-7533; (800) 288-4666
FAX (808) 595-2030

This lovely home is only a few minutes from the airport. Each of two rooms has a private entrance and shares a bath. There is also a cottage where guests may cook and do laundry. Near shopping and restaurants. $50.

Bed and Breakfast Honolulu (Statewide) JOHNM

3242 Kaohinani Drive, Honolulu, 96817
(808) 795-7533; (800) 288-4666
FAX (808) 595-2030

Two completely private units are offered, a studio and a cottage. Guests are welcome to pick citrus, bananas, papayas, and tangerines in season. Four blocks from the beach.

Bed and Breakfast Honolulu (Statewide) PISCB

3242 Kaohinani Drive, Honolulu, 96817
(808) 795-7533; (800) 288-4666
FAX (808) 595-2030

This studio is on the lower level of the host's home, complete with full kitchen, washer and dryer, phone, and cable TV. Enjoy the ocean and garden views less than a mile from the beach. $65.

Bed and Breakfast Honolulu (Statewide) SOUZC

3242 Kaohinani Drive, Honolulu, 96817
(808) 795-7533; (800) 288-4666
FAX (808) 595-2030

The guest room has sliding glass doors to a private patio. Refrigerator is stocked with food for guests to enjoy at their leisure. $45.

Bed and Breakfast Honolulu (Statewide) TYLEN

3242 Kaohinani Drive, Honolulu, 96817
(808) 795-7533; (800) 288-4666
FAX (808) 595-2030

Psychotherapists who specialize in practical application of intimate relationship skills also offer poetry readings, picnic lunches, guided tours, and therapy explorations. $40.

Bed and Breakfast Honolulu (Statewide) ROSSB

3242 Kaohinani Drive, Honolulu, 96817
(808) 795-7533; (800) 288-4666
FAX (808) 595-2030

This home is within walking distance of Old Lahaina town, and the beach and has a beautiful view of the mountains in the backdrop. May be reserved with or without breakfast. $75.

Bed and Breakfast Honolulu (Statewide) FOXF

3242 Kaohinani Drive, Honolulu, 96817
(808) 795-7533; (800) 288-4666
FAX (808) 595-2030

Two rooms with private baths are situated two miles from the beach and windsurfing in this plantation house with true Hawaiian-style country living. $80.

Bed and Breakfast Honolulu (Statewide) MCKAS

3242 Kaohinani Drive, Honolulu, 96817
(808) 795-7533; (800) 288-4666
FAX (808) 595-2030

This 1,000-square-foot cottage at the 4,000-foot level on the slope of Haleakala is beautifully decorated and has full kitchen, fireplace, and lanai with barbecue. $95.

---

welcome; 9 Social drinking allowed; 10 Tennis available; 11 Swimming available; 12 Golf available; 13 Skiing available; 14 May be booked through travel agents

OAHU—HAWAII KAI

Bed and Breakfast Honolulu (Statewide) ABEB

3242 Kaohinani Drive, Honolulu, 96817
(808) 795-7533; (800) 288-4666
FAX (808) 595-2030

Hawaii Kai is on the quiet end of Oahu. Hosts are originally from England, where the bed and breakfast tradition began. The home is on the bus line and near swimming, snorkeling, and sightseeing. $40.

Bed and Breakfast Honolulu (Statewide) CRIPJ

3242 Kaohinani Drive, Honolulu, 96817
(808) 795-7533; (800) 288-4666
FAX (808) 595-2030

This home sitting high on Mariner's Ridge offers two units and shared bath. Enjoy the lanais and an ocean-view breakfast. $45.

OAHU—KAILUA

Bed and Breakfast Honolulu (Statewide) BURRT

3242 Kaohinani Drive, Honolulu, 96817
(808) 795-7533; (800) 288-4666
FAX (808) 595-2030

This one-bedroom cottage is one block from the beach with direct beach access. The cottage has a kitchen, washer/dryer, queen bed, TV, and easy access to golf, tennis, restaurants, and shopping. $69.

Bed and Breakfast Honolulu (Statewide) NELMP

3242 Kaohinani Drive, Honolulu, 96817
(808) 795-7533; (800) 288-4666
FAX (808) 595-2030

The upstairs unit has light cooking facilities, while the larger guest room has a private bath and entrance. Ten-minute walk to beach of Kailua town. Breakfast provided first day of stay only. $55.

Bed and Breakfast Honolulu (Statewide) SHEEP

3242 Kaohinani Drive, Honolulu, 96817
(808) 795-7533; (800) 288-4666
FAX (808) 595-2030

The guest suite has a private entrance and bath, queen bed, sitting room, and kitchenette. A second room has private entrance and bath. Walk to beach or town. $40.

Bed and Breakfast Honolulu (Statewide) WARMM

3242 Kaohinani Drive, Honolulu, 96817
(808) 795-7533; (800) 288-4666
FAX (808) 595-2030

Enjoy a private entrance and on-site parking, refrigerator, microwave and toaster oven, glassware and dishes, phone, and tourist information. $50.

Bed and Breakfast Honolulu (Statewide) WIEDP

3242 Kaohinani Drive, Honolulu, 96817
(808) 795-7533; (800) 288-4666
FAX (808) 595-2030

Enjoy the peace and privacy of this cottage in an exclusive residential area adjacent to Wailea, five minutes from beaches and golf, tennis, shops, and restaurants. $50.

Bed and Breakfast Honolulu (Statewide) WOODLO

3242 Kaohinani Drive, Honolulu, 96817
(808) 795-7533; (800) 288-4666
FAX (808) 595-2030

NOTES: Credit cards accepted: A MasterCard; B Visa; C American Express; D Discover Card; E Diners Club; F Other; 2 Personal checks accepted; 3 Lunch available; 4 Dinner available; 5 Open all year; 6 Pets welcome; 8 Children

Kailua Beach Park is one-half mile away. Continental breakfast is served in the family room or on the lanai overlooking a golf course and mountain range. Guests may borrow beach equipment. Two-night minimum stay. $40.

OAHU—KAIMUKI

Bed and Breakfast Honolulu (Statewide) GURNR

3242 Kaohinani Drive, Honolulu, 96817
(808) 795-7533; (800) 288-4666
FAX (808) 595-2030

Guest rooms with a shared bath are decorated with Tapa pieces from Fiji and Samoa. Guests may use spacious livingroom and dining room and enjoy the superb ocean view from the veranda. $40.

OAHU—KANEOHE

Bed and Breakfast Honolulu (Statewide) LAKEC

3242 Kaohinani Drive, Honolulu, 96817
(808) 795-7533; (800) 288-4666
FAX (808) 595-2030

Two guest rooms share a bath, ideal for families or couples traveling together. The home is a three-minute drive to Winward Mall, and restaurants are nearby. Continental breakfast; children welcome. $55.

OAHU—LANIKAI

Bed and Breakfast Honolulu (Statewide) EASTJ

3242 Kaohinani Drive, Honolulu, 96817
(808) 795-7533; (800) 288-4666
FAX (808) 595-2030

This studio is on the beach and has a private entrance, small refrigerator, microwave, and coffeepot. Fixings are provided for breakfast on the first day only. $45.

Bed and Breakfast Honolulu (Statewide) MAXEM

3242 Kaohinani Drive, Honolulu, 96817
(808) 795-7533; (800) 288-4666
FAX (808) 595-2030

A delightfully furnished garden studio is across the street from one of the most beautiful swimming and windsurfing beaches on Oahu. Continental breakfast is stocked for guests to enjoy at their leisure. $55.

OAHU—NORTH SHORE

Bed and Breakfast Honolulu (Statewide) LOUGB

3242 Kaohinani Drive, Honolulu, 96817
(808) 795-7533; (800) 288-4666
FAX (808) 595-2030

This 700-square-foot, two-room, upstairs studio has two queen futons on frames and a queen sofa bed. The kitchenette has a microwave, hotplate, toaster oven, and coffeepot. Enjoy the ocean views. Children welcome. $75.

Bed and Breakfast Honolulu (Statewide) MACSC

3242 Kaohinani Drive, Honolulu, 96817
(808) 795-7533; (800) 288-4666
FAX (808) 595-2030

This 10-by-20-foot studio is conveniently situated one block from the zoo, two blocks from the beach, one-half block to convenience store. Enjoy sunbathing in the yard. Host leaves continental breakfast for guests' convenience. Children welcome. $65.

welcome; 9 Social drinking allowed; 10 Tennis available; 11 Swimming available; 12 Golf available; 13 Skiing available; 14 May be booked through travel agents

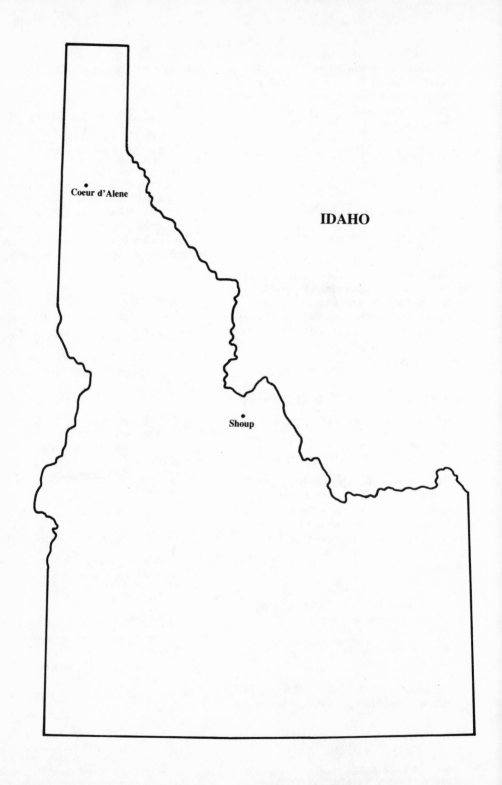

IDAHO

Coeur d'Alene

Shoup

Idaho

Katie's Wild Rose Inn
5150 Coeur d'Alene Lake Drive, 83814
(208) 765-9474; (800) 328-9474

Katie's is four minutes east of Coeur d'Alene
on a hill overlooking the lake. Rose and lilac
bushes along with tall pines line the property. A public dock is 600 feet away for
boating and swimming. The Rose Suite has
a view of the lake through sliding glass
doors, a private patio, and a Jacuzzi bath.

Hosts: Joisse and Lee Knowles
Rooms: 4 (PB) $55-75
Full Breakfast
Credit Cards: None
Notes: 2, 5, 8 (over 12), 9, 11, 12, 13

Smith House
Bed and Breakfast
49 Salmon River Road, 83469
(208) 394-2121

Since opening in 1987, Smith House has
achieved a relaxed sense of informality and
cozy comfort. This beautiful split-level log
home has five warm and distinct guest rooms.
Enjoy hot tub, orchard, library, covered
decks, homemade wines, handcrafted gifts,
fishing, float trips, hunting, and skiing. The
guest house has a kitchen, three bedrooms,
two baths, and laundry facility. Situated 50
miles from Salmon.

Hosts: Aubrey and Marsha Smith
Rooms: 5 (1 PB; 4 SB) $35-54
Full Breakfast
Credit Cards: A, B
Notes: 2, 5, 6, 8, 9, 11, 13, 14

Smith House Bed and Breakfast

NOTES: Credit cards accepted: A Master Card; B Visa; C American Express; D Discover Card; E Diners Club; F Other;
2 Personal checks accepted; 3 Lunch available; 4 Dinner available; 5 Open all year; 6 Pets welcome; 8 Children
welcome; 9 Social drinking allowed; 10 Tennis available; 11 Swimming available; 12 Golf available; 13 Skiing
available; 14 May be booked through travel agents

Galena

Oak Park •

• Port Byron

Champaign
•

• Shelbyville

• Carlyle

Maeystown •

ILLINOIS

Illinois

CARLYLE

Country Haus
1191 Franklin, 62231
(618) 594-8313

An 1890s Eastlake-style home decorated in German country tradition, Country Haus has four guest rooms. Settle into the swinging chair in the library to watch TV or enjoy a good book. Relax in the Jacuzzi or visit Carlyle Lake for swimming, boating, or hiking. Museum and golf course are nearby.

Hosts: Ron and Vickie Cook
Rooms: 4 (PB) $45-55
Full Breakfast
Credit Cards: A, B, C
Notes: 2, 4, 5, 8, 10, 11, 12, 13 (water)

CHAMPAIGN

Barb's Bed and Breakfast
606 South Russell, 61821
(217) 356-0376

This 1946 cottage is situated in a quiet, attractive neighborhood with easy access to the University of Illinois. The twin cities and nearby small communities offer many interesting things to see and do. Antique shops, museums, bike trails, small fishing lakes, and a wide variety of restaurants are all nearby. The comfortable guest rooms, featuring antiques, quilts, and ceiling fans, share a parlor and fireplace.

Hosts: Barb and Merle Eyestone
Rooms: 2 (SB) $45
Continental Breakfast
Credit Cards: None
Notes: 2, 5, 9, 10, 11, 12

GALENA

Avery Guest House
606 South Prospect Street, 61036
(815) 777-3883

Avery Guest House, built before the Civil War, is situated within a few blocks of Galena's main shopping and historical buildings. It is a homey refuge after a day of exploring, a place to share your discoveries and experiences with your hosts and other guests. Enjoy the view from the porch swing, feel free to play the piano, watch TV, or join a table game.

Hosts: Flo and Roger Jensen
Rooms: 4 (SB) $45-65
Expanded Continental Breakfast
Credit Cards: A, B, C
Notes: 2, 5, 8, 9, 10, 11, 12, 13, 14

Belle Aire Mansion Guest House

Belle Aire Mansion Guest House
11410 Route 20 West, 61036
(815) 777-0893

NOTES: Credit cards accepted: A Master Card; B Visa; C American Express; D Discover Card; E Diners Club; F Other; 2 Personal checks accepted; 3 Lunch available; 4 Dinner available; 5 Open all year; 6 Pets welcome; 8 Children welcome; 9 Social drinking allowed; 10 Tennis available; 11 Swimming available; 12 Golf available; 13 Skiing available; 14 May be booked through travel agents

Belle Aire Mansion Guest House is a Federal-style home dating back to 1836 with four rooms decorated in antiques and reproductions. A home-cooked breakfast awaits you each morning. Sit and watch TV, talk with your hosts in the parlor, or walk down the tamarack-lined drive or across the 16 acres. Special packages available.

Hosts: Jan and Lorraine Svec
Rooms: 4 (PB) $60-80
Full Breakfast
Credit Cards: A, B, D
Notes: 2, 5, 8, 9, 11, 12, 13

Brierwreath Manor Bed and Breakfast
216 North Bench Street, 61036
(815) 777-0608

Brierwreath Manor, circa 1884, is a lovely Queen Anne-style home with a wraparound porch, situated only one block from Galena's Main Street. It offers three large suites furnished in a blend of Early American and antiques, all with queen beds. Guests can partake of an early morning coffee service before a full breakfast in the formal dining room.

Hosts: Mike and Lyn Cook
Rooms: 3 (PB) $80
Full Breakfast
Credit Cards: None
Notes: 2, 5, 9, 11, 12, 13

MAEYSTOWN

Corner George Inn
Corner of Main and Mill, 62256
(800) 458-6020

The Corner George Inn is 45 minutes southeast of St. Louis, Missouri. The inn is a restored 1884 hotel and saloon and is furnished entirely with antiques. There are five unique guest rooms, each with a private bath. Bicycles and carriage rides are available upon request. Maeystown, situated in the valley of the river bluffs, is listed on the National Register of Historic Places and remains much the same as it was at its beginning.

Hosts: David and Marcia Braswell
Rooms: 5 (PB) $65-85
Full Breakfast
Credit Cards: A, B
Notes: 2, 5, 14

OAK PARK

Toad Hall
301 North Scoville Avenue, 60302
(708) 386-8623

This 1909 brick Colonial is five miles from downtown Chicago in the Frank Lloyd Wright historic district. Enjoy Old-World atmosphere and service amid antiques, Oriental rugs, and Laura Ashley furnishings. Guest rooms have comfortable reading chairs, TVs, phones, and air conditioning. Walk to 25 Frank Lloyd Wright masterpieces, Hemingway Museum, lovely shops, restaurants, and public transportation to Chicago.

Host: Cynthia Mungerson
Rooms: 3 (PB) $55-65
Full Breakfast
Credit Cards: None
Notes: 2, 10, 11

Corner George Inn

PORT BYRON _____

The Olde Brick House

502 North High, 61275
(309) 523-3236

This 1885 Greek Revival home, once a stop
for the Underground Railroad, is in a historic, picturesque Mississippi River village
and offers simple elegance, tranquil porches,
shaded yards, riverboats, eagles, antiquing,
and cultural and sporting activities. Rooms
are decorated in motifs similar to the original style and reflect the lifestyle of its residents through the years.

Hosts: Fred and LaVerne Waldbusser
Rooms: 3 (S2B) $40-45
Continental Breakfast
Credit Cards: A, B
Notes: 5, 8, 10, 12

SHELBYVILLE _____

The Williams House
Bed and Breakfast

606 South Broadway, 62565
(217) 774-2807

The house was built in 1869 and designed in
the Victorian Italianate style. It is decorated
in Victorian and country styles with antiques and crafts. Full homemade breakfast
is served in the formal dining room. Situated
less than five minutes from beautiful Lake
Shelbyville, a boater's paradise. Many antique and craft shops are nearby. Only 20
minutes from Illinois's Old Amish settlement.

Hosts: Shelby and David Williams
Rooms: 2 (SB) $35-45
Full Breakfast
Credit Cards: None
Notes: 2, 5, 8, 10, 11, 12

welcome; 9 Social drinking allowed; 10 Tennis available; 11 Swimming available; 12 Golf available; 13 Skiing
available; 14 May be booked through travel agents

Bristol •

South Bend

Middlebury

• Lagrange

• Schererville

• Huntington

• Indianapolis

• Attica

• Nashville

INDIANA

Indiana

The Apple Inn
604 South Brady, 47918
(317) 762-6574

Step back into a time when the host's grandmother lived in this 1903 Colonial Revival home and be guided through four generations of antiques. Rest comfortably in one of five unique bedrooms: Train Room, Sewing Room, Music Room, Toy Room, and Antique Doll Room. Sleep with down comforters and pillows. Breakfast is served by candlelight on fine china.

Hosts: Carolyn Borst Carlson and Donald L. Martin
Rooms: 5 (1 PB; 4 S2B) $60-75
Expanded Continental Breakfast
Credit Card: D
Notes: 2, 5, 10, 11, 12, 14

Tyler's Place
19562 State Road 120, 46507
(219) 848-7145

Originally the home of the Raber greenskeeper, Tyler's Place offers a pleasant view of the 27-hole rolling golf course and plenty of warm Hoosier hospitality. The common room is decorated with an Amish flavor. Breakfast is served in the sun room, and evenings are enjoyed around the backyard fire ring. Conveniently situated minutes from the Indiana toll road.

Host: Esther Tyler
Rooms: 2 (1 PB; 1 SB) $45
Full Breakfast
Credit Cards: None
Notes: 2, 5, 8, 10, 11, 12, 13

Purviánce House
326 South Jefferson, 46750
(219) 356-4218; (219) 356-9215

Built in 1859 and listed on the National Register of Historic Places, this home has been lovingly restored and cheerfully decorated with antiques and period furnishings. Conveniently located on U.S. 224 and State Route 5, near Interstate 69, it is close to Huntington Lake with swimming, boating, hiking, and beautiful nature trails. The fourth weekend in September features the Pioneer Festival with crafts, quilts, and traditional music.

Hosts: Bob and Jean Gernand
Rooms: 5 (2 PB; 3 SB) $40-50
Full Breakfast
Credit Cards: None
Notes: 2, 5, 8, 9, 10, 11, 12

The Hoffman House
P. O. Box 906, 46206-0906
(317) 635-1701; FAX (317) 635-1701

Hoffman House is an American foursquare-style house built in 1903 situated one and one-half miles from Monument Circle in downtown Indianapolis. The home features oak woodwork, antiques, and handmade quilts. Four cats and a dog are in residence.

Host: Laura Arnold
Rooms: 2 (SB) $50-75
Continental Breakfast
Credit Cards: A, B
Notes: 2, 9, 10, 11, 12, 14

NOTES: Credit cards accepted: A Master Card; B Visa; C American Express; D Discover Card; E Diners Club; F Other; 2 Personal checks accepted; 3 Lunch available; 4 Dinner available; 5 Open all year; 6 Pets welcome; 8 Children welcome; 9 Social drinking allowed; 10 Tennis available; 11 Swimming available; 12 Golf available; 13 Skiing available; 14 May be booked through travel agents

Varns Guest House

LAGRANGE

The 1886 Inn

212 West Factory Street, 46761
(219) 463-4227

The 1886 Inn offers historical charm and
elegance. Every room is aglow with old-
fashioned beauty. It is the finest lodging in
the area, yet affordable and only ten minutes
from Shipshewana flea market.

Host: Duane Billman
Rooms: 5 (3 PB; 2 SB) $69-79
Expanded Continental Breakfast
Credit Cards: A, B
Notes: 2, 5, 10, 11, 12, 13

MIDDLEBURY

Bee Hive Bed and Breakfast

P.O. Box 1191, 46540
(219) 825-5023

The Bee Hive is situated in the Amish
community with easy access from the Indiana toll road.   Snuggle under handmade
quilts and wake to the smell of fresh muffins
baking in the oven. Enjoy breakfast around
a 12-foot harvest table. It's like visiting a
relative in the country.

Hosts: Herb and Treva Swarm
Rooms: 4 (1 PB; 3 SB) $50-60
Full Breakfast
Credit Cards: A, B
Notes: 2, 5, 8, 10, 11, 12, 13

Varns Guest House

205 South Main Street, 46540
(219) 825-9666

Built circa 1898, this fourth-generation home
has been restored to feature five rooms
named after relatives and childhood memories. Situated in the heart of Amish country,
guests enjoy many fine restaurants and
quaint shops nearby. Relax on the porch
swing as horse-drawn buggies clip along.
Area attractions include Shipshewana flea
market and Amish communities.

Hosts: Carl and Diane Eash
Rooms: 5 (PB) $65
Expanded Continental Breakfast
Credit Cards: A, B
Notes: 2, 5, 8, 9, 11, 12, 14

NASHVILLE

Russell's Roost
Bed and Breakfast

Route 4, Box 68A, 47448
(812) 988-1600

The master bedroom features a queen bed,
hot tub overlooking the lake, remote control
TV, private entrance off porch facing lake.
This bed and breakfast is three miles north
of Nashville, Brown County. Two hundred
arts and crafts shops are nearby; guests
enjoy a free profile silhouette cut by resident artist. The house is furnished in Norwegian and English themes and is set on 17
acres of woods.

Hosts: Roy and Mary Lou Russell
Rooms: 4 (3 PB; 1 SB) $45-70
Full Breakfast
Credit Cards: None
Notes: 2, 5, 8, 9, 11, 12

NOTES: Credit cards accepted: A Master Card; B Visa; C American Express; D Discover Card; E Diners Club; F Other.
2 Personal checks accepted; 3 Lunch available; 4 Dinner available; 5 Open all year; 6 Pets welcome; 8 Children

Story Inn

P. O. Box 64, 47448
(812) 988-2273

Situated on the southern edge of the Brown County State Park, this historic Dodge City-design general store is now a country inn housing a critically acclaimed full-service restaurant. Overnight lodging is upstairs and in the surrounding village cottages. Rooms are furnished with period antiques, original artwork, fresh flowers, and have air conditioning.

Hosts: Benjamin and Cynthia Schultz
Rooms: 13 (PB) $65-85
Full Breakfast
Credit Cards: A, B, C, D, E
Notes: 3, 4, 5, 6 (limited), 8 (limited), 9, 10, 11, 12, 13

SCHERERVILLE

Sunset Pines

862 Sunset Drive, 46375-2991
(219) 322-3322

Three wooded acres of country comfort are hidden away in the city, situated one-half mile south of the "Crossroads of America," at U.S. Routes 30 and 41. Fifteen minutes from the Star Theater at Interstate 65, 35 miles from the Chicago Loop, 20 miles from Indiana State Dunes. In-ground pool and other outdoor activities available.

Hosts: Clay and Nikki Foster
Rooms: 2 (1 PB; 1 SB) $45-50
Expanded Continental Breakfast
Credit Cards: A, B
Notes: 2, 5, 8, 9, 10, 11, 12, 13

SOUTH BEND

The Book Inn

508 West Washington, 46601
(219) 288-1990

This elegant, urban Second Empire home has been professionally restored. Twelve-foot ceilings, irreplaceable butternut woodwork, comfortable antiques, and fresh flowers welcome guests. A quality used bookstore is downstairs. Breakfast is served in the formal dining room on crystal, china, and silver.

Host: Peggy Livingston
Rooms: 5 (PB) $75
Expanded Continental Breakfast
Credit Cards: A, B, C
Notes: 2, 5, 9, 14

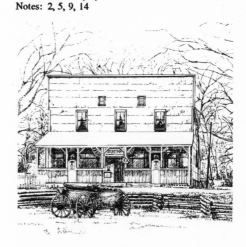

Story Inn

Home Bed and Breakfast

21166 Clover Hill Court, 46614
(219) 291-0535

Experience a European-style bed and breakfast as part of the family on a quiet residential court overlooking a pond. Guest rooms are the "empty nest" rooms. Eight miles south of the University of Notre Dame, one mile west of U.S. 31 South. Advance reservations only.

Hosts: Mark and Joyce Funderburg
Rooms: 3 (1 PB; 2 SB) $45-60
Full Breakfast
Credit Cards: None

welcome; 9 Social drinking allowed; 10 Tennis available; 11 Swimming available; 12 Golf available; 13 Skiing available; 14 May be booked through travel agents

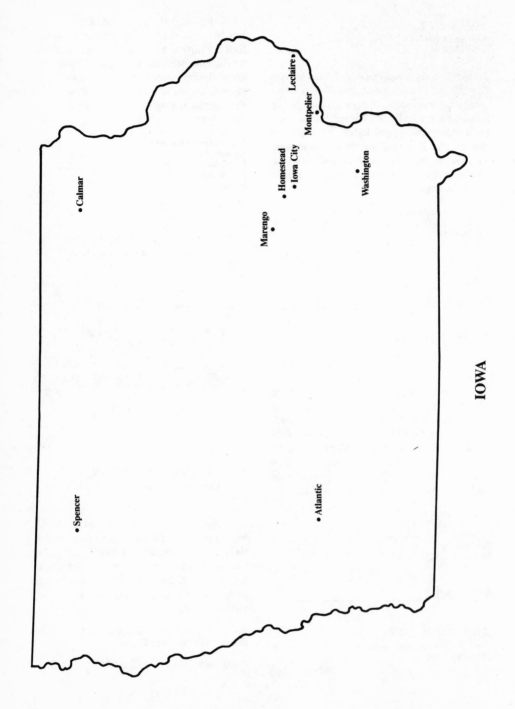

IOWA

Iowa

ATLANTIC

Chestnut Charm
Bed and Breakfast
1409 Chestnut Street, 50022
(712) 243-5652

A magical world of fantasy and romance awaits you at an elegant 1898 Victorian mansion with serene surroundings. The inn offers five richly decorated guest rooms, two relaxing sun rooms, and a patio with a fountain. Awake to the aroma of gourmet coffee and home baking. Gourmet dining and gift certificates are available. Leave your cares behind as you enter a Camelot world. Air conditioned.

Hosts: Bruce and Barbara Stensvad
Rooms: 5 (3 PB; 2 SB) $55-75
Full Breakfast
Credit Cards: A, B
Notes: 4, 5, 10, 11, 12, 14

Die Heimat Country Inn

CALMAR

Calmar Guesthouse
Rural Route 1, Box 206, 52132
(319) 562-3851

This newly remodeled Victorian home with antiques and beautiful woodwork is situated near Luther College in Decorah and Northeast Iowa Community College. It is close to the world-famous Bily Clocks in Spillville, Niagara Cave, Lake Meyer, world's smallest church, and more. Wake up to a fresh country breakfast and enjoy a variety of area restaurants. Air conditioned.

Hosts: Art and Lucille Kruse
Rooms: 5 (SB) $40-50
Full Breakfast
Credit Cards: A, B
Notes: 2, 5, 8, 10, 11, 12, 13

HOMESTEAD

Die Heimat Country Inn
Main Street, Amana Colonies, 52236
(319) 622-3937

Die Heimat, meaning "the home place," is situated in Homestead, one of the famous Amana Colonies. The inn was built in 1854, and all rooms are decorated with locally handcrafted walnut and cherry furniture, quilts, and heirlooms. Some canopy beds are available.

Hosts: Don and Sheila Janda
Rooms: 19 (PB) $37-65
Full Breakfast
Credit Cards: A, B, D
Notes: 2, 5, 6, 8, 9, 10, 11, 12, 13

IOWA CITY

Sugar Woods
Bed and Breakfast
4848 Sand Road Southeast, 52240
(319) 351-6233

NOTES: Credit cards accepted: A Master Card; B Visa; C American Express; D Discover Card; E Diners Club; F Other; 2 Personal checks accepted; 3 Lunch available; 4 Dinner available; 5 Open all year; 6 Pets welcome; 8 Children welcome; 9 Social drinking allowed; 10 Tennis available; 11 Swimming available; 12 Golf available; 13 Skiing available; 14 May be booked through travel agents

This new two-story country home is set on a hill with a panoramic view of the 45-acre farm. Guests can watch the sunrise in the sun room or from the deck, enjoy the sunset from the front porch, and relax near the family room fireplace. Bicycling and golf are nearby, or simply walk around the meadow. Quaintly furnished with antiques and collectibles. The owner is a lifelong area resident.

Hosts: David and Karen Long
Rooms: 2 (SB) $55-75
Full Breakfast
Credit Cards: None
Notes: 2, 5, 10, 11, 12

LECLAIRE

The Monarch Bed and Breakfast Inn

303 South Second Street, P.O. Box 227, 52753
(319) 289-3011; (800) 772-7724

The Monarch Bed and Breakfast Inn was built in the late 1850s and has been restored. It boasts wood floors and high ceilings and is decorated with antiques and mementos from Europe. It overlooks the mighty Mississippi River on the point where the rapids once began. LeClaire is a quaint historical town and is the birthplace of Buffalo Bill. River cruises are available May to October. Two miles north off of I-80, Exit 306. French and Polish spoken here.

Hosts: David and Emilie Oltman
Rooms: 4 (SB) $45-55
Full and Continental Breakfast
Credit Cards: A, B
Notes: 2, 5, 8, 12

MARENGO

Loy's Bed and Breakfast

Rural Route 1, Box 82, 52301
(319) 642-7787

This is a beautiful farm home situated in the heartland of Iowa County. Cornfields or white snow cover the rolling countryside. A tour of the hog facilities is offered. Recreation facilities include swing set, sand box, croquet, horseshoes, pool table, table tennis, and shuffleboard. Visit the Amana Colonies, Kalona, Herbert Hoover Memorial, Iowa City, Cedar Rapids, and Marengo. I-80, Exit 216N.

Hosts: Loy and Robert Walker
Rooms: 3 (1 PB; 2 SB) $50-60
Full Breakfast
Credit Cards: None
Notes: 2, 4 (on request), 5, 6 (caged), 8, 9, 10, 11, 12

MONTPELIER

Varner's Caboose Bed and Breakfast

204 East Second, P. O. Box 10, 52759
(319) 381-3652

Stay in a real Rock Island Lines caboose set on its own track behind a home. The caboose is a self-contained unit with complete kitchen and bath and sleeps four. There is color TV, central air conditioning, and heat. A fully prepared country breakfast is left in the caboose kitchen to be enjoyed by guests whenever they choose. Situated just a few minutes from Quad Cities area.

Host: Nancy Varner
Room: 1 (PB) $55
Full Breakfast
Credit Cards: None
Notes: 2, 8

SPENCER

Hannah Marie Country Inn

Route One, Highway 71 South, 51301
(712) 262-1286; (712) 332-7719

An inspiring bed and breakfast, this country Victorian has down comforters, polished brass, rocking chairs on the porch, and a swing on the old tree. Three-course tea/luncheons are served to the public. Open April to mid-December.

NOTES: Credit cards accepted: A Master Card; B Visa; C American Express; D Discover Card; E Diners Club; F Other; 2 Personal checks accepted; 3 Lunch available; 4 Dinner available; 5 Open all year; 6 Pets welcome; 8 Children

Host: Mary Nichols
Rooms: 3 (PB) $55-65
Full Breakfast
Credit Cards: A, B, C
Notes: 2, 3, 8, 10, 11, 12, 14

Hannah Marie Country Inn

WASHINGTON

Quiet Sleeping Rooms
125 Green Meadows Drive, 52353
(319) 653-3736

Enjoy a completely modern home with a private entrance, electric heat, air conditioning, shower, and large lawn. Only one block from the highway and 30 miles from the University of Iowa. Private livingroom for guests. Warm hospitality.

Host: Lois Williams
Rooms: 2 (SB) $30
Full Breakfast
Credit Cards: None
Notes: 2, 5, 6, 8, 9, 10, 11, 14

Lenexa

• Peabody

KANSAS

Kansas

Bed and Breakfast Kansas City

P. O. Box 14781, 66215
(913) 888-3636

This is a reservation service for 40 elegant pre-Civil War Victorian and contemporary homes and inns in the Kansas City area and in St. Louis, Missouri. Most have private baths and are priced from $40 to $125. Several have hot tubs or Jacuzzis or pools. All serve full gourmet breakfasts.

Jones Sheep Farm Bed and Breakfast

Rural Route 2, Box 185, 66866
(316) 983-2815

Enjoy a turn-of-the-century home in a pastoral setting. Situated on a working sheep farm "at the end of the road," the house is furnished in 1930s style (no phone or TV). Quiet, private. Historic small town nearby.

Hosts: Gary and Marilyn Jones
Rooms: 2 (SB) $35
Full Breakfast
Credit Cards: None
Notes: 2, 5, 6, 10, 11, 12

NOTES: Credit cards accepted: A MasterCard; B Visa; C American Express; D Discover Card; E Diners Club; F Other; 2 Personal checks accepted; 3 Lunch available; 4 Dinner available; 5 Open all year; 6 Pets welcome; 8 Children welcome; 9 Social drinking allowed; 10 Tennis available; 11 Swimming available; 12 Golf available; 13 Skiing available; 14 May be booked through travel agents

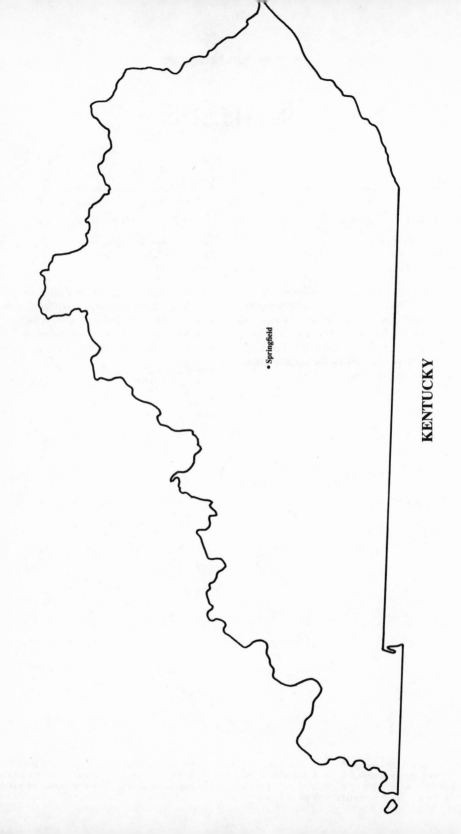

• Springfield

KENTUCKY

Kentucky

Maple Hill Manor

Perryville Road, Highway 150 East, 40069
(606) 336-3075

This stately hilltop manor built in 1851 is listed on the National Register of Historic Places. Situated on 14 tranquil acres in the scenic Bluegrass region, its Italianate design features thirteen-and-one-half-foot ceilings, a profusion of fireplaces, and a free-standing solid cherry staircase. The bedrooms are large, airy, and beautifullly furnished with carefully chosen antiques. The romantic honeymoon suite has a canopy bed, Jacuzzi, and private entrance.

Maple Hill Manor

Hosts: Bob and Kay Carroll
Rooms: 7 (PB) $55-85
Full Breakfast
Credit Cards: A, B
Notes: 2, 5, 8, 9, 10, 11, 12, 14

NOTES: Credit cards accepted: A Master Card; B Visa; C American Express; D Discover Card; E Diners Club; F Other; 2 Personal checks accepted; 3 Lunch available; 4 Dinner available; 5 Open all year; 6 Pets welcome; 8 Children welcome; 9 Social drinking allowed; 10 Tennis available; 11 Swimming available; 12 Golf available; 13 Skiing available; 14 May be booked through travel agents

LOUISIANA

• Shreveport

• Vinton

Port Vincent •

New Orleans •

Louisiana

NEW ORLEANS

St. Charles Guest House
1748 Prytania Street, 70130
(504) 523-6556

The St. Charles Guest House is a simple, cozy affordable bed and breakfast situated in the lower Garden District of New Orleans. Tea and cookies are served in the late afternoon. It is just one block from the St. Charles streetcar, which takes guests to the French Quarter. The pool and patio are surrounded by banana trees.

Host: Dennis Hilton
Rooms: 28 (22 PB; 6 SB) $25-60
Continental Breakfast
Credit Cards: A, B, C
Notes: 2, 5, 8, 9, 10, 11, 12, 14

PORT VINCENT

Tree House in the Park
Mailing address: 16520 Airport Road
Prairieville, 70769
(504) 622-2850

This Cajun cabin has kitchen, dining room, and livingroom with fireplace. With all picture windows, it is set high among cypress trees with moss swaying in the breeze. The large bedroom has a queen waterbed and double Jacuzzi. A private hot tub is on the sun deck, a pool (heated in season) is on the lower deck. The Tree House is surrounded by three acres with ponds and a foot bridge. Feed the ducks and geese and enjoy a double kayak float trip on the Amite River.

Hosts: Fran and Julius Schmieder
Rooms: 2 (PB) $60-100
Full Breakfast
Credit Cards: A, B
Notes: 2, 4 (included), 5, 11, 14

SHREVEPORT

Fairfield Place
2221 Fairfield Avenue, 71104
(318) 222-0048

This 1880s Victorian inn in the historic district near downtown is beautifully restored with private phones, cable, European and American antiques, wonderful wallpapers, and accessories. The inn has an interesting collection of paintings and porcelains. Breakfast varies each day. Porches, balcony, and courtyard are ideal for relaxation.

Host: Jane Lipscomb
Rooms: 9 (PB) $79-145
Full Breakfast
Credit Cards: A, B, C
Notes: 5, 9, 10, 11, 12

Fairfield Place

NOTES: Credit cards accepted: A Master Card; B Visa; C American Express; D Discover Card; E Diners Club; F Other; 2 Personal checks accepted; 3 Lunch available; 4 Dinner available; 5 Open all year; 6 Pets welcome; 8 Children welcome; 9 Social drinking allowed; 10 Tennis available; 11 Swimming available; 12 Golf available; 13 Skiing available; 14 May be booked through travel agents

VINTON

Old Lyons House
1335 Horridge Street, 70668-4531
(318) 589-2903

This Queen Anne Victorian with elaborate Eastlake trim is beautifully restored—homey and comfortable in a relaxing, easygoing, small-town ambience. A massage therapist is on the premises. Owners will loan bicycles or canoe. Historic homes, museums, and nature trails are close by.

Host: Daniel Cooper
Rooms: 4 (2 PB; 2 SB) $40-75
Full Breakfast
Credit Cards: None
Notes: 2, 4, 5, 6, 8, 9, 11, 14

Maine

Andover Arms Family Style Bed and Breakfast

Newton Street, P. O. Box 387, 04216
(207) 392-4251

Discover Maine the way it used to be. Stay in this comfortable 1800s farmhouse in the village and feel right at home with the warm hospitality, country breakfasts, and cozy guest rooms with oil lamps for added charm. Relax by the wood stove or play the piano. Snowmobiling and cross-country skiing from the door; 20 minutes to downhill ski areas, including Sunday River; excellent hunting, fishing, biking, foliage.

Hosts: Pat and Larry Wyman
Rooms: 4 (1 PB; 3 SB) $50
Full Breakfast
Credit Cards: A, B, D
Notes: 2, 5, 6, 8, 10, 11, 12, 13

BAILEY ISLAND

Captain York House Bed and Breakfast

Route 24, P. O. Box 32, 04003
(207) 833-6224

Enjoy true island atmosphere on scenic Bailey Island, an unspoiled fishing village accessible solely by car over the only cribstone bridge in the world. Near Brunswick, Freeport, and Portland, this former sea captain's home is tastefully restored to its original charm and furnished with antiques. Enjoy an informal, friendly atmosphere and an ocean view from every room. From the deck, see memorable sun-

sets and lobstermen hauling traps. Fine dining and summer nature cruise are nearby.

Hosts: Charles and Ingrid DiVita
Rooms: 3 (1 PB; 2 SB) $55-75
Full Breakfast
Credit Cards: None
Notes: 2, 5, 9, 11, 14

The Lady and the Loon

Main Street, P. O. Box 98, 04003
(207) 833-6871; (207) 288-3869 winter

This late-1800s seacoast inn perched on a bluff overlooking Casco Bay and its Calendar Islands is furnished with antiques and hosted by a wildlife artist. A staircase leads down to a rocky Maine beach and the Atlantic's waves, birds, and lobster boats. Home-baked blueberry muffins are the breakfast specialty.

Host: Gail F. Sprague
Rooms: 4 (S2B) $60-75
Continental Breakfast
Credit Cards: A, B
Notes: 2, 9, 11

BAR HARBOR

Castlemaine Inn

39 Holland Avenue, 04609
(207) 288-4563; (800) 338-4563

Old-World charm awaits travelers at the Castlemaine Inn, nestled on a quiet side street in Bar Harbor, minutes from downtown and Acadia National Park. Built in 1886, the inn has 12 delightful rooms, including two apartments and a cozy two-room suite. Rooms with fireplaces, canopy beds,

welcome; 9 Social drinking allowed; 10 Tennis available; 11 Swimming available; 12 Golf available; 13 Skiing available; 14 May be booked through travel agents

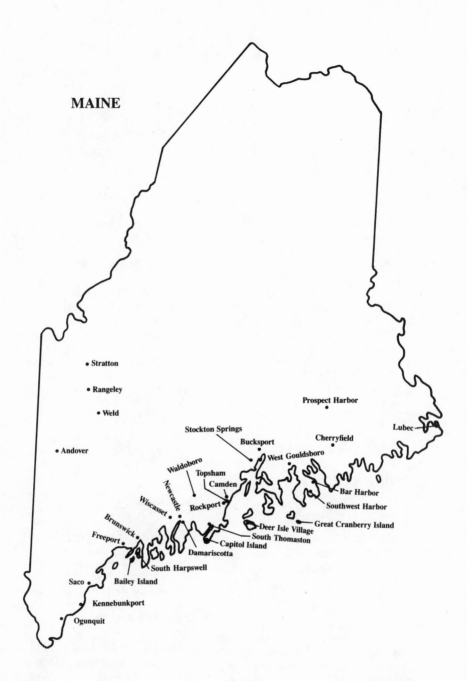

MAINE

- Stratton
- Rangeley
- Weld
- Andover

Prospect Harbor •

Stockton Springs
Bucksport
Cherryfield
West Gouldsboro
Lubec

Waldoboro
Topsham
Camden
Bar Harbor
Newcastle
Southwest Harbor
Wiscasset
Rockport
Great Cranberry Island
Brunswick
Deer Isle Village
Freeport
South Thomaston
Capitol Island
Damariscotta
South Harpswell
Saco •
Bailey Island
Kennebunkport
Ogunquit

and private balconies are available. Each room is uniquely furnished.

Hosts: Norah O'Brien and Terry O'Connell
Rooms: 12 (PB) $85-135
Expanded Continental Breakfast
Credit Cards: A, B
Notes: 2, 9, 11, 12, 13

Hearthside Bed and Breakfast

7 High Street, 04609
(207) 288-4533

Stay in this in-town turn-of-the-century home situated on a quiet side street within walking distance of shops, restaurants, and the waterfront, and a short car ride to the national park. The newly decorated rooms feature queen beds, and three rooms have fireplaces. Afternoon tea and cookies and evening refreshments are served.

Hosts: Susan and Barry Schwartz
Rooms: 9 (PB) $75-110
Full Breakfast
Credit Cards: A, B
Notes: 2, 5, 9, 10, 11, 12, 13

Manor House Inn

106 West Street, 04609
(207) 288-3759

This 22-room Victorian mansion, built in 1887, is situated in Bar Harbor's national historic district. All of the guest rooms and suites have private baths and authentic turn-of-the-century decor. Listed on the National Register of Historic Places. Situated on an acre of landscaped grounds and within walking distance of town and Acadia National Park.

Host: Mac Noyes
Rooms: 12 (PB) $85-150
Full Breakfast
Credit Cards: A, B
Notes: 2, 8, 9, 10, 11, 12, 13, 14

Town Motel and Guest House

12 Atlantic Avenue, 04609
(207) 288-5548; (800) 458-8644

The Town Guest House provides comfort, convenience, and relaxation in a quiet in-town neighborhood. Relax amid the Victorian comfort of period furnishings, marble sinks, porches, and working fireplaces while watching cable TV. Enjoy the spacious and well-shaded grounds, drink morning coffee on the front porch or gazebo. Open May through October; breakfast served only May, June, September, and October.

Hosts: Joe and Paulette Paluga
Rooms: 9 (PB) $75-110
Continental Breakfast
Credit Cards: A, B, C
Notes: 2, 8, 9, 10, 11, 12, 14

BRUNSWICK—SEE ALSO TOPSHAM

Samuel Newman House

7 South Street, 04011
(207) 729-6959

Adjoining Bowdoin College campus, a handsome Federal-style house built in 1821 by noted Brunswick architect Samuel Melcher features seven unique guest rooms comfortably furnished in antiques. Breakfast features scones, muffins, and pastry freshly baked at the inn, homemade jams, and fresh fruit. It is a pleasant walk through the campus to Brunswick's shops and restaurants one-half mile away, and a short drive to Freeport, Bailey Island, and Orrs Island.

Hosts: John and Jana Peirce
Rooms: 7 (1 PB; 6 SB) $40-55
Expanded Continental Breakfast
Credit Cards: A, B
Notes: 2, 5, 8, 9, 10, 11, 12, 13

NOTES: Credit cards accepted: A Master Card; B Visa; C American Express; D Discover Card; E Diners Club; F Other; 2 Personal checks accepted; 3 Lunch available; 4 Dinner available; 5 Open all year; 6 Pets welcome; 8 Children welcome; 9 Social drinking allowed; 10 Tennis available; 11 Swimming available; 12 Golf available; 13 Skiing available; 14 May be booked through travel agents

BUCKSPORT

The River Inn
210 Main Street, P.O. Box 1657, 04416-1657
(207) 469-3783

This spacious old Colonial home on the river in a historic area is conveniently situated, offering easy access to east and west bay tour areas and antique and craft shopping. The inn features a rare player grand piano with an antique roll collection and is owned and operated by three generations of the Stone family.

Hosts: Audrey Stone and Richard Stone
Rooms: 3 (1 PB; 2 SB) $40-55
Full Breakfast
Credit Cards: None
Notes: 2, 5, 6 (advance arrangement), 9, 10, 11, 12, 13

CAMDEN

Blackberry Inn
82 Elm Street, 04843
(207) 236-6060

Blackberry Inn is a restored Victorian inn just a short stroll from Camden's harbor and shops. Featured in *Daughters of Painted Ladies: America's Resplendent Victorians* and many fine guide books, the inn has two sunny parlors for guests, an outdoor courtyard, guest phone, and many amenities. An afternoon wine and cheese hour is featured.

Hosts: Vicki and Ed Doudera
Rooms: 8 (PB) $45-100
Full Breakfast
Credit Cards: A, B
Notes: 2, 5, 8, 9, 10, 11, 12, 13

A Little Dream
66 High Street, 04843
(207) 236-8742

Sweet dreams and little luxuries abound in this lovely white Victorian with a wraparound porch. Noted for its delicious breakfasts, beautiful rooms, and charming atmosphere, A Little Dream's English country-Victorian decor has been featured in *Country Inns* magazine and *Glamour's 40 Best Getaways Across the Country*. Situated in the affluent coastal community of Camden, it is close to the harbor and shops.

Hosts: Joanna Ball and Bill Fontana
Rooms: 5 (3 PB; 2 SB) $89-139
Full Breakfast
Credit Cards: A, B, C
Notes: 2, 5, 10, 11, 12, 13

CAPITOL ISLAND

Albonegon Inn
Capitol Island, 04538
(207) 633-2521

The Albonegon Inn is four miles from Boothbay Harbor on a small private island accessible by car. Perched on the rocks with wraparound porches, the inn offers fabulous views of nearby islands and harbors. Built in the 1880s, the Albonegon has an antique cottage feel and is a quiet and simple place to relax and vacation.

Hosts: Kim and Bob Peekham
Rooms: 15 (3 PB; 12 SB) $62-100
Continental Breakfast
Credit Cards: None
Notes: 2, 8, 9, 10, 11, 12

CHERRYFIELD

Ricker House
P. O. Box 256, 04622
(207) 546-2780

Built in 1803 and on the National Register of Historic Places, this comfortable home was selected in 1991 as one of the top 50 inns in America. Situated in a quaint and historic town on the Narraguagus River, Ricker House offers a central place for enjoying the many wonderful activities in Down East Maine, including rugged coastal shorelines, lakes, rivers, mountains, and scenic coastal villages.

NOTES: Credit cards accepted: A Master Card; B Visa; C American Express; D Discover Card; E Diners Club; F Other;
2 Personal checks accepted; 3 Lunch available; 4 Dinner available; 5 Open all year; 6 Pets welcome; 8 Children

Hosts: Jean and Bill Conway
Rooms: 3 (SB) $50
Full Breakfast
Credit Cards: None
Notes: 2, 5, 8, 9, 10, 11, 12, 13 (XC)

DAMARISCOTTA

Brannon-Bunker Inn

HCR 64, Box 045, Route 129, 04543
(207) 563-5941

This quaint inn with sleeping rooms decorated in different periods from Colonial to
Victorian is situated in an 1820s Cape, converted barn, and carriage house. The Inn
reflects the charm of yesterday and the comforts of today with a selection of queen,
double, and twin beds. The quiet beauty of
stenciled walls, quaint wallpapers, homemade quilts, dried flowers, and country crafts
sets off the warmth and solid comfort of
selected antique furniture.

Hosts: Jeanne and Joe Hovance
Rooms: 7 (4 PB; 3 SB) $50-60
Continental Breakfast
Credit Cards: A, B
Notes: 2, 5, 8, 9, 10, 11, 12, 14

DEER ISLE VILLAGE

Laphroaig
Bed and Breakfast

State Route 15, P. O. Box 489, 04627
(207) 348-6088

At Deer Isle's finest year-round accommodations, treat yourself to bed and breakfast
in this 1854 Greek Revival home in one of
Maine's loveliest locales. Lighted private
parking, flannel sheets in cool weather, a
well-stocked library, porch swings and rockers, garden benches, flowers, handmade
afghans, and antiques are featured.

Hosts: John and Andrea Maberry
Rooms: 2 (PB) $75-90
Full Breakfast
Credit Cards: None
Notes: 2, 5, 9, 10, 11, 12, 14

FREEPORT

Captain Josiah Mitchell
House

188 Main Street, 04032
(207) 865-3289

The house is in Freeport, just two blocks
from L. L. Bean and more than 100 discount
stores, and a five-minute walk past centu-
ries of old sea captains' homes and shady
trees to all shops in town. Come back and
relax on the beautiful, peaceful veranda
with antique wicker furniture and "remember when" swing porch. Meander through
the traditional flower gardens. Reduced
rates in winter.

Hosts: Loretta and Alan Bradley
Rooms: 6 (PB) $78-82
Full Breakfast
Credit Cards: A, B
Notes: 2, 5, 10, 11, 12, 13, 14

Laphroaig Bed and Breakfast

Country at Heart
Bed and Breakfast

37 Bow Street, 04032
(207) 865-0512

This cozy 1870 home is situated off Main
Street but only two blocks from L. L. Bean.
Park and walk to the restaurants and many
outlet stores. Stay in the Shaker Room,
Quilt Room, or Teddy Bear Room, all with

double beds. Rooms have stenciled borders, handmade crafts, and antique or reproduction furnishings. There is a gift shop for guests.

Hosts: Roger and Kim Dubay
Rooms: 3 (2 PB; 1 SB) $55-75
Full Breakfast
Credit Cards: A, B (for reservations only)
Notes: 2, 5, 8, 9, 10, 11, 12, 14

Holbrook Inn

7 Holbrook Street, 04032
(207) 865-6693

Holbrook Inn has wonderful, spacious, air-conditioned rooms in a 125-year-old Victorian home. Hosts are lifelong residents. It is an easy two-minute walk to Freeport's many shops.

Hosts: Ralph and Bea Routhier
Rooms: 3 (PB) $75
Full Breakfast
Credit Cards: None
Notes: 2, 5, 9, 11, 12

Isaac Randall House— 1823 Inn

5 Independence Drive, 04032
(207) 865-9295

The inn features charming, antique-furnished rooms with Oriental rugs and lovely old quilts. It is a historic farmhouse situated on five wooded acres with a spring-fed pond within walking distance of downtown Freeport and only a short drive to Maine's fabled rockbound coast and beaches. Hiking, sailing, fishing, and pleasure driving are nearby. Hosts will share their knowledge of seacoast Maine to make your stay enjoyable. Wheelchair access.

Hosts: Cynba and Shannon Ryan
Rooms: 10 (8 PB; 2 SB) $85-115
Full Breakfast
Credit Cards: A, B
Notes: 2, 3 (picnic), 5, 6 (limited), 8, 9, 10, 11, 12, 13, 14

GREAT CRANBERRY ISLAND

The Red House

Great Cranberry Island, 04625
(207) 244-5297

A charming shorefront saltwater farm of yesteryear with all the necessities of today offers traditionally decorated rooms. Guests may prepare meals in a separate kitchen as desired. The Red House is a two-mile boat ride by passenger ferry from Northeast Harbor.

Hosts: Dorothy and John Towns
Rooms: 6 (3 PB; 3 SB) $60-75; $50-60 off-season
Full Breakfast
Credit Cards: A, B
Notes: 2, 3, 4, 9, 11, 12

The Inn on South Street

KENNEBUNKPORT

The Inn on South Street

P.O. Box 478A, 04046
(207) 967-5151

Combine charm and romance in this 19th-century Greek Revival home fully restored and listed on the National Register of Historic Places. Queen-size beds and private baths in each room. Beautifully decorated with antiques and traditional furnishings. Breakfast is always special. Early risers find hot coffee at 7:00 A.M. Convenient, in a quiet location, the inn is within easy walking distance of shops, restaurants, beaches, and the village area.

Hosts: Jacques and Eva Downs
Rooms: 3 (PB) $85-99
Suite: 1 (PB) $155
Full Breakfast
Credit Cards: A, B
Notes: 2, 10, 11, 12, 13, 14

LUBEC

Breakers by the Bay
37 Washington, 04652
(207) 733-2487

Enjoy the breathtaking views of the sea from private decks in this blue and white New England home. Rooms have antique beds, handmade quilts, and hand-crocheted tablecloths. Breakfast is at guest convenience in the formal dining room. Guests may use the gas barbecue. The inn is situated close to International Bridge leading to Campobello Island and Franklin D. Roosevelt's house. Enjoy Quoddy Head State Park and four lighthouses in the area.

Host: E. M. Elg
Rooms: 5 (2 PB; 3 SB) $40-50
Full Breakfast
Credit Cards: None

NEWCASTLE

The Newcastle Inn
River Road, 04553
(207) 563-5685

Newcastle Inn is a country inn of distinction on the picturesque Damariscotta River neighboring the four-season coastal village of Damariscotta. Enjoy romantic, pampering ambience (some canopy beds) and truly memorable European cuisine. AAA rated three diamonds. Complimentary hors d'oeuvres are served by the hearth in winter or on the sun porch in summer to dinner guests.

Hosts: Ted and Chris Sprague
Rooms: 15 (PB) $70-115
Full Breakfast
Credit Cards: A, B
Notes: 2, 4, 5, 10, 11, 12, 13 (XC), 14

OGUNQUIT

Beauport Inn
96 Shore Road, P. O. Box 1793, 03907
(207) 646-8680

This cozy inn furnished with antiques includes a pine-paneled livingroom with fireplace and piano. Baked goods are prepared by the host, and an antique shop is attached. It is within easy walking distance of beaches, Marginal Walkway, Perkins Cove, playhouse, art galleries, and restaurants.

Host: Dan Pender
Rooms: 4 (2 PB; 2 SB) $48-78
Continental Breakfast
Credit Cards: A, B, C
Notes: 5, 9, 10, 11, 12

Hartwell House
118 Shore Road, P. O. Box 393, 03907
(207) 646-7210; (800) 235-8883

Hartwell House is a fine country inn in the European tradition, tastefully furnished with American and English antiques. Regardless of seasonal preference, the Hartwell House will provide the finest lodging experience: summer beach days; crisp, invigorating fall weather; quiet, wintry weekends. Hosts are happy to accommodate guests.

Hosts: Alec and Renee Adams
Rooms: 16 (PB) $90-175
Full Breakfast
Credit Cards: A, B, C
Notes: 2, 5, 9, 10, 11, 12, 14

PROSPECT HARBOR

Oceanside Meadows Inn
P. O. Box 90, 04669
(207) 963-5557

This lovely 19th-century home overlooks Sand Cove in picturesque Prospect Harbor. Seven rooms, including one suite, await the weary traveler, along with a private sand beach and refreshingly cool sea breezes. Whether an individual guest or an entire family, Oceanside Meadows will provide a memorable seaside experience.

Hosts: Norm and Marge Babineau
Rooms: 7 (1 PB; 6 SB) $50-70
Full Breakfast
Credit Cards: A, B, F
Notes: 2, 5, 6, 8, 11, 12

RANGELEY

Northwoods Bed and Breakfast
Main Street, 04970
(207) 864-2440

This historic 1912 home centrally situated in Rangeley Village is convenient to shops, restaurants, and a variety of activities: tennis, boat launch, swimming, hiking, snowmobiling, cross-country or downhill skiing. At the end of the day relax on the front porch or in a sitting room in front of a roaring fire, or enjoy the privacy of the guest rooms.

Host: Carol Scofield
Rooms: 4 (3 PB; 1 SB) $60-75
Full Breakfast
Credit Cards: None
Notes: 2, 9, 10, 11, 12, 13

Northwoods Bed and Breakfast

ROCKPORT

Sign of the Unicorn Guest House Bed and Breakfast
191 Beauchamp Avenue, 04856
(207) 236-8789

Enjoy an ambience of warmth and wit, two miles from Camden on a quiet lane overlooking Rockport Harbor. "Sleep-in late" gourmet breakfasts include blueberry-orange whole-grain pancakes and French toast dripping with maple syrup. Wine and cheese are served at sunset. Nearby are restaurants, galleries, plays, lobster feasts, antiquing, sailing, biking, jogging, skiing, photo workshop, tennis, golf, and shopping. Special rates for winter and extended stays available. French spoken.

Hosts: Winnie Easton-Jones and Howard Jones
Rooms: 5 (2 PB; 3 SB) $65-100
Full Breakfast
Credit Cards: None
Notes: 2, 3 (by arrangement), 4 (by arrangement), 5, 8, 9, 10, 11, 12, 13, 14

SACO

Crown 'n' Anchor Inn
121 North Street, P. O. Box 228, 04072
(207) 282-3829

This restored home listed on the National Register of Historic Places has two acres of landscaped lawns. Guest rooms combine the comforts of the modern age with the exuberant elegance of the Victorian period or the quiet charm of country antiques. After a bountiful breakfast or a busy day, socialize in the parlors, curl up with a good book in the library, or relax and enjoy the tree-shaded lawns.

Hosts: John Barclay; Jim and Martha Forester
Rooms: 6 (PB) $55-75
Full Breakfast
Credit Cards: A, B
Notes: 2, 5, 9, 10, 11, 12, 14

NOTES: Credit cards accepted: A Master Card; B Visa; C American Express; D Discover Card; E Diners Club; F Other; 2 Personal checks accepted; 3 Lunch available; 4 Dinner available; 5 Open all year; 6 Pets welcome; 8 Children

SOUTH HARPSWELL

Harpswell Inn

Rural Route 1, Box 141, Lookout Point, 04079
(207) 833-5509

Situated by the sea in Harpswell, this historical 1761 inn at Lookout Point dominates a knoll overlooking a quaint cove that serves as a snug harbor for lobster boats. Explore the local islands and villages and enjoy interesting day trips to historical sites and attractions. Freeport shopping is just 25 minutes away; Bowdoin College and Brunswick summer theater only 10 minutes away. Fine restaurants, swimming, boating, and bicycling available.

Hosts: Bill and Susan Menz
Rooms: 12 (2 PB; 10 SB) $60-105
Full Breakfast
Credit Cards: A, B
Notes: 2, 5, 9, 10, 11, 14

SOUTH THOMASTON

Weskeag at the Water

Route 73, P.O. Box 213, 04858
(207) 596-6676

A mid-coast Maine inn in an exceptional setting, Weskeag is a large, beautifully renovated, 1830s Greek Revival home on the edge of the Weskeag Estuary at its reversing falls. From the deck, guests enjoy watching lobstermen tending their traps and osprey fishing. Nearby is Birch Point State Park Beach, Owls Head Transportation Museum, and a wealth of seaside activities. It's also a perfect respite halfway between Freeport and Acadia National Park.

Hosts: Gray and Lynne Smith
Rooms: 8 (2 PB; 6 S3B) $55-75
Full Breakfast
Credit Cards: None
Notes: 2, 5, 8, 9, 10, 11, 12, 13

SOUTHWEST HARBOR

The Island House

Clark Point Road, P.O. Box 1006, 04679
(207) 244-5180

Begun as the first summer hotel on Mount Desert Island in the mid-1800s, the Island House retains its charm as a gracious seacoast home. Spacious, simply decorated rooms, a comfortable veranda, large garden, and tasty breakfasts in the sunny dining room all add up to a homey and restful atmosphere. A cozy loft efficiency in the old carriage house is also available. It is adjacent to Acadia National Park and 15 miles from Bar Harbor.

Host: Ann Gill
Rooms: 4 plus apartment (1 PB; 4 SB) $45-60
Full Breakfast
Credit Cards: None
Notes: 2, 8, 9, 10, 11, 12, 14

Island Watch

Freeman Ridge Road, 04679
(207) 244-7229

Island Watch is on the ridge overlooking the Great Harbor of Mount Desert Island and the village of Southwest Harbor. It features an unmatched coastal panorama, privacy, and comfort, and is only a five-minute walk to Acadia National Park or town.

Host: Maxine Clark
Rooms: 6 (PB) $55-65
Full Breakfast
Credit Cards: None
Notes: 2, 5, 9, 10, 11, 12, 13, 14

The Lambs Ear Inn

Clark Point Road, 04679
(207) 244-9828

This stately old Maine house was built in 1857 and is comfortable and serene away

welcome; 9 Social drinking allowed; 10 Tennis available; 11 Swimming available; 12 Golf available; 13 Skiing available; 14 May be booked through travel agents

from the hustle and bustle in the village of Southwest Harbor. It features comfortable beds, crisp fresh linens, a sparkling harbor view, and a breakfast to remember. Be a part of this special village in the heart of Acadia National Park. Reservations required in winter.

Hosts: Elizabeth and George Hoke
Rooms: 6 (PB) $65-125
Full Breakfast
Credit Cards: A, B
Notes: 2, 5 (winter by reservation), 8 (over 10), 9, 10, 11, 12, 13, 14

The Lambs Ear Inn

Lindenwood Inn

Clark Point Road, P. O. Box 1328, 04679
(207) 244-5335

This lovely sea captain's home overlooks the harbor on the quiet side of the island, offering a warm, cozy atmosphere. Explore nearby Acadia National Park, with its wide variety of activities and scenic beauty, then come home to swing on the porch, relax in the parlor, or play the harpsichord.

Hosts: Marilyn and Gardiner Brower
Rooms: 7 (3 PB; 4 SB) $42.80-123.05
Cottage: 1 (PB) $80.25-112.35
Full Breakfast
Credit Cards: None
Notes: 2, 5, 8 (over 12), 9, 10, 11, 12, 13, 14

STOCKTON SPRINGS _____

The Hichborn Inn

Church Street, P. O. Box 115, 04981
(207) 567-4183

Be pampered in relaxed Victorian elegance. This stately cupola-topped mansion was built in 1849 for shipbuilder N. G. Hichborn and is listed on the National Register of Historic Places. Visit the Penobscot Marine Museum, go treasure hunting in coastal Maine's best antiquing country, and enjoy fine dining, all just minutes from the inn.

Hosts: Nancy and Bruce Suppes
Rooms: 3 (1 PB; 2 SB) $55-70
Full Breakfast
Credit Card: D
Notes: 2, 5, 11

Whistlestop Bed and Breakfast

Rural Free Delivery 1, Box 639, 04981
(207) 567-3726

Beautiful ocean views, quiet, and seclusion await you in this comfortable New England home. Two large rooms, one with twin beds, one double. Awake to homemade muffins and granola. Your hosts enjoy hiking, running, art, and classical music. They are eager to help you enjoy coastal Maine. Situated between Camden and Acadia National Park, only one-half mile from Route 1.

Hosts: David and Katherine Christie-Wilson
Rooms: 2 (SB) $50-65
Expanded Continental Breakfast
Credit Cards: None
Notes: 2, 5, 8, 9, 11

STRATTON _____

The Widow's Walk

P. O. Box 150, 04982
(207) 246-6901

The steamboat gothic architecture of this Victorian home led to its listing in the National Register of Historic Places. Nearby Bigelow Mountain, the Appalachian Trail, and Flagstaff Lake present many opportunities for boating, hiking, and fishing. In the winter, Sugarloaf/U.S.A., Maine's biggest ski resort, offers both alpine and cross-country skiing and dogsled rides. Dogs and cats in residence.

Hosts: Mary and Jerry Hopson
Rooms: 6 (SB) $30; $44 in winter
Full Breakfast
Credit Cards: None
Notes: 2, 5, 8, 9, 11, 12, 13

TOPSHAM

Middaugh Bed and Breakfast
36 Elm Street, 04086
(207) 725-2562

Situated in the historic district and listed on the National Register of Historic Places, this 150-year-old Federal Greek Revival home is ten minutes from L. L. Bean and Freeport, convenient to Camden, Booth Bay Harbor, and Portland. It is a Maine coastal route home with a family atmosphere.

Hosts: Dewey and Mary Kay Nelson
Rooms: 2 (PB) $50-60
Full Breakfast
Credit Cards: A, B
Notes: 2, 5, 8

WALDOBORO

The Roaring Lion Bed and Breakfast
995 Main Street, P. O. Box 756, 04572
(207) 832-4038

Hosts are well-traveled with 20 mailing addresses in the last 30 years with two years in West Africa. Both cook from scratch, serve homemade bread, like people, books, movies, gardening, children, and animals. The house is a 1905 Victorian with fireplaces, tin ceilings, and wood paneling; on one acre near the village center. In-room flowers, afternoon tea, and special year-end holiday dinners are featured. Hosts cater to special and vegetarian diets.

Hosts: Robin and Bill Branigan
Rooms: 4 (1 PB; 3 SB) $55-65

Full Breakfast
Credit Cards: None
Notes: 2, 5, 8, 9, 10, 11, 13

WELD

Kawanhee Inn Lakeside Lodge
Route 142, Webb Lake, 04285
(207) 585-2243 summer; (207) 778-4306 winter

Lakeside Lodge is in the western mountains, snuggled among cathedral pines. The main lodge has a huge fieldstone fireplace and original furniture of the 1920s.

Host: Martha Strunk
Rooms: 9 (5 PB; 4 SB) $50-65
Continental Breakfast
Credit Cards: A, B
Notes: 3, 4, 8, 9, 10, 11, 12, 14

The Roaring Lion Bed and Breakfast

WEST GOULDSBORO

The Sunset House
Route 186, 04607
(207) 963-7156

This late Victorian home offers a choice of seven spacious bedrooms over three floors. Four have ocean views, a fifth overlooks Jones Pond. Common rooms include a large dining room, comfortable double parlor, and sun porch. Sunset House is situated on the Schoodic Peninsula, the quiet side of Acadia National Park.

welcome; 9 Social drinking allowed; 10 Tennis available; 11 Swimming available; 12 Golf available; 13 Skiing available; 14 May be booked through travel agents

Hosts: Carl and Kathy Johnson
Rooms: 7 (SB) $39-65
Full Breakfast
Credit Cards: A, B
Notes: 2, 5, 8, 9, 11, 12, 13

WISCASSET

The Stacked Arms

Rural Route 2, Box 146, Birch Point Road, 04578
(207) 882-5436; (800) 621-1517

Experience hospitality-plus in this country setting with lots of flower gardens. Rooms have twin or queen beds and small refrigerators. Upstairs rooms have ceiling fans. Guests enjoy a beautiful view of Wiscasset Harbor and part of the town from the back part of the property.

Hosts: Dee, Sean, and Pat Maguire
Rooms: 6 (1 PB; 5 SB) $85
Full Breakfast
Credit Cards: A, B
Notes: 2, 5, 8 (over five), 9, 11, 12, 14

Maryland

Ark and Dove
Bed and Breakfast
149 Prince George Street, 21401
(410) 268-6277

This home is decorated with Colonial and English flair, including antique and fishnet canopy beds. Oriental and braided rugs adorn original pine floors. Special touches, such as candies, baskets filled with toiletries, and cushy bathrobes, are thoughtfully provided. Breakfast is served from the Sheraton sideboard laden with seasonal morning gourmet fare.

Hosts: Susan Liedlich, Sandy Huffer, Flora Liedlich
Rooms: 4 (1 PB; 3 SB) $70-95
Full Breakfast
Credit Cards: A, B
Notes: 2, 5, 9, 10, 11, 12, 14

The Barn on Howard's Cove
500 Wilson Road, 21401
(410) 266-6840

This secluded 1850 converted barn is in a setting of beautiful trees on a cove of the Severn River and features country decor, antiques, old quilts, and choice of farm breakfast. It is near historic Annapolis, United States Naval Academy, sailing schools, interesting shops, and historical buildings. Each room has private half bath; shower is shared.

Hosts: Graham and Libbie Gutsche
Rooms: 2 (SB) $60
Full Breakfast
Credit Cards: None
Notes: 2, 5, 8, 9, 10, 11, 12

Casa Bahia
Bed and Breakfast
The Traveller in Maryland, Inc.
P.O. Box 2277, 21404
(301) 269-6232; FAX (301) 263-4841

This 1880s three-story home is within walking distance of the city dock, United States Naval Academy, shopping, and dining. It is across the street from Saint John's College. Guests may enjoy a quiet moment beside the koi pond, or relax by a fire in the livingroom. There are four guest rooms, one with private bath. Resident cat. $65-85.

Chez Amis
Bed and Breakfast
The Traveller in Maryland, Inc.
P.O. Box 2277, 21404
(301) 269-6232; FAX (301) 263-4841

This turn-of-the-century home was originally Sam's grocery. Completely restored, this home still reveals original woodwork and brick walls and the original tin ceiling in the livingroom and diningroom. Two blocks from city dock. All rooms have cable TV and beverage, and most have private bath. $65-85.

College House Suites
One College Avenue, 21401-1603
(410) 263-6124

This elegant brick town home is situated in the historic district between the United States Naval Academy and Saint John's College. Two suites are featured, one with fireplace and private entrance. Personal touches in-

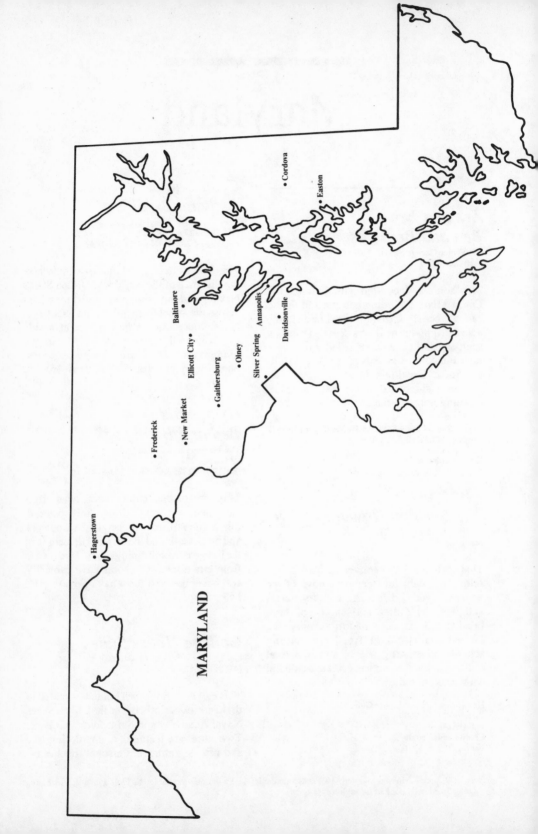

clude fresh flowers, fruit baskets, and special chocolates. A "breakfast out" option is available.

Hosts: Don and JoAnne Wolfrey
Suites: 2 (PB) $140
Continental Breakfast
Credit Cards: None
Notes: 5, 9, 14

Dean Street Bed and Breakfast

The Traveller in Maryland, Inc.
P.O. Box 2277, 21404
(301) 269-6232; FAX (301) 263-4841

This town home offers quiet and serenity, yet is only steps from the center of town. The two-story home is furnished eclectically. Off-street parking, deck surrounding in-ground pool, and two guest rooms with private bath in the hall. Full breakfast. $70.

Eastport Bed and Breakfast

The Traveller in Maryland, Inc.
P.O. Box 2277, 21404
(301) 269-6232; FAX (301) 263-4841

This contemporary home offers the pleasures of home away from home. Walk to the historic district or take a water taxi across the harbor to the city dock. Walk to Annapolis Sailing School and fine restaurants. Private hall bath. $60.

Heron's Watch Bed and Breakfast

The Traveller in Maryland, Inc.
P.O. Box 2277, 21404
(301) 269-6232; FAX (301) 263-4841

This bed and breakfast is a contemporary home on Church Creek and is landscaped for seclusion. Two guest rooms with private baths are available. Guests have use of livingroom, waterside deck, and gardens. Close to historic area. $75.

College House Suites

Keith's Bed and Breakfast

The Traveller in Maryland, Inc.
P.O. Box 2277, 21404
(301) 269-6232; FAX (301) 263-4841

This contemporary condominium overlooks the waters of Spa Creek. Upstairs guest rooms share a bath. Waterfront balconies with each room. A short walk to city dock, dining, and shopping. $65.

Magnolia House Bed and Breakfast

The Traveller in Maryland, Inc.
P.O. Box 2277, 21404
(301) 269-6232; FAX (301) 263-4841

This three-story Georgian Revival-style brick home is just outside the main entrance of the United States Naval Academy. Three rooms are available: one can accommodate up to six people, one has a fireplace, and two overlook the private garden with southern magnolia tree. Full breakfast is served on the patio. $65-75.

Mary and Rob's Bed and Breakfast

The Traveller in Maryland, Inc.
P.O. Box 2277, 21404
(301) 269-6232; FAX (301) 263-4841

NOTES: Credit cards accepted: A Master Card; B Visa; C American Express; D Discover Card; E Diners Club; F Other; 2 Personal checks accepted; 3 Lunch available; 4 Dinner available; 5 Open all year; 6 Pets welcome; 8 Children welcome; 9 Social drinking allowed; 10 Tennis available; 11 Swimming available; 12 Golf available; 13 Skiing available; 14 May be booked through travel agents

This Italianate Victorian home, circa 1864, is within walking distance of city docks. It is comfortably furnished with antiques and circular mahogany staircase. There is also a brick patio. Full breakfast is served in the dining room with bay window and garden view. There are three guest rooms, one with private bath. Resident cat. $50-80.

Riverwatch
Bed and Breakfast
The Traveller in Maryland, Inc.
P.O. Box 2277, 21404
(301) 269-6232; FAX (301) 263-4841

From subtle sunrises to fiery sunsets, the views from this riverfront contemporary home are spectacular. With private baths, pool, hot tub, waterfront balconies, and boat dock. $75.

Sailor's Wharf
Bed and Breakfast
The Traveller in Maryland, Inc.
P.O. Box 2277, 21404
(301) 269-6232; FAX (301) 263-4841

This waterfront contemporary home is within five miles of historic Annapolis. Guests enjoy the covered waterfront deck or visiting with boat owners on the deck. Guest rooms with private baths, $60-65; ground-level cottage with fireplace, livingroom, private bath, kitchenette. $80.

Southgate Bed and Breakfast
The Traveller in Maryland, Inc.
P.O. Box 2277, 21404
(301) 269-6232; FAX (301) 263-4841

This is a turn-of-the-century waterfront home overlooking Spa Creek. The large and gracious home is filled with antiques and family heirlooms. A white picket fence encloses the yards. Full breakfast; two guest rooms with private baths. $65.

William Page Inn
8 Martin Street, 21401
(410) 626-1506; FAX (410) 263-4841

Built in 1908, this dark brown, cedar shingle, wood frame structure was the local Democratic Party clubhouse for more than 50 years. Today, its wraparound porch is furnished with Adirondack chairs. Inside are appropriate Victorian reproductions. The third-floor suite has a whirlpool tub and TV. Breakfast is served in the common room.

Hosts: Robert Zuchelli and Greg Page
Rooms: 5 (3 PB; 2 SB) $75-120
Continental Breakfast
Credit Cards: A, B
Notes: 2, 5, 9, 14

BALTIMORE

Mr. Mole Bed and Breakfast
1601 Bolton Street, 21217
(301) 728-1179

In the city on historic Bolton Hill, amid tree-lined streets, is an 1870s row house with 14-foot ceilings, marble fireplaces, and many antiques. The home features a concert grand piano in the music room; suites, some with two bedrooms and sitting room; and attached garage parking. Walk to symphony, opera, and Metro; close to Johns Hopkins University, University of Baltimore, University of Maryland Medical School, but without congestion. Wheelchair accessible.

Host: Collin Clarke
Rooms: 5 (PB) $75-130
Continental Breakfast
Credit Cards: A, B
Notes: 2, 5, 9, 14

Mulberry House
Bed and Breakfast
The Traveller in Maryland, Inc.
P.O. Box 2277, Annapolis, 21404
(301) 269-6232; FAX (301) 263-4841

NOTES: Credit cards accepted: A Master Card; B Visa; C American Express; D Discover Card; E Diners Club; F Other; 2 Personal checks accepted; 3 Lunch available; 4 Dinner available; 5 Open all year; 6 Pets welcome; 8 Children

Built in 1830 by an officer of George Washington's army, this Italianate home has a delightful courtyard and antique-filled sitting room and dining room. There are four guest rooms that share two baths. Full breakfast. $65.

CORDOVA

The Traveller in Maryland, Inc.

P.O. Box 2277, Annapolis, 21404
(301) 269-6232; FAX (301) 263-4841

This bed and breakfast is a farmhouse on 200 acres where harness racing horses are raised. Two guest rooms share a hall bath. In-ground pool; full breakfast. $65.

Middle Plantation Inn

DAVIDSONVILLE

The Traveller in Maryland, Inc.

P.O. Box 2277, Annapolis, 21404
(301) 269-6232; FAX (301) 263-4841

This rambling country-style home is on three acres on the outskirts of Annapolis and is 16 miles to Washington, D.C. Families welcome; full breakfast. $50.

EASTON

John S. McDaniel House Bed and Breakfast

The Traveller in Maryland, Inc.
P.O. Box 2277, Annapolis, 21404
(301) 269-6232; FAX (301) 263-4841

This charming Victorian home, circa 1890, has an octagonal tower, dormers, and a wraparound porch. It is within walking distance of historical points of interest and is available for meetings, seminars, and retreats. $75 private bath; $65 shared bath.

ELLICOTT CITY

The Wayside Inn

4344 Columbia Road, 21043
(410) 461-4636

A stately Federal-period stone farmhouse situated on two acres with a pond features two suites, two guest rooms, fireplaces, antiques, and air conditioning. The inn is convenient to historic Ellicott City, Columbia, Baltimore, Annapolis, and Washington, D. C. Breakfast is served in the dining room. The livingroom, music room, and tavern room are available to guests.

Hosts: Margo and John Osantowski
Rooms: 4 (2 PB; 2 SB) $70-90
Continental Breakfast
Credit Cards: A, B, C
Notes: 2, 5, 12, 14

FREDERICK

Middle Plantation Inn

9549 Liberty Road, 21701
(301) 898-7128

The inn is a rustic building of stone and log. Drive through horse country to the village of Mount Pleasant. Situated several miles east of Frederick on 26 acres, the inn offers rooms furnished with antiques, air conditioning, and TV. The Keeping Room, a public room, has stained glass and a stone fireplace. Nearby are antique shops, museums, and historic attractions.

Hosts: Shirley and Dwight Mullican
Rooms: 4 (PB) $75-85
Continental Breakfast ($15 discount without breakfast)
Credit Cards: A, B
Notes: 2, 5, 9, 10, 11, 12, 14

GAITHERSBURG

The Traveller in Maryland, Inc.

P.O. Box 2277, Annapolis, 21404
(301) 269-6232; FAX (301) 263-4841

This two-story brick contemporary home is near a community lake and is ten minutes to shops and restaurants. Three guest rooms with private baths are available. TV and laundry, full breakfast. $55.

HAGERSTOWN

Lewrene Farm Bed and Breakfast

9738 Downsville Pike, 21740
(301) 582-1735

This spacious Colonial country farm home near interstates 70 and 81 has a large livingroom, fireplace, piano, antique family heirlooms, canopy beds, four-poster beds, bedside snacks, and a whirlpool bath. It is a home away from home for tourists, business people, and families. Room for small seminars and gatherings. Peacocks, old-fashioned swing, gazebo. Quilts for sale.

Host: Irene R. Lehman
Rooms: 6 (3 PB; 3 SB) $50-80
Full Breakfast
Credit Cards: None
Notes: 2, 5, 8, 10, 11, 12

NEW MARKET

National Pike Inn

9 West Main Street, P. O. Box 299, 21774
(301) 865-5055

This is a Federal-style inn circa 1796-1804. The completely restored inn has four beautifully furnished, air-conditioned guest rooms, each representing a different period from the past. Enjoy the Colonial sitting room or retreat outdoors in the private courtyard surrounded by lavish azalea gardens, sculptured bird baths, and fountain. New Market, founded in 1793, offers antique shopping and dining within easy walking distance.

Hosts: Tom and Terry Rimel
Rooms: 4 (2 PB; 2 SB) $75-100
Full Breakfast
Credit Cards: A, B
Notes: 2, 5, 9, 10, 12

OLNEY

Thoroughbred Bed and Breakfast

16410 Batchellor's Forest Road, 20832
(301) 774-7649

This is a beautiful 175-acre estate where some of the finest racehorses in the country have been raised, situated only 12 miles from Washington, D. C., and six miles from Metrorail. Guests enjoy swimming pool, hot tub, pool table, piano, and gazebo. Choose to stay in the main house or the newly renovated turn-of-the-century farmhouse annex.

Host: Helen Polinger
Rooms: 9 (3 PB; 6 SB) $60-85
Full Breakfast
Credit Cards: A, B
Notes: 2, 5, 10, 11, 12, 14

NOTES: Credit cards accepted: A Master Card; B Visa; C American Express; D Discover Card; E Diners Club; F Other;
2 Personal checks accepted; 3 Lunch available; 4 Dinner available; 5 Open all year; 6 Pets welcome; 8 Children

Thoroughbred Bed and Breakfast

SILVER SPRING

The Traveller in Maryland, Inc.
P.O. Box 2277, Annapolis, 21404
(301) 269-6232; FAX (301) 263-4841

This bed and breakfast home is in a quiet residential neighborhood, just minutes from I-495 and Washington, D.C. Metro station. The local neighborhood has a nice shopping district and restaurants. Two guest rooms share a hall bath. $55.

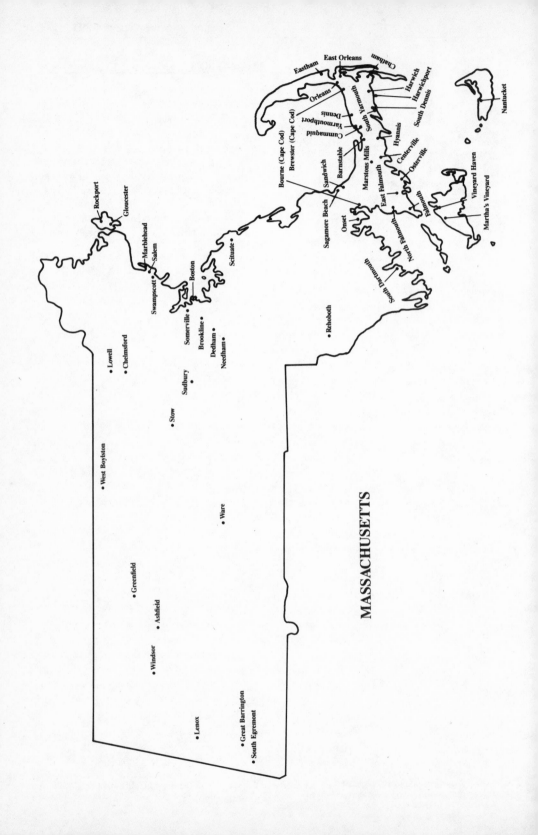

MASSACHUSETTS

Massachusetts

The Ashfield Inn
Main Street, P. O. Box 129, 01330
(413) 628-4571; (800) 428-8325 reservations

Built in 1919, The Ashfield Inn is a
Georgian-Colonial mansion resting atop a
hill on nine acres. It boasts eight guest
rooms, all with antiques. The first floor
includes a foyer with fireplace, dining room
for 24, library/TV room with fireplace, and
great room with fireplace. The inn is perfect
for weddings, business and social func-
tions, and retreats. Freshly baked goods
with coffee and tea are served nightly.

Hosts: Susan and Michael Brakefield
Rooms: 8 (S4B) $65-95
Full Breakfast; Continental on weekdays
Credit Cards: A, B, C
Notes: 2, 3 (by request), 4 (by request), 5, 6, 8, 9, 10,
  11, 12, 13, 14

Bed and Breakfast Cape Cod #14
Box 341, West Hyannisport, 02672
(508) 775-2772

This circa-1821 barn has been converted
into a comfortable home with a natural
country feeling. Three guest rooms with
private baths feature Victorian decor and
furnishings. Children over 12 welcome. $75.

Bed and Breakfast Cape Cod #35
Box 341, West Hyannisport, 02672
(508) 775-2772

This charming building, constructed in 1695,
was part of the Cape Cod designers house
tour in 1989. The grounds are a rural wooded
setting. Children over 12 welcome. $60.

Bed and Breakfast Cape Cod #46
Box 341, West Hyannisport, 02672
(508) 775-2772

In this quiet village setting within walking
distance of shops, restaurants, and the Cape
Cod Bay is a ten-year-old Cape-style house
with a spacious second-floor suite. Children over 12 welcome. $75.

A Bed & Breakfast Above the Rest
50 Boatswains Way #105, 02150
(800) 677-2262

A Bed & Breakfast Above the Rest is a
reservation liaison service providing gracious and distinctive accommodations in
the greater Boston area. Accommodations
are scrupulously selected and include pri-

NOTES: Credit cards accepted: A MasterCard; B Visa; C American Express; D Discover Card; E Diners Club; F Other;
2 Personal checks accepted; 3 Lunch available; 4 Dinner available; 5 Open all year; 6 Pets welcome; 8 Children
welcome; 9 Social drinking allowed; 10 Tennis available; 11 Swimming available; 12 Golf available; 13 Skiing
available; 14 May be booked through travel agents

vate homes, Beacon Hill brownstones, Victorian townhouses, elegant apartments, and historic mansions. More than 120 locations to choose from ranging from $50 to $100.

Beacon Hill Bed and Breakfast

27 Brimmer Street, 02108
(617) 523-7376

This 1869 spacious Victorian town house overlooks the Charles River within an elegant downtown historic neighborhood of brick sidewalks, gas lamps, and tree-lined streets. Two blocks from Cheers, easy walk to Boston Common, Freedom Trail, connecting historic sites, Quincy Market, Filene's Basement, Convention Center, subway, garages, restaurants, and shops. Large double beds and sitting rooms, fireplaces, TV, air conditioning.

Host: Susan Butterworth
Rooms: 3 (PB) $90-120
Full Breakfast
Credit Cards: None
Notes: 2, 9, 14

Bed and Breakfast Associates #M128

P.O. Box 57166, Babson Park Branch, 02157-0166
(617) 449-5302; (800) 347-5088

This 1835 Federal town house has all its original architectural detail and two fireplaces. Guests enjoy the use of the entire second floor. Continental breakfast is served in the room. $90.

Bed and Breakfast Associates #M131

P.O. Box 57166, Babson Park Branch, 02157-0166
(617) 449-5302; (800) 347-5088

This lovingly restored inn has 20 distinctive rooms overlooking the State House and the

Boston Common. Modern bath and central air conditioning enhance the beauty of the Victorian architecture. Continental self-prepared breakfast. $99.

Bed and Breakfast Associates #M133

P.O. Box 57166, Babson Park Branch, 02157-0166
(617) 449-5302; (800) 347-5088

The fourth-floor guest room with cathedral ceiling and rooftop deck overlooks a quiet street behind the State House near Faneuil Hall waterfront area. Continental self-serve breakfast. $95.

Bed and Breakfast Associates #M314

P.O. Box 57166, Babson Park Branch, 02157-0166
(617) 449-5302; (800) 347-5088

This fine 1863 brick town house has been meticulously restored. Hospitality, convenience, and attention to guest comfort are the hallmarks. Full breakfast. $97.

Bed and Breakfast Associates #M319

P.O. Box 57166, Babson Park Branch, 02157-0166
(617) 449-5302; (800) 347-5088

This 19th-century brick town house is on a pretty street near Copley Square. Victorian and contemporary furnishings are tastefully blended. Continental breakfast. $65-78.

Bed and Breakfast Associates #M322

P.O. Box 57166, Babson Park Branch, 02157-0166
(617) 449-5302; (800) 347-5088

This restored bowfront Victorian town house is on a quiet road in the up-and-coming

---

NOTES: Credit cards accepted: A Master Card; B Visa; C American Express; D Discover Card; E Diners Club; F Other;
2 Personal checks accepted; 3 Lunch available; 4 Dinner available; 5 Open all year; 6 Pets welcome; 8 Children

Tremont Street neighborhood. The guest room includes an antique spool bed and Oriental rug. Continental breakfast. $85.

Bed and Breakfast Associates #M323

P.O. Box 57166, Babson Park Branch, 02157-0166
(617) 449-5302; (800) 347-5088

This 1869 Victorian town house is close to the city's newest restaurant area and five blocks from Copley Square. Guest room features gracious bow window and antique furnishings. Continental breakfast. $68.

Bed and Breakfast Associates #M356

P.O. Box 57166, Babson Park Branch, 02157-0166
(617) 449-5302; (800) 347-5088

This third-floor apartment offers bedroom, livingroom with queen sleep sofa, and fully equipped kitchen. Continental self-serve breakfast. $75.

The Emma James House

Bed and Breakfast Associates #M357

P.O. Box 57166, Babson Park Branch, 02157-0166
(617) 449-5302; (800) 347-5088

This 1860s bowfront town house is four blocks from Copley Square and regularly

featured on historic house tours. It is furnished with Federal period antiques and has 12-foot ceilings. Continental breakfast. $68.

Bed and Breakfast Associates #M412

P.O. Box 57166, Babson Park Branch, 02157-0166
(617) 449-5302; (800) 347-5088

This stunning waterfront condominium with lovely decor has a nice view of Boston Harbor from the balcony. Continental breakfast. $80.

82 Chandler Street Bed and Breakfast

82 Chandler Street, 02116
(617) 482-0408

This 1863 red-brick row house is situated downtown in a historic residential neighborhood, just off famous Copley Square, near Hynes Convention Center, public gardens, Freedom Trail, Quincy Market, Back Bay subway/Amtrak station. Each room is finely furnished, with air conditioning and phone. A car is not necessary to see the sights. Breakfast is served in the penthouse kitchen.

Hosts: Denis F. Coté and Dominic C. Beraldi
Rooms: 5 (PB) $75-95
Full Breakfast
Credit Cards: None
Notes: 2, 5, 9

The Emma James House

47 Ocean Street, 02124
(617) 288-8867; (617) 282-5350

This spacious 1894 Victorian home offers six guest rooms, large livingroom, paneled library, sunny dining room, and adjoining breakfast kitchen (with self-serve breakfast). Gleaming woodwork and stained-glass windows. Enjoy convenient subway access to downtown Boston's historic sights, museums, restaurants, schools, and shopping, as well as the Kennedy library, Bayside Exposition Center, and the University of Massachusetts/Boston. Cape Cod is one hour's drive away, and historic Plymouth is 45 minutes away. Free parking is available.

Hosts: Vicki and Bob Rugo, Moo Bishop, and
 Michael Stella
Rooms: 6 (2 PB; 4 S2B) $50-70
Expanded Continental Breakfast
Credit Cards: None
Notes: 2, 5, 8, 9, 14

La Maison Caché

A Beacon Hill Guest House
P.O. Box 732, 02146
(617) 884-7748; (800) 677-2262 outside
 Massachusetts

Enter this historic home through a black wrought-iron gate, walk down a quaint brick passageway, and take a few steps back in time as you find yourself in this wonderfully cozy Victorian bed and breakfast. The well-appointed rooms have comfortable beds, fluffy pillows and down comforters, lace curtains, and lots of charm. Each morning a delicious gourmet breakfast is brought to your room. Come and pamper yourself at La Maison Caché.

Hosts: Glenn Sprenger and Helen Benliga
Rooms: 2 (PB; 3 SB) $50-100
Full Breakfast
Credit Cards: A, B, C, D
Notes: 2, 3, 4, 5, 6, 8, 9, 10, 11, 12, 14

Captain Freeman Inn

BOURNE (CAPE COD) _____

Cape Cod Canalside Bed and Breakfast

7 Coastal Way, 02532
(508) 759-6564

See a "billion dollar view" of the busiest canal in the world. See huge ships, private yachts, and multi-sailed schooners. The entire first floor of this new contemporary home is for guests only. Seven rooms include a two-room suite and kitchenette. Fireplace, cable TV, refrigerator, cook-out, picnic table. Abuts canal and bicycle path. Free bikes, fishing, jogging, all sports nearby. AARP and military discount.

Hosts: Terry and Paul Deasy
Rooms: 3 (1 PB; 2 SB) $40-90
Full Breakfast
Credit Cards: None
Notes: 5, 9, 10, 11, 12, 14

BREWSTER (CAPE COD) _____

Bed and Breakfast Cape Cod #41

Box 341, West Hyannisport, 02672
(508) 775-2772

This property dating back to 1854 was rebuilt in 1973 with all modern amenities. Situated in the heart of the village, it is a two-block walk to Cape Cod Bay beaches. Children over 12 welcome. $68-98.

Captain Freeman Inn

15 Breakwater Road, 02631
(508) 896-7481

This charming old sea captain's mansion offers luxury suites with balcony, private spa, fireplace, canopy bed, TV, and air conditioning. Enjoy the wraparound porch, outdoor pool, and full breakfast. Centrally situated on Cape Cod's historic north side, close to beaches, restaurants, and shopping.

NOTES: Credit cards accepted: A Master Card; B Visa; C American Express; D Discover Card; E Diners Club; F Other;
2 Personal checks accepted; 3 Lunch available; 4 Dinner available; 5 Open all year; 6 Pets welcome; 8 Children

Hosts: John and Barbara Mulkey
Rooms: 12 (9 PB; 3 SB) $50-185
Full Breakfast
Credit Cards: A, B, D
Notes: 2, 5, 9, 10, 11, 12, 14

Ocean Gold

74 Locust Lane, 02631
(508) 255-7045; (800) 526-3760

This residential bed and breakfast is in a restful setting next to Nickerson State Park, with miles of blacktop trails and ponds nearby. Hosts raise chickens for fresh eggs and offer homemade breads, jams, and berries. Breakfast is served in the formal dining room.

Hosts: Marge and Jim Geisler
Rooms: 3 (1 PB; 2 SB) $65-95
Full Breakfast
Credit Cards: None
Notes: 2, 5, 9, 10, 11, 12, 13, 14

BROOKLINE

Bed and Breakfast Associates #M617

P.O. Box 57166, Babson Park Branch
Boston, 02157-0166
(617) 449-5302; (800) 347-5088

Near Boston University, this Victorian bed and breakfast is a haven for guests visiting both Boston and Cambridge. The decor is enhanced by 19th-century antiques throughout. Full breakfast. $50-70.

Bed and Breakfast Associates #M642

P.O. Box 57166, Babson Park Branch
Boston, 02157-0166
(617) 449-5302; (800) 347-5088

Sparkling, bright, and cheerful, this spacious condominium occupies the second floor of a fine Old-World-style brownstone in the Washington Square area. Full breakfast. $50-75.

The Carriage House

Greater Boston Hospitality
P. O. Box 1142, 02146
(617) 277-5430

This nonsmoking home is listed exclusively with Greater Boston Hospitality. On a separate guest floor of a carriage house, there are two bedrooms, one with a queen bed and the second with twin beds, a bath, and den with piano. Each room leads out onto a large patio exclusively for guest use. Parking included.

Host: Lauren Simonelli
Rooms: 2 (SB) $63
Full Breakfast
Credit Cards: None
Notes: 2, 5, 9, 10, 11, 12, 14

CAMBRIDGE

Bed and Breakfast Associates #M804

P.O. Box 57166, Babson Park Branch
Boston, 02157-0166
(617) 449-5302; (800) 347-5088

Near Harvard Yard, this impeccable Philadelphia-style Victorian, circa 1890, is situated among the finest homes in Cambridge. A two-room suite features sitting room with sleep sofa and fireplace. Continental breakfast. $85.

Bed and Breakfast Associates #M813

P.O. Box 57166, Babson Park Branch
Boston, 02157-0166
(617) 449-5302; (800) 347-5088

This 60-year-old home has been newly renovated maximizing light and natural wood while preserving the original design. Continental breakfast. $70.

welcome; 9 Social drinking allowed; 10 Tennis available; 11 Swimming available; 12 Golf available; 13 Skiing available; 14 May be booked through travel agents

Bed and Breakfast Associates #M885

P.O. Box 57166, Babson Park Branch
Boston, 02157-0166
(617) 449-5302; (800) 347-5088

This Greek Revival home is just outside Harvard Square and is accented by a mix of country antiques. It is a convenient setting for activities in Boston or Cambridge. Full breakfast. $55-75.

CENTERVILLE

Bed and Breakfast Cape Cod #43

Box 341, West Hyannisport, 02672
(508) 775-2772

This home overlooks Lake Wequaquet, the largest freshwater lake on Cape Cod. Guests may swim, fish, or boat on the beautiful lake. $55-65.

CHATHAM

Bed and Breakfast Cape Cod #12

Box 341, West Hyannisport, 02672
(508) 775-2772

Early American Cape Cod designs have been built into this 12-year-old house featuring wide-board floors, huge fireplace in the common room, and braided rugs. Walk to village, fishing pier, and beach. $65.

Bed and Breakfast Cape Cod #49

Box 341, West Hyannisport, 02672
(508) 775-2772

This 25-year-old Cape Cod-style home features wide-board floors, two fireplaces, and a den for guest use. Rooms are furnished in traditional decor. View a lighthouse in the distance. Children over 12 welcome. $65-95.

Bed and Breakfast Cape Cod #60

Box 341, West Hyannisport, 02672
(508) 775-2772

This two-story Garrison Colonial stands three miles from the village center along the warm water sound. The rear deck overlooks a saltwater march. Children over four welcome. $55-60.

Moses Nickerson House Inn

364 Old Harbor Road, 02633
(800) 628-6972

This historic sea captain's house built in 1839 includes seven guest rooms with private baths, canopy beds, fireplaces, and period antiques. Within walking distance of the village and fishing pier activities. AAA three-diamond rating. Featured in *Fodor's Cape Cod.*

Hosts: Carl and Elsie Piccola
Rooms: 7 (PB) $69-139
Full Breakfast
Credit Cards: A, B, C
Notes: 2, 5, 10, 11, 12, 14

CHELMSFORD

Westview Landing

4 Westview Avenue, P. O. Box 4141, 01824
(508) 256-0074

Westview Landing is a large contemporary home set on a tranquil pond. Unwind on a private beach, with swimming, boating, and fishing. Bicycling and hot spa are available. Situated three miles from Routes 495 and 3, 30 miles north of Boston, and 15 miles south of Nashua, New Hampshire, close to historic Lexington, Concord, and Lowell.

NOTES: Credit cards accepted: A Master Card; B Visa; C American Express; D Discover Card; E Diners Club; F Other; 2 Personal checks accepted; 3 Lunch available; 4 Dinner available; 5 Open all year; 6 Pets welcome; 8 Children

Hosts: Lorraine and Robert Pinette
Rooms: 2 (SB) $50
Full Breakfast
Credit Cards: None
Notes: 2, 5, 6, 8, 9, 10, 11, 12, 13, 14

CUMMAQUID

Bed and Breakfast Cape Cod #61

Box 341, West Hyannisport, 02672
(508) 775-2772

Just east of Barnstable on the Olde Kings Highway stands this lovely home built in 1950 in typical Cape Cod style on two and one-half acres. No children. $75-85.

DEDHAM

Bed and Breakfast Associates #IW757

P.O. Box 57166, Babson Park Branch
Boston, 02157-0166
(617) 449-5302; (800) 347-5088

Thirty minutes from Boston, this lovely home sits on 13 acres with landscaping and natural views. Master bedroom has working fireplace and Jacuzzi. Continental breakfast. $65-90.

DENNIS

Bed and Breakfast Cape Cod #4

Box 341, West Hyannisport, 02672
(508) 775-2772

The local postmaster built and occupied this Victorian cottage for many years following its construction in 1860. It has been restored with Victorian antiques and is near shops, restaurants, and summer theater. Children over 13 welcome. $65-95.

EAST FALMOUTH

Bed and Breakfast Cape Cod #44

Box 341, West Hyannisport, 02672
(508) 775-2772

This picturesque modern-design home features cathedral ceilings, glass walls, and magnificent waterviews of Waquoit Bay and beyond to Martha's Vineyard. The private beach is steps away. Children over 11 welcome. $85.

EASTHAM

Great Pond House

Great Pond Road, P. O. Box 351, 02642
(508) 255-2867; (802) 988-4300

This traditional two-story modern home is situated in a secluded area on the shore of Great Pond. Beaches, restaurants, antiques, art galleries, fishing, and Whale Watch cruises are nearby. The Cape Cod National Seashore and bike trails are one mile away. Guests may relax in the TV room or livingroom and are invited to play the 1927 Chickering grand piano.

Host: Camilla Mead
Rooms: 2 (PB) $75-85
Continental Breakfast
Credit Cards: None
Notes: 2, 9, 10, 11, 12, 14

EAST ORLEANS

Ivy Lodge

194 Main Street, P.O. Box 1195, 02643
(508) 255-0119

Enjoy casual, relaxed lodging in this early-19th-century home featuring cheery rooms and spacious grounds with a picnic area and within walking distance of restaurants and shops, one and one-half miles to the ocean

welcome; 9 Social drinking allowed; 10 Tennis available; 11 Swimming available; 12 Golf available; 13 Skiing available; 14 May be booked through travel agents

and bay beaches. Two-bedroom efficiency unit available.

Hosts: Barbara and David McCormack
Rooms: 3 (1 PB; 2 SB) $50-70
Continental Breakfast
Credit Cards: None
Notes: 2, 5, 8, 9, 10, 11, 12

The Parsonage Inn
202 Main Street, P. O. Box 1501, 02643
(508) 255-8217

Originally a parsonage, circa 1770, this full Cape home is now a cozy romantic inn only one and one-half miles from one of Cape Cod's most beautiful beaches, Nauset Beach. All seven rooms are decorated with country antiques, quilts, and stenciling. A bountiful breakfast is served either in the dining room or under sunny skies on the patio. Appetizers are served in the evening in the parlor where guests can peruse menus of many fine restaurants.

Hosts: Ian and Elizabeth Browne
Rooms: 7 (PB) $55-85
Expanded Continental Breakfast
Credit Cards: A, B
Notes: 2, 5, 8 (over 5), 9, 10, 11, 12, 14

FALMOUTH

Captain Tom Lawrence House Bed and Breakfast Inn
75 Locust Street, 02540
(508) 540-1445

This authentic 1861 Victorian whaling captain's residence is now an intimate inn for those who appreciate warm hospitality and delicious breakfasts. It is close to the beach, bikeway, island ferries, shops, restaurants, and bus station. Explore the entire Cape, Vineyard, and Plymouth by day trips. Beautiful, spacious corner guest rooms have firm beds and canopies. Other features in-

clude a Steinway piano, antiques, and fireplace. German spoken.

Host: Barbara Sabo-Feller
Rooms: 6 (PB) $75-95
Full Breakfast
Credit Cards: A, B
Notes: 2, 5, 9, 10, 11, 12

Captain Tom Lawrence House
Bed and Breakfast Inn

Grafton Inn
261 Grand Avenue South, 02540
(508) 540-8688; FAX (508) 540-1861

This oceanfront historic Queen Anne Victorian looks on miles of beautiful beach and breathtaking views of Martha's Vineyard. Eleven airy rooms are furnished with period antiques. A sumptuous breakfast is served at private tables on the enclosed porch overlooking Nantucket Sound. Thoughtful amenities, complimentary bicycles, short walk to restaurant, shops, and island ferry.

Hosts: Liz and Rudy Cvitan
Rooms: 11 (PB) $75-115
Full Breakfast
Credit Cards: A, B, C
Notes: 2, 5, 9, 10, 11, 12, 14

Mostly Hall Bed and Breakfast Inn
27 Main Street, 02540
(508) 548-3786

NOTES: Credit cards accepted: A Master Card; B Visa; C American Express; D Discover Card; E Diners Club; F Other; 2 Personal checks accepted; 3 Lunch available; 4 Dinner available; 5 Open all year; 6 Pets welcome; 8 Children

This romantic 1849 southern plantation-style Cape Cod home has a wraparound veranda and widow's walk sitting room. Set back from the road across from the village green on one acre of beautiful gardens with a gazebo, it is close to beaches, shops, restaurants, bike path, island ferries, whale watches, and offers spacious corner rooms with queen canopy beds, reading chairs, ceiling fans, and air conditioning. Breakfast is served on the veranda in warm weather.

Hosts: Caroline and Jim Lloyd
Rooms: 6 (PB) $80-105
Full Breakfast
Credit Cards: A, B
Notes: 2, 9, 10, 11, 12

Mostly Hall Bed and Breakfast Inn

GLOUCESTER

Bed and Breakfast Associates #NS500
P.O. Box 57166, Babson Park Branch
Boston, 02157-0166
(617) 449-5302; (800) 347-5088

Walk to the beach from this white frame house 30 miles north of Boston in the delightful village of Lanesville. Continental breakfast. $60.

GREAT BARRINGTON

Round Hill Farm Non-Smokers' Bed and Breakfast
17 Round Hill Road, 01230
(413) 528-3366

This classic 19th-century Berkshires hilltop farm overlooks 300 enchanting acres with panoramic views. The 1920s Uttermost Barn has two luxurious suites, one with kitchen and deck. The 1907 farmhouse has sunny, immaculate, warmly furnished guest rooms filled with antiques and books. Walks, wildlife, swimming, fishing, bicycling, and cross-country skiing. Five minutes from routes 7 and 23. Reservations required.

Hosts: Thomas and Margaret Whitfield
Rooms: 8 (3 PB; 5 SB) $65-150
Full Breakfast
Credit Cards: A, B, C
Notes: 2, 5, 6 (horses only), 8 (over 16), 9, 10, 11, 12, 13, 14

Seekonk Pines Inn
142 Seekonk Cross Road, 01230
(413) 528-4192

This 1830s homestead has extensive gardens, meadows, picnic tables, swimming pool, and a large common room with fireplace, piano, and library. There is also a guest pantry with refrigerator and hot water dispenser. Antique quilts, stenciling, and original artwork adorn guest rooms. Delicious whole-grain, low-fat breakfasts change daily. Cross-country skiing from the door. Featured on the cover of Bed and Breakfast American Style in 1988.

Hosts: Linda and Christian Best
Rooms: 6 (4 PB; 2 SB) $65-95
Full Breakfast
Credit Cards: A, B
Notes: 2, 5, 8, 9, 10, 11, 12, 13

welcome; 9 Social drinking allowed; 10 Tennis available; 11 Swimming available; 12 Golf available; 13 Skiing available; 14 May be booked through travel agents

Seekonk Pines Inn

The Turning Point Inn

3 Lake Buel Road, 01230
(413) 528-4777

This inn is a restored 18th-century stage-coach stop on 11 acres with nature and cross country ski trails on the premises and nearby. Sitting rooms have fireplaces. Enjoy a full, naturally delicious breakfast as reviewed in *The New York Times* and *Boston Globe,* and old-fashioned comfort in an atmosphere of informality and warmth. Near Tanglewood and adjacent to Butternut ski slope. Groups and families welcome.

Hosts: Irving, Shirley, and Jamie Yost
Rooms: 9 (1 PB; 8 SB) $75-95
Full Breakfast
Credit Cards: A, B
Notes: 2, 5, 8, 9, 10, 11, 12, 13

GREENFIELD

The Brandt House

29 Highland Avenue, 01301
(413) 774-3329

Come enjoy the hospitality of this restored turn-of-the-century classic in a spectacular setting, situated high on a hill with three and one-half acres of rolling lawns, private clay tennis courts, and trails through the woods. The comfortable spacious rooms, library with pool table, fireplaces, wraparound porches, and sumptuous breakfasts are just some of what awaits guests. Situated just five minutes from historic Deerfiefld, Route 91, and Route 2.

Hosts: Phoebe Brandt and Joan Fitzgerald
Rooms: 8 (3 PB; 5 SB) $75-95
Full Breakfast
Credit Cards: A, B
Notes: 2, 5, 8, 9, 10, 11, 12, 13, 14

HARWICH

Bed and Breakfast Cape Cod #7

Box 341, West Hyannisport, 02672
(508) 775-2772

This Cape-style home sits 100 yards from a freshwater pond. Situated on the Cape Cod Bike Trail, it is a great spot for bike riders. The beach is one mile away. Children over 11 welcome. $48.

NOTES: Credit cards accepted: A Master Card; B Visa; C American Express; D Discover Card; E Diners Club; F Other; 2 Personal checks accepted; 3 Lunch available; 4 Dinner available; 5 Open all year; 6 Pets welcome; 8 Children

Bed and Breakfast Cape Cod #16

Box 341, West Hyannisport, 02672
(508) 775-2772

Three blocks from the warm water beaches of Nantucket Sound stands this ranch-style private home with one wing set aside for accommodations. The home is immaculate in every respect. No children. $70.

The Birchwood Inn

HARWICHPORT

Bed and Breakfast Cape Cod #37

Box 341, West Hyannisport, 02672
(508) 775-2772

Wychmere Harbor is across the street from this 1880 rambling guest house originally owned by a retired seaman. It is a short walk to the best seafood restaurants on Cape Cod. Children over three welcome. $45-60.

HYANNIS

The Inn on Sea Street

358 Sea Street, 02601
(508) 775-8030

A small, elegant 1849 Victorian inn is just steps from the beach. Antiques, canopy beds, Persian rugs, and objets d'art abound in this unpretentious, hospitable atmosphere where no detail has been overlooked. Gour-met breakfast is served at individual tables set with fine sterling silver and china, crystal, and fresh flowers.

Hosts: Lois M. Nelson and J. B. Whitehead
Rooms: 9 (7 PB; 2 SB) $70-90
Full Breakfast
Credit Cards: A, B, C, D
Notes: 2, 9, 10, 11, 12

LENOX

The Birchwood Inn

7 Hubbard Street, P. O. Box 2020, 01240
(413) 637-2600

This inn is situated in the historic district of Lenox, the summer center for the arts in New England and growing in popularity for year-round sports and recreation. The spacious common areas of the inn invite guests to enjoy conversation, games, or quiet contemplation. The tastefully decorated rooms range from spacious luxury to cozy comfort. Full breakfasts and weekend dinners are showcases for the talented, European-trained chefs.

Hosts: Joan, Dick and Dan Toner
Rooms: 12 (10 PB; 2 SB) $65-185
Full Breakfast
Credit Cards: A, B
Notes: 2, 5, 9, 10, 11, 12, 13, 14

Forty-Four Saint Ann's Avenue

P.O. Box 718, 01240
(413) 637-3381

Enjoy Lenox, Tanglewood, and the Berkshires from our charming bed and breakfast located in the center of Lenox Village. Each of our rooms has a private bath, air conditioning, and a truly comfortable bed. The elegant, expanded continental breakfast includes fresh fruit, fresh orange juice, homemade muffins, pastries, granola, tea, and coffee. Your enthusiastic hosts combine a warm, friendly environment with a genuine

welcome; 9 Social drinking allowed; 10 Tennis available; 11 Swimming available; 12 Golf available; 13 Skiing available; 14 May be booked through travel agents

desire to assist newcomers in their discovery of the cultural and scenic joys of the Berkshires.

Hosts: Barbara and Milton Kolodkin
Rooms: 3 (PB) $80-170
Expanded Continental Breakfast
Credit Cards: None
Notes: 2, 9, 10, 11, 12

Rookwood Inn

19 Old Stockbridge Road, P. O. Box 1717, 01240
(413) 637-9750

This charming 1885 Victorian "painted lady" is like something out of a storybook and a haven of relaxation and fun for all who come. It is on a quiet road, yet one-half block to shopping and dining in the town center. Rookwood has 15 lovely guest rooms decorated in period antiques and furnishings, some with canopy beds, fireplaces, and porches. A buffet breakfast is served, and the congenial hospitality of the owners is always present.

Hosts: Tom and Betsy Sherman
Rooms: 15 (PB) $70-180
Full Breakfast
Credit Cards: C
Notes: 2, 5, 8, 9, 10, 11, 12, 13, 14

LOWELL

Sherman-Berry House

163 Dartmouth Street, 01851-2425
(508) 459-4760

The Victorian Sherman-Berry House has operated as a historic bed and breakfast since 1985. Guests enjoy this charming, unique home and its large collection of Victoriana year-round. Near Lexington, Concord, Andover, and southern New Hampshire, with easy access to Boston. Delicious breakfasts are served in the Victorian style. The hostess is a delegate to the fifth world conference on smoking and health.

Hosts: Susan Scott and David Strohmeyer
Rooms: 2 (SB) $50-60
Full Breakfast
Credit Cards: None
Notes: 2, 5, 8, 9, 10, 11, 12, 13, 14

MARBLEHEAD

Bed and Breakfast Associates #NS261

P.O. Box 57166, Babson Park Branch
Boston, 02157-0166
(617) 449-5302; (800) 347-5088

This 19th-century carriage house on restored Federalist property is just two blocks to beaches, antique shops, and restaurants. It has beamed cathedral ceilings and charming decor. Continental breakfast. $80.

Stillpoint

27 Gregory Street, 01945
(617) 631-1667

This gracious 1830s home is furnished with antiques and situated in a quiet area of historic Marblehead, accessible to cultural events, interesting shops, fine restaurants, coastal walks, seaside activities, public transportation. Guest rooms feature firm mattresses and allergen-free pillows. Breakfast is served on the deck with a harbor view. Enjoy the period-furnished dining room and cozy livingroom with fireplace and piano.

Host: Sarah Lincoln-Harrison
Rooms: 3 (2 PB; 1 SB) $60-100
Continental Breakfast
Credit Cards: A, B
Notes: 2, 5, 8, 10, 11, 12, 13

MARSTONS MILLS

Bed and Breakfast Cape Cod #34

Box 341, West Hyannisport, 02672
(508) 775-2772

Built in 1986 in a shaded residential area, this ranch-style house features a suite with private entrance. The private guest deck is a great spot for relaxing. A full country breakfast is served from 8 to 10 A.M. daily. There is also a second room with a semi-private bath. Children over 11 welcome. $70.

NANTUCKET

Bed and Breakfast Cape Cod #102

Box 341, West Hyannisport, 02672
(508) 775-2772

This 16-room inn is situated close to the harbor in the village. From the widow's walk on the top floor there is a panoramic view of Nantucket Harbor. All guest rooms have private baths. Children over 11 welcome. $90-180.

Eighteen Gardner Street Inn

18 Gardner Street, 02554
(508) 228-1155

From a romantic weekend encounter to a small family gathering, the 12 unique guest rooms can accommodate all vacation needs. Many rooms offer working fireplaces and color TVs. Breakfast is served in the formal dining room. On summer holiday weekends, an old-fashioned barbecue is offered in the garden. In the cooler months, the holidays bring intimate dinner parties.

Hosts: Roger and Mary Schmidt
Rooms: 12 (PB) $55-165
Full Breakfast
Credit Cards: A, B, C
Notes: 2, 5, 9, 10, 11, 12, 14

The Quaker House Inn and Restaurant

5 Chestnut Street, 02554
(508) 228-0400

The Quaker House Inn is a charming 19th-century inn in the heart of Nantucket's historic area. Each of the eight guest rooms is decorated with antiques and period furnishings, yet with the convenience of queen-size beds and modern private baths. Its quaint restaurant is popular and highly recommended by reviewers (and is also entirely nonsmoking).

Hosts: Caroline and Bob Taylor
Rooms: 8 (PB) $75-125 plus breakfast
Full Breakfast
Credit Cards: A, B
Notes: 2, 4, 9, 10, 11, 12, 14

Eighteen Gardner Street Inn

Tuckernuck Inn

60 Union Street, 02554
(508) 228-4886; (800) 228-4886

Tuckernuck Inn is a special, quiet retreat set in a spacious relaxed atmosphere on a romantic vacation island. The immaculate rooms beckon guests to a quiet restful sleep and refresh them for a day of shopping, sightseeing, swimming, biking, and sailing. Enjoy some of the best restaurants in town, and stroll Main Street for lasting memories.

Hosts: Ken and Phyllis Parker
Rooms: 16 (PB) $75-120
Continental Breakfast
Credit Cards: A, B, C
Notes: 5, 8 (off-season October 15-May 15) ,11, 14

NEEDHAM

Brock's Bed and Breakfast

60 Stevens Road, 02192
(617) 444-6573

The Brock's home is the first Royal Barry Wills house designed in 1922 when Wills was an architecture student at Massachusetts Institute of Technology. It is Cape style with nooks and crannies, built-ins, original high ceilings, flagstone walk, landscaping, and Williamsburg decor all done by the Brocks. Breakfast is served in the dining room from 7:00 A.M. to 9:00 A.M. Twenty minutes by public transportation to historic Boston.

Hosts: Anne and Frank Brock
Rooms: 3 (SB) $55
Full Breakfast
Credit Cards: None
Notes: 2, 5, 9, 10, 12

NORTH FALMOUTH

Bed and Breakfast Cape Cod #45

Box 341, West Hyannisport, 02672
(508) 775-2772

This 14-year-old Cape Cod-style home was built amid tall trees and flourishing growth and features a parlor with fireplace and TV. The ferry to Martha's Vineyard is ten minutes away. Children over nine welcome. $55-60.

Bed and Breakfast Cape Cod #57

Box 341, West Hyannisport, 02672
(508) 775-2772

This 1806 restored farmhouse captures the flavor of a bygone era. The second-floor suite is available for guests. Two beaches are within one mile. No children. $80.

ONSET

Bed and Breakfast Cape Cod #62

Box 341, West Hyannisport, 02672
(508) 775-2772

The upper Cape offers a world of beautiful beaches, great restaurants, and water views. Built in 1880, this small inn is directly on Onset Bay. Twelve guest rooms are available with private or semi-private baths. Children over 11 welcome. $95-130.

ORLEANS

Bed and Breakfast Cape Cod #8

Box 341, West Hyannisport, 02672
(508) 775-2772

This dramatic contemporary home is built on high ground overlooking five acres of pastoral wooded land that leads to the ocean. The massive deck adjacent to the in-ground pool offers complete privacy. Children over 11 welcome. $90.

Bed and Breakfast Cape Cod #50

Box 341, West Hyannisport, 02672
(508) 775-2772

This gracious Cape-style home on a harbor in a quiet inlet is complete with deck, sunfish, and magnificent waterviews. For additional charge, harbor cruises in the host's boat are available. Children over seven welcome. $68-75.

Bed and Breakfast Cape Cod #66

Box 341, West Hyannisport, 02672
(508) 775-2772

This English Cape-design home was built in 1938 by a wealthy merchant. The rooms are tastefully decorated with traditional and Victorian furnishings. A full country breakfast is served in the dining room. Children over 11 welcome. $65.

OSTERVILLE

Bed and Breakfast Cape Cod #65

Box 341, West Hyannisport, 02672
(508) 775-2772

This is one of the most spectacular villages on the Cape with lovely estates, private homes, and a warm water beach. The house was built in 1730 and was the town's first library and later a coach stop. Two guest rooms and one bath are rented to one party at a time. $65.

PLYMOUTH

Bed and Breakfast Associates #SS765

P.O. Box 57166, Babson Park Branch
Boston, 02157-0166
(617) 449-5302; (800) 347-5088

This spectacular restoration of an 1820 Cape-style home provides gracious accommodations with American and English antiques. The home is set on 40 acres six minutes from Plymouth Rock. Full breakfast. $68.

REHOBOTH

Gilbert's Bed and Breakfast

30 Spring Street, 02769
(508) 252-6416

This 150-year-old farmhouse features original floors, doors, windows, and hardware. The in-ground pool is open from mid-June through August. Hiking is available through the 100-acre tree farm. Nearby activities include bicycling, antique shopping, and

museum touring. The house is situated 12 miles east of Providence, Rhode Island, at the hub of many southeastern Massachusetts tourist attractions.

Host: Jeanne Gilbert
Rooms: 3 (SB) $45-50
Full Breakfast
Credit Cards: None
Notes: 2, 5, 8, 9, 10, 11, 12, 14

ROCKPORT

The Inn on Cove Hill

37 Mount Pleasant Street, 01966
(508) 546-2701

A friendly atmosphere with the option of privacy is available in this painstakingly restored 200-year-old Federal home in a perfect setting two blocks from the harbor and shops. Cozy bedrooms are meticulously appointed with antiques, and some have canopy beds. Wake up to the aroma of hot muffins, and enjoy breakfast at the umbrella tables in the Pump Garden.

Hosts: John and Marjorie Pratt
Rooms: 11 (9 PB; 2 SB) $45-93
Continental Breakfast
Credit Cards: None
Notes: 2, 9, 10, 11, 12

Mooringstone for Nonsmokers

12 Norwood Avenue, 01966
(508) 546-2479

The Mooringstone for Nonsmokers is on a quiet side street centrally situated a three- to five-minute walk to beach, restaurants, shops, and the scenic Headlands. Comfortable new ground-floor rooms have twin, king, or queen beds. Air conditioning, cable TV, refrigerators, and parking included. Daily, weekly, and off-season rates. Open mid-May to mid-October.

Hosts: David and Mary Knowlton
Rooms: 3 (PB) $70-79
Expanded Continental Breakfast

welcome; 9 Social drinking allowed; 10 Tennis available; 11 Swimming available; 12 Golf available; 13 Skiing available; 14 May be booked through travel agents

Credit Cards: A, B, C
Notes: 2, 9, 10, 11, 12, 14

SAGAMORE BEACH

Bed and Breakfast Cape Cod #36

Box 341, West Hyannisport, 02672
(508) 775-2772

Situated on the banks of beautiful Cape Cod bay is this luxurious two-story beach house with spectacular water views. It is a short drive to fine restaurants and shops. Breakfast is served with home-baked goods in the dining room overlooking the ocean. $75-95.

SALEM

Amelia Payson Guest House

16 Winter Street, 01970
(508) 744-8304

Built in 1845, the Amelia Payson Guest House is one of Salem's finest examples of Greek Revival architecture. Elegantly restored and beautifully decorated, each room is furnished with period antiques and warmed by a personal touch. Situated in the heart of Salem's historic district, a five-minute stroll finds downtown shopping, historic houses, museums, and Pickering Wharf's waterfront dining. Seaside towns are nearby. Boston is easily reached by car, train, or bus.

Hosts: Ada and Donald Roberts
Rooms: 4 (PB) $75-85
Expanded Continental Breakfast
Credit Cards: A, B, C
Notes: 5, 9, 10, 11, 12

The Inn at Seven Winter Street

7 Winter Street, 01970
(508) 745-9520

The inn is situated in the heart of historic Salem within walking distance of all that Salem's rich heritage has to offer, including museums, shops, and quaint restaurants. The building is a magnificently restored French Second Empire home built in 1870 by a wealthy merchant. All rooms have something beautifully unique, such as working marble fireplaces, canopy beds, or Victorian bath. Breakfast is served in the main parlor.

Hosts: Sally Flint, Dee and Jill Coté
Rooms: 9 (PB) $65-125
Continental Breakfast
Credit Cards: A, B, C, D
Notes: 2, 5, 10, 11, 12, 13

The Inn at Seven Winter Street

SANDWICH

Bed and Breakfast Cape Cod #1

Box 341, West Hyannisport, 02672
(508) 775-2772

This elegant Victorian-style home is situated in the heart of Sandwich, the oldest village on Cape Cod. It was built in 1849 and meticulously restored in 1987 and is convenient to many fine restaurants and attractions. Children over 11 welcome. $80-110.

Bed and Breakfast Cape Cod #15

Box 341, West Hyannisport, 02672
(508) 775-2772

NOTES: Credit cards accepted: A Master Card; B Visa; C American Express; D Discover Card; E Diners Club; F Other; 2 Personal checks accepted; 3 Lunch available; 4 Dinner available; 5 Open all year; 6 Pets welcome; 8 Children

High on Academy Hill sits this beautifully maintained 60-year-old Cape Cod house. Classic design and traditional furnishings create a gracious yet relaxing atmosphere. Children over 11 welcome. $65-70.

Bed and Breakfast Cape Cod #22

Box 341, West Hyannisport, 02672
(508) 775-2772

This early-1800s home was built by a sea captain and has been restored with Victorian decor. The location provides a perfect setting for reflection on the past. Children over five welcome. $50-75.

Bed and Breakfast Cape Cod #55

Box 341, West Hyannisport, 02672
(508) 775-2772

This beautiful three-level contemporary home overlooks the entrance to the Cape Cod Canal. One room has a whirlpool tub for two. No children. $100-150.

Captain Ezra Nye House

152 Main Street, 02563
(508) 888-6142; (800) 388-2278

A sense of history and romance fills this 1829 Federal home, built by the distinguished sea captain Ezra Nye. The inn was chosen one of the top 50 inns in America and one of five Cape Cod best bed and breakfasts. It has been featured in *Glamour, Innsider,* and *Cape Cod Life* magazines. Rooms are uniquely decorated with antiques in soft pastel tones.

Hosts: Elaine and Harry Dickson
Rooms: 7 (5 PB; 2 SB) $50-85
Full Breakfast
Credit Cards: A, B, C, D
Notes: 2, 5, 8, 9, 10, 14

The Summer House

158 Main Street, 02563
(508) 888-4991

This elegant Greek Revival home, circa 1835, featured in *Country Living* magazine, is situated in the heart of historic Sandwich Village, Cape Cod's oldest town (settled 1638). The house has antiques, hand-stitched quilts, fireplaces, flowers, large sunny rooms, and English-style gardens. It is within strolling distance of dining, museums, shops, pond and grist mill, and boardwalk to the beach. Afternoon tea in the garden is included.

Hosts: David and Kay Merrell
Rooms: 5 (1 PB; 4 SB) $50-75
Full Breakfast
Credit Cards: A, B, C, D
Notes: 2, 5, 8, 9, 10, 11, 12, 14

SCITUATE

Bed and Breakfast Cape Cod #64

Box 341, West Hyannisport, 02672
(508) 775-2772

Ocean views and English elegance can be found in the heart of this New England fishing village. The 1905 Victorian inn has a commanding view of Scituate Harbor. Children over 15 welcome. $75.

SOMERVILLE

Bed and Breakfast Associates #IN176

P.O. Box 57166, Babson Park Branch
Boston, 02157-0166
(617) 449-5302; (800) 347-5088

This pleasant, modern, two-bedroom apartment has a full kitchen, livingroom, dining area, and small balcony. Continental self-serve breakfast. $85.

welcome; 9 Social drinking allowed; 10 Tennis available; 11 Swimming available; 12 Golf available; 13 Skiing available; 14 May be booked through travel agents

SOUTH DARTMOUTH

The Little Red House

631 Elm Street, 02748
(508) 996-4554

A charming, gambrel Colonial home situated in the lovely coastal village of Pandanaram is beautifully furnished with country accents, antiques, fireplace, luxurious four-poster or brass and iron beds. The back yard gazebo offers a perfect setting for relaxing moments. Breakfast in the romantic candlelit dining room is a delectable treat. Close to harbor, beaches, restaurants, historic sites, Newport, Plymouth, Boston, and Cape Cod.

Hosts: Meryl and Dan Scully
Rooms: 2 (SB) $65
Full Breakfast
Credit Cards: A, B
Notes: 2, 5, 11, 12, 14

SOUTH DENNIS

Bed and Breakfast Cape Cod #42

Box 341, West Hyannisport, 02672
(508) 775-2772

This nicely restored 1840 Greek Revival home is filled with Queen Anne and Chippendale formal antiques and reproductions. Rooms are individually decorated in a warm country style. Children over nine welcome. $58-75.

SOUTH EGREMONT

Bed and Breakfast USA

P.O. Box 418, 01258
(413) 528-2113; (800) 255-7213 reservations
FAX (413) 528-6133

Bed and Breakfast USA is a professional reservation service representing bed and breakfasts, guest houses, private home accommodations, farms, private cottages, and apartments in New York, the Berkshires, parts of Connecticut, Vermont, Pennsylvania, Florida, and the Carribean. Modest to elegant, casual to Art Deco. 80 percent or more of the accommodations are nonsmoking. Catalog $6; reservation fee $15; annual travel membership $25.

SOUTH YARMOUTH

Bed and Breakfast Cape Cod #2

Box 341, West Hyannisport, 02672
(508) 775-2772

This 1820s sea captain's house is complete with wide-board floors and widow's walk. It is restored and in immaculate condition. Walk to the beach; only a short distance to fine restaurants and shops. Children over 11 welcome. $60-70.

STOW

Bed and Breakfast Associates #CW325

P.O. Box 57166, Babson Park Branch
Boston, 02157-0166
(617) 449-5302; (800) 347-5088

This 1734 rural Colonial farmhouse has been authentically restored and is beautifully furnished with antiques, quilts, and modern conveniences. Full breakfast. $75-90.

SUDBURY

Bed and Breakfast Associates #CW640

P.O. Box 57166, Babson Park Branch
Boston, 02157-0166
(617) 449-5302; (800) 347-5088

This exquisite 1929 Dutch Colonial features a world-class collection of antique carousel horses tastefully integrated with traditional furnishings. Set on several acres with an in-ground pool. Continental breakfast. $85-95.

Wildwood Inn

SWAMPSCOTT

Oak Shores
Bed and Breakfast

64 Fuller Avenue, 01907
(617) 599-7677

This 61-year-old Dutch Colonial is on Boston's lovely North Shore. Rooms are filled with fine restored furniture. Sleep in the comfort of old brass and iron beds, relax in the private garden, or stroll the two blocks to the beach. Near public transportation and restaurants and just 25 minutes from Boston's Logan Airport.

Host: Marjorie McClung
Rooms: 2 (SB) $60
Continental Breakfast
Credit Cards: None
Notes: 2, 8 (over 8), 10, 11, 12

VINEYARD HAVEN, MARTHA'S VINEYARD

Crocker House Inn

4 Crocker Avenue, P. O. Box 1658, 02568
(508) 693-1151

A charming Victorian inn with eight unique rooms and suites, all with private baths.

Some rooms feature private entrances with balconies and a fireplace. A homemade breakfast is served in the cozy common area. The inn is just a short walk to ferry, shops, restaurant, golf, tennis, and theater.

Host: Darlene Stavens
Rooms: 8 (PB) $85-140
Expanded Continental Breakfast
Credit Cards: A, B
Notes: 2, 9, 10, 11, 12, 14

WARE

Wildwood Inn

121 Church Street, 01082
(413) 967-7798

This 1880 Victorian has a comfortably furnished wraparound porch. American primitive antiques, early cradles, and heirloom quilts add coziness to seven rooms with four shared baths. Set on a residential street bordered by a 110-acre park, Wildwood offers two acres of woods and yards for recreation or quiet solitude. Free tennis, swimming, canoeing, hiking, and other outdoor sports are available. It is an easy drive to historic sights and museums.

Hosts: Fraidell Fenster and Richard Watson
Rooms: 7 (S4B) $38-75
Full Breakfast
Credit Cards: C, F
Notes: 2, 5, 8 (over 6), 9, 10, 11, 12, 13, 14

WEST BOYLSTON

The Rose Cottage

24 Worcester Street, Routes 12 and 140, 01583
(508) 835-4034

Enjoy the quiet elegance of a 19th-century cottage and furnishings with wide-board floors, marble fireplaces, gaslight hanging lamps, and gabled roof. The Rose Cottage offers five lovely guest rooms and an executive three-room apartment. There is also a music room that is ideal for daytime meetings. Air-conditioned.

welcome; 9 Social drinking allowed; 10 Tennis available; 11 Swimming available; 12 Golf available; 13 Skiing available; 14 May be booked through travel agents

Hosts: Michael and Loretta Kittredge
Rooms: 5 (1 PB; 4 S2B) $65
Apartment: 1 (PB) $65
Full Breakfast
Credit Cards: None
Notes: 2, 5, 8, 10, 11, 12, 13, 14

WINDSOR

Windfields Farm

Bush Road, Rural Route 1, Box 170
Cummington, 01026
(413) 684-3786 before 9 P.M.

A highland homestead up a dirt road with trails to hike or ski, swimming pond, blueberry pastures, organic gardens, and solar greenhouses. The secluded 1830 farmhouse provides guests with a separate entrance to their own quarters; a book-lined livingroom with stereo, piano, and stone fireplace; dining room; and two spacious corner bedrooms with shared bath. Family antiques, paintings, and fresh flowers throughout. Breakfast features homegrown eggs, maple syrup, and raspberry breads and jams. Walk to nearby state forest and waterfall. Near Tanglewood. Two-night minimum stay most weekends.

Hosts: Carolyn and Arnold Westwood
Rooms: 2 (SB) $60
Full Breakfast
Credit Cards: None
Notes: 2, 9, 11, 13

YARMOUTHPORT

Bed and Breakfast Cape Cod #63

Box 341, West Hyannisport, 02672
(508) 775-2772

This Georgian Colonial-style house features the characteristic columns of the period and offers an interesting variety of beds. The decor is primarily Victorian. $65-95.

NOTES: Credit cards accepted: A Master Card; B Visa; C American Express; D Discover Card; E Diners Club; F Other;
2 Personal checks accepted; 3 Lunch available; 4 Dinner available; 5 Open all year; 6 Pets welcome; 8 Children

Michigan

BIG BAY

Big Bay Lighthouse Bed and Breakfast
3 Lighthhouse Road, 49808
(906) 345-9957

This 1896 brick, working lighthouse, on the National Register of Historic Places, is on the craggy photogenic shore of Lake Superior. Surrounded by 100 wooded acres with two and one-half miles of groomed trails and pristine nature path, it has a livingroom, fireplace, library, and a ghost. The home is chock-full of art and history, with unrestricted use of the tower 120 feet above the lake. Packages with Huron Mountain Waterfall tours, canyons, panoramic vistas, hiking, and biking.

Hosts: Marilyn and Buck Gotschall
Rooms: 6 (4 PB; 2 SB) $95-165
Continental Breakfast
Credit Cards: None
Notes: 2, 9, 10, 11, 14

CADILLAC

Hermann's European Inn
214 North Mitchell Street, 49601
(616) 775-9563

This restored early-1900s inn is above Hermann's European Cafe and Chef's Deli. All the amenities have a European flair. Parking is available, and rates include an extensive continental breakfast. Chef Hermann is a certified Austrian pastry chef. Affordable luxuries at a comfortable price.

Host: Hermann Suhs
Rooms: 7 (PB) $50-80

Continental Breakfast
Credit Cards: A, B
Notes: 2, 3, 4, 5, 8, 9, 10, 11, 12, 13, 14

CALUMET

Calumet House
1159 Calumet Avenue, Box 126, 49913
(906) 337-1936

The Calumet House is a typical example of a mining official's home of the 1890s, featuring original woodwork, butler's pantry, and a Victorian bathroom. The home is furnished with antiques. House breakfast specialties incorporate native wild berries into breads and muffins, all homemade. Ethnic foods are also featured.

Hosts: George and Rose Chivses
Rooms: 2 (SB) $30
Full Breakfast
Credit Cards: None
Notes: 2, 5, 10, 11, 12, 13

DEWITT

Griffin House
303 North Bridge Street, 48820
(517) 669-9486

This lovely 1871 house is situated in historic DeWitt, a quiet town with country atmosphere ten miles north of Lansing, just off U.S. 27, the route to Traverse City and the Upper Peninsula. Michigan State University on the scenic Red Cedar River is only 15 minutes away, and the airport is ten minutes away. Canoeing, golfing, and antique shopping are within 15 minutes. Hosts love to travel and enjoy swapping stories.

welcome; 9 Social drinking allowed; 10 Tennis available; 11 Swimming available; 12 Golf available; 13 Skiing available; 14 May be booked through travel agents

Hosts: Phyllis and Roger Griffin
Room: 1 (PB) $50-60
Continental or Full Breakfast
Credit Cards: None
Notes: 2, 9, 12

FENNVILLE

The Kingsley House Bed and Breakfast

626 West Main Street, 49408
(616) 561-6425

This 1886 elegant Queen Anne Victorian was built by the prominent Kingsley family. It has been featured in *Innsider* magazine and selected by *Inn Times* and *Frommers* as one of the top 50 inns in America. Situated near Holland, Saugatuck, South Haven, Allegan State Forest, sandy beaches, cross-country or downhill skiing, bicycling. Beautiful surroundings, family antiques. The honeymoon getaway suite has a whirlpool bath.

Hosts: David and Shirley Witt
Rooms: 7 (PB) $50-125
Full Breakfast
Credit Cards: A, B

FRUITPORT—GRAND HAVEN

Village Park Bed and Breakfast

60 West Park Street, 49415
(616) 865-6289

Overlooking the welcoming waters of Spring Lake and Village Park where guests can picnic, play tennis, or use the boat launch to enjoy Spring Lake with access to Lake Michigan. Pedestrian/bike path, country roads, hiking/ski trails are in the area; Hoffmaster Park is nearby. The inn serves the Grand Haven-Muskegon area. Special wellness weekend package available.

Hosts: John and Virginia Hewett
Rooms: 6 (PB) $50-75
Full Breakfast
Credit Cards: A, B
Notes: 2, 5, 9, 10, 11, 12, 13, 14

The Kingsley House Bed and Breakfast

HOLLAND

The Parsonage 1908

6 East 24th Street, 49423
(616) 396-1316 (9-12 A.M. and 5-9 P.M.)

Experience a charming European-style bed and breakfast home situated in a beautiful residential neighborhood near Hope College and Lake Michigan. Holland's first bed and breakfast was built in 1908 as the parsonage for one of the early Dutch churches. Guests who look for history, quality, and pampering will enjoy this bed and breakfast and waking up to a delicious breakfast served in the formal dining room. AAA approved. Featured in *Country Folk Art* magazine March/April 1992.

Hosts: Bonnie, Wendy, Kimberly, and Heather Verwys
Rooms: 4 (2 PB; 2 SB)
Full Breakfast
Credit Card: A
Notes: 2, 5, 8, 9, 10, 11, 12, 13, 14

NOTES: Credit cards accepted: A Master Card; B Visa; C American Express; D Discover Card; E Diners Club; F Other; 2 Personal checks accepted; 3 Lunch available; 4 Dinner available; 5 Open all year; 6 Pets welcome; 8 Children welcome; 9 Social drinking allowed; 10 Tennis available; 11 Swimming available; 12 Golf available; 13 Skiing available; 14 May be booked through travel agents

HOLLY

The Side Porch Bed and Breakfast

120 College Street, 48442
(313) 634-0740

In Holly, known as the village of festivals, is this lovely 1800s Italianate home. The guest rooms are tastefully decorated in country Victorian style with antiques and reproductions. The home is within walking distance of the village where guests may enjoy the quaint shops and gourmet dining. Guests also enjoy an expanded continental breakfast after coffee is served in their rooms.

Hosts: Sally and Dave Eyberse
Rooms: 2 (PB) $55-65
Expanded Continental Breakfast
Credit Cards: A, B
Notes: 2, 9, 10, 11, 12, 13

The Side Porch Bed and Breakfast

HUDSON

Sutton's Weed Farm Bed and Breakfast

18736 Quaker Road, Box 102, 49247
(517) 547-6302; (800) 826-FARM

This farm of 170 acres has been in the same family since it was purchased by Albert Clinton-Weed in 1873. The seven-gabled Victorian house features furnishings collected from five generations. There is a secretary made without nails with poured-glass panes, a rope bed, a spinning wheel, and antique chairs and chests. The fields are planted; the trees, once tapped by the Potawatomi Indians, yield maple syrup.

Hosts: Jack and Barb Sutton
Rooms: 4 (SB) $55
Full Breakfast
Credit Cards: A, B
Notes: 2, 5, 8, 9, 10, 11, 12

LUDINGTON

Bed and Breakfast at Ludington

2458 South Beaune Road, 49431
(616) 843-9768

"Next on the Hesslund farm there was another creek with a log bridge. The creek began as a spring a bit farther west and was called Good Creek, as the water was so good to drink. Here the teams were allowed to stop and rest and take a long cool drink." Plus: 16 acres, hot tub, various trails, toboggan hill, skating pond, and big breakfast. 10 percent discount for successive nights.

Hosts: Grace Schneider and Robert Schneider
Rooms: 3 (2 PB; 1 SB); $40-55
Full Breakfast
Credit Cards: None
Notes: 2, 5, 6, 8, 9, 10, 11, 12, 13, 14

MACKINAC ISLAND

Pine Cottage

Bogan Lane, Box 519, 49757
(906) 847-3820

Situated on Mackinac Island two blocks from the ferry. Go back in time and spend a weekend in this historical setting.

Rooms: 21 (6 PB; 15 SB) $48
Continental Breakfast
Credit Cards: A, B, C, D
Notes: 2, 8

NOTES: Credit cards accepted: A Master Card; B Visa; C American Express; D Discover Card; E Diners Club; F Other; 2 Personal checks accepted; 3 Lunch available; 4 Dinner available; 5 Open all year; 6 Pets welcome; 8 Children

MANISTEE

E. E. Douville House Bed and Breakfast

111 Pine Street, 49660
(616) 723-8654

This 1879 home, with ornate handcarved woodwork, has interior shutters, a soaring staircase, and elaborate archways with original pocket doors. Charming rooms feature antiques and collectibles. The sitting room has a TV. Lake Michigan beaches, fishing, golfing, skiing, historical buildings, Victorian shopping, and restaurants are all within walking distance.

Host: Barbara Johnson
Rooms: 3 (SB) $40-45
Continental Breakfast
Credit Cards: None
Notes: 2, 5, 9, 10, 11, 12, 13

NILES

Yesterdays Inn Bed and Breakfast

518 North Fourth Street, 49120
(616) 683-6079

This elegant Italianate brick home in the historic district has 12-foot ceilings, lace in the windows, antique bedsteads, classical music, and candlelight breakfast on old china with home-baked goodies and homemade fruit sauces and syrups. Close to Lake Michigan beaches, Fernwood Nature and Art Center, Notre Dame University, 15 minutes from South Bend, Indiana airport.

Hosts: Elizabeth and Bob Baker
Rooms: 5 (3 PB; 2 SB) $50-65
Full Breakfast
Credit Cards: A, B, D
Notes: 2, 5, 8, 10, 12, 13, 14

OWOSSO

R&R Ranch

308 East Hibbard Road, 48867
(517) 723-3232 business; (517) 723-2553 home

A newly remodeled farmhouse from the early 1900s, the Rossmans' ranch sits on 150 acres overlooking the Maple River Valley. This home is a must for animal lovers. A large, concrete circle drive and white fences lead to stables for horses and cattle. The area's wildlife includes deer, fox, rabbits, pheasants, quail, and songbirds. A countrylike setting adorns the interior.

Hosts: Carl and Jeanne Rossman
Rooms: 2 (SB) $40-50
Continental Breakfast
Credit Cards: None
Notes: 2, 5, 6, 8, 10, 12, 13

PLAINWELL

The 1882 John Crispe House Bed and Breakfast

404 East Bridge Street, 49080
(616) 685-1293

Museum-quality Victorian elegance on the bank of the Kalamazoo River is situated between Grand Rapids and Kalamazoo on U.S. 131. The John Crispe House is close to some of west Michigan's finest gourmet dining, lakes, golfing, skiing, auto racing, fall color touring, antique shoping, and a 5K-10K run (last weekend in July). Summer theater and musical events are nearby. Air-conditioned.

Hosts: Ormand and Nancy Lefever
Rooms: 5 (3 PB; 2 SB) $55-65
Full Breakfast
Credit Cards: A, B
Notes: 2, 5, 8, 10, 12, 13

SAULT SAINTE MARIE _____

The Water Street Inn
140 Water Street, 49783
(906) 632-1900; (800) 236-1904

This restored 1900s Queen Anne home is graced by Tiffany windows, original woodwork, and Italian marble fireplaces. An aura of quiet elegance prevails. A large wraparound porch beckons guests to sit and watch the freighters on the Saint Mary's River. The Water Street Inn is situated within walking distance of tourist attractions and fine restaurants. Whatever the season, your stay in Sault Sainte Marie will be a special time to remember.

The Water Street Inn

Hosts: Phyllis and Greg Walker
Rooms: 4 (PB) $65-80
Full Breakfast
Credit Cards: A, B
Notes: 2, 5, 9, 12, 13

Minnesota

CALEDONIA

The Inn on the Green
Route 1, Box 205, 55921
(507) 724-2818

Discover the beauty of bluff country at this landmark southern Colonial home situated just one-half mile south of Caledonia on Highways 44 and 76 and overlooking the beautiful Ma Cal Grove Country Club. The wooded country estate offers comfort and luxury in a quiet and serene setting. Many furnishings are handmade, and others are family heirlooms. The handiwork that adorns the inn is available for purchase.

Hosts: Brad and Shelley Jilek
Rooms: 4 (2 PB; 2 SB) $50-65
Full Breakfast
Credit Cards: E
Notes: 2, 5, 8, 9, 10, 11, 12, 13, 14

FERGUS FALLS

Bakketopp Hus Bed and Breakfast
Rural Route 2, Box 187A, 56537
(218) 739-2915

Overlooking Long Lake on a wooded hilltop is Bakketopp Hus Bed and Breakfast. Here guests sleep under a skylight and view the galaxy, sit on the decks at dusk and hear the loons calling, or relax on the patio and enjoy the birds that grace the sunken flower gardens. After a busy day, relax in the spa or in front of the fireplace. Nearby are antique shopping, golfing, hiking, and cross-country skiing at Maplewood State Park.

Hosts: Judy and Dennis Nims
Rooms: 3 (1 PB; 2 SB) $55-85
Full Breakfast
Credit Cards: None
Notes: 2, 5, 8, 9, 10, 11, 12, 13

HIBBING

Adams House Bed and Breakfast
201 East 23rd Street, 55746
(218) 263-9742

This English Tudor-style manor house is situated in the central area of Hibbing. There are many tourist and business areas in the immediate vicinity. Rooms are furnished with chintz and antiques. A lounge with a TV is available, as well as a kitchenette. A little bit of England in northern Minnesota.

Hosts: Merrill and Marlene Widmark
Rooms: 5 (1 PB; 4 SB) $37
Continental Breakfast
Credit Cards: None
Notes: 2, 5, 8, 9, 10, 11, 12, 13

LAKE CITY

The Pepin House Bed and Breakfast
120 South Prairie, 55041
(612) 345-4454

This elegant 1905 Victorian home is situated in the scenic Hiawatha Valley near beautiful Lake Pepin. Three bedrooms have queen beds and are beautifully decorated. There is a carved, open staircase, pocket doors, fireplace, stained-glass windows, and air conditioning. Reservations requested.

welcome; 9 Social drinking allowed; 10 Tennis available; 11 Swimming available; 12 Golf available; 13 Skiing available; 14 May be booked through travel agents

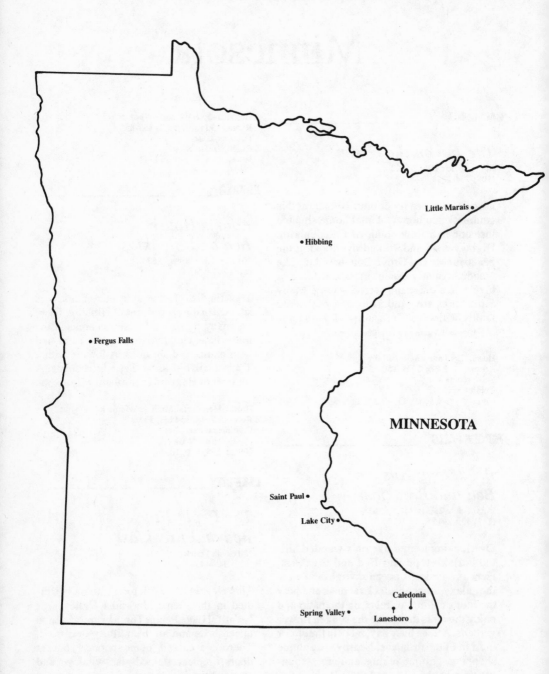

Little Marais •

• Hibbing

• Fergus Falls

MINNESOTA

Saint Paul •

Lake City •

Caledonia

Spring Valley •

Lanesboro

Hosts: Jim and Darlyne Lyons
Rooms: 3 (1 PB; 2 SB) $50-90
Full Breakfast
Credit Cards: A, B, D, E
Notes: 2, 5, 9, 10, 11, 12, 13

LANESBORO

Historic Scanlan House Bed and Breakfast Inn

708 Parkway Avenue South, 55949
(507) 467-2158

This unique 1889 Queen Anne Victorian home was built by the founder of Lanesboro, John Scanlan. It features large luxurious rooms filled with antiques and personal touches, elaborate woodwork, stained-glass windows, fireplaces, and balcony. Complimentary champagne and full gourmet breakfast. Six blocks from historic downtown, paved bike trail, antique shops, winery, sports.

Hosts: Kirsten, Mary, and Gene Mensing
Rooms: 5 (2 PB; 3 SB) $55-90
Full Breakfast
Credit Cards: A, B, C
Notes: 2, 5, 9, 10, 11, 12, 13, 14

Historic Scanlan House Bed and Breakfast Inn

LITTLE MARAIS

The Stone Hearth Inn

1118 Highway 61 East, 56431
(218) 226-3020

Enjoy four unique seasons in a romantic 1920s-style country inn on the shore of Lake Superior. Relax on the old-fashioned front porch or in front of the huge stone fireplace. Guest rooms are uniquely furnished with Old-World antiques. A breakfast of regional cuisine and American favorites is served in the lakeside dining room.

Hosts: Charlie and Susan Michels
Rooms: 5 (PB) $75-85
Full Breakfast
Credit Cards: A, B, C
Notes: 2, 5, 9, 12, 13

SAINT PAUL

Chatsworth Bed and Breakfast

984 Ashland Avenue, 55104
(612) 227-4288

This spacious 1900 Victorian home is a pleasant urban alternative. Its five rooms include two with private double whirlpool baths. It is situated in a quiet residential neighborhood near the governor's mansion with easy access to Interstates 94 and 35. Excellent restaurants and unique shops are within walking distance on Grand Avenue.

Hosts: Donna and Earl Gustafson
Rooms: 5 (3 PB; 2 SB) $60-100
Expanded Continental Breakfast
Credit Cards: None
Notes: 2, 5, 9, 10, 11, 12, 13

SPRING VALLEY

Chase's

508 North Huron Avenue, 55975
(507) 346-2850

NOTES: Credit cards accepted: A Master Card; B Visa; C American Express; D Discover Card; E Diners Club; F Other; 2 Personal checks accepted; 3 Lunch available; 4 Dinner available; 5 Open all year; 6 Pets welcome; 8 Children welcome; 9 Social drinking allowed; 10 Tennis available; 11 Swimming available; 12 Golf available; 13 Skiing available; 14 May be booked through travel agents

This quiet, romantic Victorian mansion has porches and antiques throughout. Near Mystery Cave, Forestville State Park, Meighan Store, Laura Ingalls Wilder sites, Amish areas, hiking and biking trails, trout fishing, and numerous golf courses.

Hosts: Bob and Jeannine Chase
Rooms: 5 (PB) $75
Full Breakfast
Credit Cards: A, B, D
Notes: 2, 9, 10, 11, 12

Chase's

Mississippi

FRENCH CAMP

Lincoln, Ltd. #59
2303 23rd Avenue, P.O. Box 3479, Meridian, 39303
(601) 482-5483; (800) 633-MISS reservations
FAX (601) 679-7747

Enjoy the spacious view of forest and wildlife from the wide windows of this two-story log home. The home was reconstructed from two log cabins more than 100 years old. Awake to a traditional country breakfast and the scent of cypress and sweet pine. Four guest rooms with private baths. $53.

HATTIESBURG

Lincoln, Ltd. #61
2303 23rd Avenue, P.O. Box 3479, Meridian, 39303
(601) 482-5483; (800) 633-MISS reservations
FAX (601) 679-7747

This cottage offers one to three bedrooms, each with a private bath, phone, and TV. The central livingroom has a wood-burning fireplace, library, and VCR. Enjoy fishing or boating in the one and one-half-acre pond, watching the Australian swans, or picnicking beside a mountain laurel-lined creek. Full breakfast; Cajun dinner available with advance reservations. $45-50.

JACKSON

Lincoln, Ltd. #50
2303 23rd Avenue, P.O. Box 3479, Meridian, 39303
(601) 482-5483; (800) 633-MISS reservations
FAX (601) 679-7747

Step through the door and step back across 100 years into a graceful world of sparkling chandeliers and finely crafted furnishings in this 19th-century home. Convenient to Jackson's finest shopping, dining, and entertainment. Eleven guest rooms with private baths. $87-142.

KOSCIUSKO

Lincoln, Ltd. #63
2303 23rd Avenue, P.O. Box 3479, Meridian, 39303
(601) 482-5483; (800) 633-MISS reservations
FAX (601) 679-7747

One of the finest examples of Queen Anne architecture, this historic inn stands as a visual example of the lifestyle and culture of 1884. Four bedrooms furnished with antiques are available. Lunch and dinner are available by reservation. $75.

LONG BEACH

Red Creek Colonial Inn
7416 Red Creek Road, 39560
(601) 452-3080

This circa-1899 three-story raised French cottage with a 64-foot front porch is situated on 11 acres of live oaks and magnolias one and one-half miles south of Interstate 10, Long Beach, Exit 28. Just five miles north of Gulf beaches, this tranquil inn is furnished in Victorian, French, English, and country antiques, including an organ, Victrola, and wooden radios.

Hosts: Philip Hansen and Denise Gazso
Rooms: 7 (5 PB; 2 SB) $44-64
Expanded Continental Breakfast
Credit Cards: A, B
Notes: 2, 5, 8, 9, 10, 11, 12, 14

welcome; 9 Social drinking allowed; 10 Tennis available; 11 Swimming available; 12 Golf available; 13 Skiing available; 14 May be booked through travel agents

Oxford

Slate Springs

French Camp

Kosciusko

Yazoo City

Vicksburg

Jackson

Meridian

Port Gibson

Natchez

Hattiesburg

MISSISSIPPI

Long Beach

MERIDIAN

Lincoln, Ltd. #18

2303 23rd Avenue, P.O. Box 3479, 39303
(601) 482-5483; (800) 633-MISS reservations
FAX (601) 679-7747

In one of Meridian's loveliest neighborhoods, this home is set among flowering shrubs and dogwood trees. Two attractively furnished bedrooms share a bath, perfect for family or four people traveling together. Full breakfast. $55-70.

NATCHEZ

Lincoln, Ltd. #46

2303 23rd Avenue, P.O. Box 3479, Meridian, 39303
(601) 482-5483; (800) 633-MISS reservations
FAX (601) 679-7747

One of the finest examples of early southern plantation-style architecture, this lovely home is situated on a promontory overlooking the Mississippi River. Abounding in history, the antique-filled rooms offer guests a time to relax and enjoy the very room where Jefferson Davis was married in 1845. Thirteen guest rooms, some with private baths. $90-135.

Lincoln, Ltd. #69

2303 23rd Avenue, P.O. Box 3479, Meridian, 39303
(601) 482-5483; (800) 633-MISS reservations
FAX (601) 679-7747

Once owned by the last territorial governor and the first U.S. governor of Mississippi, this home built in 1794 is in the heart of Natchez, one block from Pilgrimage headquarters. Many of the rooms have original 18th-century paneling and are furnished in period antiques. Full breakfast. Five guest rooms $75-85; suite $110.

OXFORD

Lincoln, Ltd. #23

2303 23rd Avenue, P.O. Box 3479, Meridian, 39303
(601) 482-5483; (800) 633-MISS reservations
FAX (601) 679-7747

Built in 1838, this antebellum home is made entirely of native timber and is listed on the National Register of Historic Places. In an attic, 150 years of fashion are displayed on mannequins. Guests can enjoy cakes that are still warm and have breakfast on the balcony on warm mornings. Convenient to the University of Mississippi and the William Faulkner home. $55-70.

PORT GIBSON

Oak Square Plantation

1207 Church Street, 39150
(601) 437-4350; (800) 729-0240

This antebellum mansion in the town General U. S. Grant said was "too beautiful to burn" is listed on the National Register of Historic Places and features heirloom antiques and canopy beds. Beautiful grounds with courtyard, fountain, and gazebo are a fitting complement to this impressive home that exemplifies the grandeur of antebellum days. It has been restored to its original elegance by the present owners.

Hosts: Mr. and Mrs. William Lum
Rooms: 9 (PB) $75-95
Full Breakfast
Credit Cards: A, B, C, D
Notes: 2, 5, 8, 9, 10, 11, 12

SLATE SPRINGS

Lincoln, Ltd. #65

2303 23rd Avenue, P.O. Box 3479, Meridian, 39303
(601) 482-5483; (800) 633-MISS reservations
FAX (601) 679-7747

NOTES: Credit cards accepted: A Master Card; B Visa; C American Express; D Discover Card; E Diners Club; F Other; 2 Personal checks accepted; 3 Lunch available; 4 Dinner available; 5 Open all year; 6 Pets welcome; 8 Children welcome; 9 Social drinking allowed; 10 Tennis available; 11 Swimming available; 12 Golf available; 13 Skiing available; 14 May be booked through travel agents

Circa 1890, this lovely farmhouse with curved staircase has been restored to its present beauty with half-tester Victorian beds and heirloom antiques. Walk the 150-acre farm with its beautiful wildflowers, colorful birds, and trees. Enjoy a full southern breakfast and a full-course dinner (included in price). Three guest rooms. $110-125.

Cedar Grove Mansion

VICKSBURG

Cedar Grove Mansion
2300 Washington Street
Mailing address: P. O. Box B, 39181
(800) 862-1300; (800) 448-2820 Mississippi

Cedar Grove was built by John A. Klein as a wedding present to his bride. Since then, it has established itself as a well-known bed and breakfast throughout the South and the United States. The grounds, furnishings, and staff provide guests with a feeling of comfort and enjoyment. All accommodations are furnished in period pieces and contain modern conveniences.

Host: Ted Mackey
Rooms: 20 (PB) $95-145
Full Breakfast
Credit Cards: A, B, C
Notes: 2, 5, 8, 9, 10, 11, 12

Lincoln, Ltd. #27
2303 23rd Avenue, P.O. Box 3479, Meridian, 39303
(601) 482-5483; (800) 633-MISS reservations
FAX (601) 679-7747

True southern hospitality is found in this Federal-style home. History combines with modern amenities, including a hot tub and a swimming pool. Eleven antique-filled guest rooms. A full plantation-style breakfast is served in the formal dining room. A tour of the home and a welcoming beverage are included. $75-115.

Lincoln, Ltd. #32
2303 23rd Avenue, P.O. Box 3479, Meridian, 39303
(601) 482-5483; (800) 633-MISS reservations
FAX (601) 679-7747

Situated on six acres, this outstanding home designed in the Federal style hosts exquisite milled woodwork, sterling silver doorknobs, French bronze chandeliers, and a lonely ghost. Three guest rooms all furnished with antiques. A tour of the home, plantation breakfast, and mint juleps included. $85.

Lincoln, Ltd. #35
2303 23rd Avenue, P.O. Box 3479, Meridian, 39303
(601) 482-5483; (800) 633-MISS reservations
FAX (601) 679-7747

Circa 1873, this home was built as a wedding present from father to daughter. An interesting mixture of Victorian and Greek Revival architectural styles. The home is listed on the National Register of Historic Places and offers six guest rooms with private baths. Some have fireplaces and TVs. $75-130.

Lincoln, Ltd. #36
2303 23rd Avenue, P.O. Box 3479, Meridian, 39303
(601) 482-5483; (800) 633-MISS reservations
FAX (601) 679-7747

This lavish antebellum mansion was built between 1840 and 1858 and offers *Gone with the Wind* elegance. The home is exquisitely furnished with many original antiques. Enjoy the beautiful formal gardens, gazebos, and fountains. Relax in the courtyard. Pool and spa are available. Seventeen guest rooms. $75-140.

YAZOO CITY _____

Lincoln, Ltd. #70

2303 23rd Avenue, P.O. Box 3479, Meridian, 39303
(601) 482-5483; (800) 633-MISS reservations
FAX (601) 679-7747

Step back into history and walk among azaleas and spectacular day lilies. This plantation home was built in 1860 with four bedrooms that are tastefully decorated with period antiques. Relax in two gazebos and enjoy a panoramic view of the entire front garden from the sitting room. A full breakfast and plantation dinner are included. $90-110.

MISSOURI

- Independence
Kansas City

- Mexico

Saint Louis •

- Osage Beach
  - Camdenton

Sainte Genevieve•

- Springfield   Jackson •
- Carthage

- Branson
          • Point Lookout

Missouri

Gaines Landing Bed and Breakfast

521 West Atlantic Street, P. O. Box 1369, 65616
(800) 825-3145

This contemporary home within easy walking distance of downtown Branson and Lake Taneycomo features a suite with private entrance and hot tub, two rooms on the lower level with private entrances, large patio, hot tub, and swimming pool. Full breakfast is served in the formal dining room or on the deck overlooking the pool and patio. Complimentary refreshments upon arrival.

Host: Jeanne Gaines
Rooms: 3 (PB) $65-90
Full Breakfast
Credit Cards: None
Notes: 2, 5, 9, 11, 14

Ozark Mountain Country #106

Box 295, 65616
(417) 334-4720; (800) 695-1546

Up the hill from Table Rock Lake are accommodations with a view of the lake, near marina and swimming area. $35-40.

Ozark Mountain Country #107

Box 295, 65616
(417) 334-4720; (800) 695-1546

Two blocks from Table Rock Lake with easy access to Silver Dollar City. Special breakfast on weekends. $50.

Ozark Mountain Country #111

Box 295, 65616
(417) 334-4720; (800) 695-1546

This 1800s suite has a private entrance and an antique, four-poster bed and unique decor. Sitting area has leather furnishings. The English Garden suite has Victorian furnishings. Smoking permitted on deck. $50-65.

Ozark Mountain Country #116

Box 295, 65616
(417) 334-4720; (800) 695-1546

On Indian Point two miles from Silver Dollar City, enjoy a lake-view guest suite and a full breakfast with homemade breads. Smoking on patio. $55.

Ozark Mountain Country #117

Box 295, 65616
(417) 334-4720; (800) 695-1546

This bed and breakfast is on Indian Point three miles from Silver Dollar City. Great room and fireplace are available, along with a lake-view deck. $45-85.

NOTES: Credit cards accepted: A Master Card; B Visa; C American Express; D Discover Card; E Diners Club; F Other; 2 Personal checks accepted; 3 Lunch available; 4 Dinner available; 5 Open all year; 6 Pets welcome; 8 Children welcome; 9 Social drinking allowed; 10 Tennis available; 11 Swimming available; 12 Golf available; 13 Skiing available; 14 May be booked through travel agents

Ozark Mountain Country #118

Box 295, 65616
(417) 334-4720; (800) 695-1546

Charming, contemporary accommodations with suite or rooms available. Guests enjoy fireplace, microwave, gas grill, picnic table. $65-90.

Ozark Mountain Country #126

Box 295, 65616
(417) 334-4720; (800) 695-1546

This contemporary home has a view of Table Rock Lake. Full gourmet breakfast with homemade breads. Smoking permitted on porch. $50.

Ozark Mountain Country #128

Box 295, 65616
(417) 334-4720; (800) 695-1546

In the Shell Knob area on Table Rock Lake, enjoy 2,000 square feet of deck overlooking the lake, petting zoo, row boat, and swimming area. Smoking permitted on deck. $55.

CAMDENTON

Ozark Mountain Country #203

Box 295, Branson, 65616
(417) 334-4720; (800) 695-1546

Fifty feet from the Lake of the Ozarks. Hearty continental breakfast. $40.

Ozark Mountain Country #207

Box 295, Branson, 65616
(417) 334-4720; (800) 695-1546

Two guest rooms with hall bath. Full hearty breakfast in the dining room. Smoking permitted on deck. $40.

CARTHAGE

Brewer's Maple Lane Farm Bed and Breakfast

Rural Route 1, Box 203, 64836
(417) 358-6312

On the National Register of Historic Places, this Victorian home has 20 rooms furnished with family heirlooms. One of many detailed features shines through in the 200 hand-turned staircase spindles leading to the third floor. The 240-acre farm is ideal for family vacations and campers, with fishing, hunting, barnyard animals, playground. Nearby are artist Lowell Davis, Red Oak II, and Butcher's Precious Moments Chapel.

Hosts: Arch and Renee Brewer
Rooms: 4 (SB) $45
Expanded Continental Breakfast
Credit Cards: None
Notes: 2, 5, 8, 10, 11, 12

Hill House

1157 South Main, 64836
(417) 358-6145

Hill House is a brick Victorian mansion, circa 1887, with ten fireplaces, stained glass, and pocket doors. Unusual antiques are on display. Guest rooms have antique furniture and feather beds. Situated five miles from Precious Moments Chapel and Red Oak II. Breakfast features home-baked muffins,

---

NOTES: Credit cards accepted: A Master Card; B Visa; C American Express; D Discover Card; E Diners Club; F Other; 2 Personal checks accepted; 3 Lunch available; 4 Dinner available; 5 Open all year; 6 Pets welcome; 8 Children

doughnuts, waffles, specialty jams, fruit, juice, bacon. An antique and gift shop is on the third floor.

Hosts: Dean and Ella Mae Scoville
Rooms: 4 (PB) $40
Full Breakfast
Credit Cards: None
Notes: 2, 5, 10, 11, 12

INDEPENDENCE

Woodstock Inn Bed and Breakfast
1212 West Lexington, 64050
(816) 833-2233

Woodstock Inn is located in the heart of historic Independence and close to the Truman library and home, historic mansions, sports stadiums, theme parks, and Latter Day Saints centers. The new, architecturally unique Reformed Latter Day Saints temple is two blocks from the inn and open to the public. Eleven guest rooms are tastefully furnished and air conditioned. Excellent food, private parking, personalized touring directions.

Hosts: Ben and Mona Crosby; Lane and Ruth Harold
Rooms: 11 (PB) $45-65
Full Breakfast
Credit Cards: A, B
Notes: 5, 8, 9

JACKSON

Trisha's Bed and Breakfast
203 Bellevue, 63755
(314) 243-7427

Welcome to southern hospitality at its finest just four miles off Interstate 55 near Cape Girardeau. Gourmet breakfasts accented with fruits have become a trademark. Hosts are volunteers with a historic steam train only three blocks away. Enjoy a 1905 Victorian home furnished with antiques and full of charm.

Hosts: Gus and Trisha Wischmann
Rooms: 4 (3 PB; 1 SB) $55-65
Full Breakfast
Credit Cards: None

Hill House

KANSAS CITY

Milford House
3605 Gillham Road, 64111
(816) 753-1269

Guest rooms at Milford House are reached by climbing the 100-year-old spiral staircase enclosed in the Queen Anne tower. Rooms are decorated with many personal touches. Downstairs parlors feature a woodburning fireplace and baby grand piano, and the game room is available with a pool table, dart board, and exercise equipment. Centrally situated, it is five minutes from both Crown Center and the Plaza.

Hosts: Ian and Pat Mills
Rooms: 4 (PB) $75-85
Full Breakfast weekends; Continental weekdays
Credit Cards: A, B, C
Notes: 2, 5, 9, 10, 14

Ozark Mountain Country #131
Box 295, Branson, 65616
(417) 334-4720; (800) 695-1546

welcome; 9 Social drinking allowed; 10 Tennis available; 11 Swimming available; 12 Golf available; 13 Skiing available; 14 May be booked through travel agents

This quaint farmhouse was built in 1987. A honeymoon suite is available with a private entrance and Jacuzzi. $45-65.

MEXICO

Hylas House Bed and Breakfast

811 South Jefferson, 65265
(314) 581-2011

Quality service and warm hospitality are the first priorities of this inn featuring Italianate architecture, unique scroll work, mantels of cherubs, antique fireplaces, cherry wood, and white carpeting. One suite and three rooms have phones, stereo remote cable TV, and VCR. Popular with romantics.

Hosts: Tom and Linda Hylas
Rooms: 4 (1 PB; 3 SB) $55-95
Full Breakfast
Credit Cards: A, B
Notes: 2, 4, 5, 8 (over eight), 9, 10, 12, 14

OSAGE BEACH

Ozark Mountain Country #228

Box 295, Branson, 65616
(417) 334-4720; (800) 695-1546

Contemporary lakeside home with a sitting area and fireplace. Smoking allowed on decks. $60.

POINT LOOKOUT

Cameron Crag

P.O. Box 526, 65726

Enjoy a spectacular view high on a bluff overlooking Lake Taneycomo and valley. Two suites with private bath, deck, TV/VCR are available. There is also a guest room with private bath and TV where school-age children are welcome. Dinner is avail-

able for guest staying three nights in a suite. Three miles south of Branson.

Host: Kay Cameron
Rooms: 3 (PB) $50-85
Full Breakfast
Credit Cards: A, B, C
Notes: 2, 4, 5, 8 (over 6), 14

Hylas House Bed and Breakfast

SAINTE GENEVIEVE

Southern Hotel

146 South Third Street, 63670
(800) 275-1412

Step gently into the time when riverboats plied the mighty Mississippi and weary travelers looked forward to the hospitality of this famous hotel. This graceful Federal building operated as a hotel from the 1820s and was known for the finest accommodations, fine food, busy gambling rooms, and the first pool hall west of the Mississippi. A total renovation has restored this magnificent inn.

Hosts: Mike and Barbara Hankins
Rooms: 8 (PB) $65-105
Full Breakfast
Credit Cards: A, B
Notes: 2, 5, 9

SAINT LOUIS—SEE ALSO LENEXA, KANSAS

The Winter House

3522 Arsenal Street, 63118
(314) 664-4399

This ten-room 1897 Victorian features a pressed tin ceiling in the lower bedroom and a suite on the second floor. Fresh-squeezed orange juice is always served for breakfast in the dining room using crystal and antique china. Tea is served with live piano music available by reservation.

Hosts: Sarah and Kendall Winter
Rooms: 2 (PB) $52-65
Expanded Continental Breakfast
Credit Cards: A, B, C, E
Notes: 2, 5, 8, 9, 10, 11, 12, 14

SPRINGFIELD

Ozark Mountain Country #202

Box 295, Branson, 65616
(417) 334-4720; (800) 695-1546

This authentic Victorian home is furnished and accessorized with antiques. One guest room is on the main floor, three are upstairs. $35.

Ozark Mountain Country #206

Box 295, Branson, 65616
(417) 334-4720; (800) 695-1546

Take a step back in time into this 1894 mansion in the historic district. It has been redecorated with antiques and stained glass. Smoking permitted on veranda. $70-95.

Ozark Mountain Country #211

Box 295, Branson, 65616
(417) 334-4720; (800) 695-1546

This charming country home full of antiques is four miles south of Springfield and features antique china and queen canopy bed. $55.

Ozark Mountain Country #216

Box 295, Branson, 65616
(417) 334-4720; (800) 695-1546

An 1867 farmhouse features antiques, parlor, and sitting room for guest use. A country breakfast is served. Smoking permitted on porch. $40.

Ozark Mountain Country #221

Box 295, Branson, 65616
(417) 334-4720; (800) 695-1546

A traditional home on a private lake near Kansas City features balcony and library. Smoking permitted on patio. $55.

Ozark Mountain Country #222

Box 295, Branson, 65616
(417) 334-4720; (800) 695-1546

An 1896 Victorian with antiques and next to an antique shop. Shared hall bath. Smoking permitted on porches. $35.

Ozark Mountain Country #231

Box 295, Branson, 65616
(417) 334-4720; (800) 695-1546

This charming reproduction Victorian house is within walking distance of Mount Vernon's historic town square. Bridal suite available. Smoking permitted on patio. $55-70.

welcome; 9 Social drinking allowed; 10 Tennis available; 11 Swimming available; 12 Golf available; 13 Skiing available; 14 May be booked through travel agents

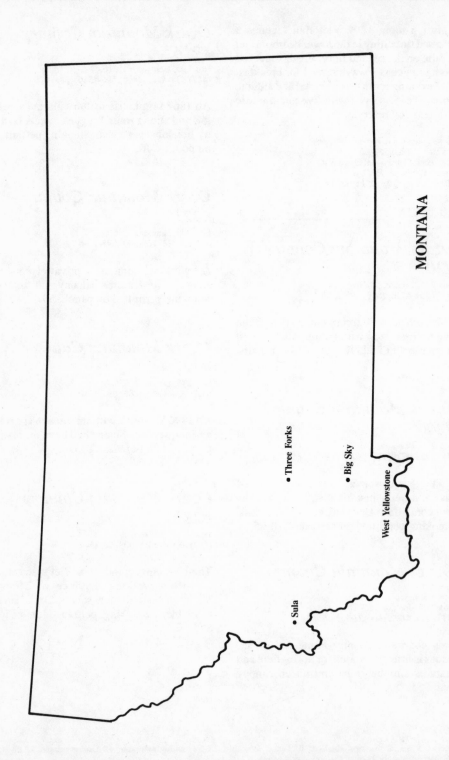

MONTANA

Three Forks

Big Sky

West Yellowstone

Sula

Montana

BIG SKY

Lone Mountain Ranch
P. O. Box 69, 59716
(406) 995-4451

Enjoy comfortable ranch cabin accommodations nestled in a secluded valley. Horseback riding, Yellowstone Park interpretive trips, ORVIS-endorsed fly fishing, kids' activities, nature hikes in summer, cross-country skiing, sleigh-ride dinner, Yellowstone ski tours in winter. The ranch features nationally acclaimed cuisine in spectacular log dining lodge. All meals included in weekly rate.

Hosts: Bob and Vivian Schaap
Rooms: 23 (PB) $850-1075 per week
Full Breakfast
Credit Cards: A, B
Notes: 2, 3, 4, 8, 9, 10, 11, 12, 13

SULA

Camp Creek Inn Bed and Breakfast Guest Ranch
7674 Highway 93 South, 59871
(406) 821-3508

Camp Creek Inn was one of the original homesteads and a stage stop in the Sula Basin in southwestern Montana. The 120-acre ranch is surrounded by the Bitterroot National Forest and is near the Selway Bitterroot and Anaconda Pintlar Wilderness areas. Guided horseback rides and stalls for guest horses are available at additional charge. Nearby river float trips, hiking, hunting, downhill and cross-country skiing are available.

Host: Sandy
Rooms: 3 (2 PB; 1 SB) $50-55
Full Breakfast
Credit Cards: None
Notes: 2, 3, 4, 5, 8, 9, 11, 13

THREE FORKS

Sacajawea Inn
5 North Main Street, P. O. Box 648, 59752
(406) 285-6934

A registered national landmark since 1978. Peace and history abound in this gracious old railroad hotel built in 1910. A warm Montana welcome awaits guests who enjoy nostalgic, comfortable guest rooms and fine dining. Just minutes from blue ribbon trout streams, Lewis and Clark caverns, hunting, and canoeing. Or just relax on the porch in a rocking chair.

Hosts: Jane and Smith Roedel
Rooms: 34 (PB) $40-85
Expanded Continental Breakfast
Credit Cards: A, B, C, D
Notes: 2, 4, 5, 6 (limited), 8, 9, 12, 13, 14

Lone Mountain Ranch

NOTES: Credit cards accepted: A Master Card; B Visa; C American Express; D Discover Card; E Diners Club; F Other; 2 Personal checks accepted; 3 Lunch available; 4 Dinner available; 5 Open all year; 6 Pets welcome; 8 Children welcome; 9 Social drinking allowed; 10 Tennis available; 11 Swimming available; 12 Golf available; 13 Skiing available; 14 May be booked through travel agents

WEST YELLOWSTONE _____

Sportsman's High
750 Deer Street, 59758
(406) 646-7865

This spacious country-style home with spectacular views and wraparound porch sits on three acres of aspen and pines. Abundant wildlife includes varieties of birds, moose, deer, squirrels, and chipmunks. Situated eight miles from the west entrance to Yellowstone National Park. Guest rooms have been lovingly decorated with country colors, fabrics, and antiques. Feather pillows, terry robes, and hot tub are just a few of the amenities.

Hosts: Diana and Gary Baxter
Rooms: 5 (3 PB; 2 SB) $50-75
Full Breakfast
Credit Cards: A, B
Notes: 2, 5, 14

Nebraska

GRAND ISLAND

Kirschke House
1124 West Third Street, 68801
(308) 381-6851

Enjoy and experience yesterday today! A 1902 Victorian home decorated in period furnishings and antiques. A wooden hot tub adds to the Old World charm in the lantern-lit brick wash house.

Host: Lois Hank
Rooms: 4 (SB) $45-55
Full Breakfast
Credit Cards: A, B
Notes: 2, 5, 9, 14

PAWNEE CITY

My Blue Heaven Bed and Breakfast
1041 Fifth Street, 68420
(402) 852-3131; (402) 852-9914

Conversation, relaxation, and a quiet place to sleep will be found here. There are three places to dine in Pawnee City in the evenings. Arrangements can be made to tour the 15-building museum. Directions can be obtained to the three lakes 15 minutes away where you can fish, water ski, and swim. Just a few blocks from shopping, two city parks, a sand greens golf course, municipal swimming pool, pet hospital, and an airport. Two rooms are decorated with antiques, tatting, quilts for your enjoyment.

Hosts: Duane and Yvonne Dalluge
Rooms: 2 (SB) $30-35
Full Breakfast
Credit Cards: A, B
Notes: 2, 5, 10, 11, 12

welcome; 9 Social drinking allowed; 10 Tennis available; 11 Swimming available; 12 Golf available; 13 Skiing available; 14 May be booked through travel agents

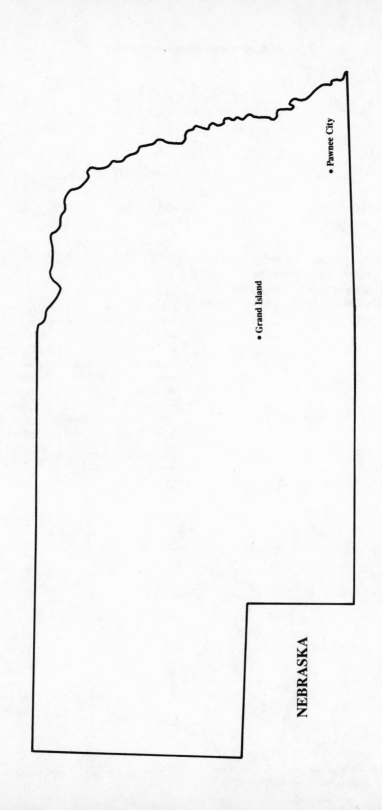

Grand Island

• Pawnee City

NEBRASKA

Nevada

CARSON CITY

Deer Run Ranch
Bed and Breakfast
5440 Eastlake, 89704
(702) 882-3643

Guests enjoy informal western ambience in a unique architect-designed and built ranch house on spacious grounds situated between Reno and Carson City and just minutes from Virginia City, Lake Tahoe's skiing and summer fun, and many great restaurants. Two hundred acres include pond with boat (summer), skating (winter), above-ground pool, and lots of privacy.

Hosts: David and Muffy Vhay
Rooms: 2 (PB) $75-85
Full Breakfast
Credit Cards: A, B
Notes: 2, 5, 9, 11, 12, 13

RENO

Bed and Breakfast
South Reno
136 Andrew Lane, 89511
(702) 849-0772

This ranch home decorated in Early American antiques with four-poster beds and beamed ceilings is surrounded by unbroken vistas of Mount Rose and Slide Mountain, over 10,000 feet high. Reno, full of showrooms, casinos, and all dining possibilities, is only ten miles away. Lake Tahoe is an easy drive, and Virginia City is just over the hill. Discount for a two-night stay.

Host: Caroline S. Walters
Rooms: 3 (2 PB; 1 SB) $64-74
Full Breakfast
Credit Cards: C
Notes: 2, 5, 8, 9, 10, 11, 12, 13, 14

Deer Run Ranch Bed and Breakfast

NOTES: Credit cards accepted: A Master Card; B Visa; C American Express; D Discover Card; E Diners Club; F Other; 2 Personal checks accepted; 3 Lunch available; 4 Dinner available; 5 Open all year; 6 Pets welcome; 8 Children welcome; 9 Social drinking allowed; 10 Tennis available; 11 Swimming available; 12 Golf available; 13 Skiing available; 14 May be booked through travel agents

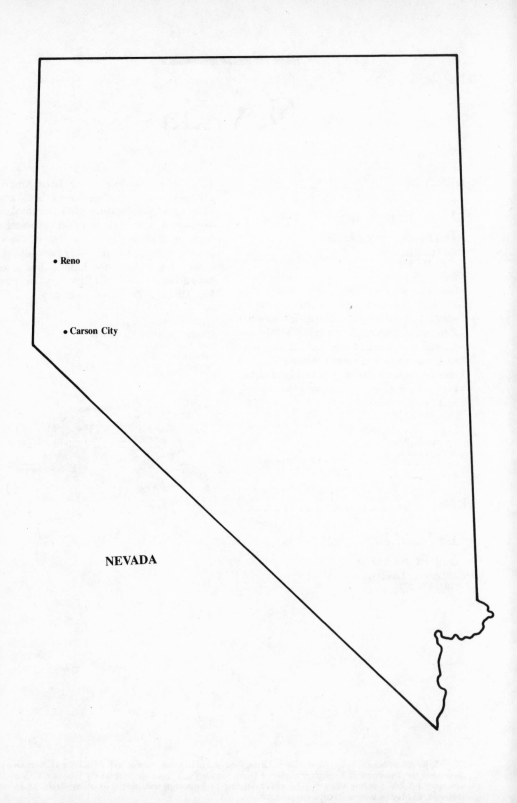

• Reno

• Carson City

NEVADA

New Hampshire

Amber Lights Inn
Bed and Breakfast

Rural Free Delivery 1, Box 828, 03223
(603) 726-4077

The newest bed and breakfast in the White Mountains in Thornton, this lovingly restored 1815 Colonial offers a sumptuous six-course breakfast, homemade bread and muffins like Grandma made, queen country beds with handmade quilts, meticulously clean guest rooms, Hannah Adams dining room with fireplace, guest library, and garden room. Hors d'oeuvres served nightly. Conveniently situated between Loon Mountain and Waterville Valley.

Hosts: Paul V. Sears and Carola L. Warnsman
Rooms: 5 (1 PB; 4 SB) $55-70
Full Breakfast
Credit Cards: A, B, D
Notes: 2, 5, 8, 9, 10, 11, 12, 13, 14

Goddard Mansion Bed and Breakfast

Mountain-Fare Inn

Mad River Road, P. O. Box 553, 03223
(603) 726-4283

Truly a country cottage and charming in style, Mountain-Fare is host to the year-round beauty of the White Mountains. Find both peace and exhilaration. Explore, hike, bike, ski. Specializing in small groups (20), family reunions, guided hikes, dinner.

Hosts: Susan and Nick Preston
Rooms: 8 (5 PB; 3 SB) $48-64
Full Breakfast
Credit Cards: None
Notes: 2, 4, 5, 8, 9, 10, 11, 12, 13, 14

The Lavender Flower Inn

Main Street, P.O. Box 328, 03813
(800) 729-0106

The inn is a newly restored 1840 farmhouse at the foot of the White Mountains, furnished with a mix of Victorian and country antiques. Floral and herb gardens dress out the two acres in the warmer seasons, with cross-country skiing available in the winter. A full country breakfast is always offered.

Hosts: Noreen and Ray Berthiaume
Rooms: 8 (4 PB; 4 SB) $45-95
Full Breakfast
Credit Cards: B, C, D
Notes: 2, 5, 8, 10, 11, 12, 13, 14

Goddard Mansion
Bed and Breakfast

25 Hillstead Road, 03743
(603) 543-0603; (800) 736-0603

Delightful, beautifully restored, early-1900s English manor-style 18-room mansion with

NOTES: Credit cards accepted: A Master Card; B Visa; C American Express; D Discover Card; E Diners Club; F Other; 2 Personal checks accepted; 3 Lunch available; 4 Dinner available; 5 Open all year; 6 Pets welcome; 8 Children welcome; 9 Social drinking allowed; 10 Tennis available; 11 Swimming available; 12 Golf available; 13 Skiing available; 14 May be booked through travel agents

NEW HAMPSHIRE

• Jefferson

• Franconia

Jackson
•

• Glen

North Conway •

Center Conway •
•

Wentworth • • Campton

Plymouth • • Holderness

Mirror Lake
•

East Andover
•

• Claremont • North Sutton

Portsmouth •

• Marlborough

• Wilton Center   Hampton Beach •

New Ipswich
•

expansive porches and tea house. Situated on seven acres with panoramic mountain views. Eight guest rooms, including a bridal suite, are available. A full, natural breakfast starts each day. Four-season activities are nearby.

Hosts: Frank and Debbie Albee
Rooms: 8 (2 PB; 6 SB) $65-95
Full Breakfast
Credit Cards: A, B, D, E
Notes: 2, 5, 8, 9, 10, 11, 12, 13

EAST ANDOVER

The Patchwork Inn

Maple Street, P.O. Box 107, 03231
(603) 735-6426

This 1805 Colonial farmhouse has been restored and furnished with antique and country furniture, pewter pieces, and braided rugs. Guest rooms overlook Highland Lake and Mount Kearsarge. Close to downhill and cross-country skiing; walk to the beach; near White Mountain attractions. The common room features fireplaces and piano. Breakfast includes cheese strata, baked eggs, French toast, waffles or pancakes, and maple syrup from trees on the premises.

Hosts: Brad and Ethelyn Sherman
Rooms: 7 (3 PB; 4 SB) $50-65
Full Breakfast
Credit Cards: A, B
Notes: 2, 5, 8, 9, 10, 11, 12, 13, 14

FRANCONIA

Blanche's Bed and Breakfast

351 Easton Valley Road, 03580
(603) 823-7061

A century-old farmhouse restored to a glory it probably never had, the inn is set in the Easton Valley and looks up on the Kinsman Ridge, a section of the Appalachian Trail. In the English tradition, the inn offers cotton linens and a breakfast that will get most

people through lunch. There is decorative painting throughout. Gather 'round the wood-burning stove for live folk music or storytelling.

Hosts: Brenda Shannon and John Vail
Rooms: 5 (1 PB; 4 SB) $55-85
Full Breakfast
Credit Cards: None
Notes: 2, 4 (for groups), 5, 8, 9, 10, 11, 12, 13

Bungay Jar
Bed and Breakfast

Easton Valley Road, P.O. Box 15, 03580
(603) 823-7775

Five miles south of Franconia in Robert Frost's Easton Valley. Guests are greeted by a crackling fire and the aroma of mulled cider and homemade snacks in this home built from a century-old barn. Four large guest rooms include king canopy bed with antiques throughout. Sauna and balconies with mountain views on eight private, wooded acres.

Hosts: Kate Kerivan and Lee Strimbeck
Rooms: 6 (4 PB; 2 SB) $60-105
Full Breakfast
Credit Cards: A, B, C
Notes: 2, 5, 9, 10, 11, 12, 13

Lovetts' Inn by
Lafayette Brook

Route 18, Profile Road, 03580
(603) 823-7761; (800) 356-3802

Lovetts' is a charming 1784 inn listed in the National Register of Historic Places with beautifully appointed rooms with antiques. Also cottages, some with fireplaces. Situated at the head of Franconia Notch, there is excellent sightseeing, hiking, biking, walking tours, and photography trips. Both downhill and cross-country skiing on the premises. A three-star restaurant offers great country food.

NOTES: Credit cards accepted: A Master Card; B Visa; C American Express; D Discover Card; E Diners Club; F Other; 2 Personal checks accepted; 3 Lunch available; 4 Dinner available; 5 Open all year; 6 Pets welcome; 8 Children welcome; 9 Social drinking allowed; 10 Tennis available; 11 Swimming available; 12 Golf available; 13 Skiing available; 14 May be booked through travel agents

Hosts: Anthony and Sharon Avrutine
Rooms: 30 (22 PB; 8 SB) $40-146
Full Breakfast
Credit Cards: A, B, C
Notes: 2, 9, 10, 11, 12, 13

Sugar Hill Inn

Route 117, 03580
(603) 823-5621; (800) 548-4748

A welcoming 18th-century farmhouse
nestled in the White Mountains has
antique-filled guest rooms with magnificent mountain views. Enjoy superb dining
and country breakfasts served by the hearth
in an unhurried setting. Situated minutes
from Franconia State Park with all its attractions. Golf, hike, swim, or tennis nearby.

Hosts: Jim and Barbara Quinn
Rooms: 10 (PB) $90-125
Full Breakfast
Credit Cards: A, B
Notes: 2, 4, 10, 11, 12, 13, 14

GLEN

The Bernerhof Inn

Route 302, P.O. Box 240, 03838
(603) 383-4414

An elegant, small hotel in the foothills of the
White Mountains. Deluxe accommodations feature antique-filled rooms, many
with private spa tubs. Enjoy the European-
style taproom or savor the chef's virtuoso
skills featuring Central European classics,
such as wiener schnitzel and emince de
veau. The Bernerhof also hosts its renowned
Taste of the Mountains Cooking School.
Operating each spring, fall, and winter, it
offers weekend, five-day, and daily ses-
sions.

Host: Sharon Wroblewski
Rooms: 10 (8 PB; 2 SB) $75-135
Full Breakfast
Credit Cards: A, B, C
Notes: 2, 3 (summer and fall), 4, 5, 8, 9, 11, 12, 13

Sugar Hill Inn

HAMPTON BEACH

The Oceanside

365 Ocean Boulevard, 03842
(603) 926-3542

The Oceanside overlooks the Atlantic Ocean
and its beautiful sandy beaches. Each of the
ten rooms is tastefully and individually decorated. Many have period antiques, quilts,
and collectibles. The intimate cafe is open
for breakfast during July and August featuring homemade breads and pastries. At other
times a complimentary continental breakfast is served. The inn is within easy walking distance of restaurants, shops, and attractions.

Hosts: Skip and Debbie Windemiller
Rooms: 10 (PB) $80-110
Expanded Continental Breakfast
Credit Cards: A, B, C, D

HOLDERNESS

The Inn on Golden Pond

Route 3, P.O. Box 680, 03245
(603) 968-7269

An impressive country home built in 1879
has grounds spotted with stone walls, antique split-rail fences, and a variety of flowering bushes and shade trees. Nearby is
Squam Lake, the setting for the classic film
On Golden Pond. The inn is known for its
refreshingly friendly yet professional atmosphere. Each room is decorated in traditional country style.

NOTES: Credit cards accepted: A Master Card; B Visa; C American Express; D Discover Card; E Diners Club; F Other;
2 Personal checks accepted; 3 Lunch available; 4 Dinner available; 5 Open all year; 6 Pets welcome; 8 Children

Hosts: Bill and Bonnie Webb
Rooms: 9 (PB) $95-135
Full Breakfast
Credit Cards: A, B, C
Notes: 2, 5, 9, 10, 11, 12, 13, 14

JACKSON

Inn at Thorn Hill

Thorn Hill Road, Box A, 03846
(603) 383-4242; (800) 289-8990

Savor the pleasures of country life amid
Victorian splendor, spectacular views,
antique-filled rooms, and creative cuisine
by candlelight in an inn originally designed
by Stanford White in 1895. Additional accommodations are available in the carriage
house and three cottages. Enjoy the outdoor
pool and air conditioning in the summer;
skiing, sleigh rides, skating, or tobogganing
in the winter.

Hosts: Peter and Linda La Rose
Rooms: 20 (18 PB; 2 SB) $80-162
Full Breakfast
Credit Cards: A, B, C
Notes: 2, 4, 5 (except April), 8 (over 12), 9, 10, 12,
    13, 14

Nestlenook Farm on the River

Dinsmore Road, 03846
(603) 383-9443

Escape into a Victorian past on a 65-acre
estate. Seven elegant rooms with private
Jacuzzis, canopy beds, 19th-century parlor
stoves, unique cuisine, intimate pub, five
working fireplaces. Also gazebo, nightly
bonfires, farm animals, award-winning gardens, year-round Austrian sleigh rides, cross-
country skis and skate rentals and lessons.

Hosts: Robert and Nancy Cyr
Rooms: 7 (PB) $95
Full Breakfast
Credit Cards: A, B
Notes: 5, 9, 10, 11, 12, 13, 14

JEFFERSON

The Jefferson Inn

Route 2, 03583
(603) 586-7998; (800) 729-7908

This charming 1896 Victorian inn near
Mount Washington offers 360-degree mountain views and nightly sunset from the wraparound porch. Excellently situated for outdoor activities, superb hiking, swimming
pond, cycling trails, golf courses, cross-
country and downhill skiing, skating. Afternoon tea served daily. Breakfast is both
hearty and unique.

Hosts: Greg Brown and Bertie Koelewÿn
Rooms: 10 (8 PB; 2 SB) $46-68
Full Breakfast
Credit Cards: A, B, C
Notes: 2, 8, 9, 10, 11, 12, 13, 14

Nestlenook Farm on the River

MARLBOROUGH

Peep-Willow Farm

51 Bixby Street, 03455
(603) 876-3807

A working Thoroughbred horse farm. There
is no riding, but guests may help with chores,
or just watch the horses frolicking in the
fields. There is a beautiful view all the way
to the Connecticut River valley, and cross-
country skiing is nearby.

welcome; 9 Social drinking allowed; 10 Tennis available; 11 Swimming available; 12 Golf available; 13 Skiing
available; 14 May be booked through travel agents

Host: Noel Aderer
Rooms: 3 (SB) $40
Full Breakfast
Credit Cards: None
Notes: 2, 5, 6 (prior arrangement), 8, 9, 10, 11, 12, 13 (XC)

MIRROR LAKE

Pick Point Lodge, Inc.

Windleblo Road, P.O. Box 220, 03853
(603) 569-1338

Pick Point's main lodge is situated on 113 acres of pine forest and one-half mile of the best shoreline that Lake Winnipesaukee offers. The nonsmoking main lodge rooms feature king beds, color cable TV, AM/FM radio. The lodge has a game room, library, main livingroom, and 60-foot deck all with spectacular views of the lake. The resort also features tennis, beach, boats, dock space, walking trails, cookouts.

Host: Jeffrey Newcomb
Rooms: 2 (PB) $105-125
Full Breakfast
Credit Cards: None
Notes: 2, 10, 11, 12, 14

NEW IPSWICH

The Inn at New Ipswich

Porter Hill Road, P.O. Box 208, 03071
(603) 878-3711

The inn is situated at the heart of New England, in New Hampshire's Monadnock region. The 1790 Colonial, with classic red barn, set amid stone walls and fruit trees, heartily welcomes guests. Guest rooms feature firm beds and country antiques. Also featured are wide pine floors and six original fireplaces. Downhill and cross-country skiing, hiking, antique shops, concerts, auctions are all nearby.

Hosts: Steve and Ginny Bankuti
Rooms: 6 (PB) $60
Full Breakfast
Credit Cards: A, B
Notes: 2, 5, 12, 13, 14

NORTH CONWAY

Nereledge Inn

River Road, P.O. Box 547, 03860
(603) 356-2831

Enjoy the charm, hospitality, and relaxation of this small, traditional 1787 inn overlooking Cathedral Ledge. Walk to Seco River and village; close to all activities. A comfortable, casual atmosphere at affordable rates includes delicious breakfast with warm apple pie. The English-style pub is open weekends.

Hosts: Valerie and Dave Halpin
Rooms: 9 (4 PB; 5 SB) $59-85
Full Breakfast
Credit Cards: A, B, C
Notes: 2, 5, 8, 10, 11, 12, 13

The Victorian Harvest Inn

The Victorian Harvest Inn

Locust Lane, Box 1763, 03860
(603) 356-3548

The comfortably elegant inn is at the edge of quaint North Conway village featuring European shops, outlets, and national forest trails. The large, country Victorian-decorated rooms all have mountain views. Start a romantic adventure with a bounteous breakfast and hospitality as it was meant to be. Fireplace, in-ground pool, air conditioning. AAA triple-diamond award.

NOTES: Credit cards accepted: A Master Card; B Visa; C American Express; D Discover Card; E Diners Club; F Other;
2 Personal checks accepted; 3 Lunch available; 4 Dinner available; 5 Open all year; 6 Pets welcome; 8 Children

Hosts: Linda and Robert Dahlberg
Rooms: 6 (4 PB; 2 SB) $55-75
Full Breakfast
Credit Cards: A, B, C
Notes: 2, 5, 8 (over 10), 11, 13

NORTH SUTTON

Follansbee Inn

P. O. Box 92, 03260
(603) 927-4221; (800) 626-4221

This is a great place to take a step into the past. The Follansbee is an authentic 1840 New England inn with a comfortable porch, sitting rooms with fireplaces, and charming antique-furnished bedrooms. It is situated on peaceful Kegas Lake and offers something for all seasons: swimming, boating, hiking, skiing, and golf nearby. The absence of TV and phones reveals the art of conversation and slower pace of living.

Hosts: Dick and Sandy Reilein
Rooms: 23 (11 PB; 12 SB) $70-90
Full Breakfast
Credit Cards: A, B
Notes: 2, 5, 10, 11, 12, 13

PLYMOUTH

Colonel Spencer Inn

Rural Route 1, Box 206, 03264
(603) 536-3438

Colonel Spencer Inn is hosted by college professors interested in antiques, house restoration, and travel. It is a 1764 center-chimney Colonial with antique furnishings, four fireplaces, and views of the Pemigewasset River and White Mountains. Special rates for stays of two or more days. Children and teenagers stay free in room with parents.

Hosts: Carolyn and Alan Hill
Rooms: 7 (PB) $35-75
Full Breakfast
Credit Cards: None
Notes: 2, 5, 8, 9, 10, 11, 12, 13, 14

PORTSMOUTH

The Bow Street Inn

121 Bow Street, 03801
(603) 431-7760

This inn occupies the second floor of a historic brick brewery situated on the Piscataqua River and personifies comfort and charm throughout its ten cozy rooms and bright breakfast nook. Each room has color TV, phone, and air conditioning. The inn shares the building with a performing arts theater, and the convenience adds to a pleasant stay. Situated downtown, it is just a few steps from a number of unusual shops and many restaurants.

Host: Jann Bora
Rooms: 10 (PB) $69-119
Expanded Continental Breakfast
Credit Cards: A, B
Notes: 5, 8, 9, 12

WENTWORTH

Mountain Laurel Inn Bed and Breakfast

Route 25 at 25A, 03282-0147
(603) 764-9600; (800) 338-9986

This 1840 Colonial was built by the prominent Webster family and has romantically appointed, comfortable rooms. Enjoy a leisurely breakfast in the dining room before the day's activities. The inn overlooks the White Mountains and is minutes away from the famous Kancamagus Highway, the Appalachian Trail, major ski areas, excellent fishing, cycling routes, and lakes. Many fine antique shops, restaurants, and specialty shops are nearby.

Hosts: Don and Daine LaBrie
Rooms: 4 (2 PB; 2 SB) $65-75
Full Breakfast
Credit Cards: A, B
Notes: 2, 11, 13

welcome; 9 Social drinking allowed; 10 Tennis available; 11 Swimming available; 12 Golf available; 13 Skiing available; 14 May be booked through travel agents

Stepping Stones Bed and Breakfast

Bennington Battle Trail, 03086
(603) 654-9048

Stepping Stones is owned by a garden designer and weaver. The house is surrounded by pathways through extensive gardens. Breakfast may be served on the garden terrace in summer or in the solar garden room year-round. Working looms, handwoven materials, and a craft collection make interesting furnishings. The cozy livingroom provides good reading, TV, and an atmosphere of civilized quiet.

Host: D. Ann Carlsmith
Rooms: 3 (1 PB; 2 SB) $45-50
Full Breakfast
Credit Cards: None
Notes: 2, 5, 6, 8, 9, 12, 13

New Jersey

Bay Head Harbor Inn
676 Main Avenue, 08742
(908) 899-0767

Originally built in the 1890s, this bed and breakfast has become a comfortable shore home. The inn reflects the hosts' interests in folk art, antiques, and shore living. The decor is country and casual. You'll want to make this your home away from home as the echo of the surf beckons and the sea breezes surround you.

Hosts: Dan and Janice Eskesen
Rooms: 12 (SB) $75-100
Expanded Continental Breakfast
Credit Cards: A, B
Notes: 5, 8, 9, 10, 11, 12

CAPE MAY

The Abbey
34 Guerney Street, 08204
(609) 884-4506

In a national historic landmark city, the Abbey stands out as one of the finest examples of Gothic Revival architecture in the East. Enjoy comfortable bed and sumptuous breakfast, laughter, and fun amid Victorian ambience. One block to the beach, two blocks to the shopping mall, restaurants within easy walking distance. Tours and afternoon tea are available to the public. Open April through November.

Hosts: Jay and Marianne Schatz
Rooms: 14 (PB) $90-175
Full Breakfast in spring and fall
Continental Breakfast in summer

Credit Cards: A, B, C
Notes: 2 (for deposit only), 8 (over 12), 9, 10, 11, 12, 14

The Albert Stevens Inn
127 Myrtle Avenue, 08204
(609) 884-4717

Built in 1889 by Dr. Albert G. Stevens as a wedding gift for his bride, Bessie, this elegant Queen Anne home is decorated with period antiques and crystal. Serving a succulent two-course hot breakfast every day, the inn offers complimentary four-course gourmet dinners from November to April. A large 102-degree hot tub, classic movies, and quiet seclusion make a memorable stay. Just two blocks from historic shopping and a ten-minute walk to beaches.

Hosts: Curt and Diane Rangen
Rooms: 6 (PB) $85-125
Full Breakfast
Credit Cards: A, B, C, D
Notes: 2, 4, 5, 6 (call), 9, 10, 11, 12, 14

Captain Mey's Bed and Breakfast Inn
202 Ocean Street, 08204
(609) 884-7793; (609) 884-9637

Dutch heritage is evident in the delft blue china collection and authentic European antiques. Victorian bedroom suites are accented with handmade quilts, fresh flowers, and imported Dutch lace curtains. Breakfast is a special time with candlelight and classical music. The wraparound sun-and-shade veranda furnished with wicker and Victorian wind curtains adds a romantic touch.

welcome; 9 Social drinking allowed; 10 Tennis available; 11 Swimming available; 12 Golf available; 13 Skiing available; 14 May be booked through travel agents

Midland Park

Stanhope

Frenchtown

Ocean Grove

Bay Head

Haddonfield

Ocean City

NEW JERSEY

Cape May

Hosts: Milly LaCanfora and Carin Fedderman
Rooms: 9 (6 PB; 3 SB) $75-145
Full Breakfast
Credit Cards: A, B
Notes: 2, 5, 8, 10, 11, 12

Colvmns by the Sea

1513 Beach Drive, 08204
(609) 884-2228

This elegant turn-of-the-century mansion on the ocean in a landmark Victorian village has large, airy rooms decorated with antiques and featuring wonderful ocean views. Gourmet breakfast, high tea, and evening snacks are served. Complimentary bikes and beach badges. Hot tub. Great for history buffs, to bird-watch, or just to relax.

Hosts: Barry and Cathy Rein
Rooms: 11 (PB) $110-150
Full Breakfast
Credit Cards: None
Notes: 2, 9, 10, 11, 12

Colvmns by the Sea

Leith Hall Historic Seashore Inn

22 Ocean Street, 08204
(609) 884-1934

Visit this elegantly restored 1880s home in the heart of the Victorian historic district.

Only one-half block from the beach, Leith Hall features Aesthetic Movement antiques and wallpapers with comfy couches and Oriental carpets. Full gourmet breakfast and afternoon English tea are offered. Enjoy ocean views.

Hosts: Susan and Elan Zingman-Leith
Rooms: 8 (6 PB; 2 SB) $75-150
Full Breakfast
Credit Cards: None
Notes: 2, 5, 9, 10, 11, 12

The Mason Cottage

625 Columbia Avenue, 08204
(609) 884-3358

The Mason Cottage is an elegant Victorian seaside inn built in 1871 as the summer residence for a wealthy Philadelphia entrepreneur. The inn is French Second Empire with a curved roof and offers superior accommodations. Breakfast is served in the parlor or on the veranda.

Hosts: Dave and Joan Mason
Rooms: 5 (4 PB; 1 SB) $75-145
Expanded Continental Breakfast
Credit Cartds: A, B
Notes: 2, 9, 10, 11, 12, 14

The Queen Victoria

102 Ocean Street, 08204
(609) 884-8702

The Wells family welcomes guests as friends and treats them royally with unpretentious service and attention to detail. Four restored buildings, furnished with antiques, are in the center of the historic district. The inn is nationally recognized for special Christmas activities.

Hosts: Dane and Joan Wells
Rooms: 22 (PB) $75-250
Full Breakfast
Credit Cards: A, B
Notes: 2, 5, 8, 9, 10, 11, 12

NOTES: Credit cards accepted: A Master Card; B Visa; C American Express; D Discover Card; E Diners Club; F Other; 2 Personal checks accepted; 3 Lunch available; 4 Dinner available; 5 Open all year; 6 Pets welcome; 8 Children welcome; 9 Social drinking allowed; 10 Tennis available; 11 Swimming available; 12 Golf available; 13 Skiing available; 14 May be booked through travel agents

Woodleigh House

808 Washington Street, 08204
(609) 884-7123

Nestled prominently in Cape May's historic district, within easy walking distance to everything and surrounded by comfortable porches, gardens, and courtyards. Woodleigh House Bed and Breakfast is an attractive example of the country Victorian style. Enjoy a stroll in the courtyard, wander through the garden area, or enjoy rocking and people watching from the spacious porches.

Hosts: Buddy and Jan Wood
Rooms: 5 (PB) $70-110
Expanded Continental Breakfast
Credit Cards: A, B
Notes: 2, 5, 8 (over 5), 9, 10, 11, 12

The Queen Victoria

FRENCHTOWN

The Old Hunterdon House

12 Bridge Street, 08825
(908) 996-3632

Travelers may choose from seven distinctively appointed guest rooms, each with its own style and characteristics. Guests find chilled juice and a newspaper at their door early in the morning before a full breakfast in the high-ceiling dining room is served. Frenchtown is home to fine restaurants, interesting shops, and galleries and is across the river from Bucks County, with its many historic and scenic attractions.

Hosts: Tony Cappiello and Larry Miller
Rooms: 7 (PB) $70-115
Full Breakfast
Credit Cards: A, B, C
Notes: 2, 5, 9, 11, 12

HADDONFIELD

Bed and Breakfast of Valley Forge

P. O. Box 562, Valley Forge, Pennsylvania 19481
(215) 783-7838; (800) 344-01231

This charming turn-of-the-century Victorian guest house is ideally suited for the overnight traveler or business person requiring temporary accommodations. Just 20 minutes to Philadelphia. $80.

MIDLAND PARK

Bed and Breakfast Adventures

103 Godwin Avenue, Suite 132, 07432
(800) 992-2632

More than 700 sleeping rooms available at gold-medallion, certified properties throughout New Jersey, New York, Pennsylvania, and southern Florida. Each accommodation has been inspected for cleanliness, comfort, hospitality, safety, and amenities. Indulge in a high-rise luxury view of the metropolitan skyline, relax on a yacht, or hide away at a mountain cottage. Aster Mould, general manager. Rates from $50 to $200.

OCEAN CITY

BarnaGate
Bed and Breakfast
637 Wesley Avenue, 08226
(609) 391-9366

This 1895 seashore Victorian, painted a soft peach with mauve and burgundy trim, is only three blocks from the ocean. The attractively furnished rooms have paddle fans, antiques, quilts, and wicker accessories. Enjoy the homey atmosphere and sensitive hospitality. Privacy is respected, company is offered. Near Cape May and ten miles south of Atlantic City.

Hosts: Lois and Frank Barna
Rooms: 5 (1 PB; 4 S2B) $50-70
Expanded Continental Breakfast
Credit Cards: A, B
Notes: 2, 5, 8 (over 10), 10, 11, 12

BarnaGate Bed and Breakfast

OCEAN GROVE

Cordova
26 Webb Avenue, 07756
(908) 774-3084 summer; (212) 751-9577 winter

This century-old Victorian inn in historic Ocean Grove has a friendly atmosphere with Old World charm. It was recently featured in *New Jersey* magazine as one of the seven best places on the Jersey shore. Kitchen, barbecue, and picnic area are available for guests. Only 90 minutes from New York City and Atlantic City.

Host: Doris Chernik
Rooms: 15 (3 PB; 12 SB) $35-60
Expanded Continental Breakfast
Credit Cards: None
Notes: 2, 8, 9, 10, 11, 14

STANHOPE

The Whistling Swan Inn Bed and Breakfast Guesthouse
110 Main Street, P.O. Box 791, 07874
(201) 347-6369

This large, family Victorian home has been restored and has ten guest rooms, all with private baths and queen-size beds. It is only one mile north of I-80 at Exit 27. A full buffet-style breakfast is presented. Special rates for senior citizens, single guests, and corporate travelers are available.

Hosts: Paula Williams and Joe Mulay
Rooms: 10 (PB) $65-95
Full Breakfast
Credit Cards: A, B, C, D, E
Notes: 2, 5, 8 (over 11), 9, 10, 11, 12, 13, 14

welcome; 9 Social drinking allowed; 10 Tennis available; 11 Swimming available; 12 Golf available; 13 Skiing available; 14 May be booked through travel agents

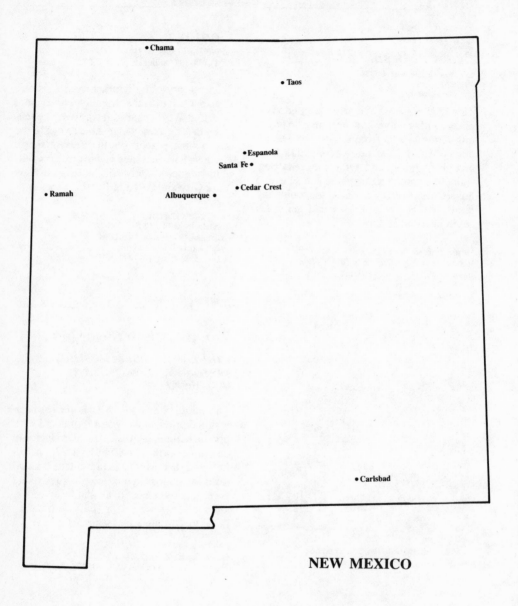

• Chama

• Taos

• Espanola

Santa Fe •

• Ramah

• Cedar Crest

Albuquerque •

• Carlsbad

NEW MEXICO

New Mexico

Casas de Sueños
Bed and Breakfast Inn
310 Rio Grande Boulevard Southwest, 87104
(505) 897-2280

Enjoy fresh flowers, rambling gardens, waterfalls, and hospitality at this inn that adjoins Albuquerque's famous Old Town, with museums, theater, fine dining and fast food, galleries, shops, parks, nature trails, the world's longest aerial tramway, and zoo. Santa Fe is only one hour away by car. World-famous architecture is combined with superb locale and southwestern hospitality.

Hosts: Steven Barnard and Susan Keller
Rooms: 12 (PB) $65-250
Full Breakfast
Credit Cards: A, B, C
Notes: 2, 5, 9, 10, 11, 12, 13, 14

Sandcastle
Bed and Breakfast
327 Arizona Southeast, 87108
(505) 256-9462

With a convenient metropolitan location, the Sandcastle has large rooms and common areas and off-street parking. It is close to airport, shopping, restaurants, University of New Mexico, Sandia Corporation, and fairgrounds. Enjoy a friendly, quiet atmosphere.

Hosts: Mary and John Cosgrove
Rooms: 4 (PB) $55-75

Continental Breakfast
Credit Cards: A, B
Notes: 2, 5, 9, 10, 11, 12, 13

Windmill Ranch
Bed and Breakfast
6400 Coors Road Northwest, 87120
(505) 898-6864

Enjoy bicycling, jogging, or just walking along secluded paths under ancient cottonwoods in the Bosque. Each room provides views of glorious sunrises over the Sandia Mountains, large private baths, and Southwest flavor with antiques collected from ghost towns all over New Mexico. A romantic hideaway for lovers, a chance to herd cattle for city-slickers, a place to take off your boots and rest your horse, or just plain soak up New Mexico.

Hosts: Bob and Margaret Cover
Rooms: 4 (PB) $65-95
Full Breakfast
Credit Cards: A, B
Notes: 2, 5, 9, 10, 11, 12, 13, 14

Mi Casa Su Casa #1806
P. O. Box 950, Tempe, Arizona 85280
(800) 456-0682

There is a waist-high stone wall surrounding the property of this 1929 Spanish-style house, only a short walk to downtown area, churches, and library. Short drive to golf, tennis, fishing, swimming, boating, and picnic areas. Continental breakfast. $65.

NOTES: Credit cards accepted: A Master Card; B Visa; C American Express; D Discover Card; E Diners Club; F Other; 2 Personal checks accepted; 3 Lunch available; 4 Dinner available; 5 Open all year; 6 Pets welcome; 8 Children welcome; 9 Social drinking allowed; 10 Tennis available; 11 Swimming available; 12 Golf available; 13 Skiing available; 14 May be booked through travel agents

CEDAR CREST

Apple Tree
Bed and Breakfast
12050 Highway 14 North, Box 287, 87008
(505) 281-3597; (800) 648-4262

The Apple Tree welcomes guests to this
Territorial-style adobe home in the Sandia
Mountains east of Albuquerque on the scenic Turquoise Trail, offering two guest units
with private entrance, kitchenette, and deck
or patio. Fragrant piñon and cedar burn in
the fireplaces of these rustic units as guests
enjoy antiques and country decor, cable TV,
stereo, phone, and library. Try blue corn
waffles or breakfast burritos, delivered to
guest room.

Hosts: Garland and Norma Curry
Rooms: 2 (PB) $65-85
Full Breakfast
Credit Cards: None
Notes: 2, 5, 6, 8, 9, 10, 11, 12, 13, 14

CHAMA

Jones House
Bed and Breakfast
311 Terrace Avenue, P.O. Box 887, 87520
(505) 756-2908

Come and enjoy the friendly, comfortable
atmosphere at this bed and breakfast across
from the Cumbres and Toltec Scenic Railroad. This Tudor-style home is the train
buff's dream, with a library full of books
and videos about trains. In the winter, cross-
country ski at Cumbres Pass, or find an
oversized chair in the livingroom by the fire
where you can curl up and read. The flowering yard with benches and picnic table is
a peaceful spot to watch the birds and enjoy
the apple trees and lilac bushes.

Hosts: Phil and Sara Cole
Rooms: 4 (2 PB; 2 SB) $55-70
Full Breakfast
Credit Cards: A, B, C

ESPANOLA

La Puebla House
Route 3, Box 172A, 87532
(505) 753-3981

La Puebla House is a ten-room traditional
adobe with vigas and latillas, flagstone and
brick floors. It is situated in a small Spanish
village between Santa Cruz and Chimayo.
This is a lovely country setting from which
to explore the many attractions of northern
New Mexico. Nearby are Indian pueblos
and ruins, the Santa Fe opera, Taos, Abiqui,
Ojo Caliente, and many other small villages
in the Espanola Valley.

Host: Elvira Bain
Rooms: 4 (1 PB; 3 SB) $45-70
Full Breakfast
Credit Cards: A, B
Notes: 2, 5, 6, 8, 9, 13

RAMAH

Mi Casa Su Casa #1805
P. O. Box 950, Tempe, Arizona 85280
(800) 456-0682

Enjoy warm hospitality on this working
cattle ranch. The house was built in 1915 of
rocks from the nearby Indian ruin and has
wood floors, Navajo rugs, large garden, and
big elm trees. Full breakfast. $58.

SANTA FE

Alexander's Inn
529 East Palace Avenue, 87501
(505) 986-1431

The inn, built in 1903, is made of brick and
wood in a southwestern Victorian style.
Situated five blocks from the plaza and two
blocks from Canyon Road, it is still in a
quiet neighborhood. It is furnished with
antiques, lace, and chintz, and it abounds
with lovely detail in each of five spacious,
sunny bedrooms. Breakfast is served on the

NOTES: Credit cards accepted: A Master Card; B Visa; C American Express; D Discover Card; E Diners Club; F Other;
2 Personal checks accepted; 3 Lunch available; 4 Dinner available; 5 Open all year; 6 Pets welcome; 8 Children

Alexander's Inn

veranda in the summer and in front of a crackling fire in the winter.

Hosts: Carolyn Lee and Mary Jo Schneider
Rooms: 5 (3 PB; 2 SB) $65-105 off-season; $75-115 in-season
Expanded Continental Breakfast
Credit Cards: A, B
Notes: 2, 5, 8 (over 5), 9, 10, 11, 12, 13, 14

Canyon Road Casitas

652 Canyon Road, 87501
(800) 279-0755

This is a small, luxurious inn on Santa Fe's historic Canyon Road, a restored adobe with the finest southwestern decor and amenities. It offers accommodations with queen feather beds, quilts, guest robes, and private garden and is within walking distance of all attractions. Wine and cheese are served upon arrival in this four-season retreat.

Host: Trisha Ambrose
Rooms: 2 (PB) $85-165
Continental Breakfast
Credit Cards: A, B, C, D, E
Notes: 2, 5, 8, 9, 10, 11, 12, 13, 14

El Paradero

220 West Manhattan, 87501
(505) 988-1177

El Paradero was originally a Spanish farmhouse built between 1800 and 1820. In the 1880s, Territorial-style details were added to the old adobe, and Victorian touches were added in 1912. The innkeepers remodeled the building but kept the eccentric, rambling character. The thick adobe walls provide a quiet, relaxing, and nurturing space.

Hosts: Ouida MacGregor and Thom Allen.
Rooms: 14 (10 PB; 4 SB) $50-130
Full Breakfast
Credit Cards: None
Notes: 2, 6 (by arrangement), 8 (over 4), 9, 10, 11, 12, 13, 14

Jean's Place

2407 Camino Capitan, 87505
(505) 471-4053

A modest home and vibrational healing center, Jean's Place is situated in a quiet neighborhood 10 to 15 minutes from the town plaza. A deck above the patio overlooks the greenbelt with views of the mountains on each side. Guests have a queen bed. Those attracted to crystals will enjoy the energy here. Cat and dog in residence.

Host: Jean Gosse
Room: 1 (PB) $40
Continental Breakfast
Credit Cards: None
Notes: 2, 5, 10, 11, 12, 13, 14

welcome; 9 Social drinking allowed; 10 Tennis available; 11 Swimming available; 12 Golf available; 13 Skiing available; 14 May be booked through travel agents

Sunset House
436 Sunset, 87501
(505) 983-3523

This private home is four blocks from the plaza and one block from a sports complex and swimming pool. Also close to ski area. There is a baby grand piano in the living room, and art is displayed throughout. Separate, unhosted casitas are also available without bed and breakfast service.

Host: Gloria Bennett
Rooms: 2 (PB) $75-85
Continental Breakfast
Credit Cards: None
Notes: 2, 10, 11, 13, 14

El Paradero

Water Street Inn
427 West Water Street, 87501
(505) 984-1193

This intimate, restored adobe in an award-winning complex is decorated with southwestern furnishings and antiques and features fireplaces, cable TV, air conditioning, and complimentary refreshments. Near historic downtown.

Hosts: Dolores and Albert Dietz
Rooms: 6 (PB) $85-125
Continental Breakfast

Credit Cards: A, B
Notes: 2, 5, 9, 13, 14

TAOS

Blue Star
Bed and Breakfast/Retreat
P. O. Box 800, El Prado, 87529
(505) 758-4634

The Blue Star in Taos is a lovely private studio with kitchenette and bath. It offers a choice of king bed or single beds, and is in full view of the Sangre de Cristo Mountain Range. Relax in the shadow of Taos's sacred mountain. Cash payment requested.

Host: Lee Hester
Room: 1 (PB) $49-59
Continental Breakfast
Credit Cards: None
Notes: 5, 6, 8, 10, 11, 12, 13

Casa de las Chimeneas
Bed and Breakfast Inn
405 Cordoba Road, Box 5303, 87571
(505) 758-4777

Details and special amenities abound in the "House of Chimneys" featuring spectacular gardens, in-room fireplaces, cable color TV, outdoor hot tub, and complimentary hors d'oeuvres. Guests rave about the bed linens. The inn was named one of the ten "inns for romance" in the West by the *Denver Post*, and breakfast has been featured in *Bon Appetit*. Mobil two-star rating.

Hosts: Susan Vernon and Ron Rencher
Rooms: 3 (PB) $103-130
Full Breakfast
Credit Cards: A, B
Notes: 2, 5, 8, 9, 10, 11, 12, 13, 14

Casa Zia
Box 5497, 87571
(505) 758-7536; (505) 751-0697

NOTES: Credit cards accepted: A Master Card; B Visa; C American Express; D Discover Card; E Diners Club; F Other; 2 Personal checks accepted; 3 Lunch available; 4 Dinner available; 5 Open all year; 6 Pets welcome; 8 Children

This artist's home and gallery on a quiet corner near the plaza is a short drive to Taos ski area and river rafting. Amenities include hot tub and TV/VCR. Host specializes in portrait painting and furniture design. The ambience is focused on warmth and hospitality.

Host: George Reed
Rooms: $65-90
Expanded Continental Breakfast
Credit Cards: A, B
Notes: 2, 5, 10, 11, 13

Orinda
Box 4451, 87571
(505) 758-8581

Orinda is called a "bed and breakfast paradise" by the *Rocky Mountain News*. Surrounded by open meadows and towering cottonwood trees, Orinda is a dramatic adobe estate that combines spectacular views and country privacy, all within walking distance of Taos Plaza. Enjoy a spacious two-bedroom suite with livingroom, or a distinctive one-bedroom suite. Each has a kiva fireplace, Mexican-tile bath, and private entrance.

Hosts: Dave and Karol Dondero
Rooms: 2 (PB) $75-85
Continental Breakfast
Credit Cards: A, B
Notes: 2, 5, 8, 9, 12, 13, 14

Salsa del Salto
Bed and Breakfast Inn
P.O. Box 1468, El Prado, 87529
(505) 776-2422

Salsa del Salto is an exquisite southwestern inn situated between Taos Plaza and Toas Ski Valley. Eight spacious rooms, king-size beds, private baths, and spectacular views, all surrounded by flowers from spring to fall. Private tennis court, swimming pool, and hot tub. The elegant lobby has room for everyone to meet, relax, or read. Gourmet breakfast and afternoon snacks are served. Ski packages are available in winter.

Hosts: Dadou Mayer and Mary Hockett
Rooms: 8 (PB)
Full Breakfast
Credit Cards: A, B
Notes: 2, 5, 9, 10, 11, 14

Orinda

Stewart House
Gallery and Inn
P. O. Box 2326, 87571
(505) 776-2913

Built by a local artist 20 years ago from reclaimed parts of history, the inn is an extraordinary mixture of styles and textures, combining architectural elements from Spanish to Scandinavian, Moorish to Mayan. More surprises come via the owners' 20 years in the art business. Each room is filled with art, antiques, and handcrafted furniture. Situated minutes from Ski Valley, Pueblo, and town in a quiet country setting.

Hosts: Don and Mildred Cheek
Rooms: 5 (PB) $65-80
Full Breakfast
Credit Cards: A, B
Notes: 2, 5, 9, 10, 12, 13, 14 (off-season only)

welcome; 9 Social drinking allowed; 10 Tennis available; 11 Swimming available; 12 Golf available; 13 Skiing available; 14 May be booked through travel agents

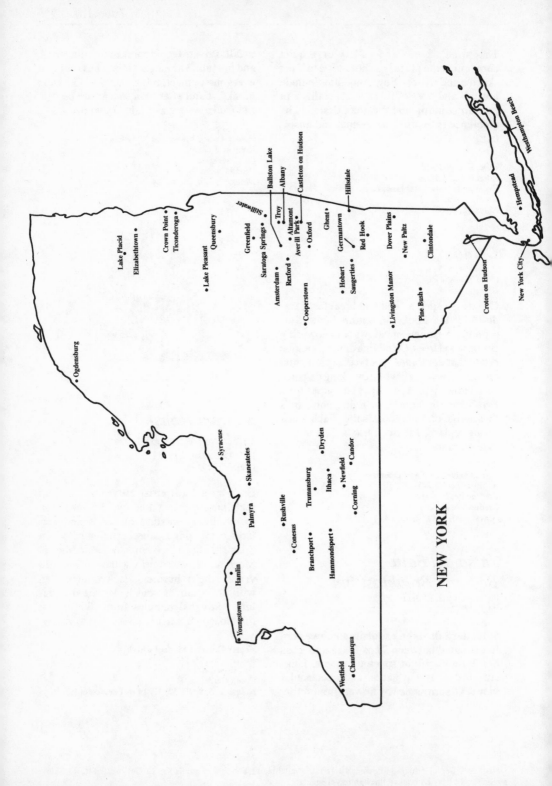

New York

The American Country Collection 097

4 Greenwood Lane, Delmar, 12054
(518) 439-7001

This bed and breakfast has an open stair-case, ten-foot ceilings, carved mantles, origi-nal oak woodwork, and pocket doors. Iron beds trimmed with brass are topped with feather mattresses. Just two miles from the New York State Thruway and one mile from the bus route. Continental breakfast; chil-dren over 12 welcome. $49.

The American Country Collection 110

4 Greenwood Lane, Delmar, 12054
(518) 439-7001

City convenience combined with quiet resi-dential living makes this suburban ranch home an ideal capital region location. In the summer, breakfast is served on the screened porch that overlooks the landscaped lot. Bedrooms are attractive and have desks and radios. Full breakfast on weekends; conti-nental breakfast on weekdays; children wel-come. $45-60.

Mansion Hill Inn

155 Philip Street at Park Avenue, 12202
(518) 465-2038; (518) 427-7358

This urban inn is nestled in a quiet residen-tial neighborhood within walking distance of the New York state governor's executive mansion and state capitol complex. The Victorian-era buildings have been renovated with charm. Dinner is served with an Ameri-can flair prepared by Chef David K. Martin from Monday through Saturday. Please re-quest nonsmoking upon reservation.

Hosts: Maryellen and Steve Stofeland, Jr.
Rooms: 12 (PB) $95-145
Full Breakfast
Credit Cards: A, B, C, E
Notes: 2, 3, 4, 5, 6, 8, 9, 10, 11, 12, 13, 14

The American Country Collection 045

4 Greenwood Lane, Delmar, 12054
(518) 439-7001

This 75-year-old Colonial is just 20 miles from the hustle and bustle of the state capi-tal. It is situated on 15 acres that include well-groomed lawns, old shade trees, barns, a swimming pool, patio, and orchards. Con-venient to Albany and Schenectady. Laun-dry facilties and kitchen use are available for long-term guests. One suite with private bath, one single room with shared bath. Full breakfast; children welcome. $45.

Pine Haven Bed and Breakfast

531 Western Avenue, 12203
(518) 482-1574

Pine Haven is a century-old Victorian home in the heart of Albany's prettiest area. Fur-nished with antiques, feather mattresses, and brass and iron beds, it has the ambience

NOTES: Credit cards accepted: A Master Card; B Visa; C American Express; D Discover Card; E Diners Club; F Other; 2 Personal checks accepted; 3 Lunch available; 4 Dinner available; 5 Open all year; 6 Pets welcome; 8 Children welcome; 9 Social drinking allowed; 10 Tennis available; 11 Swimming available; 12 Golf available; 13 Skiing available; 14 May be booked through travel agents

of Grandma's house. Pine Haven is on the main artery, is served by bus lines in every direction, has off-street parking, and is close to restaurants, a theater, bookstore, and other attractions.

Host: Janice Tricarill
Rooms: 4 (SB) $49
Continental Breakfast
Credit Cards: None
Notes: 2, 5, 9, 14

AMSTERDAM

The American Country Collection 118
4 Greenwood Lane, Delmar, 12054
(518) 439-7001

This historic home, circa 1830, retains all of its original architectural features. Rooms in this brick Federal Colonial have wide-pine floors, fireplaces, and a mix of antiques and country furnishings. Three guest rooms with shared bath. Afternoon tea; full breakfast; children welcome. $35-45.

AVERILL PARK

Ananas Hus Bed and Breakfast
Route 3, Box 301, 12018
(518) 766-5035

The welcome mat is out at this hillside ranch home on 30 acres with a panoramic view of the Hudson River valley. It is informally furnished in the Early American style, accented with mementos from the hosts' international travels and lovely needlework. It is 15 minutes to Jiminey Peak and Brodie Mountain ski areas, 30 minutes to Tanglewood, Williamstown Theatre Festival, and Clark Art Institute in Massachusetts.

Hosts: Thelma Olsen Tomlinson and Clyde H. Tomlinson
Rooms: 3 (SB) $55

Full Breakfast
Credit Cards: C, F
Notes: 2, 5, 8 (over 12), 9, 11, 12, 13

BALLSTON LAKE

The American Country Collection 009
4 Greenwood Lane, Delmar, 12054
(518) 439-7001

Months of renovation restored this Second Empire Victorian to its former position as a focal point in this tiny village. The rear section has a private entrance, livingroom with fireplace, dining room, kitchen, and porch. The second floor has three guest rooms and a bath. The front section also contains a queen room with private bath and a two-room suite. Victorian roses, fresh fruit, chocolate mints, and fresh flowers help to make your stay memorable. Continental buffet breakfast; children over 11 welcome. $65-135.

The American Country Collection 012
4 Greenwood Lane, Delmar, 12054
(518) 439-7001

A separate entrance leads to the first-floor suite that consists of a bedroom, a library with a collection of treasured books, a cozy livingroom with fireplace, and a private terrace. A selection of family antiques reflects a New England heritage. Swimming, canoeing, sailing, and windsurfing are available on the lake during the summer. Expanded continental breakfast. $75 October 23 to July 1; $95 July 1 to October 22.

The American Country Collection 119
4 Greenwood Lane, Delmar, 12054
(518) 439-7001

This working farm and girls' summer riding academy is on 100 acres of rolling meadows and scenic farmland. More than 30 horses and foals, a goat dairy, and a private flock of ducks and geese ensure a true farm experience. Riding lessons are available at the indoor riding area. Full breakfast from 7:30 to 8:30 A.M., continental breakfast other times; children welcome. $70-95 July and August; $50-65 September to June.

BRANCHPORT

Gone with the Wind on Keuka Lake

453 West Lake Road 54A, 14418
(607) 868-4603

The name paints the picture of this 1887 stone Victorian on 14 acres on a slight rise overlooking a quiet lake cove that is adorned by an inviting gazebo. Feel the magic of total relaxation and peace of mind while enjoying the solarium hot tub, nature trails, three fireplaces, delectable breakfasts, private beach, and dock. Rooms have queen and king beds and are of varied decor: southwestern, French, antique, Victorian.

Hosts: Linda and Robert Lewis
Rooms: 6 (S4B) $65-95
Full Breakfast
Credit Cards: None
Notes: 2, 5, 10, 11, 12, 13

CANDOR

The Edge of Thyme Bed and Breakfast

6 Main Street (Junction Routes 96 and 96 B), 13743
(607) 659-5155

Candor is a rural village situated 17 miles south of Ithaca featuring this gracious turn-of-the-century Georgian home with leaded-glass windowed porch, marble fireplaces, period sitting rooms, gardens, and pergola. It is central to Cornell University, Ithaca College, Corning, Elmira, Watkins

Glen, wineries. Antiques, tea room, and gift shop are on premises.

Hosts: Eva Mae and Frank Musgrave
Rooms: 6 (2 PB; 4 SB) $45-70
Full Breakfast
Credit Cards: A, B
Notes: 2, 5, 8, 10, 12, 13, 14

CASTLETON ON HUDSON

The American Country Collection 071

4 Greenwood Lane, Delmar, 12054
(518) 439-7001

The atmosphere at this country-style ranch home is warm and welcoming. Just a ten-minute drive to Albany, it is an ideal location for touring the capital district, a drive to Saratoga, or a jaunt to Lenox or Stockbridge, Massachusetts. A pool and deck are available in warm weather, and a running track and tennis court are across the street. Private bath. Continental breakfast. $60.

CHAUTAUQUA

Plumbush—A Victorian Bed and Breakfast

P. O. Box 864, 14722
(716) 789-5309

Plumbush, circa 1865, is a gracious Victorian home painstakingly authentic in its restoration and furnished with pieces from the early 19th century. A music room, piano, organ, livingroom, porches, and a savory breakfast blend to make the Plumbush a delight. Less than one mile to Chautauqua; bicycles are available. Seen in May/June 1990 issue of *Innsider* magazine, the August 1989 issue of *Victoria* magazine, and the summer 1991 issue of *Victorian Homes*.

Hosts: George and Sandy Green
Rooms: 4 (PB) $85
Full Breakfast
Credit Cards: None
Notes: 2, 5, 9, 10, 11, 12, 13, 14

CLINTONDALE

Orchard House
Route 44/55 at Eckert Place, P.O. Box 413, 12515
(914) 883-6136

This 1866 Queen Anne Victorian sits on two acres in the heart of Hudson River valley orchards, just minutes from New Paltz. Luxuriously furnished rooms have soothing garden views. The master bedroom, with private bath, includes an indoor balcony overlooking a plant-filled solarium. Nearby activities include climbing or hiking in the famous Shawangunk Mountains, horseback riding, and cross-country skiing. The Culinary Institute, Vanderbilt mansion, Hyde Park, and countless antique shops are also nearby.

Host: Carol Surovick
Rooms: 3 (1 PB; 2 SB) $70-90
Full Breakfast
Credit Cards: None
Notes: 2, 5, 9, 11, 12, 13

The Phoenix on River Road

CONESUS

Conesus Lake Bed and Breakfast
2388 East Lake Road, 14435
(716) 346-6526

Situated on beautiful Conesus Lake. A relaxing atmosphere includes large private dock; picnic facilities; and free use of canoe, paddleboat, rowboat, and overnight docking with mooring whips. Each attractive bedroom has cable TV and private balcony. Whirlpool and weekly discounts are available.

Hosts: Virginia and Dale Esse
Rooms: 2 (SB) $60
Full Breakfast
Credit Cards: A, B, D
Notes: 5, 9, 11, 12

COOPERSTOWN

The American Country Collection 014
4 Greenwood Lane, Delmar, 12054
(518) 439-7001

Guest rooms at this bed and breakfast are adorned with wildflowers freshly picked from the garden and bowls of fruit and candy. Wicker, timeless antiques, old photographs, ceiling fans, and plants tie each room to the past. In the restored barn, three guest rooms have private baths. In the main house, a two-bedroom suite has a private bath. Two-night minimum stay on weekends and holidays. Continental breakfast; children welcome; resident ducks. $68.

The Phoenix on River Road
Rural Delivery 4, Box 360, 13326
(607) 547-8250

Once a Victorian hotel, the Phoenix has been completely remodeled into a charming French country inn, serving an expanded continental breakfast in what was once the tavern room. All rooms have ceiling fans. The Phoenix is situated two miles from Cooperstown on Scenic River Road, near museums and cross-country ski trails.

Hosts: Meg and Jim Myers, Mary Dunkle
Rooms: 4 (PB)
Expanded Continental Breakfast
Credit Cards: A, B
Notes: 2, 5, 8, 9, 10, 11, 12, 13 (XC), 14

NOTES: Credit cards accepted: A Master Card; B Visa; C American Express; D Discover Card; E Diners Club; F Other; 2 Personal checks accepted; 3 Lunch available; 4 Dinner available; 5 Open all year; 6 Pets welcome; 8 Children

CORNING

Delevan House
188 Delevan Avenue, 14830
(607) 962-2347

Most people call this house a small glass museum. Overlooking Corning, just five minutes away, it is set in quiet surroundings up high on a hill. Free pick-up from airport is available.

Host: Mary DePumpo
Rooms: 3 (1 PB; 2 SB) $60-65
Full Breakfast
Credit Cards: None

CROTON ON HUDSON

Alexander Hamilton House
49 Van Wyck Street, 10520
(914) 271-6737

This 1889 Victorian inn overlooking the Hudson river is 30 miles north of New York City, 12 miles from West Point, Lyndhurst, Sunnyside, and White Plaines. It features an in-ground pool, antiques, and a Shih Tzu puppy. Four rooms share two baths, and a queen suite has a private bath and sitting room with fireplace. The bridal chamber has skylights, fireplace, and private bath with Jacuzzi.

Host: Barbara Notarius
Rooms: 6 (2 PB; 4 SB) $65-250
Full Breakfast
Credit Cards: A, B, C
Notes: 2, 5, 8, 9, 11, 12, 14

CROWN POINT

The American Country Collection 095
4 Greenwood Lane, Delmar, 12054
(518) 439-7001

This 18-room Victorian mansion, circa 1887, on five and one-half acres is in the center of this small town near the Vermont state line. Carved woodwork, doors, and stair railings from oak, cherry, mahogany, and walnut grace the home. In winter, breakfast is served in front of a crackling fire in the oak-paneled dining room. The five guest rooms, two with private baths, feature period wall-papers, antiques, white wicker, custom draperies, and plush carpeting. Continental breakfast; children welcome. $40-55.

DOVER PLAINS

The Mill Farm
66 Cricket Hill Road, 12522
(914) 832-9198

A rambling Colonial situated one hour north of New York City near the Connecticut border, the home is decorated with antique furniture and linens, has a wonderful sitting porch, and offers a panoramic view of the countryside. There are many ski areas, private schools, good restaurants, and antique shops in the area.

Host: Margery Mill
Rooms: 4 (1 PB; 3 SB) $65-95
Full Breakfast
Credit Cards: None
Notes: 2, 8, 9, 10, 11, 12, 13, 14

DRYDEN

Margaret Thacher's Spruce Haven Bed and Breakfast
9 James Street, Box 119, 13053
(607) 844-8052

A log home surrounded by tall spruce trees gives a feeling of being in the woods. It is warm and friendly on a quiet side street with restaurants within two blocks. Homemade muffins and porridge are favorites with guests. Within 12 miles of Ithaca, Cortland, lakes and parks, golfing, skiing, colleges, museums, and antiques. Day trips are easy to Corning Glass, Rose Hill Mansion (Geneva), Syracuse, and Binghamton.

Host: Margaret Thacher Brownell
Rooms: 2 (SB) $55-65
Full Breakfast
Credit Cards: None
Notes: 2, 5, 8, 10, 11, 12, 13

ELIZABETHTOWN

The American Country Collection 072

4 Greenwood Lane, Delmar, 12054
(518) 439-7001

Bed and breakfast guests stay in the main house, an early-1800s Colonial that reflects gracious days of old. There is a large cozy livingroom, where classical music plays softly and a fire burns on cold winter days. In summer, breakfast is served on the covered stone patio that overlooks the grounds. Five guest rooms, three with private baths. Small cottages are also available. Full breakfast from 8:00 to 9:00 A.M.; children welcome. $64-76.

GERMANTOWN

The American Country Collection 113

4 Greenwood Lane, Delmar, 12054
(518) 439-7001

This immaculate and inviting spot is home to the town justice and his wife. The lower-level suite contains a family room with fireplace, piano, and TV; two bedrooms; and a bath. Breakfast is served on the porch or in the dining room from 8:00 to 10:00 A.M. Guests are welcome to use the in-ground swimming pool. Full breakfast on weekends; continental breakfast on weekdays; children welcome by reservation. $50 November 1 to May 30; $60 June 1 to October 31.

GHENT

The American Country Collection 082

4 Greenwood Lane, Delmar, 12054
(518) 439-7001

This early-19th-century rural farmhouse is situated on ten scenic acres for walking and picnicking. There is a private one-acre pond for fishing and paddleboating, a miniature horse farm, and an antique shop. The guest wing has a private livingroom, a bedroom with private bath, and a two-bedroom suite. Full breakfast; children welcome. $60.

GREENFIELD

The American Country Collection 112

4 Greenwood Lane, Delmar, 12054
(518) 439-7001

This bed and breakfast was an inn for British officers during the War of 1812, then a stagecoach stop in the 1820s before serving as part of the undergound railroad during the Civil War. Oriental rugs and fine antiques from Europe and the Middle and Far East furnish the home. Five guest rooms, three with private baths. Full breakfast served at 9:00 A.M.; children over 11 welcome. $50-125 seasonal.

HAMLIN

Sandy Creek Manor House

1960 Redman Road, 14464-9635
(716) 964-7528

A quiet country setting surrounds this 1910 English Tudor on six wooded acres and Sandy Creek. Stained-glass windows, natural oak woodwork, an antique player piano, and massive stone porch take guests back in time. One-half hour to Rochester and less than 90 minutes to Niagara Falls along the Seaway Trail.

Hosts: Shirley Hollink and James Krempasky
Rooms: 3 (SB) $45-60
Full Breakfast
Credit Cards: None
Notes: 2, 5, 6, 8 (over 12), 12, 13, 14

HAMMONDSPORT

The Blushing Rosé Bed and Breakfast Inn

11 William Street, 14840
(607) 569-3402; (607) 569-3483

The Blushing Rosé Bed and Breakfast is in the middle of wine country at the southern end of the Finger Lakes region. It is close to Corning, with its glass museum; Watkins Glen of auto racing fame; and Elmira, the soaring capital of the United States. Whether you spend your day driving, hiking, biking, or just enjoying the sights and sounds of Keuka Lake, you'll enjoy the ambience of this 19th-century inn. Breakfast may include baked French toast, lemon poppy seed waffles, or strawberry bread.

Host: Ellen Laufersweiler
Rooms: 4 (PB) $65-85
Full Breakfast
Credit Cards: F
Notes: 2, 5, 9, 10, 11, 12, 13

The Blushing Rosé Bed and Breakfast Inn

J. S. Hubbs Bed and Breakfast

17 Sheather Street, P.O. Box 366, 14840
(607) 569-2440; (607) 569-3629

This historic Greek Revival, built in 1840 and known as the ink bottle house, is one of the major landmarks on Sheather Street and situated in Hammondsport's oldest residential district. The original wallpaper in the foyer remains intact. The home stands detached on a large landscaped site with some plants dating from the 19th century.

Hosts: Walter, Linda, and John Carl
Rooms: 4 (2 PB; 2 SB) $62
Full Breakfast
Credit Cards: A, B
Notes: 5, 9, 10, 11, 12, 13

HEMPSTEAD

Country Life Bed and Breakfast

237 Cathedral Avenue, 11550
(516) 292-9219

This 70-year-old charming Dutch Colonial is ideally situated in the center of Long Island with delightful décor and a genuine welcome. Each guest room has a special charm: hand-crocheted spreads, marble-top antique dresser, Queen Anne furnishings. All rooms have color TV and air conditioning. Breakfast is served in a sunny, plant-filled room.

Hosts: Wendy and Richard Duvall
Rooms: 4 (2 PB; 2 SB) $60-75
Full Breakfast
Credit Cards: None
Notes: 2 (for deposit only), 5, 8, 9, 11, 12, 14

HILLSDALE

The American Country Collection 106

4 Greenwood Lane, Delmar, 12054
(518) 439-7001

The inn, on one acre of lawns and flowers and surrounded by 100 acres of meadows, woodlands, and an ancient cemetery, is near where the Cranse Creek flows into the Green River. Built as a farmhouse around 1830, it was formerly the parsonage to the old church next door. Antiques and country Victorian furniture rest on polished floors and Oriental rugs. Four guest rooms, one with private bath. Continental breakfast; children welcome. $70-95.

HOBART

Breezy Acres Farm Bed and Breakfast
Rural Delivery 1, Box 191, 13788
(607) 538-9338

Enjoy everything one could look for in a bed and breakfast. This beautifully remodeled 1850s farmhouse features personalized attention by friendly hosts, incredible homemade breakfasts with maple products, spa, fireplace, perennial gardens, deck, and pillared porches, surrounded by 300 acres of woods and rolling hills. Skiing, golfing, tennis, swimming nearby. Pond on premises for fishing and swimming.

Hosts: Joyce and David Barber
Rooms: 3 (PB) $50-60
Full Breakfast
Credit Cards: A, B
Notes: 2, 5, 9, 10, 11, 12, 13, 14

ITHACA—SEE ALSO NEWFIELD

Rose Inn
Route 34 North, P. O. Box 6576, 14851-6576
(607) 533-7905; FAX (607) 533-4202

Rose Inn is the only Mobil four-star and AAA four-diamond country inn in the state of New York. It has been selected two years in a row by Uncle Ben's as one of the ten best inns in America. Rose Inn is an elegant 1840s Italianate mansion close to Cornell University and the Finger Lakes wineries. A

prix fixe dinner is served Tuesday through Saturday.

Hosts: Charles and Sherry Rosemann
Rooms: 15 (PB) $100-150; suites $175
Full Breakfast
Credit Cards: None
Notes: 2, 4, 5, 9, 10, 11, 12, 13, 14

Rose Inn

LAKE PLACID

South Meadow Farm Lodge
Cascade Road, HCR 1, Box 44, 12946-9703
(518) 523- 9369

South Meadow Farm Lodge is a cozy, year-round working farm and lodge situated in the middle of the beautiful high peaks region of the Adirondack Park. The lodge lies off Route 73, halfway (seven miles) between Lake Placid and Keene, and one-half mile east of Mount Van Hoevenberg Recreation Area. This sports complex houses the Olympic bobsled and luge run as well as the Olympic cross-country ski trails (30 miles). Free passes to ski trails included.

Hosts: Tony and Nancy Corwin
Rooms: 5 (SB) $70-90
Full Breakfast
Credit Cards: A, B
Notes: 2, 3, 4, 5, 8, 10, 11, 12, 13, 14

LAKE PLEASANT

Hummingbird Hill
Route 8, Box 18, 12108
(518) 548-6386

Enjoy simple country charm in a natural setting. Wander the 40 acres and see the beauty of mother nature or relax in the backyard and watch the hummingbirds. The house is a converted Adirondack summer camp. The dining/livingroom features a huge fieldstone fireplace. The bedrooms are individually decorated with handmade afghans on the beds. Rooms may be rented with either private or shared bath. A TV room and common room provide places for relaxing, reading, or playing games.

Hosts: John and Cathy Doyle
Rooms: 3 (2 PB; 1 SB) $43-49
Full Breakfast
Credit Cards: A, B
Notes: 2, 5, 6, 8, 9, 10, 11, 12, 13

LIVINGSTON MANOR

Clarke's Place in the Country

Rural Delivery 2, Box 465A, 12758
(914) 439-5442

In a unique, contemporary rustic home on top of Shandelee, in the heart of the Catskills, the great room features a wood-burning stove and 20-foot cathedral ceiling. The interior has tongue-and-groove white pine throughout. A deep-water pond on the premises offers year-round enjoyment. Extraordinary restaurants, exquisite antiques, and cider mill are nearby.

Hosts: Robert Clarke and Nan Clarke
Rooms: 2 (PB) $55-65
Full Breakfast
Credit Cards: A, B
Notes: 2, 5, 8, 9, 10, 11, 12, 13

NEWFIELD

Decker Pond Inn

1076 Elmira Road, 14867
(607) 273-7133; (800) 564-5647 New York

Situated on ten acres next to the Robert Treman State Park, this elegant inn is near Cornell and Ithaca colleges, Cayuga Lake, the wine country, Buttermilk Falls, and Taughannock Falls State Park. A short drive takes guests to Corning, Watkins Glen, and Seneca Lake. Come and enjoy the hospitality, beautiful antiques, and wonderful breakfast served in the dining room. Browse in the gift shop, The Blueberry Muffin.

Host: Diane Carroll-Carney
Rooms: 4 (PB) $60-130
Full Breakfast
Credit Cards: A, B, C
Notes: 2, 5, 9, 10, 11, 12, 13, 14

NEW PALTZ

The American Country Collection 117

4 Greenwood Lane, Delmar, 12054
(518) 439-7001

Original artwork and samples of fine needlework complement an eclectic blend of European and Victorian antiques and designer furnishings. A new solarium just off the kitchen provides a sunny spot for tea and conversation. Three guest rooms, one with private bath. Full breakfast; children over ten welcome. $70-80.

NEW YORK CITY

Bed and Breakfast Network of New York

134 West 32nd Street, Suite 602, 10001
(212) 645-8134

This reservation service represents more than 100 nonsmoking accommodations in New York City, both traditional homestays and entire furnished apartments. Most accommodations are in Manhattan's most exciting neighborhoods, such as Greenwich Village, Soho, and the mid-upper East and West Sides. $70-90 hosted; $80-300 unhosted.

welcome; 9 Social drinking allowed; 10 Tennis available; 11 Swimming available; 12 Golf available; 13 Skiing available; 14 May be booked through travel agents

Whitegate Bed and Breakfast in the Country

Urban Ventures, Inc.

306 West 38th, Sixth Floor, 10018
(212) 594-5650; FAX (212) 947-9320

Urban Ventures is a reservation service that represents approximately 650 accommodations in New York City. Bed and breakfasts have hosts, offer breakfast, and loan sweaters and umbrellas. Each accommodation is inspected, and accurate descriptions are offered. Urban Ventures networks with other agencies in order to make reservations in other American cities, Canada, London, and Paris. $60-125.

OGDENSBURG

Maple Hill Country Inn

Route 2, Box 21, 13669
(315) 393-3961

Situated amid 50 old maple trees high on a hill overlooking the mighty Saint Lawrence River, Ogdensburg is home to the Frederic Remington Museum and within easy driving distance of the scenic Thousand Islands and Ottawa, Canada's capital. This is the perfect spot to rock away on the porch with a cold glass of lemonade or take in the gorgeous sunsets.

Host: Marilyn Jones
Rooms: 4 (2 PB; 2 SB) $55-75
Full Breakfast
Credit Cards: None
Notes: 2, 4, 5, 8, 9, 11, 12, 13, 14

OXFORD

Whitegate Bed and Breakfast in the Country

P.O. Box 917, 13830
(607) 843-6965

Country elegance sets the style at this restored 1820 Greek Revival house. Situated on 196 acres of serene meadows and lush woodlands midway between the Finger Lakes and Cooperstown. Stroll on hiking paths, bask in the sun by one of the ponds, sit by the fire, enjoy the big open sky from the solarium, or take advantage of one of the nearby activities, including antique shopping, golfing, swimming, and tennis.

Hosts: Paul and Wanda Mitten
Rooms: 4 (2 PB; 2 SB) $55-65
Full Breakfast
Credit Cards: None
Notes: 2, 10, 11, 12, 13, 14

PALMYRA

Canaltown Bed and Breakfast

119 Canandaigua Street, 14522
(315) 597-5553

This 1850s historic village home of Greek Revival architecture is situated near antique stores, Erie Coverlet Museum, country store museum, Erie Canal hiking trail, canoe rental. Rooms are furnished with iron and brass beds and antiques. Livingroom fireplace. New York wine tasting available by request.

Hosts: Robert and Barbara Leisten
Rooms 3 (1 PB; 2SB) $50-60
Full Breakfast
Credit Cards: C
Notes: 2, 5, 8, 9, 10, 12, 13, 14,

NOTES: Credit cards accepted: A Master Card; B Visa; C American Express; D Discover Card; E Diners Club; F Other;
2 Personal checks accepted; 3 Lunch available; 4 Dinner available; 5 Open all year; 6 Pets welcome; 8 Children

PINE BUSH

Sunrise Farm
Rural Delivery 1, Box 433A
Bruyn Avenue, 12566-9801
(914) 361-3629

Sunrise Farm is a 30-acre certified organic farm featuring Scottish highland cattle, vegetables and fruit, lawns, flower beds, cross-country skiing, and ice skating on the large pond. The guest room on second floor has a ceiling fan and skylight. There is a wood-burning stove in the livingroom, where guests are welcome to join hosts for tea and wine. Dinner is available by arrangement.

Hosts: Janet and Fred Schmelzer
Room: 1 (PB) $45
Full Breakfast
Credit Cards: None
Notes: 2, 4, 5, 8, 9, 10, 11, 12, 13

QUEENSBURY

The American Country Collection 126
4 Greenwood Lane, Delmar, 12054
(518) 439-7001

Original gingerbread accents this 100-year-old farmhouse on a working berry farm. The home features hardwood floors, a dining room that overlooks gardens, lawns, and meadows. Two guest rooms with private baths. Full breakfast; children over six welcome. $45-55.

RED HOOK

The American Country Collection 115
4 Greenwood Lane, Delmar, 12054
(518) 439-7001

This home was built in 1821 in the Federal style. Guest quarters feature wide-board floors, beamed ceiling, wainscoting, plaster walls, original fireplace, and beehive oven. One guest suite with private bath. Full breakfast; children welcome. $75.

REXFORD

The American Country Collection 123
4 Greenwood Lane, Delmar, 12054
(518) 439-7001

Rolling hills, grassy fields, woodlands, and flowers surround this private suite on seven country acres. The house is a passive-solar saltbox built into a hill. The suite features colonial and antique furnishings on Oriental rugs. Continental breakfast; children over six welcome. $65; $85 in August; $200 weekly; $500 monthly.

RUSHVILLE

Lakeview Farm Bed and Breakfast
4761 Route 364, 14544
(716) 554-6973

Hospitality and nature are at their best in this country home on the east side of Canandaigua Lake on 170 acres of woods, fields, and streams. Two lake-view bedrooms are furnished in family antiques and share an upstairs sitting room. Enjoy the pond, beautiful ravine, cross-country skiing. Two minutes to public beach, lakeside restaurant. Ten minutes to Canandaigua shops and restaurants. Air conditioned.

Hosts: Betty and Howard Freese
Rooms: 2 (SB) $45-50
Full Breakfast
Credit Cards: C
Notes: 2, 5, 8 (older), 9, 11, 14

welcome; 9 Social drinking allowed; 10 Tennis available; 11 Swimming available; 12 Golf available; 13 Skiing available; 14 May be booked through travel agents

SARATOGA SPRINGS _____

The American Country Collection 107
4 Greenwood Lane, Delmar, 12054
(518) 439-7001

This cozy, restored Victorian cottage with gingerbread millwork is within walking distance of the downtown shops and Skidmore College. Wicker, hardwood floors, lace curtains, and hand-embroidered bed coverlets combine with unusual artwork and an eclectic mix of antiques. Two guest rooms share one bath with host. Continental breakfast from 8:00 to 9:00 A.M.; children welcome. $55-85 seasonal.

Six Sisters Bed and Breakfast
149 Union Avenue, 12866
(518) 583-1173

Uniquely styled, elegant 1880 Victorian, conveniently situated within walking distance of museums, downtown specialty shops, and restaurants. Luxurious suites and spacious rooms, all with private baths and king or queen beds, prepare you for a leisurely home-cooked breakfast. Breakfast includes honey-nut French toast with apple crisp, or a fresh vegetable and jalapeño cheese omelet with corn bread. Mineral bath and massage package available from November to April.

Hosts: Kate Benton and Steve Ramirez
Rooms: 4 (PB) $65-90 seasonal
Full Breakfast
Credit Cards: None
Notes: 2, 5, 8 (over 10), 9, 10, 11, 12, 13, 14

SAUGERTIES _____

Bed by the Stream
7531 George Sickle Road, 12477
(914) 246-2979

Five acres of streamside property is the setting for this working farm three miles from Exit 20 off the New York State Thruway, seven miles from Woodstock. In-ground pool. Rooms have a private entrance.

Host: Odette Reinhardt
Rooms: 2 (SB) $60
Full Breakfast
Credit Cards: None
Notes: 2, 8, 10, 11, 12, 13

SKANEATELES _____

Cozy Cottage
4987 Kingston Road, 13060
(315) 689-2082

Relax in a quiet, casual atmosphere in this remodeled ranch house on 41 acres five miles from Skaneateles Village. Cozy Cottage is 20 minutes from downtown Syracuse and 15 minutes from Auburn, yet worlds away from city life on a quiet country road. Guest rooms are secure and individually decorated. Nearby are cycling, antiques, boating, swimming, fishing, shopping, and restaurants. Cat in residence.

Host: Elaine Samuels
Rooms: 3 (SB) $ 45-50
Expanded Continental Breakfast
Credit Cards: None
Notes: 2 (two weeks in advance), 5, 6 (cats), 9, 10, 11, 12, 13

STILLWATER _____

The American Country Collection 005
4 Greenwood Lane, Delmar, 12054
(518) 439-7001

This mammoth barn, circa 1800, is an exquisite home that features some original barnboard and exposed beams. Convenient to Saratoga Lake and Saratoga National Historical Park, the two spacious suites are accented with fresh garden flowers and

NOTES: Credit cards accepted: A Master Card; B Visa; C American Express; D Discover Card; E Diners Club; F Other; 2 Personal checks accepted; 3 Lunch available; 4 Dinner available; 5 Open all year; 6 Pets welcome; 8 Children

bowls of fruit and candy. Two suites with private baths; two guest rooms with private baths. Full or continental breakfast; children over nine welcome. $65-105 seasonal.

Bed and Breakfast Wellington

707 Danforth Street, 13208
(315) 474-3641

This historic 1914 brick and stucco Tudor home is one of the most interesting in Syracuse. Designed by the prolific architect Ward Wellington Ward, it represents one of the finest arts and crafts homes of the era. The home contains rich wood interiors, ample interior glass, fireplaces, arched foyer, and many porches. Antiques abound throughout.

Hosts: Wendy Wilber and Ray Borg
Rooms: 3 (PB) $55-65
Full Breakfast
Credit Cards: C
Notes: 2, 5, 9, 10, 11, 12, 13

The American Country Collection 046

4 Greenwood Lane, Delmar, 12054
(518) 439-7001

Enjoy a horsedrawn sleigh ride on this 52-acre farm, or cross-country ski past pond and through pastures on a sunny afternoon. Summer brings wagon rides and the activities of this family-operated farm. Small, cozy guest rooms are filled with nostalgic country touches and have fresh fruit and mints. Three rooms share a bath. Full breakfast at 8:00 A.M.; candlelight dinner available; children welcome. $40.

The American Country Collection 108

4 Greenwood Lane, Delmar, 12054
(518) 439-7001

Westwind Bed and Breakfast

This luxurious new apartment is part of a reborn parochial school. Ethan Allen furnishings, pianos, cathedral ceiling, and solarium create a sophisticated private living area for guests. Unhosted; self-serve continental breakfast; no children. $65; $650-675 monthly without breakfast.

TRUMANSBURG

Westwind Bed and Breakfast
1662 Taughannock Boulevard, 14886
(607) 387-3377

This 1870 Victorian farmhouse is situated on a hillside above Cayuga Lake on 11 acres of land, one-half mile from Taughannock State Park on Route 89N. Nearby are Cornell University, Ithaca College, Hangar Theatre, Cass Park, Treman Marina, many golf courses, antique shops, museums, and excellent restaurants. On the Cayuga wine trail.

Host: Sharon Scott
Rooms: 4 (S2B) $55-75
Full Breakfast
Credit Cards: A, B
Notes: 2, 5, 8, 9, 10, 11, 12, 13

WESTFIELD

Westfield House
East Main Road, Route 20, P. O. Box 505, 14787
(716) 326-6262

Westfield House was built in 1840 as part of the Granger homestead. In 1860 a Gothic Revival addition was built. A complete renovation was completed in 1988. The large common rooms have huge Gothic windows and are furnished with antiques. A lovely carriage barn is full of unfinished furniture. There are several exceptional wineries in the area. Westfield is a national antique center.

Hosts: Betty and Jud Wilson
Rooms: 6 (PB) $60-85

Full Breakfast
Credit Cards: A, B
Notes: 2, 5, 9, 10, 11, 12, 13

WESTHAMPTON BEACH

1880 Seafield House
2 Seafield Lane, 11978
(516) 288-1559; (800) 346-3290

This 100-year-old country retreat is the perfect place for a romantic hideaway, a weekend of privacy, or a change of pace from city life. Only 90 minutes from Manhattan, the estate includes a swimming pool and tennis court, and is only a short walk to the beach. Eclectic furnishings harmonize to create a casual, country inn atmosphere. The Hamptons offer numerous outstanding restaurants and shops.

Host: Elsie Pardee Collins
Suites: 2 (PB) $100-200
Full Breakfast
Minimum stay: 2 nights
Credit Cards: C
Notes: 2, 5, 9, 10, 11

YOUNGSTOWN

The Cameo Inn
3881 Lower River Road (Route 18F), 14074
(716) 754-2075

Situated just four miles north of Lewiston, this English manor house is the perfect spot for that quiet getaway. On three secluded acres, the manor offers a great room with fireplaces at both ends, solarium, library with fireplace, and a terrace. The beautifully appointed guest rooms include suites with private sun rooms, cable TV, and private phones.

Hosts: Greg and Carolyn Fisher
Rooms: 6 (3 PB; 3 SB) $65-125
Full Breakfast
Credit Cards: None
Notes: 2, 5, 8, 9, 10, 11, 12, 13, 14

NOTES: Credit cards accepted: A Master Card; B Visa; C American Express; D Discover Card; E Diners Club; F Other; 2 Personal checks accepted; 3 Lunch available; 4 Dinner available; 5 Open all year; 6 Pets welcome; 8 Children

North Carolina

Blake House Inn
150 Royal Pines Drive, 28704
(704) 684-1847

Circa 1847 and situated in a quiet grove of 200-year-old boxwood trees, the inn has five guest rooms and a restaurant open to the public. It was voted one of the top 50 inns in America. Used as a field hospital during the Civil War, it is decorated in country antiques. Biltmore House is five miles away, Asheville is seven miles away. Close to hiking, swimming, Blue Ridge Parkway, and other area attractions.

Hosts: Bob, Eloise, and Pati Roesler
Rooms: 5 (PB) $60-80
Full Breakfast
Credit Cards: A, B
Notes: 4, 5, 10, 11, 12, 13

Cairn Brae

Cairn Brae
217 Patton Mountain Road, 28804
(704) 252-9219

Cairn Brae, Scottish for rocky hillside, describes the mountain retreat situated above Asheville. Nestled on three acres of woods offering views of the Blue Ridge countryside, Cairn Brae has quiet seclusion, yet is only minutes from downtown Asheville. Guests have a private entrance to a charming sitting room with fireplace, cable TV, and game table. Seasonal.

Hosts: Milli and Ed Adams
Rooms: 3 plus suite (PB) $80-95
Full Breakfast
Credit Cards: A, B
Notes: 2, 3, 8 (over 5), 9, 10, 11, 12, 14

Corner Oak Manor
53 Saint Dunstans Road, 28803
(704) 253-3525

This lovely English Tudor home is situated minutes away from the famed Biltmore estate and gardens. Antiques, handmade wreaths, weavings, and stitchery complement the restored elegance of this 1924 home. There is a gourmet breakfast, livingroom with fireplace, baby grand piano, deck, and Jacuzzi for guest use. It is convenient to downtown shops and restaurants and the Blue Ridge Parkway.

welcome; 9 Social drinking allowed; 10 Tennis available; 11 Swimming available; 12 Golf available; 13 Skiing available; 14 May be booked through travel agents

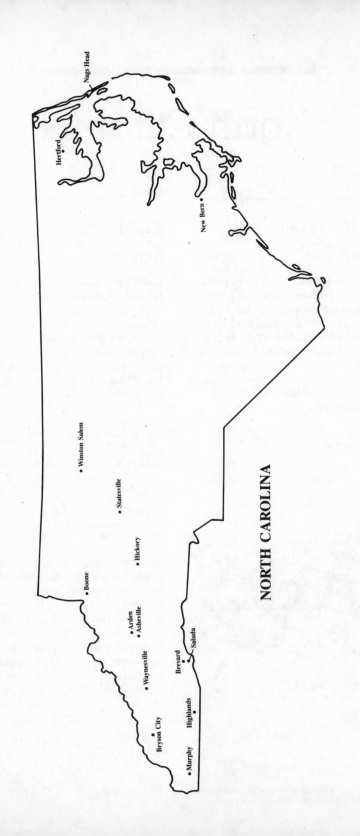

NORTH CAROLINA

Nags Head

Hertford

New Bern

Winston Salem

Statesville

Hickory

Boone

Arden
Asheville

Waynesville

Saluda

Brevard

Bryson City

Highlands

Murphy

Hosts: Karen and Andy Spradley
Rooms: 4 (PB) $80-95
Full Breakfast
Credit Cards: A, B, C, D
Notes: 2, 3, 5, 8, 9, 10, 11, 12, 14

BOONE

Grandma Jean's Bed and Breakfast
209 Meadowview Drive, 28607
(704) 262-3670

This charming 62-year-old country home is on a quiet residential street in the heart of the Blue Ridge Mountains, near Linville Caverns, Tweetsie Railroad, Appalachian State University, and Grandfather Mountain. Lots of craft shops are nearby. Wicker furniture, rockers; Blue Ridge Parkway only three miles away.

Host: Dr. Jean Probinsky
Rooms: 4 (S2B) $40-55
Continental Breakfast
Credit Cards: None
Notes: 2, 8, 9, 10, 11, 12, 13, 14

Gingerbread Inn

BREVARD

The Red House Inn
412 West Probart Street, 28712
(704) 884-9349

Built in 1851, the Red House has been restored and is now furnished with antiques

and open to the public. It is in the Blue Ridge Mountains and Pisgah National Forest, convenient to downtown shops and restaurants, waterfalls, hiking trails, and the Brevard Music Center.

Hosts: Lynne Ong and Mary MacGillycuddy
Rooms: 7 (3 PB; 4 SB) $47-59
Full Breakfast
Credit Cards: A, B
Notes: 2, 9, 11, 12, 14

BRYSON CITY

Folkestone Inn
767 West Deep Creek Road, 28713
(704) 488-2730

Built as a country farmhouse in the mid-1920s, the inn has nine guest rooms decorated with a variety of country antiques. Guests use the parlor with its potbelly stove and adjacent library with a wide selection of books on mountains, trails, wildlife, and birds. It is adjacent to the walking entrance into the Great Smoky Mountains National Park. Streams, waterfalls, white-water rafting, tubing, and hiking.

Hosts: Norma and Peter Joyce
Rooms: 9 (PB) $59-79
Full Breakfast
Credit Cards: None
Notes: 2, 5, 9, 10, 11, 14

HERTFORD

Gingerbread Inn
103 South Church Street, 27944
(919) 426-5809

This beautifully restored turn-of-the-century Victorian home is on the local historic tour and boasts a wraparound porch with paired columns. The comfortably furnished, centrally air-conditioned rooms with cable TV are spacious with single, queen, or king beds, and plush carpeting. The aroma of

NOTES: Credit cards accepted: A Master Card; B Visa; C American Express; D Discover Card; E Diners Club; F Other; 2 Personal checks accepted; 3 Lunch available; 4 Dinner available; 5 Open all year; 6 Pets welcome; 8 Children welcome; 9 Social drinking allowed; 10 Tennis available; 11 Swimming available; 12 Golf available; 13 Skiing available; 14 May be booked through travel agents

freshly baked gingerbreads is something guests will not miss. There is even a souvenir cookie for the ride home.

Host: Jenny Harnisch
Rooms: 3 (PB) $45
Full Breakfast
Credit Cards: A, B
Notes: 2, 9, 11, 12

HICKORY

The Hickory Bed and Breakfast

464 Seventh Street Southwest, 28602
(704) 324-0548; (800) 654-2961

Southern hospitality and friendly hosts welcome you to this country-furnished home. Rest comfortably in one of four bedrooms decorated with antiques and collectibles. The homemade breakfast is an experience long remembered. Homemade iced tea and lemonade with something from the oven are served in the late afternoon. Relax in the sunbeams that stream through the beveled-glass windows, shop for furniture, go fishing or climbing.

Hosts: Suzanne and Bob Ellis
Rooms: 4 (2 PB; 2 SB) $45-55
Full Breakfast
Credit Cards: None
Notes: 2, 5, 11, 12, 13, 14

HIGHLANDS

Colonial Pines Inn

Route 1, Box 22B, 28741
(704) 526-2060

A quiet country guest house on two acres with a lovely mountain view is just one-half mile from Highlands' great shopping and dining. It features an expansive porch with rockers, cozy guest parlor with fireplace, grand piano, TV. All rooms are different and furnished with antiques, interesting fabrics, and accessories. Afternoon refresh-

ments are always available in the guest pantry.

Hosts: Donna and Chris Alley
Rooms: 6 (PB) $55-85
Houses: 2 (PB) $65-95
Full Breakfast
Credit Cards: A, B
Notes: 2, 5, 8 (in guest houses, under 6), 9, 10, 11, 12, 13

The First Colony Inn

MURPHY

Hill Top House

104 Campbell Street, 28906
(704) 837-8661

Built circa 1900, Hill Top House is a step back into a turn-of-the-century home. It offers the comfort of a large dining room for the delicious breakfast. Rooms have queen or twin beds. Each room is spacious and tastefully decorated in period and antique pieces.

Hosts: Don and Jacqueline Heinze
Rooms: 3 (1 PB; 2 SB) $45-50
Full Breakfast
Credit Cards: None
Notes: 2, 5, 8 (over 6)

Hoover House

306 Natural Springs Drive, 28906
(704) 837-8734

Hoover House, an elegant country inn, is situated in the Great Smoky Mountains, two hours from Atlanta, on a private six-and-one-half acre estate. The large, red brick inn has a gorgeous interior decor and furnishings, with guest spa and exercise room. Enjoy the moderate year-round climate, close to airport, golf, hiking, water sports, tourist areas, and national forest.

Host: Sugie Kovach
Rooms: 4 (PB) $50-75
Full Breakfast
Credit Cards: A, B
Notes: 5, 9, 10, 11, 12, 14

NAGS HEAD

The First Colony Inn
6720 South Virginia Dare Trail, 27959
(919) 441-2343; (800) 368-9390 reservations

Enjoy an old-fashioned vacation at this historic inn. A two-story veranda encircles the beautiful building. The inn has a sun deck, pool, and boardwalk across the street to a private gazebo and beach. English antiques fill the rooms. Luxuries available include kitchenettes, microwaves, wet bars, VCRs, and Jacuzzis. Guests may use the library with a fireplace.

Hosts: The Lawrences
Rooms: 26 (PB) $50-100 winter; $60-110 spring and fall; $100-200 in-season
Expanded Continental Breakfast
Credit Cards: A, B, C, D
Notes: 4 (except January and February), 5, 8, 9, 11, 12, 14

NEW BERN

New Berne House Inn
709 Broad Street, 28560
(800) 842-7688

This is an inn for the young and young at heart, with its particularly pleasing English country decor. Authentically restored, it has hardwood floors, antiques, working fireplaces, and a friendly ghost. Guest rooms feature antique beds and vintage baths. Scrumptious breakfasts include pralines and cream waffles, honey-glazed ham, and spiced apple crepes. Afternoon tea, mystery weekends, tour packages. The closest accommodation to Tryon Palace.

Hosts: David and Gina Hawkins
Rooms: 7 (PB) $75
Full Breakfast
Credit Cards: A, B, C, D
Notes: 2, 5, 6, 8, 9, 10, 11, 12, 14

SALUDA

The Oaks
P. O. Box 1008, 28773
(704) 749-9613

A turreted Victorian home benefits from the Saluda mountain breezes. Rooms are decorated in the period with interesting antiques. The Oaks provides a warm and welcoming atmosphere. The surrounding porch offers a place to relax and mull before ambling down to the many antique and craft shops on Main Street. Saluda is situated between Hendersonville and Tryon.

Hosts: Ceri and Peggy Dando
Rooms: 5 (PB) $55-85
Full Breakfast
Credit Cards: A, B
Notes: 2, 5, 9, 10, 12, 14

The Oaks

STATESVILLE _____

Madelyn's Bed and Breakfast
514 Carroll, 28677
(704) 872-3973

Located at the crossroads of I-40 and I-77, Statesville's first bed and breakfast is a charming 1940s brick cottage filled with family antiques and collections. There are three lovely bedrooms with private baths. A full gourmet breakfast is served, along with sweets and fresh fruits at check-in. Of course, you will enjoy your visit in a smoke-free environment.

Hosts: Madelyn and John Hill
Rooms: 3 (PB) $55-65
Full Breakfast
Credit Cards: A, B
Notes: 2, 5, 9, 10, 12, 14

WAYNESVILLE _____

Belle Meade Inn
P. O. Box 1319, 28786
(704) 456-3234

Nestled in the mountains, Waynesville is near the Great Smoky National Park and Asheville. This craftsman-style, elegant home from yesteryear, featuring chestnut woodwork in the formal rooms and a large fieldstone fireplace, is an interesting blend of antique and traditional furnishings. It offers central air conditioning, distinctively prepared hot breakfast, golf, hiking, rafting, and the Biltmore House nearby. Open April 15 through January 15.

Hosts: Larry Hanson and William Shaw
Rooms: 4 (PB) $50-55
Full Breakfast
Credit Cards: A, B, D
Notes: 9, 10, 12, 13, 14

WINSTON SALEM _____

Wachovia Bed and Breakfast
513 Wachovia Street, 27101
(919) 777-0332

Combine the relaxed charm of a bed and breakfast with the convenience and attractions of a metropolitan area. Situated on a quiet, tree-lined street, Wachovia Bed and Breakfast is a lovely rose and white Victorian cottage with a wraparound porch furnished in white wicker. The interior contains simple yet refined furnishings. Despite the tranquil setting, it is only a few blocks to the city center and historic district.

Host: Carol Royals
Rooms: 4 (2 PB; 2 SB) $45-55
Full Breakfast
Credit Cards: None
Notes: 2, 5, 8, 9, 10, 11, 12

NOTES: Credit cards accepted: A Master Card; B Visa; C American Express; D Discover Card; E Diners Club; F Other; 2 Personal checks accepted; 3 Lunch available; 4 Dinner available; 5 Open all year; 6 Pets welcome; 8 Children

North Dakota

LUVERNE

Old West Bed and Breakfast
Box 211, Regent, 58650
(701) 563-4542

This bed and breakfast is a pleasant blending of a 1926 farmhouse and a 1978 addition, filled with antiques and collectibles that reflect 27 years in the U.S. Air Force. Situated a mile from the Sheyenne River, it offers fishing, hunting, canoeing, hiking, biking, and skiing as possible attractions. Two rooms with double beds and a bath upstairs in the old house give a measure of privacy. The entire house is open for the use of guests. Scandinavian breakfast is served. Children welcome. No credit cards. $35; $50 for a family; $50 for suite.

REEDER

Old West Bed and Breakfast
Box 211, Regent, 58650
(701) 563-4542

Five miles from a large surface coal mine, this bed and breakfast offers two bedrooms with queen-size beds and a shared bath. One bedroom has a separate entrance. Children over 12 welcome. $30.

REGENT

Old West Bed and Breakfast
Box 211, 58650
(701) 563-4542

Not far from Medora and the Badlands. Outdoor heated swimming pool available in summer. Two bedrooms with double beds. Children over 12 welcome. $40; rates not applicable during hunting season.

WING

Old West Bed and Breakfast
Box 211, Regent, 58650
(701) 563-4542

A contemporary ranch house situated on an active grain farm and ranching operation. It is a 45-minute drive to the capital, heritage center, and Garrison Dam. The family room with fireplace and hot tub is available to guests. Two guest rooms share a bath. Children welcome. No pets. $25.

welcome; 9 Social drinking allowed; 10 Tennis available; 11 Swimming available; 12 Golf available; 13 Skiing available; 14 May be booked through travel agents

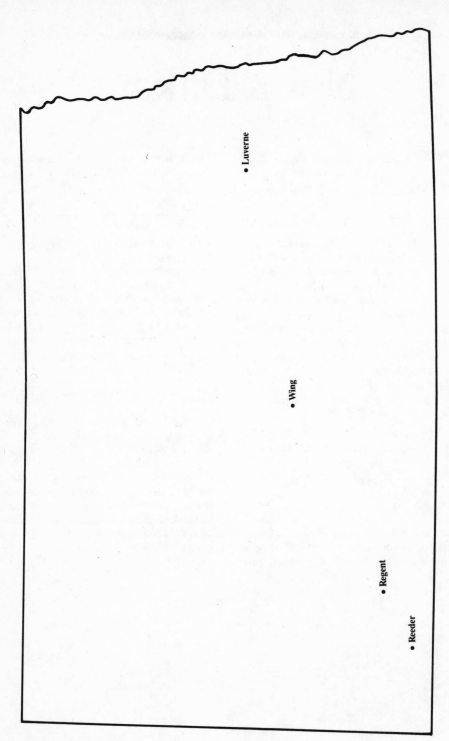

NORTH DAKOTA

Ohio

Prospect Hill
Bed and Breakfast
408 Boal Street, 45210
(513) 421-4408

The bed and breakfast is an elegantly restored 1867 Italianate Victorian town house
with spectacular views of downtown Cincinnati. For business, vacations, or a romantic weekend, there are wood-burning
fireplaces, antique furnishings, a magnificent breakfast, and proximity to downtown
and the Ohio River. The house sits on a
wooded hillside in the Prospect Hill national historical district. The zoo, University of Cincinnati, and Kings Island amuse-
ment park are nearby.

Host: Gary Hackney
Rooms: 3 (1 PB; 2 SB) $69-79
Full Breakfast
Credit Cards: A, B
Notes: 2, 5, 9, 10, 11, 13

Castle Inn
610 South Court Street, 43113
(614) 477-3986; (800) 477-1541

Arches, battlements, towers, and plenty of
stained glass adorn this romantic medieval
"castle" completed in 1899 for a beautiful
bride. All rooms feature Victorian antiques.
Breakfast is served on English china in a
museum-quality dining room overlooking
the walled Shakespeare garden in which
grow flowers and herbs mentioned in
Shakespeare's plays. Occasional weekend
events include murder mysteries and Eliza-
bethan holidays.

Hosts: Sue and Jim Maxwell
Rooms: 6 (4 PB; 2 SB) $45-75
Full Breakfast
Credit Cards: A, B
Notes: 2, 5, 8 (over 8), 14

The White Oak Inn
29683 Walhonding Road, 43014
(614) 599-6107

This turn-of-the-century farmhouse in a
quiet, wooded setting features antiques and
period decor, large common room with fireplace, front porch spanning the inn with
swings and rockers, screen house, and lawn
games. The inn is listed in 18 guidebooks
including the prestigious *Country Inns and
Back Roads* and is recommended by AAA
and *Mobil Travel Guide*. Near Amish country, Roscoe Village, antiques, golf, and canoeing.

Castle Inn

NOTES: Credit cards accepted: A Master Card; B Visa; C American Express; D Discover Card; E Diners Club; F Other;
2 Personal checks accepted; 3 Lunch available; 4 Dinner available; 5 Open all year; 6 Pets welcome; 8 Children
welcome; 9 Social drinking allowed; 10 Tennis available; 11 Swimming available; 12 Golf available; 13 Skiing
available; 14 May be booked through travel agents

OHIO

• Northfield

Millersburg
• • Dellroy
• Danville

• West Milton

• Circleville

• Cincinnati
• New Richmond

Hosts: Joyce and Jim Acton
Rooms: 10 (PB) $70-115
Full Breakfast
Credit Cards: A, B
Notes: 2, 4, 5, 9, 11, 12, 14

DELLROY

Whispering Pines Bed and Breakfast

1268 Magnolia, State Route 542
P. O. Box 340, 44620
(216) 735-2824

Discover elegance, hospitality, romance, and a tranquil setting in this 1880 Victorian home situated on seven acres and overlooking picturesque Atwood Lake. Each guest room has a magnificent view. Furnished in fine 19th-century antiques, the inn has four working fireplaces. A leisurely breakfast is served on the enclosed wraparound porch. Enjoy the large brick courtyard with Victorian lighting, seating, and gardens.

Hosts: Bill and Linda Horn
Rooms: 3 (PB) $70-80
Full Breakfast
Credit Cards: None
Notes: 2, 5, 9, 10, 11, 12, 13

MILLERSBURG

Adams Street Bed and Breakfast

175 West Adams Street, 44654
(216) 674-0766

This Victorian country home is in Holmes County, in the center of the world's largest Amish community. Amish quilts, rag rugs on hardwood floors, oak-framed fireplace, library, homebaked bread, air conditioning. One block from village shops. Host grew up Amish; recently retired as *Cleveland Plain Dealer* reporter and studied at Zona Spray Cooking School. Abigail Adams, resident cat, welcomes guests.

Host: Alma J. Kaufman
Rooms: 2 (SB) $45-55
Full Breakfast
Credit Cards: None
Notes: 2, 9, 10, 12

NEW RICHMOND

Hollyhock Bed and Breakfast

1610 Altman Road, 45157
(513) 553-6585; (513) 632-1572

A working sheep farm 25 miles east of Cincinnati, Hollyhock offers a gracious suite with a queen bed, private parlor, and excellent proximity to Kings Island, Cincinnati, Riverfront Stadium, and many golf courses. The home is an 1853 farmhouse lovingly restored.

Host: Evelyn Cutter
Suite: 1 (PB) $75
Full Breakfast
Credit Cards: None
Notes: 2, 5, 6, 8, 9, 10, 11, 12, 14

Whispering Pines Bed and Breakfast

NORTHFIELD

The Inn at Brandywine Falls

8230 Brandywine Road, 44067
(216) 467-1812

The inn, overlooking Brandywine Waterfall in the Cuyahoga Valley National Park, was built in 1848 and is on the National

NOTES: Credit cards accepted: A Master Card; B Visa; C American Express; D Discover Card; E Diners Club; F Other; 2 Personal checks accepted; 3 Lunch available; 4 Dinner available; 5 Open all year; 6 Pets welcome; 8 Children welcome; 9 Social drinking allowed; 10 Tennis available; 11 Swimming available; 12 Golf available; 13 Skiing available; 14 May be booked through travel agents

Register of Historic Places. It has been thoroughly renovated and made modern with up-to-date heating, plumbing, and air conditioning, all without changing its historic Greek Revival appearance and character. It is furnished with antiques and features quality amenities and gourmet foods. The inn enjoys local and national recognition.

Hosts: Katie and George Hoy
Rooms: 6 (PB) $85-150
Full Breakfast
Credit Cards: A, B
Notes: 2, 5, 8, 9, 11, 12, 13, 14

This delightful old Cape Cod home is tastefully decorated with family antiques. It has lots of space to roam or lounge on the screened porch, deck, patio, or gazebo. Breakfast is served in the dining room or porch. Relax in the library or in front of the fireplace. Near antique shops, nature center, golf course, canoeing, restaurants.

Host: Ruth Shoup
Rooms: 3 (1 PB; 2 SB) $45-50
Full Breakfast
Credit Cards: None
Notes: 2, 5, 8, 12

WEST MILTON

Locust Lane Farm Bed and Breakfast
5590 Kessler Cowlesville Road, 45383
(513) 698-4743

Oklahoma

Country Inn
Bed and Breakfast
Route 3, Box 1925, 74017
(918) 342-1894

Leland and Kay invite you to their country retreat. Stay in charming barn-style guest quarters, separate from the main house. Enjoy the swimming pool, relax under a big shade tree with a cool drink, or take a country walk. A delightful continental breakfast is provided. Visit the on-premises quilt and craft shop. Nearby are J. M. Davis Gun Museum, Will Rogers Memorial, and horse racing at Will Rogers Downs during August and September.

Hosts: Leland and Kay Jenkins
Rooms: 3 (PB) $47-59
Full Breakfast
Credit Cards: None
Notes: 2, 5, 9, 11

Willow Way
27 Oakwood Drive, 73121-5410
(405) 427-2133

Willow Way is a wooded town retreat in English Tudor country-style with antique decor and genuine charm. Established two-story stone, with vaulted ceiling den and picture window, guests' favorite place for breakfast. Safe and comfortable with off-street parking. Quiet, situated near nature, the race track, Cowboy Hall of Fame, and other area attractions. Three rooms with two private baths. Full breakfast; occasions and dinner by arrangement.

Hosts: Johnita and Lionel Turner
Rooms: 3 (2 PB; 1 SB) $50-80
Full Breakfast
Credit Cards: A, B
Notes: 2, 3, 5, 8, 9, 12

welcome; 9 Social drinking allowed; 10 Tennis available; 11 Swimming available; 12 Golf available; 13 Skiing available; 14 May be booked through travel agents

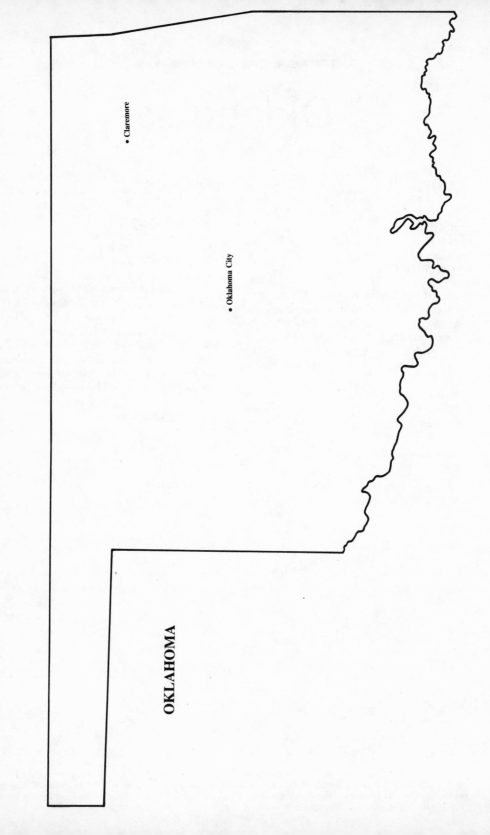

OKLAHOMA

Claremore

Oklahoma City

Oregon

Adams Cottage
Bed and Breakfast

737 Siskiyou Boulevard, 97520
(503) 488-5405; (800) 345-2570

Five blocks or less to theaters, shopping, and Southern Oregon State College, this historic 1900 vernacular-style home offers uniquely decorated guest rooms with queen beds and air conditioning. The carriage house offers junior suites with private patio or balcony and large social areas. The Shakespearean Theater is a ten-minute walk away. Adam's Cottage is the ultimate Ashland experience.

Hosts: Jeff and Amy Von Hauf
Rooms: 4 (PB) $59-105
Full Breakfast
Credit Cards: None
Notes: 2, 5, 8, 9, 10, 11, 12, 13, 14

Buckhorn Springs

2200 Buckhorn Springs Road, 97520
(503) 488-2200

The Sargent family delights in sharing this secluded mineral springs resort with guests who would enjoy a step back to simpler times. A short, picturesque drive from Ashland, this home on the National Register of Historic Places includes a century-old lodge with eight unique guest rooms and five creekside cabins. This quiet getaway offers a restaurant serving healthy meals.

Hosts: Bruce and Leslie Sargent
Rooms: 8 (4 PB; 4 SB) $65-150

Cabins: 5 (PB)
Full Breakfast
Credit Cards: A, B
Notes: 2, 3, 4, 8, 9, 11, 12, 13, 14

Cowslip's Belle
Bed and Breakfast

159 North Main Street, 97520
(503) 488-2901

The Cowslip's Belle offers teddy bears and chocolate truffles, fancy linens and snow-white laces, scrumptious breakfasts, happy faces, and is comfy and cozy in all the right places.

Hosts: Jon and Carmen Reinhardt
Rooms: 4 (PB) $50-95
Full or Continental Breakfast
Credit Cards: A, B
Notes: 2, 5, 9, 10, 11, 12, 13, 14

Mount Ashland Inn

550 Mount Ashland Road, P. O. Box 944, 97520
(503) 482-8707

Enjoy mountain serenity and warm hospitality in this handcrafted log inn 16 miles from Ashland. Attention to detail is evident in the hand carvings, finely crafted furniture, stained glass, rock fireplace, and elegant decor. Guest rooms have spectacular views. Hike, bike, or cross-country ski from the inn's door, or downhill ski nearby.

Hosts: Elaine and Jerry Shanafelt
Rooms: 5 (PB) $75-125
Full Breakfast
Credit Cards: A, B
Notes: 2, 5, 9, 13, 14

NOTES: Credit cards accepted: A Master Card; B Visa; C American Express; D Discover Card; E Diners Club; F Other; 2 Personal checks accepted; 3 Lunch available; 4 Dinner available; 5 Open all year; 6 Pets welcome; 8 Children welcome; 9 Social drinking allowed; 10 Tennis available; 11 Swimming available; 12 Golf available; 13 Skiing available; 14 May be booked through travel agents

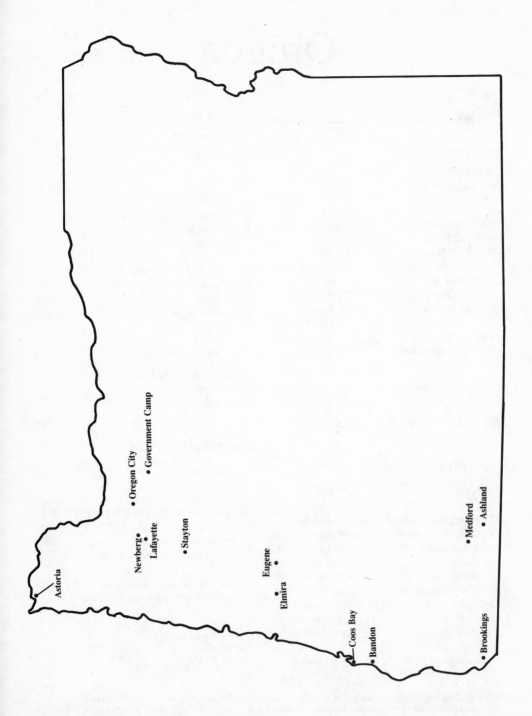

OREGON

Pinehurst Inn at Jenny Creek

17250 Highway 66, 97520
(503) 488-1002

A restored 1920s roadhouse next to a year-round creek, Pinehurst is furnished with antiques and handmade quilts. The restaurant serves American fresh cuisine dinners and breakfasts. It is 23 miles east of Ashland, 39 miles west of Klamath Falls in the Cascade Mountains. Nearby are the Pacific Crest Trail, Klamath River rafting, horseback riding, and cross-country skiing. Small plane landing one-half mile away.

Host: Delia Smith
Rooms: 6 (PB) $75-95
Full Breakfast
Credit Cards: A, B
Notes: 2, 4, 5, 6, 8, 9

ASTORIA

Grandview Bed and Breakfast

1574 Grand Avenue, 97103
(503) 325-5555; (800) 488-3250

Enjoy wonderful views from the light, cheerful rooms that have hardwood floors, lace, and fluffy comforters. This Victorian home is situated on the Historic Homes Walking Tour and is close to superb Maritime Museum, Heritage Museum, and 100-year-old churches. Breakfast includes several coffee and tea choices, fruit juice, fresh fruit, muffins, and often lox and bagels.

Host: Charleen Maxwell
Rooms: 3 (PB) $38-75
Continental Breakfast
Credit Cards: A, B, D
Notes: 2, 5, 8 (over 10), 10, 11, 12

BANDON

Lighthouse Bed and Breakfast

P. O. Box 24, 97411
(503) 347-9316

Lighthouse Bed and Breakfast is situated on the beach at the mouth of the Coquille River across from the historic Bandon lighthouse. Sunny, plant-filled rooms have ocean and jetty or river views. The master bedroom has a fireplace and whirlpool for two. King or queen beds. Walk to Old Town and gourmet restaurants.

Hosts: Bruce and Linda Sisson
Rooms: 4 (PB) $75-95
Continental Breakfast
Credit Cards: A, B
Notes: 2, 5, 9, 10, 12, 14

Sea Star Guesthouse

370 First Street, 97411
(503) 347-9632

Sea Star Guesthouse is a unique coastal getaway in historic Old Town Bandon-by-the-Sea, situated right on the harbor with an incredible view. It is only a stroll to shops, galleries, river cruises, crabbing, fishing, and the spectacular beach. Sea Star's bistro, where guests enjoy breakfast, also serves lunch and dinner, offering freshly prepared international cuisines.

Hosts: David and Monica Jennings
Rooms: 4 (PB) $55-90
Full Breakfast
Credit Cards: A, B, C
Notes: 3, 4, 5, 9, 10, 12

Pinehurst Inn at Jenny Creek

NOTES: Credit cards accepted: A Master Card; B Visa; C American Express; D Discover Card; E Diners Club; F Other; 2 Personal checks accepted; 3 Lunch available; 4 Dinner available; 5 Open all year; 6 Pets welcome; 8 Children welcome; 9 Social drinking allowed; 10 Tennis available; 11 Swimming available; 12 Golf available; 13 Skiing available; 14 May be booked through travel agents

BROOKINGS

Chetco River Inn

21202 High Prairie Road, 97415
(503) 469-8128; (800) 327-2688 Pelican Bay Travel

A private retreat along the banks of the beautiful Chetco River, the inn offers modern conveniences using alternative energy sources. The inn is small, so guest numbers are limited. Nearly 40 wooded acres are nearby for guest enjoyment. Situated a short distance from Brookings, an Oregon seacoast town with great beaches. Warm beds, good food, and peace.

Host: Sandra Brugger
Rooms: 4 (3 PB; 1 SB) $75-85
Full Breakfast
Credit Cards: A, B
Notes: 2, 3, 4, 5, 9, 11

Holmes Sea Cove Bed and Breakfast

17350 Holmes Drive, 97415
(503) 469-3025

Hosts have a separate guest cottage and two bedrooms on the lower level of their home. Each room has a spectacular ocean view, small refrigerator, color TV, queen bed. Enjoy the ocean view; walk down the winding trail through the trees to a private park and the beach.

Hosts: Lorene and Jack Holmes
Rooms: 3 (PB) $80-95
Continental Breakfast
Credit Cards: A, B
Notes: 2, 5, 10, 11

COOS BAY

Captain's Quarters Bed and Breakfast

265 South Empire Boulevard, P.O. Box 3231, 97420
(503) 888-6895

An 1892 Victorian has been lovingly restored to its original beauty. This former home of Thomas McGenn, captain of the *Breakwater*, includes some of the captain's memorabilia. Bedrooms face the colorful bay and North Spit. Homemade full breakfasts include seven-grain waffles, freshly baked breads, and freshly ground coffee. Enjoy beachcombing, clamming, crabbing, visiting the lovely botanical gardens, or exploring the nearby boat basin of South Slough.

Hosts: John and Jean Griswold
Rooms: 2 (SB) $45-55
Full Breakfast
Credit Cards: None
Notes: 2, 5, 9, 11, 12

ELMIRA

McGillivray's Log Home Bed and Breakfast

88680 Evers Road, 97437
(503) 935-3564

This unique built-from-scratch log home is situated on five acres, mostly covered with fir and pine trees in a secluded country setting. Situated 14 miles west of Eugene on the way to the Oregon coast. The best of yesterday combined with the comforts of today. King beds, air conditioning, and quiet.

Host: Evelyn R. McGillivray
Rooms: 2 (PB) $55-65
Full Breakfast
Credit Cards: A, B
Notes: 2, 5, 8, 9, 11

EUGENE

Kjaer's House in the Woods

814 Lorane Highway, 97405
(503) 343-3234

The House in the Woods is a 1910 Craftsman-style home in a peaceful setting of fir and oak trees, rhododendron, and azaleas. Wildflowers abound in the spring. A porch swing offers relaxation and opportunity for viewing birds and frequent visits of deer. The interior features hardwood floors, Oriental carpets, antique furniture, and an unusual square grand piano. Breakfast is prepared with Danish and German influences.

Hosts: George and Eunice Kjaer
Rooms: 2 (1 PB; 1 SB) $50-65
Full Breakfast
Credit Cards: None
Notes: 2, 5, 10, 11, 12, 13, 14

GOVERNMENT CAMP

Falcon's Crest Inn, Inc.
87287 Government Camp Loop Highway
P. O. Box 185, 97028
(503) 272-3403; (800) 624-7384

This elegant Mount Hood-style inn features three rooms and two suites individually decorated with family heirlooms and offering in-room phones, turn-down service, morning refreshment tray, après snacks. Situated in the heart of year-round recreation area, guests enjoy skiing, hiking, fishing, horseback riding. Corporate and private mystery parties are a specialty.

Hosts: Bob and Melody Johnson
Rooms: 5 (PB) $85-110
Full Breakfast
Credit Cards: A, B, C
Notes: 2, 4, 5, 8, 9, 10, 11, 12, 13, 14

LAFAYETTE

Kelty Estate Bed and Breakfast
675 Highway 99 West, P.O. Box 817, 97127
(503) 864-3740

Built in 1872, this early Colonial-style home is on the National Register of Historic Places. Recently remodeled and furnished with turn-of-the-century antiques. Situated in the heart of the Oregon wine country, across the street from the historic old LaFayette School

House Antique Mall. Nearby are the Yamhill County Museum and many fine wineries. One hour to the coast or mountains. Thirty minutes from Portland. Barbecue area; queen beds; afternoon tea; evening wine.

Hosts: Ron and JoAnn Ross
Rooms: 2 (PB) $55-65
Full Breakfast
Credit Cards: None
Notes: 2, 5, 8, 9, 12

Waverly Cottage and Associated
Bed and Breakfasts

MEDFORD

Waverly Cottage and Associated Bed and Breakfasts
305 North Grape, 97501
(503) 779-4716

This 1898 authentically restored Victorian is on the National Register of Historic Places. It is the most ornate Queen Anne-style cottage still standing in southern Oregon. Three adjacent suites of historical merit have air conditioning, queen beds, kitchens, livingrooms, climbing roses, appliances, TV/VCR. Home away from home. One suite is handicapped accessible.

Host: David Fisse
Rooms: 5 (4 PB; 1 SB) $55-95
Expanded Continental Breakfast
Credit Cards: A, B, C, E
Notes: 2, 5, 6 (limited), 8, 9, 10, 11, 12, 13, 14

welcome; 9 Social drinking allowed; 10 Tennis available; 11 Swimming available; 12 Golf available; 13 Skiing available; 14 May be booked through travel agents

NEWBERG

Secluded Bed and Breakfast

19719 Northeast Williamson Road, 97132
(503) 538-2635

This secluded, beautiful country home is situated on ten acres and is the ideal retreat in a wooded setting for hiking, country walks, and wildlife observation. It is ten minutes to several wineries, near Newberg, behind the beautiful Red Hills of Dundee, convenient to George Fox College, 20 minutes from McMinnville, one hour to the Oregon coast.

Hosts: Del and Durell Belanger
Rooms: 2 (1 PB; 1 SB) $40-50
Full Breakfast
Credit Cards: None
Notes: 2, 5, 8, 10, 11, 12, 14

OREGON CITY

Jagger House Bed and Breakfast

512 Sixth Street, 97045
(503) 657-7820

Furnished with antiques and reproductions, this carefully restored 1880 house has many special touches, including a garden gazebo, handmade folk art, the house jigsaw puzzle, and privacy. Twelve miles south of Portland, Oregon City is the official end of the Oregon Trail, with five museums within two blocks of the inn. The innkeeper is very knowledgeable about local history.

Host: Claire Met
Rooms: 3 (1 PB; 2 SB) $55-60
Full Breakfast
Credit Cards: A, B
Notes: 2, 5, 10, 11, 12, 13, 14

Secluded Bed and Breakfast

STAYTON

Gardner House Bed and Breakfast

633 North Third Avenue, 97383
(503) 769-6331

An extraordinary cottage has design-coordinated decor, separate entrance, off-street parking, kitchen, sitting room, phone, TV/VCR. Smoky the cat, who lives in the main house, has the last word on pets.

Host: Richard Jungwirth
Rooms: 2 (PB) $55
Full Breakfast
Credit Cards: A, B
Notes: 2, 4, 5, 6, 8, 9, 10, 11, 12

Pennsylvania

Spring House
Muddy Creek Forks, 17302
(717) 927-6906

Built in 1798 of local fieldstone by state legislator Robert Turner, Spring House is nestled in the historic and scenic valley of Muddy Creek. The innkeeper restored the house to its original whitewashed and stenciled walls. Furnished with local country antiques and art pieces from around the world, the inn offers solitude and excellent country cuisine. Pets in residence. Spanish is spoken.

Host: Ray Constance Hearne
Rooms: 5 (3 PB; 2 SB) $60-85
Full Breakfast
Credit Cards: None
Notes: 2, 5, 8, 9, 10, 11, 12, 13, 14

Spring House

Highland View
Bed and Breakfast
Highland Road, Box 154 C, 19310
(215) 593-5066

Highland View is surrounded by plenty of farmland and fields. Guests get a warm, at-home feeling when staying at this ranch-style home. Breakfast is served in a brightly lit sun room. An Amish school house and antique covered bridge are both within a mile. The Rockvale outlet mall, the village of Intercourse, Longwood Gardens, and many home-style restaurants are all within 15 minutes.

Hosts: Sam and Cora Umble
Rooms: 2 (SB) $40-45
Full Breakfast
Credit Cards: None
Notes: 2, 4, 5, 8, 9, 10, 12, 14

Ponda-Rowland
Bed and Breakfast
Inn and Farm Vacations
Rural Route 1, Box 349, 18612
(717) 639-3245

This large, scenic farm in the mountains features animals, a 30-acre wildlife refuge, ponds, hiking, canoeing, swimming, cross-

welcome; 9 Social drinking allowed; 10 Tennis available; 11 Swimming available; 12 Golf available; 13 Skiing available; 14 May be booked through travel agents

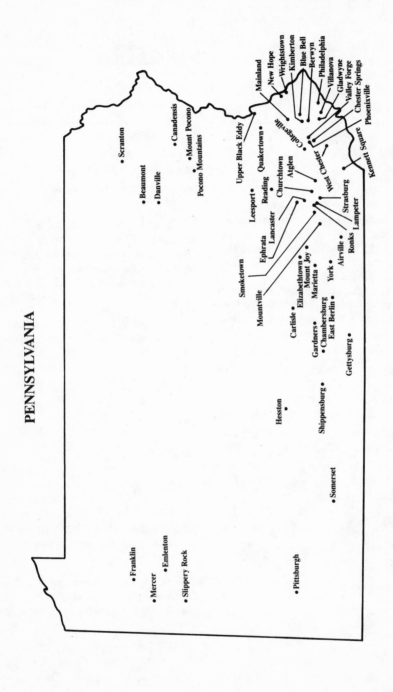

PENNSYLVANIA

Franklin
Mercer
Emlenton
Slippery Rock

Scranton

Beaumont
Danville

Canadensis
Mount Pocono
Pocono Mountains

Mainland
New Hope
Wrightstown
Kimberton
Blue Bell
Berwyn
Philadelphia
Villanova
Gladwyne
Valley Forge
Chester Springs
Phoenixville

Upper Black Eddy
Quakertown
Collegeville
Kennett Square

Leesport
Reading
Churchtown
Atglen
West Chester

Smoketown
Ephrata
Lancaster
Strasburg
Lampeter
Ronks
Airville

Mountville
Elizabethtown
Mount Joy
Marietta
York

Carlisle
Gardners
Chambersburg
East Berlin

Gettysburg

Hesston

Shippensburg

Pittsburgh

Somerset

country skiing, horseback riding, air tours, antiquing, restaurants, downhill skiing, and country fairs. The house was built circa 1850 of timberframe (post-and-beam) and double-plank construction and has a large stone fireplace.

Hosts: Jeanette and Clifford Rowland
Rooms: 5 (4 PB; 1 SB) $40-60
Full Breakfast
Credit Cards: A, B
Notes: 2, 5, 8, 9, 11, 12, 13, 14

BERWYN

Bed and Breakfast of Valley Forge #0501

P. O. Box 562, Valley Forge, 19481-0562
(215) 783-7838; (800) 344-0123
FAX (215) 783-7783

This farmhouse features beamed ceilings, stenciled walls, antique country furnishings, samplers, and local quilts. The oldest part is a restored, circa-1770 tenant house. $85-110.

Bed and Breakfast of Valley Forge #2303

P. O. Box 562, Valley Forge, 19481-0562
(215) 783-7838; (800) 344-0123
FAX (215) 783-7783

This 30-year-old two-story Colonial is situated near the Devon horse show grounds and Valley Forge Music Fair. Two guest rooms with private bath. $55.

BLUE BELL

Bed and Breakfast of Valley Forge #0705

P. O. Box 562, Valley Forge, 19481-0562
(215) 783-7838; (800) 344-0123
FAX (215) 783-7783

This magnificent 200-year-old inn sits on five peaceful acres of lawns and gardens with a pool, tennis courts, bikes, and Jacuzzi available. Two suites and three rooms with antique beds, sitting rooms, fireplace, or Jacuzzi. Continental breakfast. Three-night stay most rooms. $85-110.

Bed and Breakfast of Valley Forge #1905

P. O. Box 562, Valley Forge, 19481-0562
(215) 783-7838; (800) 344-0123
FAX (215) 783-7783

Guests' quarters are reached through a private entrance from a garden walkway and include a large, fully equipped kitchen, cozy parlor, and bedroom. Enjoy the 15 acres with barn, springhouse, orchard, stream, and pool. $75.

CANADENSIS

Nearbrook Bed and Breakfast

Rural Delivery 1, Box 630, 18325
(717) 595-3152

Situated in the heart of the recreational area of the Pocono Mountains, Nearbrook is surrounded by rose and rock gardens, woods, and a stream. There are many restaurants and tourist attractions nearby. Enjoy skiing, horseback riding, golf, swimming, and hiking on great trails. A contagious informality encourages guests to use the piano and games.

Hosts: Barb and Dick Robinson
Rooms: 3 (SB) $45
Full Breakfast
Credit Cards: None
Notes: 2, 5, 9, 11, 12, 13

NOTES: Credit cards accepted: A Master Card; B Visa; C American Express; D Discover Card; E Diners Club; F Other; 2 Personal checks accepted; 3 Lunch available; 4 Dinner available; 5 Open all year; 6 Pets welcome; 8 Children welcome; 9 Social drinking allowed; 10 Tennis available; 11 Swimming available; 12 Golf available; 13 Skiing available; 14 May be booked through travel agents

CARLISLE

Line Limousin Farmhouse
2070 Ritner Highway, 17013
(717) 243-1281

This 110-acre homestead has an 11-room brick and stone farmhouse built by Great Grandfather Line using walnut lumber for windows and doors. Furnishings include many fine antiques. Hosts raise Limousin beef cattle from France. Giant sugar maple trees make welcome shade for cookouts. Hike in the woods, play croquet, boccie ball, badminton, horseshoes, or drive golf balls.

Hosts: Bob and Joan Line
Rooms: 3 (2 PB; 1 SB) $45-55
Full Breakfast
Credit Cards: None
Notes: 2, 5, 8, 12

Line Limousin Farmhouse

CHAMBERSBURG

Falling Spring Inn
1838 Falling Spring Road, 17201
(717) 267-3654

Enjoy country living only two miles from Exit 6 off of I-81 and Route 30. On a working farm with animals and Falling Spring, a nationally renowned freshwater trout stream. Large pond, lawns, meadows, ducks, and birds all make a pleasant picture. Historical Gettysburg is only 25 miles away. Relax in the air-conditioned rooms with queen-size beds.

Hosts: Adin and Janet Frey
Rooms: 5 (PB) $49-69
Full Breakfast
Credit Cards: A, B
Notes: 2, 5, 8, 10, 11, 12, 13

CHESTER SPRINGS

Bed and Breakfast of Valley Forge #1302
P. O. Box 562, Valley Forge, 19481-0562
(215) 783-7838; (800) 344-0123
FAX (215) 783-7783

Country antiques complement this circa-1840 farmhouse on ten acres of lawn and woods that invite biking, jogging, hiking, or just appreciating. Enjoy fireplaces, porches, and patio with chairs by the stream. $65.

Bed and Breakfast of Valley Forge #1900
P. O. Box 562, Valley Forge, 19481-0562
(215) 783-7838; (800) 344-0123
FAX (215) 783-7783

This rural guest cottage on 44 acres was once a carriage house and has a livingroom with cathedral ceiling, full kitchen, and two bedrooms. Swimming pool; kitchen is fully stocked. Weekly and mothly rates available. $100.

CHURCHTOWN

Foreman House Bed and Breakfast
2129 Main Street, 17555
(215) 445-6713

The Foreman House is a turn-of-the-century home furnished with antiques and decorated with quilts and local artwork. There is a large livingroom with a piano and a side porch, both open to guests. The back yard offers a view of Amish farms, and there is a

NOTES: Credit cards accepted: A Master Card; B Visa; C American Express; D Discover Card; E Diners Club; F Other; 2 Personal checks accepted; 3 Lunch available; 4 Dinner available; 5 Open all year; 6 Pets welcome; 8 Children

picnic table where guests may enjoy eating and resting.

Hosts: Stephen and Jacqueline Mitrani
Rooms: 3 (1 PB; 2 SB) $58.30-68.90
Full Breakfast weekends; Continental Breakfast
    weekdays
Credit Cards: None
Notes: 5, 9, 10, 11, 12

COLLEGEVILLE

Bed and Breakfast of Valley Forge #1305

P. O. Box 562, Valley Forge, 19481-0562
(215) 783-7838; (800) 344-0123
FAX (215) 783-7783

Near Ursinus College, this spacious Federal-style home has a wraparound porch. In 1838, a new home was built on the original 1769 farmstead. The country kitchen has beamed ceilings and stained-glass windows. Private bath; baby equipment available. Full breakfast. $65.

Bed and Breakfast of Valley Forge #1904

P. O. Box 562, Valley Forge, 19481-0562
(215) 783-7838; (800) 344-0123
FAX (215) 783-7783

Skilled European and American craftsmen fashioned this 22-room Victorian mansion in 1897. A three-story winding chestnut staircase leads to the guest rooms that are faithfully furnished with period pieces. Private baths. Can accommodate house tours, weddings, corporate meetings. Full breakfast. $65-75.

Bed and Breakfast of Valley Forge #1908

P. O. Box 562, Valley Forge, 19481-0562
(215) 783-7838; (800) 344-0123
FAX (215) 783-7783

This Dutch Colonial home is on five acres and has a barn that houses vintage cars. The fields are a Christmas tree farm. A veranda encircles the house and is ideal for enjoying the rural surroundings. $65.

DANVILLE

Melanie Ann's Bed and Breakfast

120 Center Street, 17821
(717) 275-4147

The inn is an authentic Colonial-style house built in 1850. The original owner and builder was Alexander Montgomery, son of the founder of Danville. Five rooms are beautifully furnished in fine antiques and reproductions. Complimentary tea and homemade desserts are served upon arrival. Dinners are served in the cozy patio area from menus selected by guests.

Hosts: Ray and Melanie Rogers
Rooms: 5 (3 PB; 2 SB) $45-55
Full Breakfast
Credit Cards: None
Notes: 2, 4 (by arrangement)

EAST BERLIN

Bechtel Mansion Inn

400 West King Street, 17316
(717) 259-7760

This classic Queen Anne-style Victorian mansion has been carefully restored and furnished with quality antiques, handmade quilts, and period accessories. It is situated in the East Berlin national historic district and is popular as a honeymoon, anniversary, or romantic getaway site. It is close to excellent restaurants, antique shops, historic Gettysburg, York, and Lancaster.

Hosts: Ruth Spangler, Charles and Mariam Bechtel
Rooms: 7 (5 PB; 2 SB) $65
Suites: 2 (PB) $130

welcome; 9 Social drinking allowed; 10 Tennis available; 11 Swimming available; 12 Golf available; 13 Skiing available; 14 May be booked through travel agents

Full Breakfast
Credit Cards: A, B, C, D
Notes: 2, 5, 8, 9, 10, 11, 12, 13, 14

ELIZABETHTOWN

West Ridge Guest House

1285 West Ridge Road, 17022
(717) 367-7783

A four-star rated bed and breakfast tucked midway between Harrisburg and Lancaster, this European manor can be found four miles off Route 283 at Rheems-Elizabethtown exit. Each guest room reflects a different style. An exercise room with hot tub and a large social room are in an adjacent guest house. It is 20 to 40 minutes to local attractions, Hershey Park, Lancaster County Amish farms, and outlet shopping malls.

Host: Alice Heisey
Rooms: 7 (PB) $50-75
Full Breakfast
Credit Cards: A, B
Note: 2

Bechtel Mansion Inn

EMLENTON

Whippletree Inn and Farm

Rural Delivery 3, Box 285, 16373
(412) 867-9543

Whippletree Inn and Farm is a restored turn-of-the-century cattle farm. The house,

barns, and 100 acres of pasture sit on a hill above the Allegheny River and the town of Emlenton. There is a pleasant trail leading down to the river. Guests are welcome to use the half-mile race track for horses, carriages, and hiking. No horses for rent, but boarding for private horses is available.

Hosts: Warren and Joey Simmons
Rooms: 4 (2 PB; 2 SB) $45-50
Full Breakfast
Credit Cards: None
Notes: 2, 5, 8, 11, 12

EPHRATA

The Smithton Inn

900 West Main Street, 17522
(717) 733-6094

Smithton is a first-quality country inn with everyday prices, situated in Lancaster County, home of the Pennsylvania Dutch, where Amish and Old Order Mennonites still farm with horses. Smithton is a welcoming inn where every room has a fireplace, a four-poster or canopy bed, leather upholstered furniture, books, reading lamps, and optional feather bedding. Antiques, chamber music, candles, and quilts make a romantic setting.

Host: Dorothy Graybill
Rooms: 8 (PB) $65-115
Full Breakfast
Credit Cards: A, B, C
Notes: 2, 5, 6, 8, 9, 10, 11, 12

FRANKLIN

Quo Vadis Bed and Breakfast

1501 Liberty Street, 16323
(814) 432-4208

A stately brick and terra cotta home, Quo Vadis (Whither Goest Thou?) is an eclectic Queen Anne built in 1867 and is in the historic district of Franklin. The high-ceilinged spacious rooms, parquet floors, and detailed woodwork display Victorian elegance. The furniture has been acquired by the same family over four generations. Quilts, embroidery, and lacework are family handwork.

Hosts: Kristal and Stanton Bowmer
Rooms: 6 (PB) $60-70
Continental Breakfast
Credit Cards: A, B, C
Notes: 2, 8 (over 11), 9, 10, 11, 12, 13 (XC), 14

The Brafferton Inn

GARDNERS

Goose Chase
Bed and Breakfast

200 Blueberry Road, 17324
(717) 528-8877

This restored 18th-century stone house on 25 acres in the apple orchards of Adams County is completely private with swimming pool and walking trails. The interior is furnished in Colonial style with antiques, canopy beds, working fireplaces. Twelve miles north of Gettysburg. Air conditioned.

Host: Marsha Lucidi
Rooms: 5 (3 PB; 2 SB) $69-89
Full Breakfast
Credit Cards: A, B
Notes: 2, 5, 9, 11, 12, 13, 14

GETTYSBURG--SEE ALSO GARDNERS

The Brafferton Inn

44 York Street, 17325
(717) 337-3423

This 1786 stone building was the first home built in the historic district. A mural on the dining room walls depicts 15 other historic buildings in Gettysburg. The home has a bullet hole from the first days of the Battle of Gettysburg. It is filled with antiques, coverlets, and stenciling, and has a lovely garden in the rear, as well as a livingroom, atrium, and sitting room.

Host: Mimi Agard
Rooms: 11 (6 PB; 5 S2B) $80-95
Full Breakfast
Credit Cards: A, B
Notes: 2, 5, 8, 9, 10, 11, 12, 13, 14

Keystone Inn

231 Hanover Street, 17325
(717) 337-3888

Keystone Inn is a great three-story brick home built in 1913. This late Victorian has copious amounts of natural wood and is warmly decorated with flowered wallpapers, lace, and ruffles. Each guest room has comfortable chairs for relaxing and a writing desk. A full breakfast may include cinnamon-apple pancakes, scrapple, waffles, fruits, muffins, and juices.

Host: Doris Martin
Rooms: 5 (3 PB; 2 SB) $59-100
Full Breakfast
Credit Cards: A, B
Notes: 2, 5, 8, 10, 12, 13

The Old Appleford Inn

218 Carlisle Street, 17325
(717) 337-1711

This 1867 Victorian mansion has 12 elegant bedrooms. Common areas include a large parlor, library, dining room, sun room, and

welcome; 9 Social drinking allowed; 10 Tennis available; 11 Swimming available; 12 Golf available; 13 Skiing available; 14 May be booked through travel agents

outside porches. The antique-furnished mansion returns guests to a more elegant era with a rewarding, restful experience in Victorian surroundings. For the discriminating traveler.

Hosts: Frank and Maribeth Skradski
Rooms: 12 (PB) $83-103
Full Breakfast
Credit Cards: A, B, C
Notes: 2, 5, 8, 9, 10, 11, 12, 13, 14

The Tannery Bed and Breakfast

The Tannery Bed and Breakfast

449 Baltimore Street, P. O. Box 4565, 17325
(717) 334-2454

The Tannery has been in the Swope family since 1920. A Gothic structure built in 1868, the building has been completely refurbished over the last ten years. It is named for the tannery that stood at the side of the property and is extremely convenient for touring the Gettysburg battlefield, within four blocks of the Visitors Center, museums, shops, and restaurants.

Host: Charlotte Swope
Rooms: 5 (PB) $65-85
Expanded Continental Breakfast
Credit Cards: A, B
Notes: 2, 5, 8, 9, 10, 12, 13

GLADWYNE

Bed and Breakfast of Valley Forge #0202

P. O. Box 562, Valley Forge, 19481-0562
(215) 783-7838; (800) 344-0123
FAX (215) 783-7783

This spacious Cape Cod Colonial is situated on a large wooded lot and has fine furnishings, collectibles, art, and expanses of windows. The adjoining terrace and gardens with reflecting pool enhance the feeling of privacy. Private baths. Full breakfast. $55.

HERSHEY

Hershey Bed and Breakfast Reservation Service

P.O. Box 208, 17033
(717) 533-2928

This reservation service offers personalized service in matching guests with just the right bed-and-breakfast inn or homestay in south central Pennsylvania. Be it a family vacation, a farm experience, business meetings or transfers, a honeymoon, or weekend getaway, here is help and knowledgeable advice. Renee Deutel, coordinator. $50-125.

HESSTON

Aunt Susie's Country Vacations

Rural Delivery 1, Box 225, 16647
(814) 658-3638

Experience country living in a warm, friendly atmosphere in a Victorian parsonage or a renovated country store and post office. All rooms are furnished with antiques and oil paintings and are air conditioned. Nearby is 28-mile-long Raystown Lake for recreation; boating, swimming, and fishing are within three miles. Bring your family to the country.

Hosts: Susan, Bob, and John Wilson
Rooms: 5 (1 PB; 4 SB) $45-50
Expanded Continental Breakfast
Credit Cards: None
Notes: 2, 5, 8, 9, 10, 11, 12, 13

KENNETT SQUARE

Bed and Breakfast of Valley Forge #0302

P. O. Box 562, Valley Forge, 19481-0562
(215) 783-7838; (800) 344-0123
FAX (215) 783-7783

This solid fieldstone farmhouse, circa 1704, sits on 20 acres of rolling farmland. Amenities include pool, hot tub, and two rooms with fireplaces. Furnishings include a spool bed, rope bed, and canopy four-poster. Near Valley Forge, Lancaster, and Philadelphia. Full breakfast. $90-105.

Bed and Breakfast of Valley Forge #0805

P. O. Box 562, Valley Forge, 19481-0562
(215) 783-7838; (800) 344-0123
FAX (215) 783-7783

In the Brandywine Valley is this whitewashed stone farmhouse, circa 1729, that has been restored to authentic Colonial elegance with original locks and hardware, hand-pegged floors, and antique furnishings. Hosts raise and train horses for harness racing. Private bath. $70.

Bed and Breakfast of Valley Forge #2001

P. O. Box 562, Valley Forge, 19481-0562
(215) 783-7838; (800) 344-0123
FAX (215) 783-7783

This brick ranch home in the Brandywine Valley offers an adjoining private entrance suite and a twin room in the main house. Kitchen is stocked for long-term guests. $70-75.

KIMBERTON

Bed and Breakfast of Valley Forge

P. O. Box 562, Valley Forge, 19481-0562
(215) 783-7838; (800) 344-0123
FAX (215) 783-7783

This 18th-century stone farmhouse on five acres is in the historic village of Kimberton, an early farm settlement. It is furnished with American and European antiques. $70-95.

LAMPETER

Walkabout Inn Bed and Breakfast

837 Village Road, P. O. Box 294, 17537
(717) 464-0707

This restored Mennonite home with an Australian host in a village setting has English gardens, antique-filled rooms, canopy beds, and fireplaces. Candlelight breakfast includes homemade pastries and tea from Down Under. Specials include Amish dinner, tour, and antique auctions. Romantic honeymoon and anniversary suites are featured, and coupons are available for local restaurants and attractions.

Hosts: Richard and Margaret Mason
Rooms: 5 (PB) $59-79
Full Breakfast
Credit Cards: A, B, C
Notes: 2, 4, 5, 8, 9, 10, 11, 12, 13, 14

LANCASTER

Bed and Breakfast of Valley Forge #0303

P. O. Box 562, Valley Forge, 19481-0562
(215) 783-7838; (800) 344-0123
FAX (215) 783-7783

The inn, circa 1735, is a splendid fieldstone manor, perfectly situated overlooking picture postcard fields and farms and just min-

welcome; 9 Social drinking allowed; 10 Tennis available; 11 Swimming available; 12 Golf available; 13 Skiing available; 14 May be booked through travel agents

utes from all the attractions of Lancaster County, including antiques and Amish farms. Eight rooms with private bath. Full breakfast. $54-105.

The King's Cottage, A Bed and Breakfast Inn

1049 East King Street, 17602
(717) 397-1017; (800) 747-8717

Escape to luxurious elegance in an award-winning Spanish mansion snuggled in the Pennsylvania Dutch country. Enjoy Amish farmlands or historic homes and museums. Browse farmers' markets, outlets, antique co-ops, or quilt shops. Pamper yourselves with king or queen beds, sumptuous breakfasts, afternoon tea, fireplaces, and air conditioning. Amish dinners by pre-arrangement.

Hosts: Karen and Jim Owens
Rooms: 7 (PB) $75-115
Full Breakfast
Credit Cards: A, B
Notes: 2, 5, 9, 10, 11, 12, 14

Meadowview Guest House

2169 New Holland Pike, 17601
(717) 299-4017

Enjoy three large air-conditioned rooms on the second floor and a small, fully equipped kitchen. Centrally situated, close to historic sites, antiques, farmers' market, and flea markets. Discount of $3 after second night.

Hosts: Sheila and Ed Christie
Rooms: 3 (1 PB; 2 SB) $25
Continental Breakfast
Credit Cards: None
Notes: 2 (for reservations), 5, 9, 10, 11, 12

LEESPORT

The Sleepy Fir

Rural Delivery 2, Box 2802, 19533
(215) 926-1014

The Sleepy Fir is a very quiet and relaxing bed and breakfast situated among the rows of evergreens in the Berks County countryside just north of Reading. The guest area includes a luxurious bath with combination sauna and whirlpool; pool table and ten-speed bicycles are available for guest use. Nearby attractions include historic sites, hiking, golf, and antique and outlet shopping.

Hosts: Phil and Judy Whitmoyer
Rooms: 2 (1 PB; 1 SB) $50-55
Full Breakfast
Credit Cards: None
Notes: 2, 5, 9, 10, 11, 12, 13

The King's Cottage,
A Bed and Breakfast Inn

MAINLAND

Bed and Breakfast of Valley Forge #0703

P. O. Box 562, Valley Forge, 19481-0562
(215) 783-7838; (800) 344-0123
FAX (215) 783-7783

This circa-1880 carriage house is completely private. It has a 1940s jukebox, wood-burning stove, and kitchenette. Outside is a totally enclosed private patio with swing and pool. Full breakfast. $75.

MARIETTA

The River Inn

258 West Front Street, 17547
(717) 426-2290

NOTES: Credit cards accepted: A Master Card; B Visa; C American Express; D Discover Card; E Diners Club; F Other; 2 Personal checks accepted; 3 Lunch available; 4 Dinner available; 5 Open all year; 6 Pets welcome; 8 Children

Centrally situated for Lancaster, York, and Hershey attractions in the historic district of Marietta on the banks of the Susquehanna River, this 1790 restored home features six working fireplaces, screened porch, flower and herb gardens, large rooms, queen beds, antiques, and period reproduction furniture. Country breakfast and air conditioning.

Hosts: Joyce and Bob Heiserman
Rooms: 3 (PB) $60-65
Full Breakfast
Credit Cards: A, B
Notes: 2, 5, 8 (over 9), 9, 10, 12, 14

Vogt Farm Bed and Breakfast
1225 Colebrook Road, 17547
(717) 653-4810

Back door guests are best. Come in the back door that opens into the large farm kitchen. This is where breakfast is served. Guest rooms are pleasantly decorated with family antiques, as well as other treasures. Share the cozy living and family rooms with hosts. Enjoy the fire in winter and fresh air in summer.

Hosts: Keith and Kathy Vogt
Rooms: 3 (SB) $55
Full Breakfast
Credit Cards: A, B, C
Notes: 2, 5, 8, 12

MERCER

Magoffin Inn
129 South Pitt Street, 16137
(412) 662-4611

Visit the Magoffin Inn and be reminded of a gentler, quieter era. The house, a Queene Anne Victorian, was built in 1884 by Dr. Montrose Magoffin as a home. It has nine guest rooms for weary travelers and is completely furnished in antiques. Other amenities include clock radios and TV.

Host: Jacque McClelland
Rooms: 9 (PB) $60-100
Full Breakfast
Credit Cards: A, B, C
Notes: 2, 3, 4, 5, 8, 10, 11, 12

MOUNT JOY

Cedar Hill Farm
305 Longenecker Road, 17552
(717) 653-4655

This 1817 stone farmhouse is situated in a quiet area and was the birthplace of the host. A special room for honeymooners features a private balcony overlooking a stream. Breakfast is served beside the walk-in fireplace. Hike or bike along country roads or relax on wicker rockers on the large porch. Hershey Park, Amish country, farmers' markets, antique shops, outlets, and good restaurants nearby. Air conditioning; gift certificates.

Hosts: Russel and Gladys Swarr
Rooms: 4 (PB) $55-65
Expanded Continental Breakfast
Credit Cards: A, B, C
Notes: 2, 5, 8, 9, 10, 12

Green Acres Farm Bed and Breakfast
1382 Pinkerton Road, 17552
(717) 653-4028

This 160-acre farm has pony cart rides, trampoline, swings, kittens, chickens, goats, hogs. The house is furnished with antiques and is air conditioned. A full farmer's breakfast is served. There is also an efficiency house next door, rented by the week, that sleeps 12.

Hosts: Wayne and Yvonne Miller
Rooms: 10 (5 PB; 5 S2B) $45-55
Full Breakfast
Credit Cards: A, B
Notes: 2, 5, 6, 8, 10, 11, 12, 14

welcome; 9 Social drinking allowed; 10 Tennis available; 11 Swimming available; 12 Golf available; 13 Skiing available; 14 May be booked through travel agents

Cedar Hill Farm

MOUNT POCONO

Farmhouse Bed and Breakfast

HCR 1, Box 6B, 18344
(717) 839-0796

This 1850 homestead on six manicured acres has a separate cottage and two suites in the house with fireplaces. Farm-style breakfast is complete with original country recipes prepared by the host, a professional chef. Enjoy bedtime tea and snacks baked fresh each day. Antiques adorn each room, with cleanliness being the order of the day. Queen beds, TV, air conditioning.

Hosts: Jack and Donna Asure
Rooms: 3 (PB) $65-85
Full Breakfast
Credit Cards: A, B, D
Notes: 2, 5, 9, 10, 11, 12, 13, 14

MOUNTVILLE

Mountville Antiques Bed and Breakfast

407 East Main Street, 17554
(717) 285-5956

Breakfast is served in the antique shop that has been in business for 25 years, giving the

feel of home and Grandmother's dining room. All rooms are furnished with antique furniture, each one unique. Enjoy the herb and flower garden while sitting on the patio. Five miles west of Lancaster on Route 462. Fifteen minutes from Dutch attractions.

Hosts: Sam and Pat Reno
Rooms: 6 (4 PB; 2 SB) $55-75
Expanded Continental Breakfast
Credit Cards: A, B
Notes: 5, 8 (over 11), 10, 11, 12, 13

NEW HOPE—SEE ALSO WRIGHTSTOWN

Bed and Breakfast of Valley Forge #0809

P. O. Box 562, Valley Forge, 19481-0562
(215) 783-7838; (800) 344-0123
FAX (215) 783-7783

Forty-foot holly trees grace the entrance to this 18th-century farmhouse with an elegant country decor and a blend of period and antique furnishings. Afternoon refreshments served. Two-night stay on weekends; rates $20 less Monday through Thursday. Full breakfast. $95-120.

Bed and Breakfast of Valley Forge #1901

P. O. Box 562, Valley Forge, 19481-0562
(215) 783-7838; (800) 344-0123
FAX (215) 783-7783

This traditional 18th-century farmhouse is in the heart of Bucks County on ten wooded acres. Open-beamed ceilings and Persian carpets contribute to the rustic charm and elegance. $83-105.

Bed and Breakfast of Valley Forge #2301

P. O. Box 562, Valley Forge, 19481-0562
(215) 783-7838; (800) 344-0123
FAX (215) 783-7783

NOTES: Credit cards accepted: A Master Card; B Visa; C American Express; D Discover Card; E Diners Club; F Other;
2 Personal checks accepted; 3 Lunch available; 4 Dinner available; 5 Open all year; 6 Pets welcome; 8 Children

This inn was constructed around 1870 with a flourish of later Victorian features including cruciform floorplan, deep eaves, two-story bay window, and gazebo. $90-120.

Wedgwood Inn of New Hope

111 West Bridge Street, 18938
(215) 862-2570

This enchanting inn is situated in the heart of New Hope's historic district. It is comprised of an 1870 restored Victorian home, a stone manor, and a carriage house. A quiet celebration of nostalgia and simple luxuries, the inn is filled with country Victorian antiques, original art, handmade quilts, and Wedgwood pottery. Innkeepers are experts on the arts and attractions of historic New Hope.

Hosts: Carl Glassman and Dinie Silnutzer
Rooms: 12 (10 PB; 2 SB) $65-160
Continental Breakfast
Credit Cards: None
Notes: 2, 5, 6, 8, 9, 10, 11, 12, 13, 14

PHILADELPHIA

Bed and Breakfast of Valley Forge #0105

P. O. Box 562, Valley Forge, 19481-0562
(215) 783-7838; (800) 344-0123
FAX (215) 783-7783

This circa-1850 carriage house has been restored to a luxury accommodation. The beautiful view and lights of the city can be viewed from the roof deck. Near art museum and Franklin Institute. $100.

Bed and Breakfast of Valley Forge #0205

P. O. Box 562, Valley Forge, 19481-0562
(215) 783-7838; (800) 344-0123
FAX (215) 783-7783

The guest quarters are a private first-floor suite in an 1840 town house ideally situated in Center City. Suite with two bedrooms and two bathrooms. Full breakfast. $60.

Bed and Breakfast of Valley Forge #0305

P. O. Box 562, Valley Forge, 19481-0562
(215) 783-7838; (800) 344-0123
FAX (215) 783-7783

This inn is situated downtown four blocks from Independence Hall, one-half block to South Street, and five blocks to Penn's Landing. $50-100.

Bed and Breakfast of Valley Forge #0401

P. O. Box 562, Valley Forge, 19481-0562
(215) 783-7838; (800) 344-0123
FAX (215) 783-7783

This delightful one-bedroom suite offers the executive a place to unwind. Continental breakfast foods are provided in the kitchenette. Minimum stay one week. $300 weekly.

Bed and Breakfast of Valley Forge #0601

P. O. Box 562, Valley Forge, 19481-0562
(215) 783-7838; (800) 344-0123
FAX (215) 783-7783

This turn-of-the-century, 42-room English Tudor manor was built as a gift for a bride and groom of the rising mercantile class and was later the convent for the Sisters of the Order of Saint Francis. Wedding parties are welcome. Full breakfast. $70-110.

Bed and Breakfast of Valley Forge #0706

P. O. Box 562, Valley Forge, 19481-0562
(215) 783-7838; (800) 344-0123
FAX (215) 783-7783

welcome; 9 Social drinking allowed; 10 Tennis available; 11 Swimming available; 12 Golf available; 13 Skiing available; 14 May be booked through travel agents

This mini-estate in the English Tudor tradition was built in 1900 with paneled walls, leaded-glass windows, beamed ceilings, and fireplaces on an acre of beautifully landscaped grounds. A perfect setting for bird watching. $85.

Bed and Breakfast of Valley Forge #1401

P. O. Box 562, Valley Forge, 19481-0562
(215) 783-7838; (800) 344-0123
FAX (215) 783-7783

Situated in the heart of Center City next to Rittenhouse Square, this elegant town house has high ceilings and is furnished with antiques and artwork. Shopping and cultural events are nearby. $75.

Bed and Breakfast of Valley Forge #1601

P. O. Box 562, Valley Forge, 19481-0562
(215) 783-7838; (800) 344-0123
FAX (215) 783-7783

Built in the 1830s, this three-story Colonial town house is situated on one of Society Hill's narrow cobblestone streets just blocks from Independence Hall. A wisteria-covered patio with a bubbling fountain welcomes guests in the summer. In the winter, a Franklin stove in the guests' parlor warms them. $60.

Bed and Breakfast of Valley Forge #1907

P. O. Box 562, Valley Forge, 19481-0562
(215) 783-7838; (800) 344-0123
FAX (215) 783-7783

This is a renovated old stone schoolhouse in the historic area of Chestnut Hill. The atmosphere exudes warmth and the welcome of a cozy fire on a cold day. $65.

Bed and Breakfast of Valley Forge #1914

P. O. Box 562, Valley Forge, 19481-0562
(215) 783-7838; (800) 344-0123
FAX (215) 783-7783

The second-floor suite has a view of Rittenhouse Square, and the location is readily accessible to all Philadelphia historical sites and events. $95.

Bed and Breakfast of Valley Forge #2002

P. O. Box 562, Valley Forge, 19481-0562
(215) 783-7838; (800) 344-0123
FAX (215) 783-7783

The third floor is a charming apartment area with full kitchen that offers a family a truly private area. Old-fashioned porches shade the house, one in the front, the other off the kitchen.

Bed and Breakfast of Valley Forge #2101

P. O. Box 562, Valley Forge, 19481-0562
(215) 783-7838; (800) 344-0123
FAX (215) 783-7783

This home is situated in a small court in the Rittenhouse Square section and offers access to all attractions of the city. $75.

Bed and Breakfast of Valley Forge #2203

P. O. Box 562, Valley Forge, 19481-0562
(215) 783-7838; (800) 344-0123
FAX (215) 783-7783

This home, circa 1811, is a historic, certified home situated near Society Hill and offers a historical atmosphere. Close to all city attractions.Two guest rooms with private baths. $65.

NOTES: Credit cards accepted: A Master Card; B Visa; C American Express; D Discover Card; E Diners Club; F Other; 2 Personal checks accepted; 3 Lunch available; 4 Dinner available; 5 Open all year; 6 Pets welcome; 8 Children

Bed and Breakfast of Valley Forge #2305

P. O. Box 562, Valley Forge, 19481-0562
(215) 783-7838; (800) 344-0123
FAX (215) 783-7783

Situated in the colorful Italian Market District, this recently restored 19th-century brick rowhouse is typical of homes built to accommodate Italian immigrants who created a bustling outdoor market. $45.

PHOENIXVILLE

Bed and Breakfast of Valley Forge #0301

P. O. Box 562, Valley Forge, 19481-0562
(215) 783-7838; (800) 344-0123
FAX (215) 783-7783

Built in 1928 by an English executive, this English Tudor home is on a lovely sycamore-lined street and boasts a massive slate roof and original red oak flooring and stairway. $45-70.

Bed and Breakfast of Valley Forge #2201

P. O. Box 562, Valley Forge, 19481-0562
(215) 783-7838; (800) 344-0123
FAX (215) 783-7783

This Dutch-style farmhouse was built in 1860 and grew into a rambling home that has been lovingly restored. The Netherlands influence is evident throughout. $65-95.

PITTSBURGH

La-Fleur Bed and Breakfast

1830 Crafton Boulevard, 15205
(412) 921-8588

A large, restored Victorian built at the turn of the century, La-Fleur features four to six bedrooms with Florida rooms, private baths, and balconies. Each room is handsomely appointed. Just six minutes from the heart of Pittsburgh, Three River Stadium, and Station Square. Easy access from all interstates and airport. Pick-up if needed. Take 279 East from airport to Greentree, Exit 4. Follow Blue Belt north one-quarter mile.

Hosts: Robert and Audrey Vales
Rooms: 4-6 (PB) $59-83
Full Breakfast
Credit Cards: A, B, C
Notes: 5, 8 (over 16), 9, 10, 11, 12, 14

POCONO MOUNTAINS

Bed and Breakfast of Valley Forge #1201

P. O. Box 562, Valley Forge, 19481-0562
(215) 783-7838; (800) 344-0123
FAX (215) 783-7783

The inn was built originally as a boarding house. A charming Victorian country inn where the European tradition of attentive service is continued. $110-140.

QUAKERTOWN

Sign of the Sorrel Horse

243 Old Bethlehem Road, 18951
(215) 536-4651

This inn received its tavern license in 1749. Intricately carved French antiques include armoires and four-poster beds. The dining room atmosphere is created by its stone walls and beamed ceilings. The inn's French and Continental cuisine often features wild boar, Canadian caribou, grouse, and quail. Closed Monday and Tuesday.

Hosts: Monique Gaumont and Jon Atkin
Rooms: 5 (PB) $85-125
Full Breakfast
Credit Cards: A, B, C
Notes: 4, 6, 9, 11, 12, 13

welcome; 9 Social drinking allowed; 10 Tennis available; 11 Swimming available; 12 Golf available; 13 Skiing available; 14 May be booked through travel agents

READING

Bed and Breakfast of Valley Forge #0806

P. O. Box 562, Valley Forge, 19481-0562
(215) 783-7838; (800) 344-0123
FAX (215) 783-7783

Enjoy the time-honored European tradition of the English bed and breakfast, the French hostellerie, and the Italian pensione all in one, with warmth and friendly atmosphere. $60-70.

Bed and Breakfast of Valley Forge #1307

P. O. Box 562, Valley Forge, 19481-0562
(215) 783-7838; (800) 344-0123
FAX (215) 783-7783

The focal point of this inn is an elaborate leaded-glass doorway. The home has been kept in its original state throughout and furnished with antiques, Amish quilts, and crafts. $60.

The Inn at Centre Park

730 Centre Avenue, 19601
(215) 374-8557; (800) 447-1094
FAX (215) 374-8725

This grand Victorian mansion is beautifully furnished and decorated and has suites with down-covered beds, fireplaces, carved wood, leaded-glass windows, and hundred-year-old plaster cherubs floating overhead on the ornate ceilings. Enjoy museum quality architecture, elegant surroundings, and wonderful breakfasts all in a warm and friendly atmosphere. *Country Inns* February 1991 Inn of the Month.

Host: Andrea Smith
Rooms: 6 (4 PB; 2 SB) $75-210
Full Breakfast
Credit Cards: A, B
Notes: 5, 9, 10, 12, 13

RONKS

Candlelite Inn Bed and Breakfast

2574 Lincoln Highway East, 17572
(717) 299-6005

Surrounded by Amish farmlands in scenic Lancaster County, this 1920s farmhouse offers four clean, quiet guest rooms, a sitting room with TV, central air conditioning, phone, and full country breakfast. Close to all major attractions, there is an antique and collectibles shop on the premises.

Host: Ronald Hartzell
Rooms: 4 (SB) $55-65
Full Breakfast
Credit Cards: A, B
Notes: 2, 8 (over 11), 9, 12

SCRANTON

Bed and Breakfast of Valley Forge #2202

P. O. Box 562, Valley Forge, 19481-0562
(215) 783-7838; (800) 344-0123
FAX (215) 783-7783

This authentic English Tudor manor, circa 1883, has 28 major rooms, eight fireplaces, nine baths, and a grand salon with Tiffany windows that hosted two presidents. $150-250.

SHIPPENSBURG

Wilmar Manor Bed and Breakfast

303 West King Street, 17257
(717) 532-3784

A friendly Victorian guest house elegantly decorated with antiques offers serenity and beautiful and unusual rock gardens. Stroll down Main Street of this historic village in the midst of quiet Pennsylvania countryside.

NOTES: Credit cards accepted: A Master Card; B Visa; C American Express; D Discover Card; E Diners Club; F Other;
2 Personal checks accepted; 3 Lunch available; 4 Dinner available; 5 Open all year; 6 Pets welcome; 8 Children

Host: Wilmar Banks
Rooms: 6 (2 PB; 4 SB) $45-60
Full Breakfast
Credit Cards: None
Notes: 2, 5, 8

SLIPPERY ROCK

Applebutter Inn
152 Applewood Lane, 16057
(412) 794-1844

This charming, original 1844 farmhouse was restored and added to and now provides 11 beautifully appointed rooms with antiques and decorator linens. Breakfast is served at the adjacent Wolf Creek School Cafe. Breakfast and luncheon fare is prepared and served in the quaint atmosphere of a one-room schoolhouse recently restored to its original state.

Hosts: Gary and Sandra McKnight
Rooms: 11 (PB) $69-115
Full Breakfast
Credit Cards: A, B
Notes: 3, 4, 5, 10, 11, 12, 13

SMOKETOWN

Homestead Lodging
184 East Brook Road (Route 896), 17576
(717) 393-6927

This family-operated lodge has a homey atmosphere and country rooms. Enjoy a walk down the lane to the adjacent Amish farm or relax on the porch and listen to the clippity-clop of horse and buggies. Escorted tours are available. Shop in the outlets or visit a quilt, craft, or antique shop or farmers' market. Pennsylvania Dutch cooking is within walking distance.

Hosts: Robert and Lori Kepiro
Rooms: 4 (PB) $28-49
Continental Breakfast
Credit Cards: A, B
Notes: 2 (deposit only), 5, 8, 9, 10, 11, 12

SOMERSET

Heart of Somerset
122 West Union Street, 15501
(814) 445-6782

The Heart of Somerset is a beautifully refurbished home built circa 1839. Carefully restored antiques fill every room, and the wooden floors have been returned to their original beauty. Thomas Edison-patented light fixtures grace the lower level. Each guest room is decorated differently, with eyelet comforters and pillow shams to enhance the romantic feeling of the Victorian era.

Hosts: Hank and Phyllis Vogt
Rooms: 5 (2 PB; 3 S2B) $50-85
Continental Breakfast
Credit Cards: A, B, C, D
Notes: 2, 5, 9, 10, 11, 12, 13, 14

STRASBURG

The Decoy
958 Eisenberger Road, 17579
(717) 687-8585

Situated in Amish farm country, the Decoy has a spectacular view. Formerly an Amish home, it has five guest rooms and serves a country breakfast. Strasburg is a great area for shopping; there are wonderful craft stores, outlets, and for quilters, an ideal place to buy fabric or a quilt frame.

Hosts: Debby and Hap Joy
Rooms: 5 (PB) $50-70
Full Breakfast
Credit Cards: None
Notes: 2, 5, 8, 9

UPPER BLACK EDDY

Indian Rock Inn
Route 32, Box 42, 18972
(215) 982-5300

welcome; 9 Social drinking allowed; 10 Tennis available; 11 Swimming available; 12 Golf available; 13 Skiing available; 14 May be booked through travel agents

Indian Rock Inn is a country bed and breakfast inn that also hosts a fine dining restaurant offering continental cuisine. The inn is nestled between the Delaware River and the canal and the lush green mountainside of Ringing Rocks State Park. Prices include canoes for the canal, bicycles, and hiking. All rooms have antique furnishings and queen beds.

Hosts: Garry and Patricia Peabody
Rooms: 7 (PB) $85-95
Full Breakfast
Credit Cards: A, B, C
Notes: 2, 3, 4, 5, 9, 12

VALLEY FORGE

Bed and Breakfast of Valley Forge #0201
P. O. Box 562, 19481-0562
(215) 783-7838; (800) 344-0123
FAX (215) 783-7783

In a peaceful, heavily wooded neighborhood is this home decorated with both antique and modern furnishings. Screened patio overlooks the garden. $55.

Bed and Breakfast of Valley Forge #0203
P. O. Box 562, 19481-0562
(215) 783-7838; (800) 344-0123
FAX (215) 783-7783

This 15-room stone farmhouse on four acres is the second oldest in the state and one of the 100 oldest in the country. Original flooring, exposed beams, hand-wrought hinges, and fireplaces add to the charm. $70-75.

Bed and Breakfast of Valley Forge #0304
P. O. Box 562, 19481-0562
(215) 783-7838; (800) 344-0123
FAX (215) 783-7783

This private guest cottage is situated on a peaceful, 20-acre, pre-Revolutionary War farmstead, where horses and sheep graze and swans glide across a pond. $100.

Bed and Breakfast of Valley Forge #0306
P. O. Box 562, 19481-0562
(215) 783-7838; (800) 344-0123
FAX (215) 783-7783

Guest quarters are a home-within-a-barn in an atmosphere of quiet taste and refinement in this historic area. Close to Gulph Creek "on the path of the Revolution." $60-90.

Bed and Breakfast of Valley Forge #0702
P. O. Box 562, 19481-0562
(215) 783-7838; (800) 344-0123
FAX (215) 783-7783

This contemporary home boasts cathedral ceilings, exposed beams, and walls of windows overlooking Great Valley and Valley Forge Mountain. The enormous lower level is the guest quarters with a great room between. $75.

Bed and Breakfast of Valley Forge #0804
P. O. Box 562, 19481-0562
(215) 783-7838; (800) 344-0123
FAX (215) 783-7783

Originally part of General Anthony Wayne's estate, this 18th-century fieldstone farmhouse on two and one-half acres has 16-inch thick walls and exposed beams overhead. $60-65.

NOTES: Credit cards accepted: A Master Card; B Visa; C American Express; D Discover Card; E Diners Club; F Other; 2 Personal checks accepted; 3 Lunch available; 4 Dinner available; 5 Open all year; 6 Pets welcome; 8 Children

Bed and Breakfast of Valley Forge #0904

P. O. Box 562, 19481-0562
(215) 783-7838; (800) 344-0123
FAX (215) 783-7783

Completely private accommodations are offered in this 12-room old stone Colonial filled with antiques and country comfort. Terrace and grill are available for guest use. $100.

Bed and Breakfast of Valley Forge #1203

P. O. Box 562, 19481-0562
(215) 783-7838; (800) 344-0123
FAX (215) 783-7783

This Colonial farmhouse is on three acres of an original William Penn land grant and dates from the 1700s. Outbuildings include a smokehouse, springhouse, and outhouse. Furnished with antiques and quilts. $60-65.

Bed and Breakfast of Valley Forge #1304

P. O. Box 562, 19481-0562
(215) 783-7838; (800) 344-0123
FAX (215) 783-7783

This traditional home is on three acres of wooded land adjoining Valley Forge Park and has paths leading from the property to the park for walkers, joggers, and nature lovers. $65.

Bed and Breakfast of Valley Forge #1902

P. O. Box 562, 19481-0562
(215) 783-7838; (800) 344-0123
FAX (215) 783-7783

This modest, modern home offers a freshly decorated guest room with private bath, desk, TV, washer/dryer. Nightly, weekly, or monthly lodging. $50 nightly.

Bed and Breakfast of Valley Forge #1909

P. O. Box 562, 19481-0562
(215) 783-7838; (800) 344-0123
FAX (215) 783-7783

Behind an ivy-covered, circa-1770 house and beyond the barn is the cottage that formerly housed the master of the hounds of the old Valley Forge Hunt; with a view of the Valley Forge National Historical Park. $85-100.

VILLANOVA

Bed and Breakfast of Valley Forge #1801

P. O. Box 562, Valley Forge, 19481-0562
(215) 783-7838; (800) 344-0123
FAX (215) 783-7783

Rare swans, geese, and ducks swim in the pond of the park near this home. Relax on the terrace, on the enclosed porch, or by the fireplace or wood-burning stove. $55.

Bed and Breakfast of Valley Forge #1802

P. O. Box 562, Valley Forge, 19481-0562
(215) 783-7838; (800) 344-0123
FAX (215) 783-7783

Hosts have restored this 1890 home and furnished the interior with a bright, fully equipped kitchen, livingroom, dining room, sun room, and two bedrooms. Kitchen is stocked with breakfast foods. $100.

Bed and Breakfast of Valley Forge #1903

P. O. Box 562, Valley Forge, 19481-0562
(215) 783-7838; (800) 344-0123
FAX (215) 783-7783

This home is situated on one and one-half acres in an elegant, wooded area and is furnished with antiques, art, and Oriental rugs. The guest room has a canopied bed and leather wing chair. $70.

Bed and Breakfast of Valley Forge #2601

P. O. Box 562, Valley Forge, 19481-0562
(215) 783-7838; (800) 344-0123
FAX (215) 783-7783

This expansive English Tudor is on the original grounds of two estates owned by the brothers who made a local German beer. Guest rooms can be reached privately by a back staircase. $70.

WEST CHESTER

Bankhouse Bed and Breakfast

875 Hillsdale Road, 19382
(215) 344-7388

Discover the charm of this 18th-century bankhouse nestled in a quiet country setting overlooking horse farm and pond. Lovingly decorated with country antiques, stenciling, and folk art, it offers private entrance, porch, and sitting room/library for guests, as well as a hearty breakfast and afternoon snacks. It is conveniently situated to all Brandywine Valley attractions.

Hosts: Diane and Michael Bove
Rooms: 2 (SB; PB on request) $55-80
Full Breakfast
Credit Cards: None
Notes: 2, 5, 8 (over 11), 9, 10, 12, 13

Bed and Breakfast of Valley Forge #0204

P. O. Box 562, Valley Forge, 19481-0562
(215) 783-7838; (800) 344-0123
FAX (215) 783-7783

This modern farmhouse on property deeded from William Penn has a "long view" of the Chester County hills and is furnished with

Early American furnishings and antiques inherited over the years. $50-55.

Bed and Breakfast of Valley Forge #0208

P. O. Box 562, Valley Forge, 19481-0562
(215) 783-7838; (800) 344-0123
FAX (215) 783-7783

This 18th-century home is built into the side of a hill and features German wood lapsiding, tin roof, wooden pegs, art, antiques, crafts, and hand stenciling; private entrance. $60.

Bankhouse Bed and Breakfast

WRIGHTSTOWN

Hollileif Bed and Breakfast Establishment

677 Durham Road (Route 413), 18940
(215) 598-3100

An 18th-century farmhouse on five and one-half acres of Bucks County countryside. Romantic ambience, gourmet breakfasts, fireplaces, and air conditioning combine with gracious service and attention to detail. Each guest room is beautifully appointed with antiques and country furnishings. Enjoy afternoon refreshments by the fireside or on the arbor-covered patio. Relax in a hammock in the meadow. Six miles west of New Hope.

Hosts: Ellen and Richard Butkus
Rooms: 5 (PB) $75-120
Full Breakfast
Credit Cards: A, B, C
Notes: 2, 5, 9, 10, 11, 12, 14

YORK

Smyser-Bair House

30 South Beaver Street, 17401
(717) 854-3411

A magnificent 12-room Italianate town house
in the historic district, this home is rich in
architectural detail and contains stained-
glass windows, pier mirrors, and ceiling
medallions. There are three antique-filled
guest rooms and a two-room suite. Enjoy
the warm hospitality and player piano, walk
to farmers' markets, historic sites, and antique shops. Eight blocks to York Fairgrounds.

Host: The King family
Rooms: 4 (1 PB; 3 SB) $60-80
Full Breakfast
Credit Cards: None
Notes: 2, 5, 8, 9, 14

Smyser-Bair House

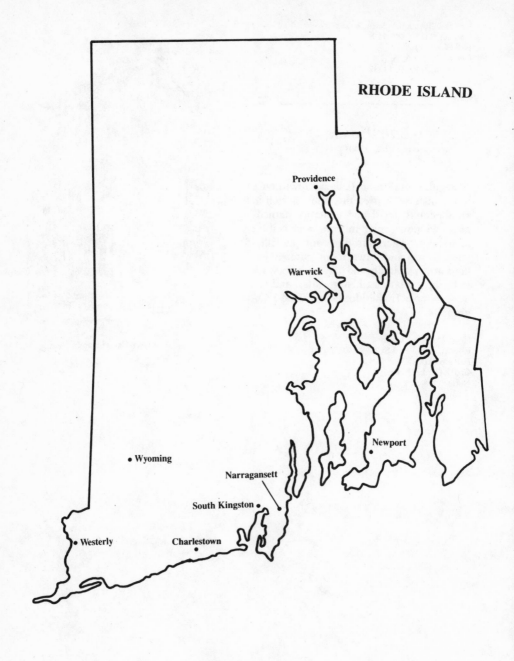

RHODE ISLAND

Providence

Warwick

Newport

Wyoming

Narragansett

South Kingston

Westerly   Charlestown

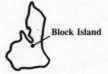

Block Island

Rhode Island

The Barrington Inn
Beach Avenue, P. O. Box 397, 02807
(401) 466-5510

On peaceful, picturesque Block Island, the inn is situated just 12 miles off the coast of Rhode Island. Bright, cheerful, corner guest rooms have lovely water views. Two housekeeping apartments are also available. Within walking distance of beach, restaurants, and shops.

Hosts: Joan and Howard Ballard
Rooms: 6 (PB) $50-145
Continental Breakfast
Credit Cards: A, B
Notes: 2, 8 (over 12), 9, 10, 11

CHARLESTOWN

Inn the Meadow
1045 Shannock Road, 02813
(401) 789-1473

Inn the Meadow is in a tranquil setting on five acres where guests can explore the wildflower meadow or the woods and watch for deer and birds. Inside, enjoy the common room with library, games, fireplace, and piano. Centrally situated between historic Newport and Mystic and near the university, beaches, summer theater, golf, shopping, and dining.

Hosts: Yolanda and Michael Day
Rooms: 4 (1 PB; 3 SB) $40-70
Full Breakfast
Credit Cards: A, B, D
Notes: 2, 5, 9, 11, 12, 14

One Willow by the Sea Bed and Breakfast
1 Willow Road, 02813-4160
(401) 364-0802

Enjoy warm year-round hospitality in peaceful surroundings. Relax with pure air, sea breezes, no pollution. Guest comfort is a top priority. Explore the pristine sandy beaches, salt ponds, and wildlife refuges. One Willow is a bird watcher's paradise. All sports are nearby. Providence, Newport, and Mystic are a short drive away. Fine restaurants, theaters, concerts, art, antique shows, historic landmarks.

Host: Denise Dillon Fuge
Rooms: 4 (S2B) $45-55 summer and fall
Full Breakfast
Credit Cards: None
Notes: 2, 5, 9, 10, 11, 12, 14 (off-season)

NARRAGANSETT

The Old Clerk House
49 Narragansett Avenue, 02882
(401) 783-8008

Enjoy English country comfort in this Victorian home. Choose from twin-, double-, or king-size beds; all with private baths, air conditioning, and one with color TV. Wake to an all-home-cooked breakfast served in a plant-filled sun room. Only one block from Narragansett Beach, movie theater, library, and fine restaurants. Ten minutes from Block Island ferry; 18 miles from Newport. Guest livingroom offers basic cable TV, VCR, and stereo. Off-street parking.

NOTES: Credit cards accepted: A Master Card; B Visa; C American Express; D Discover Card; E Diners Club; F Other; 2 Personal checks accepted; 3 Lunch available; 4 Dinner available; 5 Open all year; 6 Pets welcome; 8 Children welcome; 9 Social drinking allowed; 10 Tennis available; 11 Swimming available; 12 Golf available; 13 Skiing available; 14 May be booked through travel agents

Host: Patricia Watkins
Rooms: 2 (PB) $65-80
Full Breakfast
Credit Cards: None
Notes: 2, 5, 9, 10, 11

Stone Lea

40 Newton Avenue, 02882-1368
(401) 783-9546

Built circa 1884, this rambling Victorian estate is situated on two magnificent ocean-front acres at the mouth of Narragansett Bay. One of a handful of summer homes built during the peak period of high society in Narrangansett. Waves crashing along the rocky shore may be seen and heard from most rooms. English antiques and collections of Victorian china clocks, miniature cars, and ship models are incorporated into the decor.

Hosts: Carol and Ernie Cormier
Rooms: 4 (PB) $60-100 off-season; $85-125 in-season
Full Breakfast
Credit Cards: A, B
Notes: 2, 5, 8 (over 10), 9, 10, 11, 12, 14

Stone Lea

NEWPORT

Bellevue House

14 Catherine Street, 02840
(401) 847-1828

Originally built in 1774, Bellevue House was converted into the first summer hotel in Newport in 1828. Situated atop Historic Hill, off the famous Bellevue Avenue three blocks from the harbor, it retains a combination of ideal location, colonial history, nautical atmosphere, and Victorian charm.

Hosts: Joan and Vic Farmer
Rooms: 8 (6 PB; 2 SB) $70-95
Continental Breakfast
Credit Cards: None
Notes: 2, 8 (over 12), 9, 10, 11, 12

Jenkins Guest House

206 South Rhode Island Avenue, 02840
(401) 847-6801

The hosts built this New England Cape when they were married and raised their eight children here. The extra bedrooms are now used for traveling guests. Enjoy listening to the stories of the hosts, both native Newporters. Situated on a quiet street just a stone's throw from the ocean, yet within walking distance of mansions, cliff walk, shopping, and waterfront activities.

Hosts: David and Sally Jenkins
Rooms: 3 (1 PB; 2 SB) $60-90
Continental Breakfast
Credit Cards: None
Notes: 2, 8, 9, 10, 11, 12

Stella Maris Inn

91 Washington Street, 02840
(401) 849-2862

An elegant historic inn situated on the water in downtown Newport, the inn was built in 1861, made from Connecticut redstone with French Victorian design. Four rooms have working fireplaces. The inn is tastefully furnished with period antiques. A large porch overlooks gardens and the harbor. Homemade muffins and breads are a specialty.

Hosts: Dorothy and Ed Madden
Rooms: 8 plus cottage (PB) $75-150
Full Breakfast
Credit Cards: None
Notes: 2, 5, 8, 9, 10, 11, 12

PROVIDENCE

State House Inn

43 Jewett Street, 02908
(401) 785-1235

NOTES: Credit cards accepted: A Master Card; B Visa; C American Express; D Discover Card; E Diners Club; F Other; 2 Personal checks accepted; 3 Lunch available; 4 Dinner available; 5 Open all year; 6 Pets welcome; 8 Children

The Inn is a 100-year-old building newly renovated and restored into an urban bed and breakfast. It is situated in a quiet and quaint neighborhood, a ten-minute walk to downtown and a five-minute drive to Brown University, Rhode Island School of Design, and Providence College. Business travelers love the accommodations and corporate rates.

Host: Monica Hopton
Rooms: 10 (PB) $59-99
Full Breakfast
Credit Cards: A, B, C
Notes: 5, 8, 9, 10, 12, 14

SOUTH KINGSTON

Admiral Dewey Inn
668 Matunuck Beach Road, 02879
(401) 783-2090

The past comes alive in this 1898 Victorian that has been lovingly restored and furnished with antiques. Listed on the National Register of Historic Places, the inn offers the best of both historic interest and great location, just one block from an ocean beach. The inn is convenient to Theatre-by-the-Sea, Trustom Wildlife Refuge, and an abundance of antique shops. A shuttle bus is available to take you to the Block Island Ferry landing or to the airport.

Host: Joan LeBel
Rooms: 10 (8 PB; 2 SB) $60-120
Continental Breakfast
Credit Cards: A, B
Notes: 9, 10, 11, 12

WARWICK

The Enchanted Cottage
16 Beach Avenue, 02889-2640
(401) 732-0439

This century-old restored Cape Anne cottage is situated on a quiet tree-lined street overlooking Narragansett Bay. The Enchanted Cottage is centrally situated in Rhode Island and only five minutes from

Providence Airport in Warwick. All other points of interest, including Newport, can be reached in 15 to 45 minutes.

Hosts: Mary and Sandy Sandford
Rooms: 2 (SB) $55-75
Continental Breakfast
Credit Cards: C (for reservations)
Notes: 2, 5, 8, 9, 10, 11, 12, 14

State House Inn

WESTERLY

Grandview
Bed and Breakfast
212 Shore Road, 02891
(401) 596-6384; (800) 441-6384 outside Rhode
  Island

This stately turn-of-the-century home with a splendid ocean view has a large, comfortable livingroom with stone fireplace, cheery breakfast porch, wraparound stone porch, and spacious grounds. Walk to tennis and golf. A short drive to beaches, Watch Hill, Mystic Seaport, and Newport.

Host: Pat Grande
Rooms: 12 (2 PB; 10 SB) $55-85
Expanded Continental Breakfast
Credit Cards: A, B, C
Notes: 2, 5, 8, 9, 10, 11, 12, 14

Woody Hill
Bed and Breakfast
330 Woody Hill Road, 02891
(401) 322-0452

welcome; 9 Social drinking allowed; 10 Tennis available; 11 Swimming available; 12 Golf available; 13 Skiing available; 14 May be booked through travel agents

Close to the beaten path, yet not on it, Woody Hill offers quiet country living just two miles from the ocean. Situated on a hilltop and surrounded by rolling fields and informal gardens, the house features antiques, wide-board floors, and handmade quilts. Guests enjoy the shuttered library or rock contentedly on the porch. A 40-foot in-ground pool is also available.

Host: Ellen L. Madison
Rooms: 3 (1 PB; 2 SB) $50-90
Full Breakfast
Credit Cards: None
Notes: 2, 5, 8, 9, 10, 11, 12

The heart of this home, the livingroom, was built in 1732 as a blacksmith's shop. Later the forge was removed and a large granite fireplace was built by an American Indian stonemason. The original wood ceiling, hand-hewn beams, and granite walls remain today. The property was called the Perry Plantation, and two slaves lived above the blacksmith's shop.

Hosts: Dick and Madelein Sohl
Rooms: 3 (1 PB; 2 SB) $55
Full Breakfast
Credit Cards: None
Notes: 2, 5, 8, 9, 11, 12, 14

WYOMING

The Cookie Jar Bed and Breakfast
64 Kingstown Road, Route 138 off I-95, 02898
(401) 539-2680

South Carolina

TwoSuns Inn
Bed and Breakfast

1705 Bay Street, 29902
(803) 522-1122; (800) 532-4244
FAX (803) 522-1122

A completely restored Neoclassical Revival
home situated directly on the bay. Full personal and business amenities are offered,
including use of bicycles to explore charming, historic Beaufort, a 304-acre national
landmark area. Guest rooms feature Victorian, country, and Oriental themes, complemented by family antiques and collectibles.
A scrumptious breakfast, tea and toddy hour,
and gracious service await guests.

Hosts: Carrol and Ron Kay
Rooms: 5 (PB) $77-93
Full Breakfast
Credit Cards: A, B, C
Notes: 2, 5, 9, 10, 11, 12, 14

CHARLESTON

Brasington House
Bed and Breakfast

328 East Bay Street, 29401
(803) 722-1274; (800) 722-1274

Four elegant rooms in this antebellum residence furnished with antiques. Private baths,
central heat and air conditioning, cable TV,
king-size beds, and tea and coffee in rooms.
Also included is breakfast served in the
formal dining room, wine and liqueurs served
in the livingroom, and off-street parking.

Personalized service includes recommen-
dations for restaurants, sightseeing, shopping, and entertainment. Conveniently situated in Charleston's historic district.

Hosts: Dalton and Judy Brasington
Rooms: 4 (PB) $79-98
Full Breakfast
Credit Cards: A, B
Notes: 2, 5, 9, 10, 11, 12

Brasington House Bed and Breakfast

Country Victorian
Bed and Breakfast

105 Tradd Street, 29401-2422
(803) 577-0682

Relive the charm of the past. Relax in a
rocker on the piazza of this historic home
and watch the carriages pass by. Walk to
antique shops, churches, restaurants, art
galleries, museums, and all historic points
of interest. The house, built in 1820, is
situated in the historic district south of Broad.
Rooms have private entrances, iron and
brass beds, quilts, oak and wicker furniture,
braided rugs over heart-of-pine floors.

welcome; 9 Social drinking allowed; 10 Tennis available; 11 Swimming available; 12 Golf available; 13 Skiing
available; 14 May be booked through travel agents

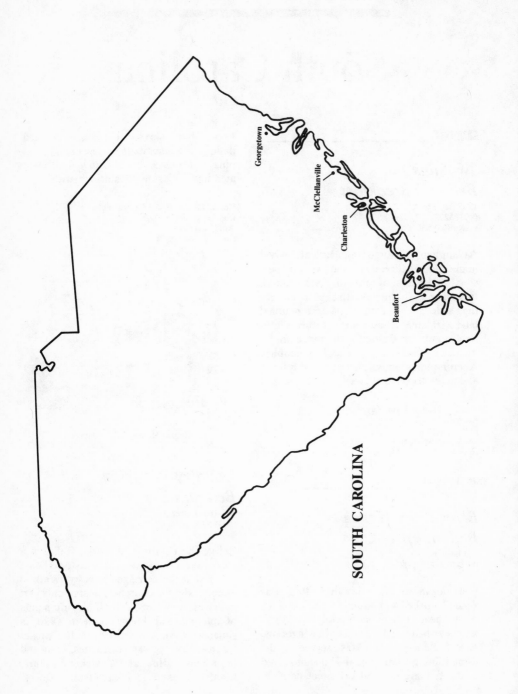

Georgetown

McClellanville

Charleston

Beaufort

SOUTH CAROLINA

Homemade cookies will be waiting. Parking and bicycles available.

Host: Diane Deardurff Weed
Rooms: 2 (PB) $65-90
Expanded Continental Breakfast
Credit Cards: None
Notes: 2, 5, 8, 9, 10, 11, 12, 14

1837 Bed and Breakfast
126 Wentworth Street, 29401
(803) 723-7166

Share and enjoy this circa-1800 home and brick carriage house, originally built and owned by a wealthy cotton planter and now owned and restored by two artists. All rooms are furnished with antiques and period pieces. Each has refrigerator and TV. It is an easy walk to the old marketplace, carriage rides, boat tours, antique shops, restaurants, the OMNI, and the College of Charleston. Afternoon tea is served.

Hosts: Sherri Weaver and Richard Dunn
Rooms: 8 (PB) $55-95
Full Breakfast
Credit Cards: A, B, C
Notes: 2, 5, 8 (limited), 9, 10, 11, 12

Historic Charleston Bed and Breakfast
43 Legare Street, 29401
(803) 722-6606

This is a reservation service for approximately 35 homes and carriage houses. Most homes are historic and situated within the historic district and within walking distance of restaurants, shops, and major points of interest. Also has listings for Columbia, Hilton Head Island, Edisto Island, Summerville. Several plantation homes are available. Charlotte Fairey, coordinator. $65-140.

Country Victorian Bed and Breakfast

King George IV Inn and Guest House
32 George Street, 29401
(803) 723-9339

The King George Inn is a 200-year-old historic home in downtown historic Charleston. It is a Federal-style home with a Greek Revival parapet roofline. There are four stories with three levels of lovely porches. All rooms have fireplaces, high ceilings, hardwood floors, and original six-foot oak doors. The inn is within walking distance of all King Street shopping and restaurants and the historic market.

Hosts: Jean, B. J., and Mike
Rooms: 8 (PB) $50-75
Continental Breakfast
Credit Cards: A, B
Notes: 2, 5, 6 (limited), 8, 9, 10, 11, 12

Rutledge Victorian Inn and Guest House
114 Rutledge Avenue, 29401
(803) 722-7551

NOTES: Credit cards accepted: A MasterCard; B Visa; C American Express; D Discover Card; E Diners Club; F Other; 2 Personal checks accepted; 3 Lunch available; 4 Dinner available; 5 Open all year; 6 Pets welcome; 8 Children welcome; 9 Social drinking allowed; 10 Tennis available; 11 Swimming available; 12 Golf available; 13 Skiing available; 14 May be booked through travel agents

For over 50 years this Italianate-style home has been an inn and boarding house in the downtown historic district. All rooms have lovely decorative fireplaces, hardwood floors, and antiques. Outside is a beautiful round porch, columns, and antique gingerbread. The inn is within walking distance of boat rides, shopping, dining, historic sights, plantations, and beaches.

Hosts: Jean, B. J., and Mike
Rooms: 10 (5 PB; 5 SB) $50-85
Continental Breakfast
Credit Cards: A, B
Notes: 2, 5, 6 (limited), 8, 9, 10, 11, 12

GEORGETOWN

Ashfield Manor

3030 South Island Road, 29440
(803) 546-0464

A Christian home offers southern hospitality in the style of a real southern plantation. In an elegant country setting, all rooms are oversized and newly redecorated in period furnishings; all have remote TV and private entrance. Breakfast is served in the guest rooms; the parlor; or on the 57-foot screened porch, complete with rocking chairs, overlooking a small lake.

Hosts: Dave and Carol Ashenfelder
Rooms: 4 (SB) $45-55
Continental Breakfast
Credit Cards: A, B, C, D, E
Notes: 2, 5, 8, 10, 11, 12, 14

The Shaw House

8 Cypress Court, 29440
(803) 546-9663

Shaw House overlooks a beautiful marsh. Built in the Colonial style, it has large rooms, a den, rocking chairs, front porch, antiques, king beds, and homemade biscuits and quiche. For eight years, the hosts have been making guests' stays special.

Hosts: Mary and Joe Shaw
Rooms: 3 (PB) $50-55
Full Breakfast
Credit Cards: None
Notes: 2, 5, 8, 9, 10, 11, 12, 14

Wade-Beckham House

LANCASTER

Wade-Beckham House

Route 7, Box 348, 29720
(803) 285-1105

This circa-1832 plantation house is listed on the National Register of Historic Places. Choose between the rose room, the summer house room, or the Wade Hampton room, all furnished with antiques. The rural setting is enhanced with the old store, barn, and barnyard animals.

Hosts: Bill and Jan Duke
Rooms: 4 (SB) $50-60
Full Breakfast
Credit Cards: None
Notes: 2

MCCLELLANVILLE

Laurel Hill Plantation

8913 North Highway 17, P.O. Box 190, 29458
(803) 887-3708

Situated between Charleston and Myrtle Beach, this reconstructed 1850s Low Coun-

NOTES: Credit cards accepted: A Master Card; B Visa; C American Express; D Discover Card; E Diners Club; F Other; 2 Personal checks accepted; 3 Lunch available; 4 Dinner available; 5 Open all year; 6 Pets welcome; 8 Children

try inn offers the romance of the past and the convenience of the contemporary. Wraparound porches overlook a sweeping panorama of salt marshes, waterways, and the Atlantic Ocean. Rooms are furnished with country antiques that reflect the historic lifestyle.

Hosts: Jackie and Lee Morrison
Rooms: 4 (PB) $65-75
Full Breakfast
Credit Cards: None
Notes: 2, 5, 9, 10, 11, 12

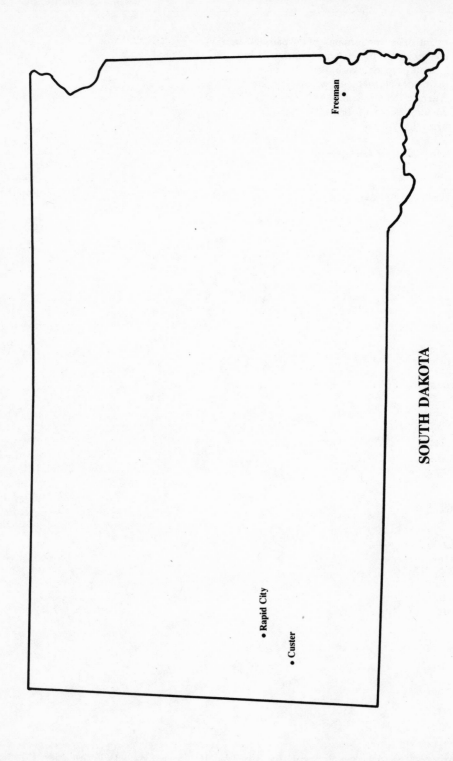

Freeman

Rapid City

Custer

SOUTH DAKOTA

South Dakota

CUSTER

Custer Mansion Bed and Breakfast

35 Centennial Drive, 57730
(605) 673-3333

This historic 1891 Victorian Gothic home on one acre is beautifully restored and decorated, including a few antiques. It offers friendly western hospitality and a delicious home-cooked breakfast in the large, gracious dining room. Enjoy the unique setting of the beautiful Black Hills near Custer State Park, Mount Rushmore, and Crazy Horse Monument. Restaurants are also nearby.

Hosts: Mill and Carole Seaman
Rooms: 5 (2 PB; 3 S2B) $45-65
Full Breakfast
Credit Cards: None
Notes: 2, 5, 8 (over 6), 10, 11, 12, 13

FREEMAN

Golden Robin Nest

1210 East Fourth Street, 57029
(605) 925-4410

One block from State Highway 81, on the edge of a small but progressive country town. This adequate facility has a quiet Christian atmosphere. Hosts are a friendly and mature couple. Guest rooms allow privacy and comfort.

Host: Goldie Boese
Rooms: 2 (SB) $20
Continental Breakfast
Credit Cards: None
Closed January to March 15
Notes: 6 (outside), 8, 10, 11

RAPID CITY

Abend Haus Cottage and Audrie's Cranbury Corner

Rural Route 8, Box 2400, 57702
(605) 342-7788

Ultimate in charm and Old World hospitality, this country home and five-acre estate is surrounded by thousands of acres of national forest in a secluded Black Hills setting. Each comfortable room, suite, or cottage has a private entrance, hot tub, patio, cable TV, refrigerator, and fireplace. Free trout fishing, hiking, and biking available on property.

Hosts: Hank and Audry Kuhnhauser
Rooms: 6 (PB) $78-85
Full Breakfast
Credit Cards: None
Notes: 2, 5, 9, 10, 11, 12, 13

NOTES: Credit cards accepted: A Master Card; B Visa; C American Express; D Discover Card; E Diners Club; F Other; 2 Personal checks accepted; 3 Lunch available; 4 Dinner available; 5 Open all year; 6 Pets welcome; 8 Children welcome; 9 Social drinking allowed; 10 Tennis available; 11 Swimming available; 12 Golf available; 13 Skiing available; 14 May be booked through travel agents

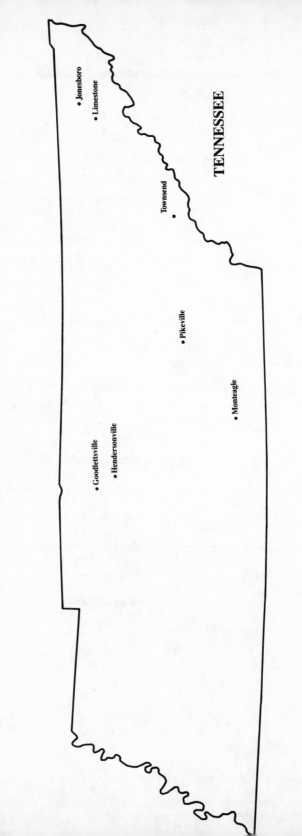

TENNESSEE

• Jonesboro
• Limestone

Townsend
•

• Pikeville

• Monteagle

Goodlettsville •
• Hendersonville

Tennessee

Woodshire
Bed and Breakfast
600 Woodshire Drive, 37072
(615) 859-7369

Eight miles from Opryland park and hotel and Andrew Jackson's Hermitage; 12 to 14 miles from Nashville's colleges and universities; 11 miles from Nashville; close to country music tours, stars' homes, and museums. This new saltbox house is filled with antiques and weavings, paintings, and woodcrafts made by the hosts, all to give it a country feel.

Hosts: John and Beverly Grayson
Rooms: 2 (PB) $45
Continental Breakfast
Credit Cards: None
Open March 1 to December 1
Notes: 2, 8, 10, 11, 12, 14

Robertson House Bed and Breakfast Inn

Monthaven
Bed and Breakfast
1154 West Main Street, 37075
(615) 824-6319

Listed on the National Register of Historic Places, Monthaven offers both the beauty of Middle Tennessee and the convenience of being only 15 minutes from downtown Nashville. Monthaven guarantees that guests will enjoy their stay. Also on this 75-acre farm is a 200-year-old log cabin rebuilt in 1938. The cabin is modern and fully furnished, only 60 yards from the main house.

Host: Hugh Waddell
Rooms: 3 (2 PB; 1 SB) $65-85
Cabin: 1 (PB)
Expanded Continental Breakfast
Credit Cards: A, B, C, E
Notes: 2, 3, 4, 5, 6, 8, 9, 10, 11, 12, 14

Robertson House
Bed and Breakfast Inn
212 East Main Street, 37659
(615) 753-3039; (800) 843-4755

A large, comfortable home built in 1925, Robertson House is unique in architectural detail reflecting the ambience of the past with modern-day amenities. The inn is conveniently situated in the heart of Jonesborough, Tennessee's oldest town. Relaxed comfort and hospitality are the

NOTES: Credit cards accepted: A Master Card; B Visa; C American Express; D Discover Card; E Diners Club; F Other; 2 Personal checks accepted; 3 Lunch available; 4 Dinner available; 5 Open all year; 6 Pets welcome; 8 Children welcome; 9 Social drinking allowed; 10 Tennis available; 11 Swimming available; 12 Golf available; 13 Skiing available; 14 May be booked through travel agents

hallmarks of the inn. Guests are invited to relax in the livingroom or in their own spacious accommodations, sip a glass of wine, or relax in the shade.

Hosts: Reva Jo Robertson and Janet O'Callaghan
Rooms: 3 (2 PB; 1 SB) $50-75
Full Breakfast
Credit Cards: None
Notes: 2, 4, 5, 8, 9, 11, 12, 14

LIMESTONE

Snapp Inn Bed and Breakfast
Route 3, Box 102, 37681
(615) 257-2482

This gracious Federal home, circa 1815, is furnished with antiques and set in farm country. Relax and enjoy the mountain views from the full back porch or front balcony, friendly family atmosphere, TV in large common room, pool table. Close to Davy Crockett's birthplace, 15-minute drive to Greeneville or historic Jonesborough.

Hosts: Dan and Ruth Dorgan
Rooms: 2 (PB) $50
Full Breakfast
Credit Cards: None
Notes: 2, 5, 9, 11, 12, 14

MONTEAGLE

Edgeworth Inn
Monteagle Assembly, 37356
(615) 924-2669

This 1896 luxurious inn, on the National Register of Historic Places, has rocking chairs, hammocks, fireplaces, a large library, 96 original paintings, and more than 200 feet of verandas. Recently redecorated with English chintz, collector quilts, fine linens, and custom-made mattresses. Breakfast is served on Wedgwood china. Atop the Cumberland Mountains, the Assembly village is an 1880 "Camelot," with more than

150 century-old Victorian homes in a 96-acre natural garden of giant trees, brooks, and wooden bridges. Near Savage Gulf, Fiery Gizzard, and many natural wonders. Literary, musical, and athletic events are frequent at Sewanee and at the Assembly during summer.

Hosts: Wendy and David Adams
Rooms: 11 (PB) $65-125
Continental Breakfast
Credit Cards: A, B
Notes: 2, 5, 9, 10, 11, 12, 14

Snapp Inn Bed and Breakfast

PIKEVILLE

Fall Creek Falls Bed and Breakfast
Route 3, P.O. Box 309, 37367
(615) 881-5494

Enjoy the country atmosphere of an English manor home situated on 40 acres of rolling hillside one mile from the nationally acclaimed Fall Creek Falls State Resort Park. All rooms have beautiful furnishings. Breakfast is served in a cozy country kitchen, an elegant dining room, or a sunny Florida room with a magnificent view. Assistance with touring, dining, and shopping is provided.

Hosts: Doug and Rita Pruett
Rooms: 8 (PB) $55-60
Continental Breakfast
Credit Cards: None
Notes: 2, 10, 11, 12

TOWNSEND _____

Smoky Bear Lodge
160 Bear Lodge Drive, 37882
(615) 448-6442

Situated in the foothills of the Great Smoky Mountains in Townsend, a 1,500-square-foot conference room complements the ideal Christian family-oriented retreat site for youth, choirs, church leaders, or family vacations. The view from the rocker-lined front porch is incredible. Enjoy the activities, pool, hot tub, and beautiful sunrises and sunsets while you learn or just relax.

Hosts: Cary and Sandy Plummer
Rooms: 11 (PB) $65-85
Full Breakfast
Credit Cards: A, B, C
Notes: 2, 5, 8, 11, 12, 13, 14

- El Paso

- Tyler

- Fredericksburg

- Houston

- San Antonio

Galveston

TEXAS

Texas

EL PASO

Sunset Heights
Bed and Breakfast Inn
717 West Yandell Avenue, 79902
(915) 544-1743

This national historic home exudes its three-story, turn-of-the-century Victorian elegance and charm from palm trees to wine cellar, with oversized Tiffany glass door and windows and crystal chandeliers throughout. Choose from the distinct bedrooms; massive cherrywood four-poster beds with fireplace, marble bath, and Jacuzzi; an Oriental motif with black marble balcony, bath, and claw foot tub; solid brass fixtures and brass beds. French dinners available by reservation.

Hosts: R. Barnett and R. Martinez
Rooms: 4 (PB) $60-150
Full Breakfast
Credit Cards: A, B, C
Notes: 3, 4, 5, 9, 11

FREDERICKSBURG

Country Cottage Inn
405 East Main, 78624
(512) 997-8549

The quaint, historic town of Fredericksburg was founded in 1846, and this lovely inn was the first two-story limestone house built in town. The walls are more than 24 inches thick, and the roof is high and peaked. All rooms are entered from a typical early-Texan porch. The handmade arched doors lead to cool whitewashed stone rooms. Ex-posed rafters are hand cut from solid oak. Rooms are furnished completely in antiques.

Host: Jeffery Webb
Rooms: 5 (PB) $65-105
Continental Breakfast
Credit Cards: A, B
Notes: 2, 5, 9, 14

GALVESTON

The White Horse Inn
2217 Broadway, 77550
(800) 762-2632; (800) 76-B AND B

This 1885 Italianate Victorian has 14-foot ceilings, antiques, art glass, slate fireplaces, gas fixtures, and authentic colors and decor. Two rooms in the main house have antique half-canopy beds, fireplaces, and clawfoot tubs. Four rooms in the carriage house at the back of the lushly landscaped garden are reminiscent of New Orleans, with reproduction furnishings. Close to historic district and beach.

Host: Robert Clark
Rooms: 6 (PB) $90-115
Full Breakfast
Credit Cards: A, B, C, D, E
Notes: 2, 4, 5, 9, 11, 12, 14

HOUSTON

Durham House
Bed and Breakfast
921 Heights Boulevard, 77008
(713) 868-4654

Durham House, a restored Queen Anne Victorian, is listed on the National Register

NOTES: Credit cards accepted: A Master Card; B Visa; C American Express; D Discover Card; E Diners Club; F Other; 2 Personal checks accepted; 3 Lunch available; 4 Dinner available; 5 Open all year; 6 Pets welcome; 8 Children welcome; 9 Social drinking allowed; 10 Tennis available; 11 Swimming available; 12 Golf available; 13 Skiing available; 14 May be booked through travel agents

of Historic Places. Antiques fill all rooms, and breakfast is served in a choice of several dining rooms. Just five minutes from downtown Houston, Durham House offers individualized service, a parlor player piano, tandem bicycle for guest use, plus a boulevard perfect for walking and jogging.

Host: Marguerite Swanson
Rooms: 5 (4 PB; 1 SB) $50-75
Full Breakfast
Credit Cards: A, B, C
Notes: 2, 5, 9, 10, 11, 12, 14

The Highlander

The Highlander
607 Highland Street, 77009
(713) 861-6110

Nestled among stately pecan trees, this creatively decorated four-square provides an oasis of tranquility almost within the shadow of dynamic downtown Houston. But at The Highlander, one senses a distance of time from such energetic activity. Here, southern charm and Christian hospitality combine to make memories beautiful. Luxurious accommodations, bountiful breakfast, congenial hosts, and convenient location all combine to make a lovely visit.

Hosts: Arlen and Georgie McIrvin
Rooms: 4 (2 PB; 2 SB) $58-75
Full Breakfast
Credit Cards: A, B, C
Notes: 2, 5, 8, 10, 11, 12, 14

Patrician
Bed and Breakfast Inn
1200 Southmore Avenue, 77004
(713) 523-1114

This inn is a large three-story mansion built in 1919 in the Colonial Revival style and originally owned by a prominent Houston attorney. It has been lovingly restored to its former grandeur and features antiques, wrought iron and brass beds, and fireplace. Breakfast is served in the dining room or the sunny solarium. Walk to Hermann Park, Houston Zoological Gardens, Rice University, and Houston Museum of Fine Arts. A perfect setting for weddings, receptions, and private parties.

Host: Pat Thomas
Rooms: 5 (PB) $65-85
Full Breakfast
Credit Cards: A, B, C, E
Notes: 2, 5, 9, 10, 12, 14

Robin's Nest
4104 Greeley, 77006
(713) 528-5821

Originally a dairy farm, this Victorian home was built in 1894 and reportedly is the oldest house in the museum district, one of Houston's first neighborhoods. It is situated between downtown, Houston's major museums, and the Texas Medical Center. Excellent restaurants are within walking distance. A wonderfully prserved Victorian in an urban, vibrant neighborhood.

Host: Robin Smith
Rooms: 2 (SB) $50-60
Full Breakfast
Credit Cards: None
Notes: 2, 5, 9, 10, 11, 12, 13, 14

SAN ANTONIO

Naegelin Bed and Breakfast
921 Matagorda, 78210
(800) 289-3041

NOTES: Credit cards accepted: A Master Card; B Visa; C American Express; D Discover Card; E Diners Club; F Other; 2 Personal checks accepted; 3 Lunch available; 4 Dinner available; 5 Open all year; 6 Pets welcome; 8 Children

This historic Colonial home built in 1910 is situated in the La Vaca historic district of downtown San Antonio. The two-story brick home is enhanced by balconies supported by fluted Corinthian columns. Guests are greeted with wood panels in the entry, as well as rich woodwork throughout the house. The home is carefully furnished with antiques to create a personal touch of the Victorian era.

Hosts: Maria R. Trevino and Annabelle R. Gomez
Rooms: 4 (1 PB; 3 SB) $55-80
Continental Breakfast
Credit Cards: A, B, C, E
Notes: 2, 5, 14

Patrician Bed and Breakfast Inn

TYLER _____

Mary's Attic
Bed and Breakfast
413 South College
Mailing address: 417 South College, 75702
(903) 592-5181; FAX (903) 592-3846

Enjoy this 1920, completely restored bungalow furnished entirely with antiques from Mary's antique shop next door. At this non-hosted bed and breakfast, guests enjoy Mary's personally baked sweet rolls and breads and a selection of teas, coffee, juice, and fresh fruit.

Host: Mary Mirsky
Rooms: 5 (2 PB; 3 SB) $75
Continental Breakfast
Credit Cards: A, B, D
Notes: 5, 10, 11, 12

Rosevine Inn
Bed and Breakfast
415 South Vine, 75702
(903) 592-2221

Rosevine Inn is situated in the historic brick street district of Tyler. Rest and relax in the lovely courtyard complete with fountain and fireplace. A hot tub is also available for guests. After seeing the sights of Tyler and enjoying a restful night's sleep, guests relish the delectable breakfast served in the dining room.

Hosts: Bert and Rebecca Powell
Rooms: 4 (PB) $65-75
Full Breakfast
Credit Cards: A, B, C, D, E
Notes: 2, 5, 9, 10, 12, 14

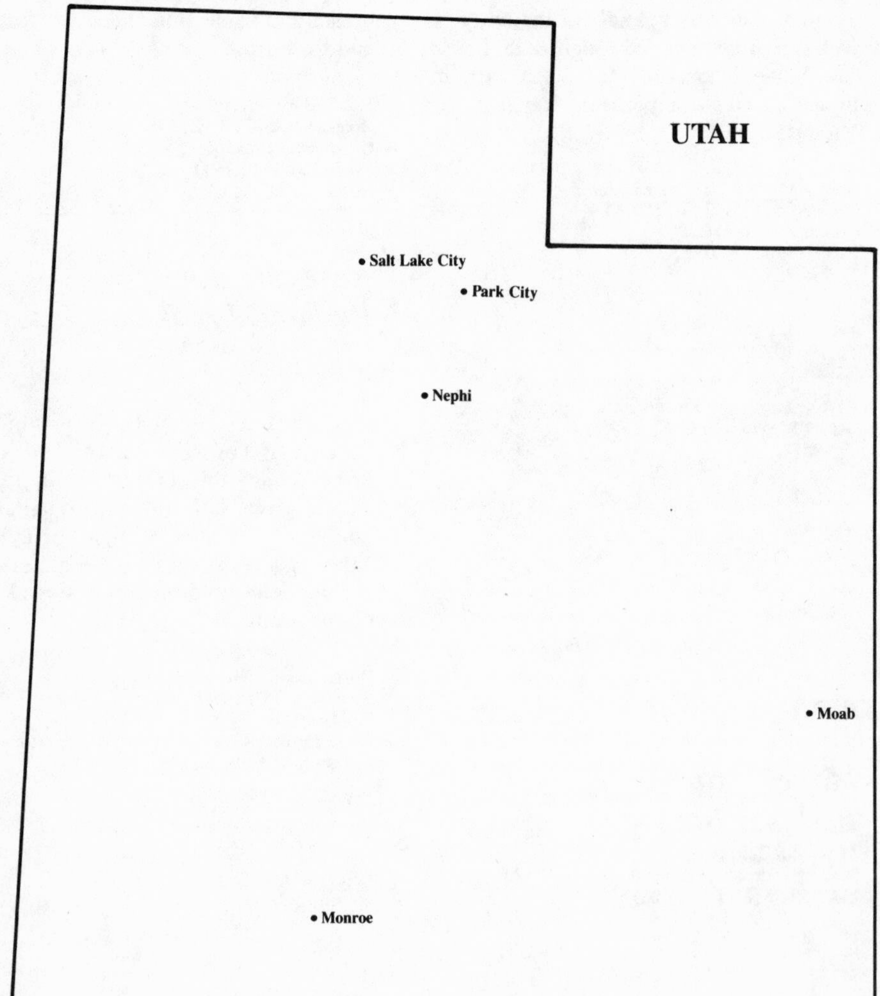

UTAH

• Salt Lake City

• Park City

• Nephi

• Moab

• Monroe

Monticello •

• Saint George

Utah

Mi Casa Su Casa #1101
P. O. Box 950, Tempe, Arizona 85280-0950
(602) 990-0682; (800) 456-0682 reservations

This ranch-style home is nestled between
the snow-capped LaSal Mountains and the
red rock canyons of the Colorado River and
is within walking distance of local shops,
museums, galleries, and restaurants. Golf,
tennis, and swimming are nearby. Full
breakfast. $65

Whitmore Mansion

MONROE _____

Mi Casa Su Casa #1093
P. O. Box 950, Tempe, Arizona 85280-0950
(602) 990-0682; (800) 456-0682 reservations

Monroe is a small farming community in
the heart of hunting and fishing country.
The house is an immaculate, casual, comfortable farmhouse near tennis courts and
golf. Full breakfast. $45.

MONTICELLO _____

Mi Casa Su Casa #1100
P. O. Box 950, Tempe, Arizona 85280-0950
(602) 990-0682; (800) 456-0682 reservations

At the foot of the Blue Mountains at 7,000
feet is the three-story building known as the
Old Monticello flour mill built in 1933,
featuring rough timber and log support
beams. It has six beautiful suites. $52.

NEPHI _____

Whitmore Mansion
110 South Main Street, P.O. Box 73, 84648
(801) 623-2047

This 1898 Queen Anne Eastlake Victorian
mansion is listed on the National Register of
Historic Places. The interior features imported oak woodwork, leaded-glass windows, a magnificent staircase, and high
ceilings. Hand-crocheted afghans and
handcrafted rugs complement antique furnishings. The hearty breakfast often includes fresh muffins or German pancakes.
In warm weather, homemade ice cream is
graciously served; during cooler months,
hot cider by the fireplace.

Hosts: Robert and Dorothy Gliske
Rooms: 6 (PB) $45-65
Full Breakfast
Credit Cards: A, B
Notes: 2, 5, 9, 10, 11, 12

NOTES: Credit cards accepted: A Master Card; B Visa; C American Express; D Discover Card; E Diners Club; F Other;
2 Personal checks accepted; 3 Lunch available; 4 Dinner available; 5 Open all year; 6 Pets welcome; 8 Children
welcome; 9 Social drinking allowed; 10 Tennis available; 11 Swimming available; 12 Golf available; 13 Skiing
available; 14 May be booked through travel agents

PARK CITY

The Old Miners' Lodge— A Bed and Breakfast Inn

615 Woodside Avenue, P.O. Box 2639, 84060-2639
(801) 645-8068; (800) 648-8068

The Old Miners' Lodge is in a restored 1893 miners' boarding house in the colorful national historic district of Park City. Ten guest rooms have private baths and are named and decorated after some of Park City's most famous characters. A full breakfast and evening refreshments complement a day of skiing, hiking, bicycling, ballooning, horseback riding, golfing, tennis, and more. An outdoor hot tub is available for guests, and the innkeepers are ready to assist with all plans.

Hosts: Hugh Daniels, Susan Wynne, and
    Jeff Sadowsky
Rooms: 10 (PB) $45-175 seasonal
Full Breakfast
Credit Cards: A, B, C, D
Notes: 2, 5, 8, 9, 10, 11, 12, 13, 14

Washington School Inn

543 Park Avenue, P.O. Box 536, 84060
(801) 649-3800; (800) 824-1672
FAX (801) 649-3802

The Washington School Inn is just 40 minutes from Salt Lake International Airport. Park City is a world-class ski and summer resort. Washington School Inn is a historic restoration of a schoolhouse built in 1889. It is on both the national and state historic registers, and it opened in June 1985 as a fully renovated inn.

Host: Nancy Beaufait
Rooms: 15 (PB) $75-240
Full Breakfast
Credit Cards: A, B, C, D
Notes: 2, 5, 8 (over 11), 9, 10, 11, 12, 13, 14

SAINT GEORGE

Greene Gate Village

76 West Tabernacle, 84770
(800) 350-6999

The inn is a cluster of nine restored pioneer homes. Each home, with a unique and interesting history, is tastefully decorated with antiques. Original fireplaces, warm quilts, pool, tennis, and a hot tub all make this a memorable escape from the fast track. The thriving community boasts an excellent regional medical center; the annual Saint George Marathon; and six national parks within a 100-mile radius, including Zion, Bryce, and Grand Canyon.

Hosts: Mark and Barbara Greene
Rooms: 16 (PB) $45-85
Full Breakfast
Credit Cards: A, B, C
Notes: 2, 3, 4 (Thurs.-Sat.), 5, 8, 9, 10, 11, 12, 13, 14

Seven Wives Inn

Seven Wives Inn

217 North 100 West, 84770
(801) 628-3737

Situated in the Saint George historical district, the inn consists of two adjacent pioneer adobe homes with massive hand-grained moldings framing windows and doors. Bedrooms are furnished with period antiques and handmade quilts. Some rooms have fireplaces; one has an adjacent whirlpool tub. There is a swimming pool on the premises.

Hosts: Donna and Jay Curtis; Alison and Jon
  Bowcutt
Rooms: 13 (PB) $35-75
Full Breakfast
Credit Cards: A, B, C, E
Notes: 2, 5, 8, 9, 10, 11, 12, 14

SALT LAKE CITY

Mi Casa Su Casa #1091

P. O. Box 950, Tempe, Arizona 85280-0950
(602) 990-0682; (800) 456-0682 reservations

Well known for its superior luxury and
hospitality, this inn takes great pride in
providing guests with one of the most beautiful settings in the Southwest. Perfect for
special occasions. Just six miles to downtown and 20 minutes to Park City. Full
breakfast. $65-160.

Saltair Bed and Breakfast

164 South 900 East, 84102
(801) 533-8184; (800) 733-8184

Saltair Bed and Breakfast is situated in a
residential area of Salt Lake City within
minutes of many prominent landmarks.
Temple Square, the Family History Library,
Symphony Hall, and the Utah state capitol
are just minutes away. Utah's virtually un-
limited outdoor recreational opportunities
are easily accessible via interstate highways. Dozens of state parks and recreation
areas are within a day's drive.

Hosts: Jan Bartlett and Nancy Saxton
Rooms: 5 (2 PB; 3 SB) $49-69
Expanded Continental Breakfast
Credit Cards: A, B, C
Notes: 2, 5, 8, 9, 10, 11, 12, 13, 14

The Spruces
Bed and Breakfast

6181 South 900 East, 84121
(801) 268-8762

The inn is set amid many tall spruces and
has four suites furnished with folk art and
southwestern touches. The largest suite has
three bedrooms, a livingroom, and kitchen.
There is easy access to ski resorts, restaurants, hospitals, and shopping. Originally
built in 1907 and renovated in 1985.

Hosts: Karl and Susan Lind
Rooms: 4 (PB) $50-90
Continental Breakfast
Credit Cards: A, B, C
Notes: 2, 5, 8, 9, 10, 11, 12, 13, 14

SPRINGDALE

Mi Casa Su Casa #1096

P. O. Box 950, Tempe, Arizona 85280-0950
(602) 990-0682; (800) 456-0682 reservations

An architect who designed many national
park lodges designed this house constructed
of timbers from Cable Mountain and sand-
stone blocks from the canyon walls. The
interior is decorated with antique furniture
with a southwestern accent. Full breakfast.
$45-65.

Mi Casa Su Casa #1098

P. O. Box 950, Tempe, Arizona 85280-0950
(602) 990-0682; (800) 456-0682 reservations

Built in contemporary pioneer ranch style,
this inn is in a quiet area of new homes. The
exterior is stucco and brick with front porch
and gabled roof, cactus garden, and views of
the park. One-half mile from the entrance to
Zion National Park. Full breakfast. $55-65.

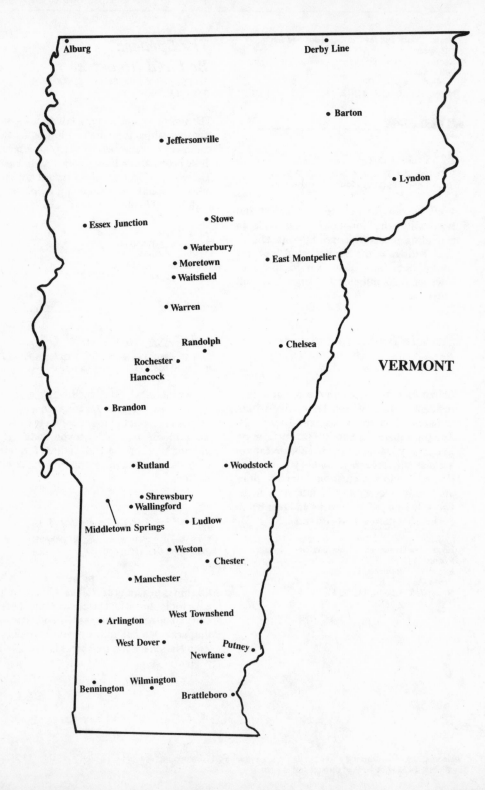

Alburg

Derby Line

Barton

Jeffersonville

Lyndon

Essex Junction   Stowe

Waterbury

Moretown   East Montpelier

Waitsfield

Warren

Randolph   Chelsea

Rochester   VERMONT
Hancock

Brandon

Rutland   Woodstock

Shrewsbury
Wallingford

Middletown Springs   Ludlow

Weston

Chester

Manchester

West Townshend

Arlington

West Dover   Putney

Newfane

Wilmington
Bennington

Brattleboro

Vermont

Thomas Mott
Bed and Breakfast

Blue Rock Road, Route 2, Box 149B, 05440
(802) 796-3736; (800) 348-0843

Hosted by a criminology and American history major and noted wine consultant, this completely restored farmhouse dates from 1838. The guest livingroom has a TV and fireplace and overlooks the northern banks of Lake Champlain. There is also a game room with bumper pool, darts, and other games. All rooms have a quilt decor and overlook the lake with full views of distant Mount Mansfield and nearby Jay Peak. One hour to Montreal/Burlington; one and one-half hours to Stowe and Lake Placid. Ben and Jerry's ice cream is always in the guest freezer. Approved by AAA, CAA, National Bed and Breakfast Association, and *Yankee* magazine.

Host: Patrick J. Schallert, Sr.
Rooms: 4 (PB) $50-65
Full Breakfast
Credit Cards: None
Notes: 2, 4, 5, 8 (over 6), 9, 10, 11, 12, 13, 14

ARLINGTON

The Inn on Covered
Bridge Green

Rural Delivery 1, Box 3550, 05250
(802) 375-9489

Unwind in country elegance in this two-century-old farmhouse and former home of Norman Rockwell. Stroll across the green from the front porch to enjoy river activities on the Battenkill. A gourmet breakfast is served.

Hosts: Anne and Ron Weber
Rooms: 5 (PB) $125-130
Full Breakfast
Credit Cards: None
Notes: 2, 5, 8, 9, 10, 11, 12, 13

BARTON

Fox Hall Inn

Willoughby Lake Road, 05822
(802) 525-6930

Enjoy warm hospitality at this whimsical cottage, which was a former girls' camp. The gambrel-roofed midsection is flanked by round towers. There are spectacular views from the veranda of Willoughby Lake surrounded by granite cliffs and gentle mountains. Designated a registered landmark, much of the lake area is protected parkland. Great hiking and biking. Many summer and winter activities.

Hosts: Ken and Sherry Pyden
Rooms: 9 (4 PB; 5 SB) $60-90
Full Breakfast
Credit Cards: A, B
Notes: 2, 5, 8, 9, 10, 11, 12, 13, 14

BENNINGTON

Molly Stark Inn

1067 East Main Street, 05201
(802) 442-9631; (800) 356-3076

This Victorian country home, circa 1860, has six warm, cozy guest rooms tastefully furnished in Americana style and decor. Antiques, claw foot tubs, hardwood floors, stenciled walls, and woodwork abound. Wraparound front porch with rocking chairs, gourmet breakfast, afternoon tea. A beautiful brick archway houses a gorgeous woodburning stove in the den. Situated one mile from the center of historic Bennington.

Host: Reed Fendler
Rooms: 6 (2 PB; 4 SB) $50-80
Full Breakfast
Credit Cards: A, B, C, D
Notes: 2, 5, 8, 9, 10, 11, 12, 13, 14

BRANDON

Hivue Bed and Breakfast Tree Farm
Rural Route 1, Box 1023
High Pond Road, 05733-9704
(802) 247-3042

Enjoy the rural surroundings of this 76-acre wildlife habitat and primitive tree farm with great views of the Pico, Killington, and Green mountains and four-season splendor. A hearty country breakfast is served.

Hosts: Wini and Bill Reuschle
Rooms: 3 (PB) $50
Full Breakfast
Credit Cards: None
Notes: 2, 5, 8, 9, 10, 11, 12, 13

Shire Inn

Rosebelle's Victorian Inn
31 Franklin Street, 05733
(802) 247-0098

This elegantly restored 1860s Victorian mansion is on the National Register of Historic Places and offers six guest rooms and a country breakfast with many choices. Relax in the warm, cozy livingroom with fireplace in the winter after a day of skiing; walk in the flower garden in the summer.

Hosts: Ginette and Norm Milot
Rooms: 6 (2 PB; 4 SB) $60-70 weekends; $50-65 midweek
Full Breakfast
Credit Cards: A, B
Notes: 2, 5, 8 (over 15), 10, 11,12, 13

BRATTLEBORO

The Green River Guest House
Rural Free Delivery 4, Box 789, 05301
(802) 254-4114

Looking for an idyllic getaway? Nestled in a valley that time appears to have passed by, the Green River Guest House, situated on 13 acres of meadowland, is the perfect place to unwind. Relax and listen to the gentle rush of the river. Take a walk down a country road to the covered bridge and old-fashioned swimming hole. Inside this charming and spacious home, comfort and warm hospitality await the guest.

Hosts: Patrick and Lorraine Ryan
Rooms: 2 (1 PB; 1 SB) $50
Full Breakfast
Credit Cards: A, B
Notes: 2, 5, 8, 9, 11, 13, 14

CHELSEA

Shire Inn
8 Main Street, 05038
(800) 441-6908

This is an 1832 historic brick Federal inn featuring 18th-century accommodations with 20th-century baths. Small and intimate, some rooms have working fireplaces. It is chef-owned and operated, with five-course dining available. The inn is centrally situated 30 miles north of Woodstock/Quechee, 33 miles to Hanover/Dartmouth, 30 miles south of Montpelier.

Hosts: James and Mary Lee Papa
Rooms: 6 (PB) $80-95
Full Breakfast
Credit Cards: A, B, C
Notes: 2, 4, 5, 10, 11, 12, 13

CHESTER

Henry Farm Inn
P.O. Box 646, 05143
(802) 875-2674

The Henry Farm Inn provides the beauty of Vermont with old-time simplicity. Nestled on 50 acres of rolling hills and meadows, assuring peace and quiet. Spacious rooms, private baths, country sitting rooms, kitchen, and sunny dining room guarantee a feeling of home. Come visit for a day or more.

Host: J. E. Bowman
Rooms: 7 (PB) $50-80
Full Breakfast
Credit Cards: A, B
Notes: 2, 5, 8, 9, 11, 12, 13, 14

The Inn at Long Last
Box 589, 05143
(802) 875-2444

This full-service inn is on the village green in unspoiled Chester with beautiful antiques, music, distinctive decor in every guest room, a 2,000-book library, and the region's most highly praised food. All that and a staff of exceptional warmth and caring.

Host: Jack Coleman
Rooms: 30 (25 PB; 5 SB) $110
Full Breakfast

Credit Cards: A, B
Notes: 2, 4, 5, 9, 10, 11, 12, 13, 14

DERBY LINE

Derby Village Inn
46 Main Street, 05830
(802) 873-3604

Enjoy this charming old Victorian mansion situated in the quiet village of Derby Line within walking distance of the Canadian border and the world's only international library and opera house. The nearby countryside offers year-round recreation: downhill and cross-country skiing, water sports, cycling, fishing, hiking, golf, snowmobiling, sleigh rides, antiques, and, most of all, peace and tranquility.

Hosts: Tom and Phyllis Moreau
Rooms: 5 (PB) $50-60
Full Breakfast
Credit Cards: A, B, D
Notes: 2, 5, 8, 9, 10, 11, 12, 13

EAST MONTPELIER

Cherry Tree Hill Bed and Breakfast
Cherry Tree Hill Road, 05651
(802) 223-0549

Beautifully restored, this Dutch-roof farmhouse with panoramic Green Mountain views is just three miles from the state capital. In summer, enjoy the heated pool with spa; during leaf season, warm before the crackling Count Rumford fireplace. Farm-fresh breakfast is served in the greenhouse dining room. Wander through 55 acres of meadows and fields. Mountain biking, hiking, cross-country and downhill skiing are all close by.

Hosts: Cheryl Potter and David Clark
Rooms: 6 (2 PB; 4 SB) $60-75
Full Breakfast
Credit Cards: None
Notes: 2, 5, 10, 11, 12, 13, 14

welcome; 9 Social drinking allowed; 10 Tennis available; 11 Swimming available; 12 Golf available; 13 Skiing available; 14 May be booked through travel agents

ESSEX JUNCTION

The Amos Bliss House
143 Weed Road, 05452
(802) 899-4577

Formerly known as Varnums, this charming farmhouse is the oldest home in town. It was built in 1792 and was originally used as a stagecoach stop. Guests can enjoy antiques, a cool swim in summer, a cozy chat in front of the wood stove in winter. Situated 20 minutes from Burlington Airport, 30 minutes from Shelburne Museum, and 50 minutes from Stowe and Sugarbush ski areas. Stunning views of the Green Mountains.

Hosts: Todd and Sheila Varnum
Rooms: 2 (SB) $65-75
Full Breakfast
Credit Cards: None
Notes: 2, 5, 10, 11, 12, 13

The Andrie Rose Inn

HANCOCK

Kincraft Inn
Route 100, P.O. Box 96, 05748
(802) 767-3734

Country hospitality on scenic Route 100 in central Vermont can be found at this 1820s farmhouse that has been refurbished and redecorated with handmade quilts and Shaker/Colonial reproduction furniture in the guest rooms, made by the hosts. Family-style dinners are available by reservation. Biking, hiking, fishing, hunting, and five major ski areas are nearby.

Hosts: Irene and Ken Neitzel
Rooms: 6 (SB) $48
Full Breakfast
Credit Cards: A, B, C
Notes: 2, 4, 5, 8, 9, 10, 11, 12, 13

JEFFERSONVILLE

Sterling Ridge Inn
Junction Hill Road, P. O. Box 5780, 05464
(802) 644-8265; (800) 347-8266

This quiet, elegant, rural inn is near Mount Mansfield, Stowe, Smugglers' Notch, and Lamoille River. Enjoy cross-country skiing, mountain and back-road biking, canoeing, and hiking vacation packages on beautiful scenic property with brooks, woods, fields, and trails. Groups and families find this ideal environment perfect for their get-togethers.

Host: Craig Kneeland
Rooms: 8 (4 PB; 4 SB) $45-65
Full Breakfast
Credit Cards: A, B
Notes: 2, 3, 4, 5, 8, 9, 10, 11, 12, 13, 14

LUDLOW

The Andrie Rose Inn
13 Pleasant Street, 05149
(802) 228-4846

Discover this gracious country inn nestled at the base of Okemo Mountain in picturesque Ludlow Village. Ten lavishly appointed, antique-filled guest rooms are all pastel-papered and have down comforters and fine designer linens. Some rooms boast mountain views, skylights, and even whirlpool tubs. Complimentary hors d'oeuvres are served, as well as hearty candlelight breakfasts and sumptuous weekend dinners. Inn bikes and picnic hampers are available.

Hosts: Carolyn and Rick Bentzinger
Rooms: 10 (PB) $70-90 summer; $90-110 fall, winter
Full Breakfast
Credit Cards: A, B, C
Notes: 2, 4, 5, 9, 10, 11, 12, 13, 14

NOTES: Credit cards accepted: A Master Card; B Visa; C American Express; D Discover Card; E Diners Club; F Other; 2 Personal checks accepted; 3 Lunch available; 4 Dinner available; 5 Open all year; 6 Pets welcome; 8 Children

The Governor's Inn

86 Main Street, 05149
(802) 228-8830; (800) 468-3766

Twice judged one of the nation's ten best inns, The Governor's Inn has an extraordinary reputation for excellence. Snuggle in a century-old four-poster bed, wake to a magnificent gourmet breakfast, order a picnic hamper, and explore flower-filled meadows. Come home to Mozart, tea, and a crackling log fire. Gather in the den for hors d'oeuvres, experience award-winning, six-course dining presented on heirloom crystal, china, and silver. Dinner included. Bed and breakfast rates available.

Hosts: Charlie and Deedy Marble
Rooms: 8 (PB) $170-200 Modified American Plan
Full Breakfast
Credit Cards: A, B
Notes: 2, 3, 4, 5, 9, 10, 11, 12, 13, 14

LYNDON

Branch Brook Bed and Breakfast

South Wheelock Road, P. O. Box 143, 05849-0143
(802) 626-8316

Enjoy this newly renovated Federal house situated in the village of Lyndon, offering the best of country surroundings in a small village setting. Breakfast is prepared on the English "AGA" cooker and served in a charming dining room. Minutes from Exit 23 off Interstate 91, Lyndon's State College, and Burke Mountain ski area.

Hosts: Ted and Ann Tolman
Rooms: 5 (3 PB; 2 SB) $55-70
Full Breakfast
Credit Cards: A, B
Notes: 2, 5, 8, 9, 11, 12, 13

MANCHESTER

Seth Warner Inn

Historic Route 7A, P. O. Box 281, 05255
(802) 362-3830

A lovely early-1800s Colonial inn is nestled between two mountain ranges. Full breakfast is served at private tables. The inn is warmly decorated with antiques and Early American decor. Guests enjoy complimentary wine in the parlor and a small library to browse through. Absolutely charming and convenient to shopping, outlets, restaurants, skiing, and golf.

Hosts: Stasia and Lee Tetreault
Rooms: 5 (PB) $70-90
Full Breakfast
Credit Cards: A, B
Notes: 2, 5, 9, 10, 11, 12, 13

MIDDLETOWN SPRINGS

Priscilla's Victorian Inn

711 South Street, 05757
(802) 235-2299

Priscilla's Victorian Inn is an 1870 Victorian house on the National Register of Historic Places, built by the inventors of the Grays horsepower machinery and filled with music boxes, photographs, and Victorian memorabilia. Breakfast is served on large porches overlooking an English garden. Close to Lake Saint Catherine, boat rentals, trout fishing; a 30-minute drive to Manchester; surrounded by some of the prettiest scenery in Vermont.

Hosts: Doyle and Priscilla Lane
Rooms: 6 (PB) $65
Full Breakfast
Credit Cards: None

MORETOWN

Camel's Hump View

Box 720, 05660
(802) 496-3614

This northern Vermont farmhouse, built about 1831, has an even older kitchen with hand-hewn wooden pegged beams and wide floor boards. Throughout the house are antiques and handmade braided rugs. Antique

welcome; 9 Social drinking allowed; 10 Tennis available; 11 Swimming available; 12 Golf available; 13 Skiing available; 14 May be booked through travel agents

copper and old brick add to the warmth of the interior. A fountain and pool surrounded by greenery are built into the livingroom. Meals are served family-style with one dinner entree offered each evening.

Hosts: Jerry and Wilma Maynard
Rooms: 8 (1 PB; 7 SB) $50
Full Breakfast
Credit Cards: None
Notes: 2, 4, 5, 9, 10, 11, 12, 13, 14

NEWFANE

The Four Columns Inn
West Street, P. O. Box 278, 05345
(802) 365-7713

The Four Columns Inn is situated in the quaint historic town of Newfane on 150 acres of gardens, woodland, and streams. This is a wonderful area for bicycling, hiking, antiquing, golfing, swimming, and skiing. The restaurant is rated four diamonds by AAA, one of two in the state of Vermont.

Hosts: Pamela and Jacques Allembert
Rooms: 15 (PB) $95-170
Continental Breakfast
Credit Cards: A, B, C
Notes: 2, 4, 5, 6, 8, 9, 10, 11, 12, 13

PUTNEY

Hickory Ridge House
Rural Free Delivery 3, Box 1410, 05346-9326
(802) 387-5709

Hickory Ridge House, a gracious 1808 Federal brick country manor set in rolling hills and fields on a quiet country road, offers the traveler a lovely way to slow down and relax. There are woodland lanes and trails to walk or ski, cozy Rumford fireplaces, and wide-ranging conversation around the great oak table or outdoor deck. The hosts have traveled widely and enjoy sharing books and ideas. One room has handicapped access.

Hosts: Jacquie Walker and Steve Anderson
Rooms: 7 (3 PB; 4 SB) $45-80
Full Breakfast
Credit Cards: A, B
Notes: 2, 5, 8, 9, 11, 13

Hickory Ridge House

RANDOLPH

Placidia Farm
Bed and Breakfast
Rural Free Delivery 1, Box 275, 05060
(802) 728-9883

Beautiful log home on 81 tranquil acres with brook, pond, hiking, cross-country skiing on property. Four-season sports nearby. Private apartment includes bedroom, livingroom, equipped kitchen, bath, private entrance, and deck. Comfortable country furnishings. Linens provided. Hearty breakfast.

Host: Viola A. Frost
Apartment: 1 (PB) $75-85
Full Breakfast
Credit Cards: None
Notes: 2, 5, 9, 10, 11, 12, 13

ROCHESTER

Liberty Hill Farm
Liberty Hill Road, 05767
(802) 767-3926

A family dairy farm nestled between the Green Mountains and the White River offers excellent country cooking. Year-round activities for children of all ages can be found on the farm and nearby sports facilities. This large 1820s farmhouse with seven guest rooms was featured on "Good Morning America" and in the *Boston Chronicle, The New York Times, Boston Globe, Family Circle,* and *Country Living.*

Hosts: Bob and Beth Kennett
Rooms: 7 (SB) $90-110 Modified American Plan
Full Breakfast
Credit Cards: None
Notes: 2, 4, 5, 8, 10, 11, 12, 13

RUTLAND

Inn at Rutland
70 North Main Street, 05701
(802) 773-0575

The inn is a distinctive 1890s Victorian mansion that has been carefully restored. The interior is rich with period architectural details. Twelve guest rooms are unique; each has TV and phone. The inn is available for social gatherings and meetings and is near Killington and Pico ski areas, Vermont Marble Exhibit, Wilson Castle, Norman Rockwell museum.

Hosts: Mark and Amber Quinn
Rooms: 12 (PB) $65-150
Continental Breakfast
Credit Cards: A, B, C, D
Notes: 2, 5, 8, 9, 10, 11, 12, 13, 14

SHREWSBURY

Buckmaster Inn Bed and Breakfast
Lincoln Hill Road, 05738
(802) 492-3485

This historic country inn features a grand staircase, spacious rooms, two large porches, lounge area, library, TV room, country

kitchen with wood-burning stove, fireplaces on main floor. Home-baked bread, muffins, and rolls are served with homemade jams and jellies, all on rolling acreage in the Green Mountains of Vermont. Vermont at its best.

Hosts: Sam and Grace Husselman
Rooms: 3 (2 PB; 1 SB) $40-60
Continental Breakfast
Credit Cards: None
Notes: 2, 5, 10, 11, 12, 13

STOWE

The American Country Collection 091
4 Greenwood Lane, Delmar, NY 12054
(518) 439-7001

This contemporary Alpine-style private home is nestled into the side of the Worcester Mountain Range just six miles from Stowe. The panoramic beauty of the countryside is enhanced by the rural charm of the ten acres of woods with a babbling brook and spruce and white pine trees. Inside, antiques blend with modern furnishings to complement the vaulted ceilings and large windows. Guest rooms have garden and mountain views, original paintings, and coordinating fabrics. Two rooms share a bath, one has a private bath. Breakfast is served in the country kitchen in front of the wood-burning stove. $65; foliage weekend (two-night minimum stay) $75.

Butternut Inn at Stowe
2309 Mountain Road, 05672
(802) 253-4277; (800) 3-BUTTER

This award-winning inn has been selected as one of the best in the northeast by *Skiing* magazine. It features a bountiful breakfast and afternoon tea with American and Tex-Mex cuisine. Situated on eight acres with gardens and pool, it is tastefully decorated with antiques, crafts, and stained glass.

welcome; 9 Social drinking allowed; 10 Tennis available; 11 Swimming available; 12 Golf available; 13 Skiing available; 14 May be booked through travel agents

A five-day honeymoon package is available. Beautiful sun room, library, billiard room, and piano parlor.

Hosts: Jim and Deborah Wimberly
Rooms: 18 (PB) $85-145
Full Breakfast
Credit Cards: A, B
Notes: 9, 10, 11, 12, 13, 14

Inn at the Brass Lantern

717 Maple Street, 05672
(802) 253-2229; (800) 729-2980

The hosts of this traditional country inn won an award for their restoration of this 1800 farmhouse and attached carriage barn that overlooks Mount Mansfield. The inn features period antiques, wide-plank floors, handmade quilts, and air conditioning. Some rooms have fireplaces; most have views. The inn has been featured in national publications. Complimentary tea offered daily on the patio or at fireside.

Hosts: Mindy and Andy Aldrich
Rooms: 9 (PB) $65-110
Full Breakfast
Credit Cards: A, B, C
Notes: 2, 5, 9, 10, 11, 12, 13, 14

The Plum Door

School Street, P. O. Box 606, 05672
(802) 253-9995; (800) 258-PLUM

This wonderful 100-year-old farmhouse has been remodeled to reflect warmth and charm while utilizing modern conveniences. Three rooms have queen beds, ceiling fans, fireplaces, and mountain views. Guest kitchen, balcony with bistro table, private livingroom with TV/VCR. Walk to village shops and restaurants. Pets on premises.

Hosts: Herb and Fran Greenhalgh
Rooms: 3 (PB) $55-110
Expanded Continental Breakfast
Credit Cards: A, B
Notes: 2, 5, 9, 10, 11, 12, 13, 14

Spruce Pond Inn

1250 Waterbury Road, 05672-9716
(802) 253-4236

This cozy country inn features six comfortable guest rooms, large livingroom with fieldstone fireplace, complimentary afternoon tea, and a large dining room serving some of Stowe's finest cuisine by Chef Patrick Miller.

Hosts: Larry, Patrick, and Susan Miller
Rooms: 6 (PB) $39-75
Full Breakfast in winter and fall
Continental Breakfast in summer
Credit Cards: A, B
Notes: 2, 4, 5, 9, 10, 11, 12, 13, 14

WAITSFIELD

Knoll Farm Country Inn

Rural Free Delivery Box 179
Bragg Hill Road, 05673
(802) 496-3939

Knoll Farm is a unique combination of country inn and working farm situated on 150 acres of hillside pastures and forest with outstanding views of valley and mountains, Scotch Highland cattle, horses, big barn, pond, spacious lawns, cross-country skiing, snowshoeing, and great sledding. The farmhouse accommodates up to ten guests in five bedrooms with cozy livingrooms and a large kitchen with wood-burning stove for winter evenings.

Host: Ann Day
Rooms: 5 (S3B) $70-100 Modified American Plan
Full Breakfast
Credit Cards: None
Notes: 2, 3, 4, 5, 8, 9, 10, 11, 12, 13

Newtons' 1824 House Inn

Route 100, Box 159, 05673
(802) 496-7555

"On the Mad River." Enjoy relaxed elegance at this epicurean bed and breakfast.

Newtons' 1824 House Inn

In winter, a warm fire glows in the living and dining rooms. In summer, iced tea is enjoyed on the back porch swing. The inn is filled with unique antiques, classical music, original art. Feast on muffins, soufflés, blueberry pancakes, and freshly squeezed orange juice. Tobogganing, skiing, golfing, fishing, tennis, horseback riding, or walking.

Hosts: Nick and Joyce Newton
Rooms: 6 (PB) $75-105
Full Breakfast
Credit Cards: A, B, C
Notes: 2, 4 (by arrangement), 5, 9, 10, 11, 12, 13, 14

Valley Inn

Rural Route 1, Box 8, Route 100, 05673
(802) 496-3450; (800) 638-8466

This is a recipe for a great Vermont vacation: take an exceptional country inn in a lovely New England village, add cozy bedrooms, stir in conversation around a warm fire or friendly breakfast table, add excellent meals, a sauna, mix in nice people, season with vacation packages to taste. Dinner is served during the ski season. Try a valley inn-terlude.

Host: The Stinson family
Rooms: 20 (PB) $40-70
Full Breakfast
Credit Cards: A, B, C
Notes: 2, 5, 8, 9, 10, 11, 12, 13, 14

WALLINGFORD

The American Country Collection 055

4 Greenwood Lane, Delmar, New York 12054
(518) 439-7001

The large, white wicker settee on the south veranda beckons you to enjoy the idyllic pastoral setting of this 1840 Colonial farmhouse. It sits on 20 acres of pastures and woods. Swim, fish for trout, or canoe for miles on quiet waters. Also, golf, tennis, and horseback riding are close by. Five guest rooms with private baths. Full breakfast; children over ten welcome. Two-night stay preferred. $65-85 seasonal.

WARREN

West Hill House Bed and Breakfast

West Hill Road, Rural Route 1, Box 292, 05674
(802) 496-7162

A charming, restored 1862 Vermont farmhouse is situated off the beaten path on a beautiful country road adjacent to Sugarbush Golf Course and only one mile from Sugarbush Ski Resort. A farmer's porch provides splendid views of surrounding meadows and mountains. The inn offers

welcome; 9 Social drinking allowed; 10 Tennis available; 11 Swimming available; 12 Golf available; 13 Skiing available; 14 May be booked through travel agents

cozy rooms, handmade quilts, antiques, country accents, guest pantry/wetbar, and massive brick fireplace. Tea and pastries in the summer; hot apple cider in the winter.

Hosts: Nina and Bob Heyd
Rooms: 4 (2 PB; 2 SB) $60-85
Full Breakfast
Credit Cards: A, B
Notes: 2, 4 (for groups), 5, 8 (over 9), 9, 10, 11, 12, 13, 14

WATERBURY

Grünberg Haus Bed and Breakfast
Route 100 South, Rural Route 2,
Box 1595, 05676-9621
(802) 244-7726; (800) 800-7760

This secluded hand-built Austrian chalet in Ben and Jerry's hometown is central to Stowe and Sugarbush resorts, Montpelier and Burlington. Innkeepers entertain at fireside grand piano and invite guests to feed the chickens and turkeys. Imaginative breakfast specialties, such as maple-poached pears, ricotta-stuffed French toast, and pumpkin-apple streussel muffins, are served overlooking the mountains. Jacuzzi, sauna, balconies.

Hosts: Christopher Sellers and Mark Frohman
Rooms: 10 (5 PB; 5 SB) $55-90
Full Breakfast
Credit Cards: A, B, C, F
Notes: 2, 3, 4, 5, 8, 9, 10, 11, 12, 13, 14

Inn at Blush Hill
Blush Hill Road, Rural Route 1, Box 1266, 05676
(802) 244-7529; (800) 736-7522

This 200-year-old Cape Cod is situated on five acres with beautiful mountain views and perennial porches. The inn features a large guest parlor with TV, games, library, roaring fires in cooler months, and antiques. Situated directly behind Ben and Jerry's ice cream factory and across from a public golf course. Guests enjoy cross-country and al-

pine skiing and nearby Stowe, Sugarbush, and Bolton Valley.

Hosts: Gary and Pamela Gosselin
Rooms: 6 (2 PB; 4 SB) $55-110
Full Breakfast
Credit Cards: A, B, C, F
Notes: 2, 5, 8 (over 6), 9, 10, 11, 12, 13, 14

WATERBURY CENTER

The Black Locust Inn
Rural Route 1, Box 715, 05677
(800) 366-5592

This beautifully restored 1832 farmhouse is set on a hill surrounded by mature black locust trees. Rooms have antique beds, lace curtains, and polished birch floors. The large livingrooms have books, music, games, large-screen TV with videos. Centrally situated near Stowe, Sugarbush, and Bolton ski areas, and all other season activities. AAA triple-diamond rating. Senior discount 10 percent.

Hosts: Anita and George Gajdos
Rooms: 6 (PB) $65-100
Full Breakfast
Credit Cards: A, B, D
Notes: 2, 5, 9, 10, 11, 12, 13, 14

The Black Locust Inn

WEST DOVER

Austin Hill Inn
Route 100, 05356
(800) 332-RELAX

Guests at Austin Hill are invited to experience a less complicated world where they can leave behind the worries and pressures of life and enjoy timeless relaxation. Austin Hill boasts 12 refreshingly different guest rooms, each with its own guest diary filled with poems, pictures, and phrases about guests, their travels, and experiences. There are afghans, antiques, and afternoon tea; peacefulness, pampering, and sumptuous home-cooked meals.

Host: Robbie Sweeney
Rooms: 12 (PB) $65-125
Full Breakfast
Credit Cards: A, B, C
Notes: 2, 4, 5, 10, 11, 12, 13

WESTON

The Wilder Homestead Inn
Lawrence Hill Road, Rural Route 1
Box 106D, 05161
(802) 824-8172

This 1827 home on the National Register of Historic Places features queen canopy beds, down comforters, Moses Eaton stenciling, antiques, five common rooms, two with fireplaces, and restored front sitting porch. Walk to village shops, summer theater, museums; skiing, hiking, golfing, and biking are nearby. Weston Priory, where Benedictine Monks sing all services, is just four miles north. The inn is peaceful, yet handy to all interests.

Hosts: Peggy and Roy Varner
Rooms: 7 (5 PB; 2 SB) $55-85
Full Breakfast
Credit Cards: A, B
Notes: 2, 5, 8 (over 6), 9, 11, 12, 13

WEST TOWNSHEND

The American Country Collection 093
4 Greenwood Lane, Delmar, New York 12054
(518) 439-7001

Steeped in history, this farmhouse, circa 1773, is reputed to be the oldest standing house in West River Valley. The owners have kept and enhanced the many original features in the house. The warmth of old wooden beams, a paneled ceiling, and original wainscoting highlight the common room and dining area. Amenities include sweets in the bedchambers and a tour of the historic property. Shopping, hiking, fishing, boating, swimming, canoeing and cross-country skiing are close by. Three guest rooms with private baths. Full or continental breakfast; children over eight welcome. $55-60.

The Wilder Homestead Inn

WILMINGTON

The Inn at Quail Run
Smith Road, HCR 63, Box 28, 05363
(800) 34-ESCAPE

Enjoy pristine mountain views, comfortable large rooms, country breakfast and après ski snacks, cross-country trails, TV, and exercise room. In the summer, enjoy the heated pool and clay tennis court. A charming and romantic getaway.

Hosts: Tom, Marie, and Molly Martin
Rooms: 15 (PB) $75-110
Full Breakfast
Credit Cards: A, B
Notes: 2, 5, 8, 9, 10, 11, 12, 13, 14

welcome; 9 Social drinking allowed; 10 Tennis available; 11 Swimming available; 12 Golf available; 13 Skiing available; 14 May be booked through travel agents

WOODSTOCK _____

Canterbury House
43 Pleasant Street, 05091
(802) 457-3077

Lovely village home four blocks from the village green. Seven sunny rooms decorated with authentic Victorian antiques and Laura Ashley furnishings, all with private bath and air conditioning. Comfortable and elegant sitting room with fireplace and color TV. Garden patio. Bicycles available, near golf, tennis, horseback riding. Excellent hiking, cross-country skiing; close to Killington. Join the innkeepers and their Golden Retriever for an unforgettable visit to Woodstock.

Hosts: John and Mary Ellen Hough
Rooms: 7 (PB) $60-125

Full Breakfast
Credit Cards: A, B
Notes: 2, 5, 8, 9, 10, 11, 12, 13, 14

The Charleston House
21 Pleasant Street, 05091
(802) 457-3843

A Greek Revival brick town house in the village has today's comforts at yesterday's standards. Seven beautiful rooms have antiques. Charleston House is listed on the National Register of Historic Places.

Hosts: Bill and Barbara Hough
Rooms: 7 (PB) $100-135
Full Breakfast
Credit Cards: A, B, C
Notes: 2, 5, 9, 10, 11, 12, 13, 14

NOTES: Credit cards accepted: A Master Card; B Visa; C American Express; D Discover Card; E Diners Club; F Other; 2 Personal checks accepted; 3 Lunch available; 4 Dinner available; 5 Open all year; 6 Pets welcome; 8 Children

Virginia

The Bed and Breakfast League, Ltd. #6

P.O. Box 9490, Washington, D.C. 20016
(202) 363-7767

A first-floor suite with an entrance through a lovely garden, only a ten-minute walk from the Ballston Metro stop in Arlington. The bedroom has a private bath and an adjacent sitting room. Full breakfast is served in the dining room. Close to many restaurants and shopping. $60-65.

Memory House

Memory House

6404 North Washington Boulevard, 22205
(703) 534-4607

Charming, ornate, restored 1899 Victorian where period antiques, stenciled walls, prize-winning handicrafts, and collectibles abound. One block from the subway; a ten-minute drive to the White House, museums, and monuments. Two guest rooms with air conditioning, TV, and claw foot tubs. Relax on the porch furnished with wicker or in double parlors. Share in the old-fashioned comfort and friendship of Memory House. Traditional lifestyles, please.

Hosts: John and Marlys McGrath
Rooms: 2 (1 PB; 1 SB) $70
Expanded Continental Breakfast
Credit Cards: None
Notes: 2, 5, 10, 11, 14

BOSTON

Thistle Hill Bed and Breakfast

Route 1, Box 291 (Route 522), 22713
(703) 987-9142

Situated on a hillside facing the beautiful Blue Ridge, Thistle Hill offers modern amenities in a rural parklike setting. Two cottages, one with fireplace, and a main house are cozily decorated with antiques and collectibles. Relax in the hot tub or wander through the lawns and woods. Enjoy afternoon tea in the gazebo and a hearty, savory breakfast in the morning. Picnics and candlelight dinners by arrangement.

Hosts: Charles and Marianne Wilson
Rooms: 4 (PB) $80-140
Full Breakfast
Credit Cards: A, B
Notes: 2, 4, 5, 8, 14

CAPE CHARLES

Pickett's Harbor

P. O. Box 97AA, 23310
(804) 331-2212

Acres of private beach on the Chesapeake Bay are the back yard for this 18th-century-

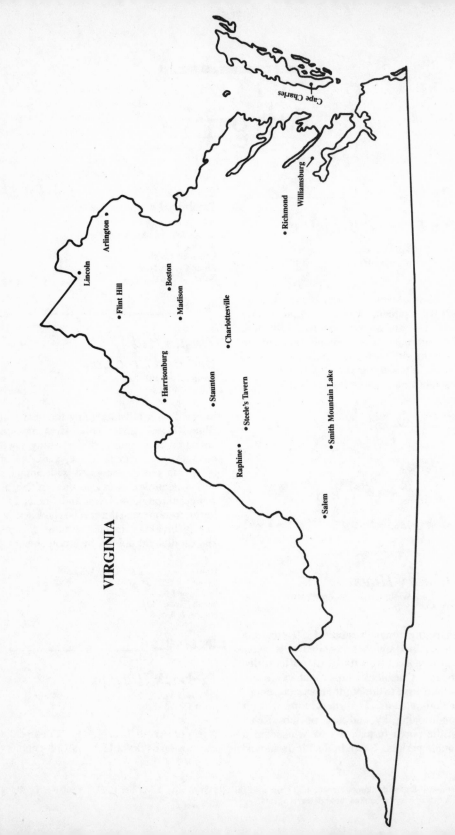

VIRGINIA

Cape Charles

Williamsburg

Richmond

Arlington

Lincoln

Flint Hill

Boston

Madison

Charlottesville

Harrisonburg

Staunton

Steele's Tavern

Smith Mountain Lake

Raphine

Salem

designed house set in the midst of pines overlooking small sand dunes. All rooms have a view of the Chesapeake. The Nature Conservancy, fish and wildlife preserves, and historic sites are nearby. This is a perfect place for retreats, beachcombing, and swimming, with reasonable seafood restaurants in the area.

Hosts: Sara and Cooke Goffigon
Rooms: 6 (2 PB; 4 SB) $65-95
Full Breakfast
Credit Cards: None
Notes: 2, 5, 9, 10, 11, 12

CHARLOTTESVILLE

Silver Thatch Inn
3001 Hollymead Drive, 22901
(804) 978-4686

Silver Thatch Inn is a white clapboard home dating from 1780. With three dining rooms and seven guest rooms, the inn is a sophisticated retreat on the outskirts of Charlottesville. Its modern American cuisine uses the freshest of ingredients, and all sauces are prepared with fruits and vegetables. The menu features grilled meats, poultry, and game in season, and there is always a vegetarian selection. The award-winning wine list features American wines. This is a wonderful respite for the sophisticated traveler who enjoys fine food and a caring atmosphere.

Hosts: Mickey and Joe Geller
Rooms: 7 (PB) $105-125
Continental Breakfast
Credit Cards: A, B
Closed late December and early August
Notes: 2, 4, 8 (over 5), 10, 11, 12, 13

FLINT HILL

Caledonia Farm
Route 1, Box 2080, 22627
(703) 675-3693

This national register landmark is adjacent to Shenandoah National Park. The 1812 stone manor house and romantic summer kitchen are magnificently situated in Virginia's Blue Ridge Mountains. Rooms have working fireplaces, air conditioning, individual heat, and a view of Skyline Drive. Full breakfast menu, evening hayride, bicycles, lawn games. Just 68 miles from Washington, D.C.

Host: Phil Irwin
Rooms: 2 plus suite (1 PB; 2 SB) $70-100
Full Breakfast
Credit Cards: A, B
Notes: 2, 3, 5, 8 (over 12), 9, 10, 11, 12, 13, 14

FREDERICKSBURG

Lavista Plantation
4420 Guinea Station Road, 22408
(703) 898-8444

This Classical Revival-style manor house, circa 1838, is situated on ten quiet, country acres and is surrounded by farm fields and mature trees. Stocked pond, six fireplaces, antiques, rich Civil War past, radio, phone, TV, bicycles. Fresh eggs and homemade jams are served for breakfast; air conditioned; close to historic attractions.

Hosts: Edward and Michele Schiesser
Room: 1 (PB) $63.90
Suite: 1 (PB) $79.88
Full Breakfast
Credit Cards: A, B
Notes: 5, 8, 9

Silver Thatch Inn

NOTES: Credit cards accepted: A Master Card; B Visa; C American Express; D Discover Card; E Diners Club; F Other; 2 Personal checks accepted; 3 Lunch available; 4 Dinner available; 5 Open all year; 6 Pets welcome; 8 Children welcome; 9 Social drinking allowed; 10 Tennis available; 11 Swimming available; 12 Golf available; 13 Skiing available; 14 May be booked through travel agents

HARRISONBURG

Kingsway Bed and Breakfast
3581 Singers Glen Road, 22801
(703) 867-9696

Enjoy a refreshing country atmosphere in
the beautiful Shenandoah Valley of Virginia. You will find a touch of home with
freshly cut flowers from around the in-ground
pool, handcrafted items of needlework and
wood, and the warm welcome of your hosts,
who enjoy people and meeting their needs.
Nearby are the scenic Skyline Drive, caverns, historic sights, antique shops, flea
markets, and national parks and forests.
Less than five miles from downtown.

Hosts: Chester and Verna Leaman
Rooms: 2 (PB) $50-55
Full Breakfast
Credit Cards: None
Notes: 2, 5, 6, 11

Abbie Hill Bed and Breakfast

LINCOLN

Springdale Country Inn
Lincoln, 22078
(800) 388-1832

Restored historic landmark just 45 miles
west of Washington, D.C. Private fireplaces, bathrooms, and Federal-period antiques grace the inn. Outside are babbling
brooks, terraced gardens, and walking paths.
An on-site management team and chef are
there to meet your needs. They can accommodate weddings, business meetings, and
family reunions. Close to shopping, sports
center, antiques, tennis, golf, and swimming.

Host: Nancy Fones
Rooms: 8 (3 PB; 5 SB) $95
Full Breakfast
Credit Cards: A, B, D, E
Notes: 2, 3, 4, 5, 9, 10, 11, 12, 14

MADISON

Shenandoah Springs Country Inn
HC 6, Box 122, 22727
(703) 923-4300

This large estate with a pre-Civil War history is situated near Skyline Drive. Mountains and lake are on the property. Rooms
have canopy beds and fireplaces, and nearby
activities include horseback riding, fishing,
swimming, and paddle boating. Two cottages are also available, one with one bedroom and one with three bedrooms and one
bath. Close to Montpelier and Monticello.
Marriage enrichment seminars are available.

Hosts: Anne and Doug Farmer
Rooms: 5 (1 PB; 4 SB) $65-125
Cottages: 2 (PB)
Full Breakfast
Credit Cards: None
Notes: 2, 3, 4, 5, 8 (in lodge), 11, 12, 13

NOTES: Credit cards accepted: A MasterCard; B Visa; C American Express; D Discover Card; E Diners Club; F Other;
2 Personal checks accepted; 3 Lunch available; 4 Dinner available; 5 Open all year; 6 Pets welcome; 8 Children

RAPHINE

Oak Spring Farm and Vineyard

Route 1, Box 356, 24472
(703) 377-2398

Oak Spring Farm is a completely restored plantation house, circa 1826, on a 40-acre working farm, including a five-acre vineyard and five acres of woods. The house is filled with antiques and family treasures and is situated halfway between historic Lexington and Staunton on U.S. 11. Modern comforts, peace and quiet, and spectacular views are found in a friendly home atmosphere.

Hosts: Pat and Jim Tichenor
Rooms: 3 (PB) $55-65
Expanded Continental Breakfast
Credit Cards: A, B
Notes: 2, 5, 9, 10, 11, 12, 13

The Emmanuel Hutzler House

RICHMOND

Abbie Hill Bed and Breakfast

P. O. Box 4503, 23220
(804) 355-5855; FAX (804) 353-4656

This lovely Federalist-style, three-story brick town house, circa 1910, is situated in the heart of Richmond's most prestigious historic district. Walk to museums, Civil War monuments, good restaurants, churches. Be spoiled in elegantly furnished guest rooms with fireplaces, four-poster beds, down comforters, overhead fans, balconies, with tea on arrival and a wonderful Virginia breakfast.

Hosts: Barbara and Bill Fleming
Rooms: 3 (2PB; 2 SB) $75-95
Full Breakfast
Credit Cards: A, B
Notes: 2, 5, 9, 10, 14

Be My Guest Bed and Breakfast

2926 Kensington Avenue, 23221
(804) 358-9901

This elegant, spacious 1918 home is furnished with lovely antiques and situated in Richmond's historic district, one block from Virginia Museum of Fine Arts, ten minutes from downtown. Many outstanding restaurants are nearby. Breakfast is served in the beautiful garden when weather permits. Southern hospitality at its best.

Hosts: Bertie and Bill Selvey
Rooms: 2 (PB) $65-80
Full Breakfast
Credit Cards: None
Notes: 2, 5, 8, 9, 10, 12, 14

The Emmanuel Hutzler House

2036 Monument Avenue, 23220
(804) 353-6900

welcome; 9 Social drinking allowed; 10 Tennis available; 11 Swimming available; 12 Golf available; 13 Skiing available; 14 May be booked through travel agents

Designed in the Italian Renaissance style, the interior of this inn has a classical, early Renaissance appearance featuring natural mahogany raised paneling, wainscoting, leaded-glass windows, and coffered ceilings with dropped beams. The large livingroom has a marble fireplace flanked by mahogany bookcases where guests can relax and converse. Centrally situated, the inn is convenient for a mid-week business trip or a lovely setting for a weekend getaway.

Host: Lyn M. Benson
Rooms: 4 (PB) $89-125
Full Breakfast
Credit Cards: None
Notes: 2, 5, 9, 10, 11, 12, 14

SALEM

The Old Manse
530 East Main Street, 24153
(703) 389-3921

The Old Manse is built on land once owned by Andrew Lewis, a Revolutionary War general. The antebellum home is furnished with antiques. Guests enjoy a leisurely home-cooked southern breakfast. The Old Manse offers a sitting room and parlor for visiting or viewing TV. Nearby are Roanoke and Hollins colleges, farmers' market, civic center, tennis, public golf, exercise trail, antique malls, and shops.

Host: Charlotte Griffith
Rooms: 3 (SB) $40
Full Breakfast
Credit Cards: None
Notes: 2, 5, 8, 10, 12

SMITH MOUNTAIN LAKE

The Manor at Taylor's Store
Route 1, Box 533, 24184
(703) 721-3951

At this secluded, historic 120-acre estate in the Blue Ridge Mountains, guests are pampered with luxurious amenities, including hot tub, exercise room, movies, and a heart-healthy gourmet breakfast. Suites are replete with antiques and special features, such as fireplaces and and private porches. Six private spring-fed ponds invite swimming, fishing, canoeing, and picnicking. Near Roanoke, Blue Ridge Parkway, and Smith Mountain Lake.

Hosts: Lee and Mary Lynn Tucker
Rooms: 6 plus cottage (5 PB; 2 SB) $65-90
Full Breakfast
Credit Cards: A, B, D
Notes: 2, 3, 5, 9, 10, 11, 12, 13, 14

STAUNTON

Ashton Country House
1205 Middlebrook Road, 24401
(703) 885-7819

Ashton Country House is a circa-1860 Greek Revival brick home situated in a peaceful setting on the outskirts of Staunton. The 19th-century heritage of the house has been carefully preserved during its adaptation as a bed and breakfast inn. A full breakfast is served accompanied by professional piano music. Explore the 20 acres of pastureland behind the barn, and enjoy afternoon tea. Open weekends and holidays September to May and all summer.

Hosts: Sheila Kennedy and Stanley Polanski
Rooms: 4 (PB) $60-75
Full Breakfast
Credit Cards: None
Notes: 2, 5, 8 (over 15), 9

Frederick House
18 East Frederick Street, P.O. Box 1387, 24401
(703) 885-4220

A small hotel and tea room offers comfortable lodgings in downtown Staunton, the oldest city in the Shenandoah Valley. Frederick House is actually five separate historic town homes with 14 rooms or suites with TV, phone, and private entrance. Walk to a

NOTES: Credit cards accepted: A Master Card; B Visa; C American Express; D Discover Card; E Diners Club; F Other; 2 Personal checks accepted; 3 Lunch available; 4 Dinner available; 5 Open all year; 6 Pets welcome; 8 Children

variety of restaurants or shops. Nearby attractions include Woodrow Wilson's birthplace, Mary Baldwin College, and the Museum of the American Frontier.

Hosts: Joe and Evy Harman
Rooms: 14 (PB) $45-95
Full Breakfast
Credit Cards: A, B, C, D, E
Notes: 2, 3, 4, 5, 8, 9, 10, 11, 12, 13, 14

The Sampson Eagon Inn

238 East Beverly Street, 24401
(703) 886-8200; FAX (703) 886-8200

Situated in the Virginia historic landmark district of Gospel Hill, this gracious residence, circa 1840, has been thoughtfully restored and transformed into a unique inn offering affordable luxury and attentive personal service in an inviting historic setting. Elegant rooms all feature sitting area, queen canopied bed, and period antique furnishings. The inn is within two blocks of downtown attractions and dining.

Hosts: Laura and Frank Mattingly
Rooms: 4 (PB) $75-95
Full Breakfast
Credit Cards: None
Notes: 2, 5, 9, 10, 11, 12, 13

STEELE'S TAVERN _____

The Osceola Mill Country Inn

State Route 56, 24476
(703) 377-6455; (800) 242-7352
FAX (703) 377-6455

Unique and gracious, yet unpretentious, the inn consists of a restored 1840s grist mill and miller house and the 1870 mill store, now an exquisite honeymoon cottage. In the heart of the Shenandoah Valley and Blue Ridge area, with 14 colleges and all major attractions within an hour, "the Mill" delivers an ambience like Grandma's house and can keep vacationers busy.

Host: Paul Newcomb
Rooms: 12 (PB) $59-89 seasonal; $99-139 cottage
Full Breakfast
Credit Cards: None
Notes: 2, 4, 5, 8, 9, 11, 12, 13, 14

The Osceola Mill Country Inn

WILLIAMSBURG _____

Legacy of Williamsburg Tavern Bed and Breakfast Inn

930 Jamestown Road, 23185
(804) 220-0524; (800) 962-4722 reservations

An 18th-century-style clapboard structure, the Tavern is complemented throughout with authentic 18th-century furnishings. It features tall poster beds, curtained canopy beds, robes, six fireplaces, library, billiards room, tavern, game room. The Tavern is pleasantly situated in a natural woodland setting overlooking an array of beautiful English gardens.

Hosts: Mary Ann and Ed Lucas
Rooms: 4 (PB) $80-125
Full Breakfast
Credit Cards: A, B
Notes: 2, 5, 9, 10, 11, 12

Liberty Rose Bed and Breakfast

1022 Jamestown Road, 23185
(804) 253-1260

This delightful old Williamsburg home is showcased on a wooded hilltop near a historic area. A charming blend of 18th century, country French, and Victorian antiques. Guest rooms include claw foot tubs, marble showers, papered walls, and queen beds. Fireplaces, chocolate chip cookies, in-room TV/VCRs, and delicious breakfasts. Awarded the highest rating by the American Bed and Breakfast Association.

Hosts: Brad and Sandi Hirz
Rooms: 4 (PB) $100-155
Full Breakfast
Credit Cards: A, B
Notes: 2, 5, 8, 9, 12, 14

Newport House

710 South Henry Street, 23185-4113
(804) 229-1775

Newport House was built in 1988 from a 1756 design by the famous architect Peter Harrison and furnished to museum standards completely in the period, including four-poster canopy beds and beautiful antiques. Breakfast features authentic colonial recipes. It is only a five-minute walk to the historic area. Colonial dancing in the ballroom every Tuesday evening. The host is an author and former museum director.

Host: John Fitzhugh Millar
Rooms: 2 (PB) $90-120
Full Breakfast
Credit Cards: None
Notes: 2, 5, 8, 10, 11, 12, 14

Williamsburg Sampler Bed and Breakfast

922 Jamestown Road, 23185
(804) 253-0398; (800) 722-1169

This elegant, plantation-style, three-story brick Colonial was awarded the AAA three-diamond rating. Richly furnished bedrooms with private baths and king- or queen-size beds. Collections of antiques, pewter, and samplers are displayed throughout this stately home. A "skip lunch" full breakfast is served. Internationally recognized as a favorite spot for a romantic honeymoon or anniversary, and for the special care given to visitors. Parallels the College of William and Mary and is within walking distance of the historic area.

Hosts: Helen and Ike Sisane
Rooms: 4 (PB) $80-85
Full Breakfast
Credit Cards: None
Notes: 2, 5, 9, 10, 11, 12, 14

Williamsburg Sampler Bed and Breakfast

Washington

Sunset Beach
Bed and Breakfast
100 Sunset Beach, 98221
(206) 293-5428

On the exciting Rosario Straits looking at seven islands. Guests can stroll on the beach adjacent to Washington Park. Enjoy the wildlife and the sunset on the deck. Five minutes to San Juan ferry, close to fine restaurants, marinas, convenience store.

Hosts: Hal and Joann Harker
Rooms: 3 (1 PB; 2 SB) $60-79
Full Breakfast
Credit Cards: A, B
Notes: 2, 5, 8, 9, 14

ANDERSON ISLAND

The Inn at Burg's Landing
8808 Villa Beach Road, 98303
(206) 884-9185

Catch the ferry from Steilacoom to stay at this contemporary log homestead. It offers spectacular views of Mount Rainier, Puget Sound, and Cascade Mountains and is situated ten miles south of Tacoma. Choose from two guest rooms, including the master bedroom with private whirlpool bath. The inn has a private beach. Collect seashells and agates, swim, or play golf or tennis.

Hosts: Ken and Annie Burg
Rooms: 2 (PB) $60-90
Full Breakfast
Credit Cards: A, B, C
Notes: 2, 5, 8, 9, 10, 11, 12

ASHFORD

Growly Bear
37311 State Road 706, 98304
(206) 569-2339

Experience a bit of history and enjoy a mountain stay at a rustic homestead built in 1890. Hike in nearby Mount Rainier National Park. Dine at unique restaurants within walking distance. Be lulled to sleep by the whispering sounds of Goat Creek just outside the window. Awake to the aroma of freshly baked bread. Indulge in a basket of warm pastries.

Host: Susan Jenny
Rooms: 2 (1 PB; 1 SB) $60-80
Full Breakfast
Credit Cards: A, B, C
Notes: 2, 5, 9, 13, 14

BELLINGHAM

BABS
(Bed and Breakfast Service)
P. O. Box 5025, 98226
(206) 733-8642

This reservations service has listings in Maui, Hawaii; Washington; Oregon; California; Florida; Vermont; Montana; Washington, D. C.; Victoria; and British Columbia. A book with complete listings may be purchased for $3.75. Dolores and George Herrmann, coordinators. Rates are modest in the European tradition: $35-50.

welcome; 9 Social drinking allowed; 10 Tennis available; 11 Swimming available; 12 Golf available; 13 Skiing available; 14 May be booked through travel agents

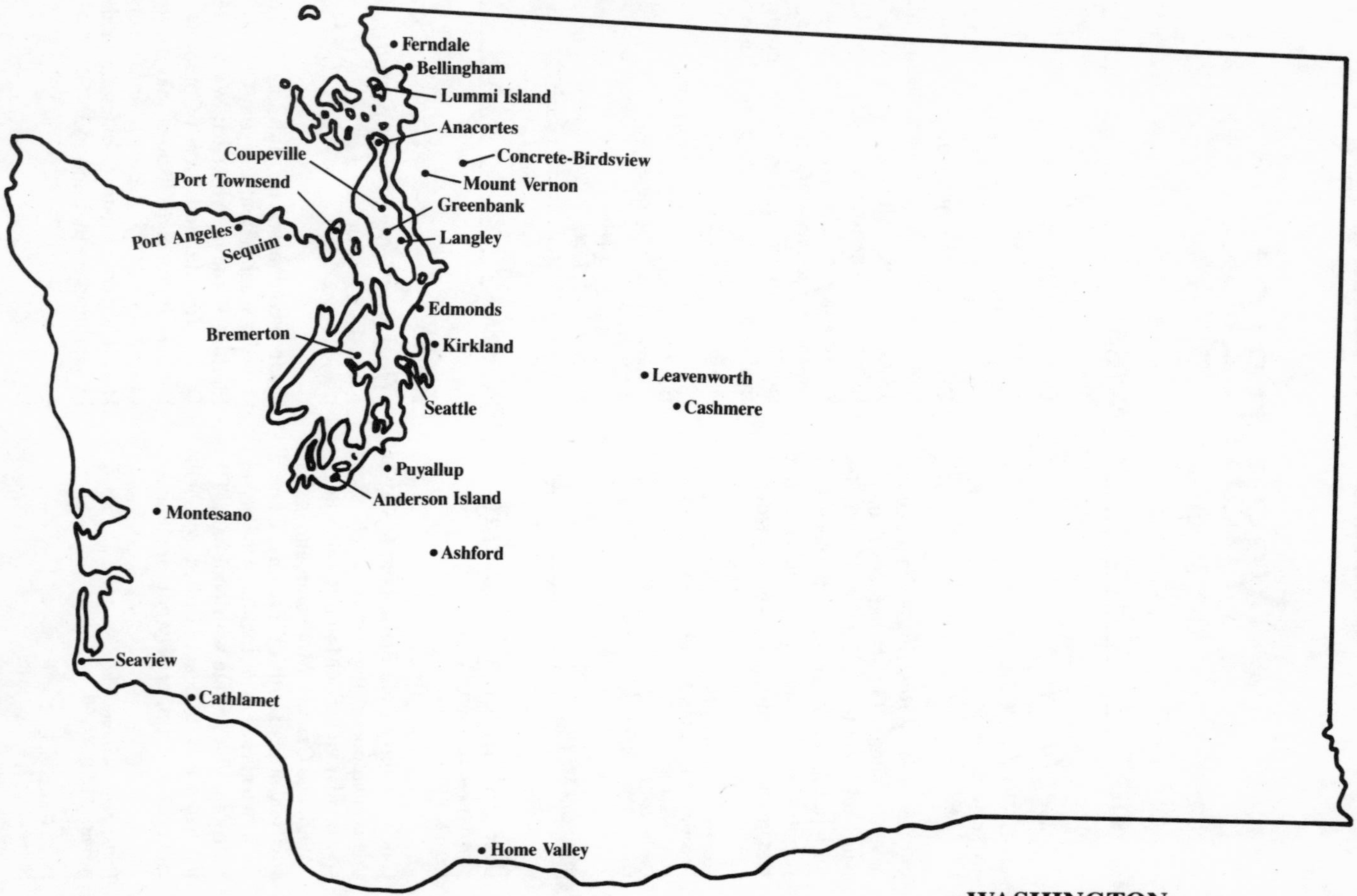

WASHINGTON

Ferndale
Bellingham
Lummi Island
Anacortes
Concrete-Birdsview
Mount Vernon
Greenbank
Langley
Coupeville
Port Townsend
Port Angeles
Sequim
Bremerton
Edmonds
Kirkland
Seattle
Puyallup
Anderson Island
Ashford
Leavenworth
Cashmere
Home Valley
Montesano
Seaview
Cathlamet

Full Breakfast
Credit Cards: A, B
Notes: 2, 5, 9, 10, 12, 13, 14

Schnauzer Crossing Bed and Breakfast

4421 Lakeway Drive, 98226
(206) 733-0055; (206) 734-2808

This luxury bed and breakfast in the Pacific Northwest has a cottage and master suite with king beds, Jacuzzis, fireplaces, and lake or garden views; queen room with lake view; outdoor spa and tennis court. Quiet and romantic, it is a splendid getaway.

Host: Donna McAllister
Rooms: 3 (PB) $95-175
Full Breakfast
Credit Cards: A, B, C
Notes: 2, 5, 8, 9, 10, 11, 12, 13

Willcox House

BREMERTON

Willcox House

2390 Tekiu Road, 98312
(206) 830-4492

Overlooking the Hood Canal and the Olympic Mountains is a place where time rests. Life is paced by the slow, steady hand of nature. It is quiet enough to hear the birds sing. Deer amble through the gardens. This elegant mansion was built in 1936 with landscaped grounds, private pier, and beach. All rooms have magnificent views of the Hood Canal and Olympic Mountains.

North Garden Inn

Bellingham's DeCann House Bed and Breakfast

2610 Eldridge Avenue, 98225
(206) 734-9172

Completely remodeled by the host, this Victorian bed and breakfast overlooks Puget Sound and the San Juan Islands, halfway between Seattle and Vancouver, Canada. The host has traveled and combines the hospitality of Europe with the conveniences Americans desire. A lifetime Washington resident, she can share favorite spots to shop, dig clams, or walk on the beach.

Host: Barbara Hudson
Rooms: 2 (PB) $55-70
Full Breakfast
Credit Cards: None
Notes: 2, 5, 9, 10, 11, 12, 13, 14

North Garden Inn

1014 North Garden, 98225
(800) 922-6414 U.S.; (800) 367-1676 Canada

North Garden Inn is a Queen Anne Victorian on the National Register of Historic Places. Several guest rooms have splendid views of Bellingham Bay. The inn boasts two grand pianos in performance condition.

Hosts: Barbara and Frank DeFreytas
Rooms: 7 winter; 10 summer (3 PB; 7 SB) $54-64

NOTES: Credit cards accepted: A Master Card; B Visa; C American Express; D Discover Card; E Diners Club; F Other; 2 Personal checks accepted; 3 Lunch available; 4 Dinner available; 5 Open all year; 6 Pets welcome; 8 Children welcome; 9 Social drinking allowed; 10 Tennis available; 11 Swimming available; 12 Golf available; 13 Skiing available; 14 May be booked through travel agents

Hosts: Cecilia and Phillip Hughes
Rooms: 5 (PB) $110-165
Full Breakfast
Credit Cards: A, B
Notes: 2, 3, 4, 5, 9, 11, 12, 14

CASHMERE

Cashmere Country Inn
5801 Pioneer Drive, 98815
(509) 782-4212

This delightful 1907 farmhouse with four bedrooms welcomes you with charm and hospitality. Every effort has been made to make your stay memorable. Among many outstanding features, the food here is superb—prepared skillfully and presented beautifully. There is a pool and hot tub; and for flower lovers, the well-kept grounds boast of country, rose, and herb gardens. If you are looking for that extra-special inn that defines a bed and breakfast, you will be pleased to discover Cashmere Country Inn.

Hosts: Dale and Patti Swanson
Rooms: 4 (2 PB; 2 SB) $60-75
Full Breakfast
Credit Cards: A, B, C
Notes: 2, 5, 9, 11, 12, 13, 14

CATHLAMET

The Gallery Bed and Breakfast at Little Cape Horn
4 Little Cape Horn, 98612
(206) 425-7395; FAX (206) 425-1351

This contemporary, elegant country home has sweeping views of the Columbia River ship channel and a large deck for relaxing or watching tug boats, seals, eagles, and windsurfers. It is surrounded by majestic cedars and fir trees and a tall cliff with waterfalls. A private beach is only steps away, and there is a warm spot on the deck for stargazing. Breakfast is served on fine crystal china. Warm, Christian hospitality.

Hosts: Eric and Carolyn Feasey
Rooms: 3 (1 PB; 2 SB) $70-80
Continental or Full Breakfast
Credit Cards: A, B, C
Notes: 2, 5, 6 (limited), 8 (over 10), 12, 14

CONCRETE-BIRDSVIEW

Cascade Mountain Inn
3840 Pioneer Lane, 98237
(206) 826-4333

Situated in the center of one of the nation's most scenic mountain areas, the inn is close to the North Cascades National Park, Baker Lake, and the Skagit River. In a pastoral setting, the inn is one of the best in the Northwest. Full, award-winning breakfast.

Hosts: Ingrid and Gerhard Meyer
Rooms: 6 (PB) $84
Full Breakfast
Credit Cards: A, B
Notes: 2, 9, 14

COUPEVILLE

Colonel Crocket Farm Bed and Breakfast Inn
1012 South Fort Casey Road, 98239
(206) 678-3711

The inn offers 135 years of Victorian/Edwardian serenity in a farm island setting with pastoral and marine views. Common areas include an oak-paneled library, a wicker-furnished solarium, and a dining room featuring individual tables. This 1855 Victorian farmhouse with period antiques is on the National Register of Historic Places. Extensive grounds, walkways, and flowerbeds.

Hosts: Robert and Beulah Whitlow
Rooms: 5 (PB) $65-95
Full Breakfast
Credit Cards: A, B
Notes: 2, 5, 8 (over 14), 9, 14

NOTES: Credit cards accepted: A Master Card; B Visa; C American Express; D Discover Card; E Diners Club; F Other; 2 Personal checks accepted; 3 Lunch available; 4 Dinner available; 5 Open all year; 6 Pets welcome; 8 Children

EDMONDS

Harrison House
210 Sunset Avenue, 98020
(206) 776-4748

This is a new waterfront home with a sweeping view of Puget Sound and the Olympic Mountains. It is one block north of the ferry dock and two blocks from the center of this historic town. There are many fine restaurants within walking distance. Spacious rooms have private deck, TV, wet bar, phone, and king bed. The University of Washington is nearby.

Hosts: Jody and Harve Harrison
Rooms: 2 (PB) $35-55
Continental Breakfast
Credit Cards: None
Notes: 2, 5, 9, 10, 11, 12, 13

FERNDALE

Anderson House
Bed and Breakfast
2140 Main Street, P.O. Box 1547, 98248
(206) 384-3450

Whatcom County's most famous inn was built in 1897, and the Andersons have restored this landmark to its original charm. All rooms are tastefully decorated in an 1890s motif. Guests from 45 states and 29 countries have left words of praise about this inn. Lumberjack breakfast included.

Hosts: Dave and Kelly Anderson
Rooms: 4 (2 PB; 2 SB) $45-75
Full Breakfast
Credit Cards: A, B, C, D
Notes: 2, 5, 9, 10, 12, 13, 14

Hill Top Bed and Breakfast
5832 Church Road, 98248
(206) 384-3619

Hill Top Bed and Breakfast is situated in the Puget Sound area close to several beautiful

state and local parks, just 12 miles from Canada. The house overlooks Mount Baker and the Cascade Mountain range. Homemade breakfast specialties include blueberry coffee cake, bran muffins, applesauce, and rhubarb from the garden. The fireside room sleeps four and is equipped with a kitchenette, perfect for families and longer stays. Lower-level rooms have cable TV and a private entrance. 10 percent discount for three-night stays or longer.

Host: Doris Matz
Rooms: 3 (2 PB; 1 SB) $44-54
Expanded Continental Breakfast
Credit Cards: A, B
Notes: 2, 5, 8, 9, 10, 11, 12, 13, 14

Anderson House Bed and Breakfast

GREENBANK

Guest House Cottages
835 East Christenson Road, Whidbey Island, 98253
(206) 678-3115

This is a romantic retreat for couples on Whidbey Island with storybook cottages or an elegant log mansion for two. Cozy settings on 25 acres. Intimate breakfast, fireplaces, VCRs, kitchens, in-room Jacuzzis, feather beds, country antiques, wildlife pond, pool, spa. Privacy, peace, and pampering. AAA four-diamond rating.

Hosts: Don and Mary Jane Creger
Suite: 1 (PB) $85-225
Cottages: 6 (PB)
Expanded Continental Breakfast
Credit Cards: A, B, C, D
Notes: 2, 5, 9, 11, 12, 14

welcome; 9 Social drinking allowed; 10 Tennis available; 11 Swimming available; 12 Golf available; 13 Skiing available; 14 May be booked through travel agents

HOME VALLEY

Home Valley Bed and Breakfast

Upper Lyons Road, P. O. Box 377, 98648
(509)427-7070

Experience a breathtaking westward view of the gorge, high above the confluence of the Wind and Columbia rivers. Stroll over five acres of grassy, private park; or relax on the sun-drenched, full-length deck that overlooks the rivers. The inn is furnished with antiques and is decorated with wood carvings and items of interest from around the world.

Host: Joan White
Rooms: 6 (1 PB; 5 SB) $45-95
Full Breakfast
Credit Cards: A, B, C
Notes: 2, 5, 6, 8, 9, 11, 12, 13, 14

Shumway Mansion

KIRKLAND

Shumway Mansion

11410 99th Place Northeast, 98033
(206) 823-2303

Overlook Lake Washington from this award-winning, 1909, 24-room mansion with seven individually decorated guest rooms and one charming corner suite. Homemade scones are prepared daily and homemade jam, evening snacks, and seasonal treats are served. Guests enjoy complimentary use of athletic club. Short distance to shopping, 20 minutes to downtown Seattle. Water and snow recreation close by.

Hosts: Richard and Salli Harris
Rooms: 8 (PB) $65-92
Full Breakfast
Credit Cards: A, B, C
Notes: 2, 5, 10, 11, 12, 13, 14

LANGLEY

Log Castle

3273 East Saratoga Road, 98260
(206) 321-5483

This unique log lodge is right on the beach. A big stone fireplace, turret bedrooms, and panoramic views of sea and mountains give this lodge rustic elegance. Eagles, loons, and seals are daily visitors.

Hosts: Senator Jack and Norma Metcalf
Rooms: 4 (PB) $80-100
Full Breakfast
Credit Cards: A, B, D
Notes: 2, 5, 10, 12

Lone Lake Cottage and Breakfast

5206 South Bayview Road, 98260
(206) 321-5325

Come to Whidbey's Shangri-La and enjoy total privacy in the waterfront cottages or tiny sternwheel houseboat. All are beautifully decorated with touches of the Orient. Each has a sweeping view, Jacuzzi, kitchen, TV/VCR, and film tapes. There are complimentary canoes, rowboat (fishing is great), bicycles, pickleball court, and bird and waterfowl aviaries.

Host: Dolores Meeks
Cottages: 2 plus houseboat (PB) $110
Continental Breakfast
Credit Cards: None
Notes: 2, 5, 9, 10, 11, 12

NOTES: Credit cards accepted: A Master Card; B Visa; C American Express; D Discover Card; E Diners Club; F Other; 2 Personal checks accepted; 3 Lunch available; 4 Dinner available; 5 Open all year; 6 Pets welcome; 8 Children

LEAVENWORTH

Pine River Ranch
19668 Highway 207, 98826
(509) 763-3959

Imagine the tranquility of an immense, serene valley with breathtaking Cascade views. Originally built in the 1940s, the huge block barn and silo serve as reminders of a bygone era. Cross-country ski, hike, bike, or fish on this historic mountain ranch. Stroll among gentle farm animals; here, the only rush hour is at feeding time.

Hosts: Mary Ann and Michael Zenk
Rooms: 4 plus guest house (2 PB; 2 SB) $65-95
Full Breakfast
Credit Cards: A, B
Notes: 2, 5, 9, 11, 12, 13

LUMMI ISLAND

West Shore Farm
Bed and Breakfast
2781 West Shore Drive, 98262
(206) 758-2600

The Hansons found this perfect place to live and then designed and built this unique octagonal home near the north tip of Lummi Island, where large windows and a wraparound deck provide a 180-degree view of islands, boats on course to Alaska or Canada, sunsets, eagles, seals, and Canadian mountains. The natural beach, farm animals, greenhouse, and orchard provide relaxation outdoors. Indoors is a stock of books and maps of local interest.

Hosts: Carl and Polly Hanson
Rooms: 2 (PB) $75
Full Breakfast
Credit Cards: A, B
Notes: 2, 3, 4, 5, 8, 9

MONTESANO

Sylvan Haus
Murphy Bed and Breakfast
P. O. Box 416, 98563
(206) 249-3453

This hilltop home with five decks overlooks the valley, the Chehalis River, and the small town of Montesano. It is five minutes to Sylvia Lake State Park and 30 minutes to Westport beaches. Country decor; close to Interstate 5.

Hosts: JoAnne and Mike Murphy
Rooms: 3 (2 PB; 2 SB) $50
Full Breakfast
Credit Cards: None
Notes: 2, 5, 8 (over 14), 11, 12

MOUNT VERNON

Whispering Firs
Bed and Breakfast
1957 Kanako Lane, 98273
(206) 428-1990

Whispering Firs is situated one mile east of Interstate 5, directly between the two La Conner exits. Set on 200 acres, high on a hill overlooking the Skagit Flats and San Juan Islands, guests enjoy miles of wooded hiking, with proximity to shops and dining. Rooms are large with astounding views. Go hot tubbing, fishing, or relax among the flowers on the deck.

Host: Linda Benson
Rooms: 3 (2 PB; 1 SB) $60-80
Full Breakfast
Credit Cards: None
Notes: 2, 4, 5, 6, 8, 11, 14

welcome; 9 Social drinking allowed; 10 Tennis available; 11 Swimming available; 12 Golf available; 13 Skiing available; 14 May be booked through travel agents

The Tudor Inn

PORT ANGELES

The Tudor Inn
1108 South Oak, 98362
(206) 452-3138; (800) 522-5174

The inn is a half-timbered Tudor-design home built in 1910. Two fireplaces grace the downstairs, one in the well-stocked library. King and queen beds have down comforters. Full breakfast entrees include scrambled eggs with smoked salmon, stuffed French toast, and sourdough pancakes.

Hosts: Jane and Jerry Glass
Rooms: 5 (1 PB; 4 S2B) $55
Full Breakfast
Credit Cards: A, B
Notes: 2, 5, 8 (over 12), 9, 10, 11, 12, 13, 14
    (winter only)

PORT TOWNSEND

Ann Starrett Mansion
744 Clay Street, 98368
(800) 321-0644 reservations

The mansion is internationally renowned for its service and its classic Victorian architecture and frescoed ceilings. A free-hung, three-tiered, spiral staircase that was handcrafted from two types of mahogany leads to an unusual domed ceiling. Inside, the mansion is exquisitely detailed with elaborate mouldings. One dozen beautiful rooms are furnished with antiques to re-create the Victorian period. A scrumptious full breakfast is served in the elegant dining room. One and one-half hours from Seattle.

Hosts: Bob and Edel Sokol
Rooms: 11 (9 PB; 2 SB) $70-150
Full Breakfast
Credit Cards: A, B, C, D
Notes: 2, 5, 9, 10, 11, 12, 14

Henry Bash House
718 F Street, 98368
(206) 385-5302

Views of the Olympic Mountains and valley can be seen from this charming Victorian home in Port Townsend's unique seaport. In a quiet area, it is only minutes to town, golf course, tennis, and Fort Worden. Come to the Gateway to the Olympic Peninsula.

Hosts: Jim and Linda Dornan
Rooms: 3 (2 PB; 1 SB) $55-65
Continental Breakfast
Credit Cards: None
Notes: 2, 5, 10, 11, 12

Trenholm House Bed and Breakfast
2037 Haines, 98368
(206) 385-6059

This 1890 Victorian farmhouse inn has five rooms plus a cottage furnished in country antiques and featuring lagoon and bay views, rose garden, herb garden, and apple and cherry trees. A gourmet breakfast is served.

Hosts: Michael and Patrice Kelly
Rooms: 6 (2 PB; 4 SB) $59-89
Full Breakfast
Credit Cards: A, B
Notes: 2, 5, 9, 10, 11, 12, 14

NOTES: Credit cards accepted: A Master Card; B Visa; C American Express; D Discover Card; E Diners Club; F Other;
2 Personal checks accepted; 3 Lunch available; 4 Dinner available; 5 Open all year; 6 Pets welcome; 8 Children

PUYALLUP

Hart's Tayberry House Bed and Breakfast

7406 80th Street East, 98371
(206) 848-4594

Nestled in the countryside overlooking the Puyallup Valley, Tayberry House is a replica of a home built by an early pioneer of the area for his daughter. The inn is a Victorian house with stained glass, open stairway, and tin ceiling in the kitchen. Guests are swept back to an age of charm, history, and romantic atmosphere. Breakfast is served in the gazebo when weather permits. Mount Rainier and Mount Saint Helens are to the south, and Tacoma and Seattle are just minutes away.

Hosts: Sandy Hart Hammer; Ray and Donna Hart
Rooms: 3 (1 PB; 2 SB) $40-60
Full Breakfast
Credit Cards: None
Notes: 2, 5, 10, 11, 12, 13

SEATTLE

Chambered Nautilus Bed and Breakfast Inn

5005 22nd Avenue Northeast, 98105
(206) 522-2536

This charming 1915 Georgian Colonial perched high on a hill is furnished with antiques, Persian rugs, a grand piano, two fireplaces, and a library with more than 2,000 books. Six spacious bedrooms, four with porches, have private or shared baths. Full, award-winning breakfasts. Close to downtown, bike and walking trails, and the University of Washington campus.

Hosts: Bunny and Bill Hagemeyer
Rooms: 6 (4 PB; 2 SB) $70-95
Full Breakfast
Credit Cards: A, B, C, E, F
Notes: 2, 5, 9, 10, 11, 12, 13, 14

Chelsea Station Bed and Breakfast

4915 Linden Avenue North, 98103
(206) 547-6077

This gracious bed and breakfast inn is nestled in a peaceful, wooded setting near Seattle's zoo and rose gardens. Each of the five comfortable guest rooms has a king bed. Enjoy the restorative calm of afternoon tea, the bottomless cookie jar, and private spa. This is a perfect place for a romantic getaway or a warm home for the tired traveler.

Hosts: Dick and Mary Lou Jones
Rooms: 5 (PB) $59-94
Full Breakfast
Credit Cards: A, B, C, D, E
Notes: 2, 5, 9, 10, 11, 12, 14

Chambered Nautilus Bed and Breakfast Inn

The Shafer-Baillie Mansion

907 Fourteenth Avenue East, 98112
(206) 322-4654; FAX (206) 329-4654

This mansion, the largest estate of historic Millionaire's Row on Seattle's Capitol Hill, was built circa 1914 for one of the Northwest's premier pioneers, Alexander Baillie. Each spacious suite in this 15,000-square-foot mansion has its own antique furnishings and ambience. Guests are just minutes from shopping and restaurants in the Emerald City, as well as nearby ski slopes and hiking or biking paths.

Host: Erv Olssen
Rooms: 11 (8 PB; 3 SB) $55-115
Continental Breakfast
Credit Cards: A, B, C
Notes: 2, 5, 8, 10, 12, 13, 14

SEAVIEW

Gumm's Bed
and Breakfast Inn
P. O. Box 447, 98644
(206) 642-8887

A lovingly restored example of northwest Craftsman architecture with a turn-of-the-century ambience, this home features a large livingroom with a great stone fireplace. A sun porch offers a warm spot for casual conversation or reading for a relaxing day. The four guest rooms are all uniquely decorated with special thought to comfort.

Hosts: Mickey and Esther Slack
Rooms: 4 (2 PB; 2 SB) $65-75
Full Breakfast

Credit Cards: A, B
Notes: 2, 5, 8, 9, 10, 12

SEQUIM

Groveland Cottage
1673 Sequim-Dungeness Way, 98382
(206) 683-3565

This historic inn is five miles north of Sequim. Ideally situated for touring the Olympic Peninsula. Within minutes, guests can enjoy beach walks, golfing, fishing, biking, and sight-seeing. Choose from four rooms; private baths and king beds are available. Coffee, tea, and the morning newspaper are delivered to each door prior to a gourmet, health-conscious breakfast that is served in the dining room.

Host: Simone Nichols
Rooms: 5 (3 PB; 2 SB) $65-85
Full Breakfast
Credit Cards: A, B, D
Notes: 2, 5, 11, 12, 13, 14

West Virginia

Gilbert House
Bed and Breakfast

P. O. Box 1104, 25414
(304) 725-0637

An American treasure, the Gilbert House, circa 1760, is a magnificent stone house listed on the Historic American Buildings Survey and the National Register of Historic Places. The house is richly decorated with European antiques, many of which came from royal courts of Europe and were collected or inherited by the hosts. Situated in the Middleway Historic District, near Antietam, Harper's Ferry, and Washington, D. C.

Hosts: Jean and Bernie Heiler
Rooms: 3 (PB) $70-150
Full Breakfast
Credit Cards: A, B, C
Notes: 2, 5, 9, 10, 11, 12, 14

Boydville Inn

Aspen Hall Inn

405 Boyd Avenue, 25401
(304) 263-4385

This romantic getaway is an exceptional setting. Rooms have queen beds. A country breakfast is served with homemade breads, as well as an English-style afternoon tea. Special requests are welcome. It is important to the hosts that guests feel as much at home as they would at their own grandmother's.

Hosts: LouAnne and Gordon Claucherty
Rooms: 3 (PB) $85-95
Full Breakfast
Credit Cards: A, B
Notes: 2, 5, 9, 10, 11, 12, 14

Boydville Inn

601 South Queen Street, 25401
(304) 263-1448

This restored 1812 mansion is on its own 14-acre park. Secluded, it is near Harper's Ferry and Antietam Battlefield. Period antiques, original wood floors, Oriental rugs, spacious garden room, livingroom, music room, huge veranda. "One of the best-appointed houses in the world," *Travel and Leisure*.

Host: Owen Sullivan
Rooms: 6 (PB) $100-120
Full Breakfast
Credit Cards: A, B
Notes: 2, 5, 9, 11, 12, 14

welcome; 9 Social drinking allowed; 10 Tennis available; 11 Swimming available; 12 Golf available; 13 Skiing available; 14 May be booked through travel agents

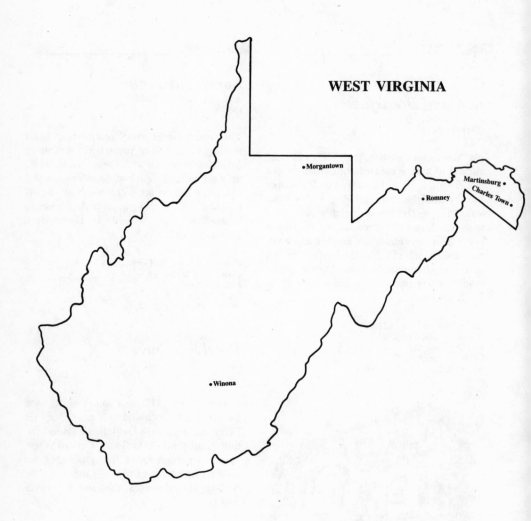

WEST VIRGINIA

Morgantown

Martinsburg

Romney

Charles Town

Winona

MORGANTOWN

Chestnut Ridge School
1000 Stewartstown Road, 26505
(304) 598-2262

Built in the 1920s, Chestnut Ridge retains the oversized windows, beadboard trim, and broad staircase that reflect its past as an elementary school. Just minutes from West Virginia University campus and Medical Center, there are natural scenic attractions and sports and recreation areas nearby. Each of four attractively furnished guest rooms has a queen bed and marble and brass bath.

Host: Sam and Nancy Bonasso
Rooms: 4 (PB) $54-60
Continental Breakfast
Credit Cards: None
Notes: 2, 5, 9, 10, 11, 12, 13

ROMNEY

Hampshire House 1884
165 North Grafton Street, 26757
(304) 822-7171

This lovely brick home was built in 1884. It is quiet, elegant, and furnished with period furniture. Two bedrooms have fireplaces. There is a large room for visiting, reading, or playing games. The grounds feature outdoor private areas. Air conditioned throughout. Bicycles available for touring West Virginia's oldest town.

Hosts: Jane and Scott Simmons
Rooms: 4 (PB) $60-75

Full Breakfast
Credit Cards: A, B, C, D, E
Notes: 2, 4, 5, 9, 10, 14

WINONA

Garvey House
Bed and Breakfast
P. O. Box 98, 25942
(800) 767-3235

Enjoy the summer evening magic of a torch-lit pond, soothing mountain sounds, and refreshing mountain air. Wake up to freshly brewed coffee and home-baked breads. Experience the adventure of whitewater rafting, hiking, and exploring ghost towns. Surrounded by mountains and beautiful forests, Garvey House will relax and refresh your spirit.

Host: Valerie Ritter
Rooms: 9 (6 PB; 3 SB) $47.50-54.50
Full Breakfast
Credit Cards: A, B
Notes: 2, 8, 9, 10, 11, 12, 14

Hampshire House 1884

NOTES: Credit cards accepted: A MasterCard; B Visa; C American Express; D Discover Card; E Diners Club; F Other;
2 Personal checks accepted; 3 Lunch available; 4 Dinner available; 5 Open all year; 6 Pets welcome; 8 Children welcome; 9 Social drinking allowed; 10 Tennis available; 11 Swimming available; 12 Golf available; 13 Skiing available; 14 May be booked through travel agents

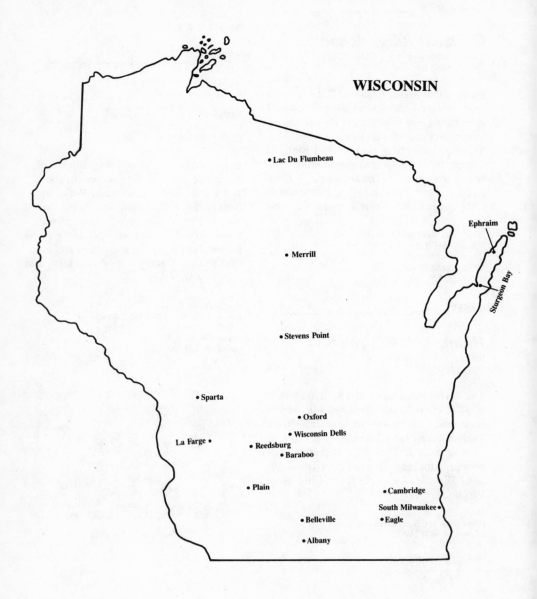

WISCONSIN

• Lac Du Flumbeau

Ephraim

Sturgeon Bay

• Merrill

• Stevens Point

• Sparta

• Oxford

• Wisconsin Dells

La Farge •   • Reedsburg

• Baraboo

• Plain

• Cambridge

South Milwaukee •

• Belleville   • Eagle

• Albany

Wisconsin

ALBANY

Albany Guest House
405 South Mill Street, 53502
(608) 862-3636

This restored 1908 home with wide front porch is situated on two acres of maple and black walnut trees and gardens. Natural woodwork and floors enhance the four bedrooms and three baths. The rooms are furnished with antiques and treasures. Canoe or tube the river, or bike, hike, or ski the Sugar River Trail. Visit the Capitol Square in Madison, 30 miles north, or New Glarus, "America's Little Switzerland."

Hosts: Bob and Sally Braem
Rooms: 4 (2 PB; 2 SB) $45-65
Full Breakfast
Credit Cards: None
Notes: 2, 5, 8, 10, 11, 12, 13

BARABOO

The Barrister's House
226 Ninth Avenue, 53913
(608) 356-3344

This comfortably elegant Colonial guest house has four uniquely decorated guest rooms. The formal dining room, library, and sitting room, all with fireplaces, provide a variety of opportunities for indoor relaxation, while a screened porch, an open veranda, and a flagstone terrace offer opportunities for whiling away the hours outdoors. Situated in a parklike setting on one of Baraboo's bluffs, the house is the perfect getaway in the heart of an all-season vacationland.

Hosts: Glen and Mary Schulz
Rooms: 4 (PB) $50-60
Continental Breakfast
Credit Cards: None
Notes: 2, 5, 9, 10, 11, 12, 13

The Grollmar Guest House
422 Third Street, 53913
(608) 356-9432

Experience Victorian beauty in this exquisite, historical circus home. Original chandeliers, beveled-glass windows, untouched oak woodwork, restored oak and maple floors, and hand-painted murals are only part of the charm of this elegant home furnished with original furniture and antiques. A guest parlor leads to a fun patio. Central air conditioning, several gardens.

Hosts: Tom and Linda Luck
Rooms: 4 (2 PB; 2 SB) $45-65
Full Breakfast
Credit Cards: A, B
Notes: 2, 5, 8, 9, 10, 11, 12, 13

BELLEVILLE

Abendruh Bed and Breakfast Swisstyle
7019 Gehin Road, 53508
(608) 424-3808

Abendruh stands for peaceful, relaxing lodging with Swiss hospitality. Guest rooms are large and uniquely decorated. Cool and relaxing in the summer, warm and cozy in the winter. Take a leisurely walk or sit by a crackling fire. Enjoy Swiss and Norwegian settlements in neighboring villages. Visit many cultural events in the capital city of

NOTES: Credit cards accepted: A Master Card; B Visa; C American Express; D Discover Card; E Diners Club; F Other; 2 Personal checks accepted; 3 Lunch available; 4 Dinner available; 5 Open all year; 6 Pets welcome; 8 Children welcome; 9 Social drinking allowed; 10 Tennis available; 11 Swimming available; 12 Golf available; 13 Skiing available; 14 May be booked through travel agents

Wisconsin. The campus, lakes, parks, shopping, biking, and cross-country ski trails are nearby.

Host: Mathilde Jaggi
Rooms: 3 (2 PB; 1 SB) $45-55
Full Breakfast
Credit Cards: A, B, C
Notes: 2, 5, 9, 10, 12, 13, 14

Whispering Pines

CAMBRIDGE

Whispering Pines

West 9442 Highway 12, 53523
(608) 423-3120

Whispering Pines is situated at Cambridge, near Lake Ripley on Highway 12, about 20 minutes east of Madison. It is a beautiful, antique, rich establishment reminiscent of a trip to Grandmother's house. The gracious rooms and general ambience hearken to an era of a slower pace of life. Close to Rowe Pottery, several antique and fine shops, local bike trails, fireside dinner theater.

Host: Patricia A. New
Rooms: 3 (2 PB; 1 SB) $50-60
Full Breakfast
Credit Cards: None
Notes: 2, 5, 10, 11, 12, 13

EAGLE

Eagle Centre House

W370 S9590 Highway 67, 53119
(414) 363-4700

A replicated Greek Revival stagecoach inn filled with antiques sits atop 16 scenic acres in the southern Kettle Moraine Forest. Two spacious chambers feature whirlpool tubs for two. Near Old World Wisconsin outdoor history museum. Horseback riding, skiing, hiking, biking, golfing all nearby. Air conditioned in summer, cozy wood-burning stoves in winter.

Hosts: Riene Wells Herriges and Dean Herriges
Rooms: 5 (PB) $69-99
Full Breakfast
Credit Cards: A, B, C
Notes: 2, 5, 9, 10, 11, 12, 13

EPHRAIM

French Country Inn of Ephraim

3052 Spruce Lane, P.O. Box 129, 54211
(414) 854-4001

Originally built as a summer cottage in 1912, the house now serves as a comfortable European-style bed and breakfast with seven guest rooms in summer and four guest rooms in winter. A large, stone fireplace and spacious common rooms add to the friendly atmosphere. Situated in the village of Ephraim in Wisconsin's famous Door County, the house has a peaceful garden setting. Enjoy Lake Michigan in summer and cross-country skiing in winter. Beautiful sunsets all year long.

Host: Walt Fisher
Rooms: 7 summer; 4 winter (2 PB; 5 SB) $50-75;
    $45-55 winter
Expanded Continental Breakfast
Credit Cards: None
Notes: 2, 5, 9, 10, 11, 12, 13

LAC DU FLAMBEAU

Ty-Bach

3104 Simpson Lane, 54538
(715) 588-7851

Ty-Bach is a modern home on a secluded northwoods lake. Guests enjoy water sports, observing loons and other wildlife, or just relaxing on the decks. Hosts will help select from the many area attractions, such as museums, theater, nature walks, wilderness cruises, tubing, and much more. Winter guests ski through the wooded 80 acres.

Hosts: Janet and Kermit Bekkum
Rooms: 2 (PB) $50-60
Full Breakfast
Credit Cards: None
Notes: 2, 5, 9, 11, 12, 13 (XC), 14

LA FARGE

Trillium

Route 2, Box 121, 54639
(608) 625-4492

A cozy, private cottage is fully furnished on this family farm. Complete with kitchen, stone fireplace, and a porch overlooking gardens and orchard, the cottage faces out over woods and fields. It is in Wisconsin's largest Amish community, near rivers, state parks, historical sites, and bike trails.

Host: Rosanne Boyett
Cottage: 1 (PB) $52-65
Full Breakfast
Credit Cards: None
Notes: 2, 5, 8, 9, 10, 11, 12, 13

Trillium

MERRILL

The Brick House Bed and Breakfast

108 South Cleveland Street, 54452
(715) 536-3230

This 1915 Prairie-style home invites guests to central Wisconsin. Sparkling beveled-glass French doors open to a glowing fireplace. Relax amid furnishings from antiques to a pink flamingo collection. The Daly Room's 1870 burled walnut bed takes guests comfortably back in time. The pastel Veranda Room's ceiling fan lazily stirs a breeze from the adjoining private porch. Air conditioned.

Hosts: Randy and Kris Ullmer
Rooms: 2 (SB) $35-50
Full Breakfast
Credit Cards: A, B, D
Notes: 2, 5, 9, 10, 11, 12, 13

Candlewick Inn

700 West Main Street, 54452
(715) 536-7744

An elegance of design and harmony has been achieved in the complete restoration of this 1883 lumber baron's mansion, situated in Merrill's historic district. Antiques, handmade quilts, massive woodwork, and collectibles combine to create a romantic masterpiece. Relax over breakfast in the formal dining room or on the wicker-filled screened porch. Browse the gift shop for a special memento. Nearby state parks lure all sports enthusiasts.

Hosts: Dan and Loretta Zimmerman
Rooms: 5 (3 PB; 2 SB) $ 55-95
Full Breakfast
Credit Cards: A, B
Notes: 2, 5, 10, 11, 12, 13, 14

Halfway House Bed and Breakfast

OXFORD

Halfway House Bed and Breakfast

Route 2, Box 80, 53952
(608) 586-5489

A big, old farmhouse has been remodeled and made comfortable, situated on a quiet and peaceful farm. Breakfast includes home-baked goods, and the house is full of books.

Hosts: J. A. and Genevieve Hines
Rooms: 4 (SB) $42
Full Breakfast
Credit Cards: None
Notes: 2, 5, 9, 10, 12, 13

PLAIN

Bettinger House Bed and Breakfast

855 Wachter Avenue (Highway 23), 53577
(608) 546-2951

This 1904 two-story brick house was purchased by Philip and Elizabeth Bettinger in 1913. Elizabeth is the present owner's grandmother. Mrs. Bettinger, a well-known midwife, delivered over 300 babies in this home. Close to The House on the Rock, American Players Theater, Frank Lloyd Wright's Taliesin. Bike quiet, paved, rural roads, canoe the Wisconsin River, or enjoy the Winter Green downhill and cross-country ski area.

Host: Marie Neider
Rooms: 6 (2 PB; 4 S2B) $45-55
Full Breakfast
Credit Cards: A, B
Notes: 2, 5, 9, 10, 11, 12, 13, 14

The Kraemer House Bed and Breakfast Inn

1190 Spruce Street, 53577
(608) 546-3161

Come and feel pampered in this traditional bed and breakfast home. The four guest rooms are lovely and bright with different colors and themes. Wake-up coffee is served right outside the door, followed by a generous breakfast that will tempt the most particular palate. Great area for biking, hiking, and cross-country skiing. Near The House on the Rock, American Players Theater, Frank Lloyd Wright's home, Taliesen.

NOTES: Credit cards accepted: A Master Card; B Visa; C American Express; D Discover Card; E Diners Club; F Other;
2 Personal checks accepted; 3 Lunch available; 4 Dinner available; 5 Open all year; 6 Pets welcome; 8 Children

Hosts: Duane and Gwen Kraemer
Rooms: 4 (1 PB; 3 SB) $42-70
Full Breakfast
Credit Cards: None
Notes: 2, 5, 10, 11, 12, 13

REEDSBURG

Parkview Bed and Breakfast
211 North Park Street, 53959
(608) 524-4333

Situated in the historic Park Street district across from the city park is this 1895 Queen Anne Victorian home with central air conditioning and ceiling fans. Fish ponds, flower gardens, and stone ornaments enhance the grounds. The home features beautiful, natural woodwork. Near Wisconsin Dells, Baraboo, Spring Green, bike trails, state parks, and skiing.

Hosts: Tom and Donna Hofmann
Rooms: 3 (SB) $52
Full Breakfast
Credit Cards: A, B, C
Notes: 2, 5, 8, 9, 10, 11, 12, 13, 14

SOUTH MILWAUKEE

Riley House Bed and Breakfast
727 Hawthorne Avenue, 53172
(414) 764-3130

Built in 1903, decorated with antiques, this bed and breakfast is in a charming residential neighborhood, just a 15-minute drive along Lake Michigan to downtown Milwaukee. A short walk to beautiful Grant Park on Lake Michigan, offering an 18-hole golf course, swimming, tennis, boat launch, hiking, biking, and cross-country skiing. Full breakfast is served in your room or in the dining room. One guest room has a whirlpool tub.

Hosts: Mark and Bert (Roberta) Tyborski
Rooms: 4 (1 PB; 3 SB) $48-78
Full Breakfast

Credit Cards: A, B, C
Notes: 2, 5, 10, 11, 12, 13, 14

SPARTA

Just-N-Trails Bed and Breakfast/Farm Vacation
Route 1, Box 274, 54656
(608) 269-4522; (800) 488-4521

Hosts specialize in offering recreation, relaxation, and a romantic atmosphere. Choose from groomed hiking and cross-country ski trails on 200 acres of lush green hills and fields or photogenic vistas. The Granary room and Little House on the Prairie room each feature a double whirlpool and fireplace in separate buildings from the 1920 farmhouse. Watch the cows being milked, pet the calves, ride the famous Elroy-Sparta bike trail, or browse the Amish community.

Hosts: Don and Donna Justin
Rooms: 6 (5 PB; 1 SB) $60-150
Full Breakfast
Credit Cards: A, B
Notes: 2, 5, 8, 13, 14

STEVENS POINT

Victorian Swan on Water
1716 Water, 54481
(715) 345-0595

Cherrywood paneling, lace curtains, and ornate crown moldings create a serene setting in this 1889 home. Read beside the fireplace, play the piano, or join in pleasant conversation. In the summer, relax in the rose garden. Breakfast is served in a sunny breakfast room. Quiet, country roads for biking; a three-inn bike tour available. Air-conditioned.

Host: Joan M. Ouellette
Rooms: 4 (PB) $45-65
Full Breakfast
Credit Cards: A, B, C, D
Notes: 2, 5, 8 (over 12), 9, 10, 11, 12, 13, 14

welcome; 9 Social drinking allowed; 10 Tennis available; 11 Swimming available; 12 Golf available; 13 Skiing available; 14 May be booked through travel agents

STURGEON BAY

The Scofield House Bed and Breakfast

908 Michigan Street, P. O. Box 761, 54235
(414) 743-7727

One of Door County's most elegant bed and breakfasts, this 1902 turn-of-the-century restored Victorian was, and still is, Sturgeon Bay's finest home. The three-story house is ornate with inlaid woodwork and carved ornamentation. Several guest rooms have double whirlpools, fireplaces, TV/VCR, stereo, movie library. Rooms are filled with fine antiques. Near shops, restaurants, museums, art galleries, state parks. Air conditioned.

Hosts: Bill and Fran Cecil
Rooms: 5 (PB) $65-125
Full Breakfast
Credit Cards: None
Notes: 2, 5, 9, 10, 11, 12, 13

WISCONSIN DELLS

Thunder Valley Bed and Breakfast Inn

W15344 Waubeek Road, 53965
(608) 254-4145

Enjoy Scandinavian hospitality in a country setting. The quaint farmhouse has six guest rooms, all with private baths. TV, refrigerator, and microwave are available. Full breakfast includes homemade whole-grain breads, pancakes, and fruit jams. Four state parks, famous Dells attractions, winter skiing are nearby. Browse the farm; pet the goats; gather an egg; or just relax with a good book, music, and hot cider. Perfect for lesiure or business getaway. *Velkommen.*

Hosts: Sigrid, Kari, and Anita
Rooms: 6 (PB) $45-80
Full Breakfast
Credit Cards: A, B
Notes: 2, 4, 5, 8, 9, 10, 11, 12, 13, 14

NOTES: Credit cards accepted: A Master Card; B Visa; C American Express; D Discover Card; E Diners Club; F Other;
2 Personal checks accepted; 3 Lunch available; 4 Dinner available; 5 Open all year; 6 Pets welcome; 8 Children

Wyoming

CHEYENNE

Drummond's Bed and Breakfast
399 Happy Jack Road, 82007
(307) 634-6042

This quiet farmhouse retreat is situated between Cheyenne and Laramie, 16 miles from Interstate 80. It is adjacent to Curt Gowdy State Park, five miles from Medicine Bow National Forest and Vedauwoo. Beverages and homemade snacks are always available. Hot tub, fishing, rock climbing, mountain biking, hiking, cross-country skiing, horseback riding, inside riding area, and barn for boarding guest horses. Bikes and horses not provided.

Host: Taydie Drummond
Rooms: 3 (1 PB; 2 SB) $50-60
Full Breakfast
Credit Cards: None
Notes: 2, 3, 4, 5, 6, 8, 9, 13

ENCAMPMENT

Platt's Rustic Mountain Lodge
Star Route 49, 82325
(307) 327-5539

The lodge offers a peaceful mountain view and wholesome country atmosphere with lots of western hospitality, horseback riding, fishing, hiking, rock hounding, guided tours, and horse-pack trips to scenic mountain areas. Enjoy the wildlife, flora and fauna, historic trails, old mines, hot springs, local museum, snowmobiling, and cross-country skiing. Situated on a working ranch.

Hosts: Mayvon and Ron Platt
Rooms: 4 plus cabin (1 PB; 3 SB) $70
Full Breakfast
Credit Cards: None
Notes: 6, 8, 9, 10, 11, 12, 13

WILSON

Teton Tree House
P.O. Box 550, 83014
(307) 733-3233

A classic bed and breakfast inn with warm, on-premises innkeepers. Rooms are large with wonderful beds, and most have decks with great views. The great room has a sweeping staircase, fireplace, piano, and walls of books. Hosts are 30-year locals/guides/travelers who delight in sharing information. For references, see *The New York Times* Sunday travel section, May 21, 1989, and the *National Geographic Traveler*, March/April 1990.

Hosts: Chris and Denny Becker
Rooms: 5 (PB) $85-115
Full Breakfast
Credit Cards: A, B, D
Notes: 2, 5, 8, 9, 10, 12, 13, 14

welcome; 9 Social drinking allowed; 10 Tennis available; 11 Swimming available; 12 Golf available; 13 Skiing available; 14 May be booked through travel agents

WYOMING

• Cheyenne

• Encampment

• Wilson

Canada

BRITISH COLUMBIA—WEST VANCOUVER

Beachside Bed and Breakfast
4208 Evergreen Avenue, V7V 1H1
(604) 922-7773; FAX (604) 926-8073

This is a quiet, beautiful waterfront home in one of the finest areas in Vancouver. A lovely sand beach is at the doorstep. Minutes from downtown and Stanley Park, this home's southern exposure affords a panoramic view of city, harbor, and Alaska cruise ships from beachside Jacuzzi and dining room. Antique stained glass, old brick, delightful decorator touches, and welcoming world travelers host you. Fishing, sailing, wilderness hiking, skiing, and excellent restaurants within ten minutes.

Hosts: Gordon and Joan Gibbs
Rooms: 3 (PB) $95-150
Full Breakfast
Credit Cards: A, B
Notes: 2, 5, 8, 9, 10, 11, 12, 13, 14

Beachside Bed and Breakfast

ONTARIO—NEW HAMBURG

The Waterlot
17 Huron Street, N0B 2G0
(519) 662-2020

The Waterlot is committed to quality in ambience and service. This 1840s house features fine French cuisine in its full-service restaurant and includes a store stocked with unique and interesting items. A great spot for birthdays, anniversaries, engagements, rehearsals, weddings, family events, or just for fun.

Host: W. Gordon Elkeer
Rooms: 3 (1 PB; 2 SB) $65-85
Continental Breakfast
Credit Cards: A, B, C, D
Notes: 2, 3, 4, 5, 9, 10, 12

ONTARIO—ST. JACOBS

Jakobstettel Guest House, Inc.
16 Isabella Street, N0B 2N0
(519) 664-2208; FAX (519) 664-1326

This turn-of-the-century estate home is where accommodations and hospitality are superb, "Where quiet can still be heard." Five treed acres, outdoor pool, tennis court, bicycles, badminton, horsehoe pits, private rose garden. Around the corner is specialty shopping in 100 shops and boutiques, restaurants, farmers' markets, and a wooded walking trail.

NOTES: Credit cards accepted: A Master Card; B Visa; C American Express; D Discover Card; E Diners Club; F Other; 2 Personal checks accepted; 3 Lunch available; 4 Dinner available; 5 Open all year; 6 Pets welcome; 8 Children welcome; 9 Social drinking allowed; 10 Tennis available; 11 Swimming available; 12 Golf available; 13 Skiing available; 14 May be booked through travel agents

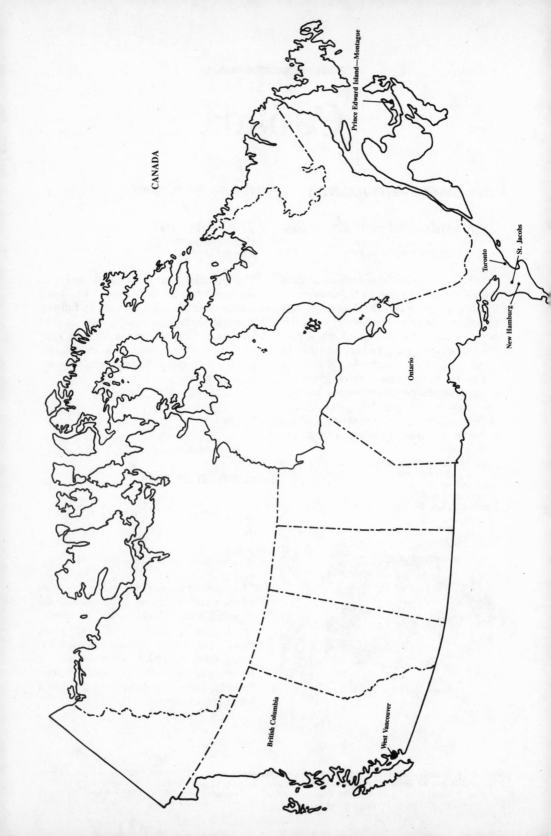

Host: Ella Brubaeker
Rooms: 12 (PB) $95-150
Continental Breakfast
Credit Cards: A, B, C
Notes: 2, 3 (by arrangement for groups), 4 (by arrangement for groups), 5, 8, 10, 11, 14

Jakobstettel Guest House, Inc.

ONTARIO—TORONTO

The Downtown Toronto Association of Bed and Breakfast Guesthouses

153 Huron Street, M5T 2B6
(416) 977-6841; FAX (416) 598-4562

Quality, charm, and location are the three main elements in this bed-and-breakfast network. All hosts are active in the arts or the hospitality industry. Locations are within 30 minutes of the Eaton Centre on 24-hour public transit lines. All homes are non-smoking. Restaurant and theater bookings, bicycle rentals, health club privileges are also available. Susan Oppenheim, coordinator. $50-80.

PRINCE EDWARD ISLAND—MONTAGUE

Partridge's Bed and Breakfast

Panmure Island, Rural Route 2, C0A 1R0
(902) 838-4687

A walk through the woods to the beach offers quiet relaxation. Clams and mussels can be dug, and Graham's Lobster Factory is nearby. Grocery stores and excellent restaurants are nearby. Babysitting and cribs are available. Bicycles, a canoe, and a rowboat are free. Seal cruises, plays, tennis, golf, and horseback riding are within 20 minutes. Cat in residence.

Hosts: Gertrude and Rod Partridge
Rooms: 7 (5 PB; 2 SB) $40-50
Full Breakfast
Credit Cards: B
Notes: 6, 8, 9, 11, 14

NOTES: Credit cards accepted: A Master Card; B Visa; C American Express; D Discover Card; E Diners Club; F Other; 2 Personal checks accepted; 3 Lunch available; 4 Dinner available; 5 Open all year; 6 Pets welcome; 8 Children welcome; 9 Social drinking allowed; 10 Tennis available; 11 Swimming available; 12 Golf available; 13 Skiing available; 14 May be booked through travel agents

Puerto Rico

Parador Martorell, Inc.
Ocean Drive 6-A, P. O. Box 384, 00773
(809) 889-2710

This small family inn in the northeast part of
the island, one block from the ocean and
beach and 45 minutes from Isla Verde Airport, has modern rooms. Breakfast is served
all year on the patio. Restaurants, golf, and
tennis are nearby.

Host: Eliud Hilerio
Rooms: 10 (4 PB; 6 SB) $58.85-69.55
Full Breakfast
Credit Cards: A, B, C
Notes: 8, 9, 10, 11, 12, 13, 14

Bed and Breakfast
Recommendation Form

As *The Non-Smokers' Guide to Bed and Breakfasts* is introduced to the traveling public, smoke-free bed and breakfasts will be asking to be included on our mailing list. If you know of another bed and breakfast who may not be on our list, give them a great business-boosting opportunity by providing us with the following information:

B&B Name_____

Address_____

City_____ State_____ Zip Code _____

Telephone_____

Name of hosts_____

B&B Name_____

Address_____

City_____ State_____ Zip Code _____

Telephone_____

Name of hosts_____

B&B Name_____

Address_____

City_____ State_____ Zip Code _____

Telephone_____

Name of hosts_____

Please, send this form to:
The Non-Smokers' Guide to Bed and Breakfasts
P.O. Box 719 • 1810 Barbour Drive
Uhrichsville, OH 44683